מקורות

ArtScroll Judaiscope Series ®

THY
BROTHER'S

by David Kranzler

Foreword by Dr. Isaac Lewin

BLOOD

קול
דמי אחיך
צועקים אלי.

The Orthodox Jewish response during the HOLOCAUST

Published by

Mesorah Publications, ltd

FIRST EDITION
First Impression ... June 1987

Published and Distributed by
MESORAH PUBLICATIONS, Ltd.
Brooklyn, New York 11223

Distributed in Israel by
MESORAH MAFITZIM / J. GROSSMAN
Rechov Harav Uziel 117 — Jerusalem, Israel

Distributed in Europe by
J. LEHMANN HEBREW BOOKSELLERS
20 Cambridge Terrace / Gateshead
Tyne and Wear / England NE8 1RP

ISBN
0-89906-858-8 (hard cover)

Typography by CompuScribe at ArtScroll Studios, Ltd.
1969 Coney Island Avenue / Brooklyn, N.Y. 11223 / (718) 339-1700

Printed in U.S.A. by NOBLE BOOK PRESS.
Bound by SEFERCRAFT, Inc., Brooklyn, N.Y.

This book is dedicated
to the memory of
Dr. Jeffery Kranzler ז״ל
Yahrtzeit Rosh Chodesh Shvat

Born June 15, 1941, he was blessed early in life
with that *rare mind and noble spirit*
whose brilliance streaked only too briefly
on this earth towards the heavens.
He was a humanitarian,
a totally dedicated physician and pediatric radiologist,
wholly devoted to curing ailing children
and constantly placing the needs of others
above his own.
An honored yeshivah graduate and talmudic scholar
he combined his healing art with a love of
Torah, Judaism, Mitzvos and Hashem.
חבל אל דאבדין ולא מישתכחין
May we, his parents, brother and sister,
who mourn him,
be inspired by his great accomplishments,
his love of humanity
and affection for his brethren of all ages.
יזכור אלקינו לטובה אם שאר צדיקי עולם
May our G-d remember him for his goodness,
honor and kindness
among all the Just and Righteous of the world.

The Kranzler Family

Acknowledgments

One of the fruits of the long, hard process of producing a book is the opportunity to extend one's gratitude to the numerous individuals who have contributed to every stage of its conception, gestation and birth. As a pioneering work, many years in the making, it was, perhaps, more than most, the beneficiary of a host of wonderful people.

Among the most knowledgable and cooperative were the librarians and archivists at numerous public and private institutions as well as the families of some of the rescue personalities, who gave me unrestricted access to the various collections and permitted me to photocopy or microfilm tens of thousands of documents. They have made my long and arduous task inmeasurably easier.

In Washington D.C.: the staffs of The Library of Congress and The National Archives. In Hyde Park, N.Y., Mr. Ray Teichman of the FDR Library. In New York: Mrs. Helen Ritter and her assistant Mrs. Ruth Rausch, at the document center and Ms. Sima Horowitz in the library, of the American Jewish Committee; Mr. Emanuel Muravchick and Mr. Aaron Silbermintz of the Jewish Labor Committee, Dr. Benjamin Nadel and Mr. Leon Greenbaum of the Bund Archives; Rabbi Moshe Kolodny of the Orthodox Jewish Archives; Mr. Marek Webb of YIVO and Ms. Esther Togman of the Zionists Archives.

In Jerusalem: Dr. Michael Heyman and Dr. I. Phillippe of the Central Zionist Archives; Mrs. Nechama A. Chalom of the Weizmann Institute and Dr. Shmuel Krakowski of Yad Vashem. In London: Dr. Elizabeth Eppler, director of the World Jewish Congress Archives.

A special note of appreciation to my many colleagues and friends who for years served as sounding boards for new ideas, and provided countless hours of fruitful discussion, constructive criticism and numerous suggestions. They have surely added inmeasurably to the value of the book and prevented many pitfalls of style and substance, inherent in a pioneering work of this nature. One must include my colleagues and friends, such as Profs. Alois Chmela, Catherine Sestay, Mary Nutley and her ever helpful assistant May O'Daugherty; Joseph Friedenson, Gertrude Hirschler, Dr. Abby Mendelson, Dr. Yaakov Petroff, Rabbi Joseph Elias, Rabbi Boruch B. Borchard and Ernest Seewald.

Special kudos to Rebbetzin Dr. Judith Grunfeld, whose keen historical sense was always a source of intellectual stimulation, and who helped make accessible, through personal introduction, the people and collections that were invaluable. Moreover her hospitality made my stays in London most memorable.

Eli Matzozki, with whom I conducted a good exchange of documents. Over the years, he proved to be a good student in absorbing my "lectures" and analysis of the ideological factor in rescue.

I am most indebted to my numerous interviewees; rescue activists, their families and friends, who shared their memories on tapes. There are listed in the footnotes of this and my other two forthcoming volumes on the Holocaust. One must single out, however, the families of Rabbi Solomon Schonfeld, Recha and Yitzchok Sternbuch, Mike Tress, Harry Goodman (a special thanks to Simon for the original newspaper volumes). They made their major collections readily available without restrictions.

One cannot say the same for the papers of Natan Schwalb (of Hechalutz) which were shown only to a few select researchers. Even the more public archives of the Joint Distribution Committee, which had been closed to all scholars during Prof. Yehuda Bauer's research for his "official" history of the Joint, are now open only for perusal. No one but Prof. Bauer may duplicate any documents, especially from the valuable Saly Mayer papers. This is a changed policy from the late sixties when I was permitted to photocopy hundreds of documents for my research on the Shanghai Jewish Community.

My gratitude is also extended to those individuals and publications which permitted the use of their material as the base for several units; to Prof. Isaac Lewin, scholar, leader, and rescue activist, for his gracious foreword and permission to use his article on Rabbi Eliezer Silver; Joseph Friedenson, editor, colleague, (and co-author on *Heroine of Rescue*), for permission to use the article in *Der Yiddisher Vort*, by Sonnenfeld, on Julius Steinfeld; Asher (Siegmund) Forst, artists, thinker and friend, for the use of Andre Steiner's cartoon of Rabbi Weissmandl, and his own vignettes of that genius of rescue; Dr. Shulamit Eliash, and the publishers of *Modern Judaism* for permission to utilize her article on Chief Rabbi Yitzchok Isaac Halevy Herzog.

I must single out Al Lipson, a truly outstanding friend, scholar, editor and a gentleman of the first order, who always came through thick and thin with constructive criticism, suggestions and a helpful hand, down to the final set of galleys. May the Al-mighty repay his kindness.

To Mesorah Publications: Rabbi Nosson Scherman and Rabbi Meir

Zlotowitz, for their keen interest in my manuscript from its earliest, brief stage throughout its nine years of development; my friend Rabbi Avie Gold, for his valuable editorial facility, steady cooperation and common sense; Rabbi Shea Brander and his assistant Eli Kroen, whose graphics and production talents are justifiably legendary; Shimon Golding and Shmuel Klaver for their skillful handling of publicity and sales; to the indefatigable proofreading expertise of Mrs. Feygie Weinbaum and Mrs. Judi Dick, as well as the skillful typing team of Mrs. Esther Feierstein, Mrs. Simie Korn and Menucha Marcus; and of course kudos to my own supertypist, Mrs. Simi Eichhorn, whose dedication to this project went far beyond the call of duty.

May I also extend my appreciation to Rabbi Yisroel Lefkowitz for his interest in dissenimating this volume among the Jewish leadership.

My great indebtedness to all of these makes it all the more necessary to emphasize that the full responsibility for the entire work is mine alone.

On a more personal level, I want to thank my family for the whole-hearted support. they provided throughout; my wife Judy תחי׳, whose father Rabbi Yaakov Bein ז״ל set a good example of *mesiras nefesh* on behalf of the *klal*. My brother, Dr. Gershon Kranzler and brother-in-law, Rabbi Alex Weisfogel, whose own involvement with *hatzalah* inspired me to plough through the documentation in search of the lacuna in the heroic epic of World War II missing in all general accounts of the Holocaust; to Moishy and Feigi, Shani and Yaakov Meir, תחי׳, who served as permanent sounding boards for all the issues raised by this work. May the heroic acts of *mesiras nefesh* portrayed by the men and women in this book serve as inspiration to them and their generation.

ᴄ§ Table of Contents

Part One: Analysis

Part One: Analysis

Part Two: Personality Portraits

Foreword

by Dr. Isaac Lewin

Professor of History, Yeshiva University

For too long has the role of the Orhodox rescue efforts during the Holocaust been neglected, distorted or denigrated by historians of that tragic era. As a historian as well as a participant in the events recounted so admirably by Dr. David Kranzler, I can fully attest to the lucunae left wittingly or unwittingly by the chroniclers of this great drama.

The author has done an outstanding job of researching, sifting and analyzing a wealth of documents, both well-known and some not so well-known, to create a totally new work of history and to provide another historic perspective. Dr. Kranzler clearly shows how the classic Jewish *weltanschauung* was undermined by the rising secular Jewish ideologies of the early 20th-century and how this affected rescue efforts during the Hitler era.

Soon after my arrival in the States in 1941 I became directly involved with the rescue apparatus as representative of World Agudath Israel and Vaad Hatzalah to the Polish Embassy in Washington as well as to the various Jewish cooperative rescue efforts such as the Joint Emergency Committee, etc.

How well do I remember the secret cables sent clandestinely via the Polish diplomatic pouch from Bern, Switzerland, to Washington D.C., detailing the latest information of the Nazi massacres, which at times left even the members of the War Refugee Board in utter amazement. Nor could I forget the expressions of anguish and anxiety in the faces of the *roshei yeshiva* or *Moreinu* Rosenheim when I showed them these evidences of the new tragedies or a faint glimmer of hope when rescue opportunities opened up.

For the first time, a trained historian has attempted to do justice to the extraordinary rescue efforts of the valiant few Orthodox personalities throughout the world. Yet, for all his labor, Dr. Kranzler has not said the final word. He himself is completing, as I am informed, a more detailed scholarly work in this field. Moreover, as I peruse my own collection of documents, remnants of that tragic period, I realize how much work must still be done to bring to light the Orthodox rescue efforts during the most tragic period of Jewish history.

I warmly recommend this book to all Jewish readers, Orthodox and non-Orthodox alike.

PART I:
ANALYSIS

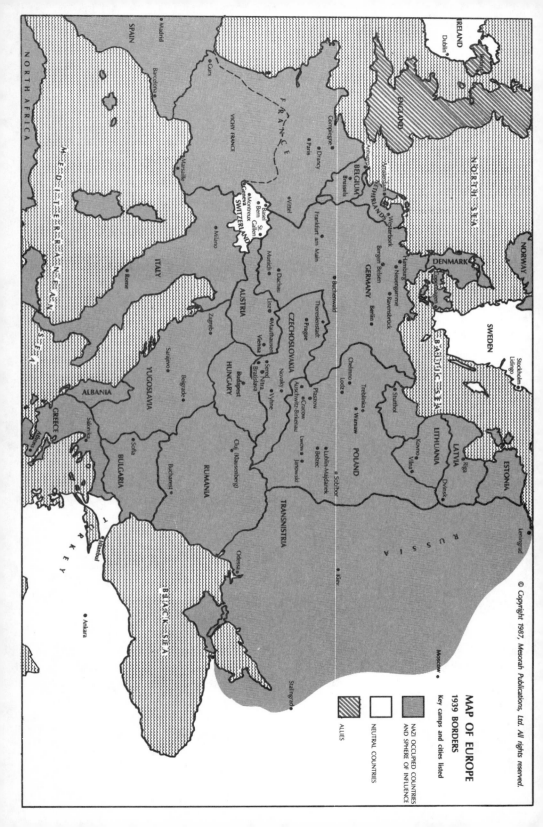

MAP OF EUROPE
1939 BORDERS

Key camps and cities listed

NAZI OCCUPIED COUNTRIES
AND SPHERE OF INFLUENCE

NEUTRAL COUNTRIES

ALLIES

© Copyright 1987, Mesorah Publications, Ltd. All rights reserved.

Introduction

AT A TIME WHEN millions were dying, only united Jewish efforts could have had a major impact upon events. But just the opposite was the case. American Jews split along ideological lines and clung stubbornly to courses of action dictated by their loyalties — the assimilationists to government policy and the greater war effort, most of the Zionists to the goal of a postwar Jewish state, most of the Orthodox to the imperatives of Torah law for immediate rescue. The battles were often bitter, the wounds deep and slow to heal. Yet the passions are understandable, even after forty years, for the issues were paramount to each participant. At stake was the fate of European Jewry as well as the role and standing of the Jew in his most populous home, America.

The Orthodox, so often denigrated for being anti-progressive, presented the greatest paradox, for while their formulas for rescue were rooted in the past, their demands and thoughts were simultaneously the most immediate and realistic. Quite simply, they demanded action *now*, to correspond virtually minute-by-minute with the deepening mire in Europe. While other activists were content to do little or nothing about rescue, Orthodox activists fought for more visas, for relaxed entry requirements, for illegal food shipments, and increased Allied action and ransom. While others chose to remain passing and obey the laws, the Orthodox created fictitious bank accounts, forged papers, used illegal cash transfers and secret cables, pleaded and wept before high government officials, and risked imprisonment and death to save lives. Indeed, the stories would be fit material for pulp thrillers — were they not so hollow in the face of millions whom they failed to reach.

At the start of World War II the Orthodox community in America was insignificant numerically and powerless politically and economically. By the end of 1943, however, the Orthodox activists had developed a sophisticated and efficient rescue apparatus as well as a small international network that at times accomplished far more than the larger, wealthier arms of the Jewish establishment.

Yet that achievement is virtually absent from the historical record. A volume published by Yad Vashem, the preeminent Israeli Holocaust Center, a book based on a symposium of historians of the Holocaust on rescue activities, contains not a single chapter on Orthodox activities.[1] The work of Rabbi Michoel Ber Weissmandl is given only incidental mention in that work, despite the fact that among his many rescue activities, Rabbi Weissmandl created the plans to ransom Slovakian Jewry, followed by all captive Jewry, and was the first to urge that the crematoria and the railway lines to Auschwitz be bombed. Professor Yehudah Bauer, in *Holocaust in Historical Perspective*, admits that he is somewhat astonished by the breadth of Rabbi Weissmandl's efforts. "It seems strange," he writes, "that the very sensible idea of using Allied military power to prevent the murder of Hungarian Jews should have occurred first to an ultra-Orthodox Slovak rabbi, but that is a fact."[2]

Bernard Wasserstein, in *Britain and the Jews of Europe 1939-1945*, does not even mention the name of Rabbi Solomon Schonfeld, despite the fact that Schonfeld worked every corridor of power and influence, raised enormous sums, and rescued thousands of Jews.[3]

Rabbi Weissmandl predicted that such readings would occur, that the role of the Orthodox would be lost in the larger, secularist histories. In discussing such matters with Dr. Yaakov Griffel, another rescue activist, in Switzerland after the war, Rabbi Weissmandl said:

> Now many of those party people are coming to me, looking for an alibi, to appease me into keeping quiet about their guilt. But later, it will be *they* who will write history, and they will try to obliterate their faults and their guilt, to monopolize every positive achievement, and put in the shadow any achievements of non-party members.[4]

Why was a separate Orthodox response necessary in the first

place? Major organizations already existed, such as the American Jewish Joint Distribution Committee (called the Joint or JDC), which spent millions of dollars to help European Jews; the Hebrew Sheltering and Immigrant Aid Society (or HIAS in this country, HICEM in Europe), the World Jewish Congress; and the American Jewish Labor Committee — all of which made diligent relief efforts. There were also Jewish defense organizations that spoke out against European oppression, notably the American Jewish Committee, B'nai Brith, and the American Jewish Congress, the latter headed by Dr. Stephen Wise, president of the Zionist Organization of America and of the World Jewish Congress, arguably the most powerful and influential American Jew of his day and a confidant of President Franklin Delano Roosevelt.

Secularists like Hillel Storch in Sweden and Gerhard Riegner in Switzerland (both of the World Jewish Congress) and Dr. Joseph J. Schwartz, who was affiliated with the Joint in Portugal, played major roles in relief and rescue.[5] And more than once the Vaad Hatzalah — the united Orthodox rabbinical relief and rescue group, created during the Holocaust — had to seek large sums of money from the Joint. Clearly, in the words of Herman Landau, an ally of the Sternbuch family and one of the principal activists in Switzerland, "Orthodoxy did not have a monopoly on relief or rescue."[6]

Yet despite the significant efforts of some established groups, many problems involving potential rescue were left unattended — and so the Orthodox groups found their role. The secularist organizations generally refused to go as far as breaking the law to provide aid or attempt rescue. Then, as the lives of more and more Jews were being swallowed, many Jewish groups in the U.S. concentrated not on immediate rescue, but on the plans for postwar reconstruction and the creation of a Jewish state. The Orthodox groups, on the other hand, were bound by the higher moral laws of the Torah's imperative of *pikuach nefesh* (saving a life), so their behavior often incurred the wrath of their fellow Jews. Throughout the Holocaust, however, the Orthodox groups usually sought unity on rescue and were willing to cooperate with any others, including the atheist leaders of the Jewish Labor Committee and the outcast Bergson group, to save Jewish lives.

One caveat. Although *Thy Brother's Blood* examines the successes of the Orthodox rescue movement, it does not by any means suggest that the personalities involved in rescue activities were flawless in their planning and execution, especially regarding a proper response to Rabbi Weissmandl's desperate pleas and rescue proposals. Cincinnati's Rabbi Eliezer Silver, founder of Vaad Hatzalah and one of the most dedicated Orthodox rescue savants, alluded to this when he wrote how he grieved for

> hundreds of thousands of chaste and pure souls that cried out for help and rescue and were not answered ... perhaps there was some possibility to rescue them and it was not properly exploited; or there was a propitious moment for snatching them from the jaws of doom and we missed the opportunity, even if unwittingly.[7]

Arguments over methodology didn't stop with the end of the war. Although many believe that the right effort at the right time would have spared untold lives, some critics hold today that if unlimited funds had been available, only a handful more could have been saved. Such critics miss the point. For Orthodox Jews it is a Torah dictum that if even one more Jewish life had been spared, then all the money and effort would have been worthwhile — and mandatory. Indeed, the Torah* says that "whoever saves one life is considered as if he had saved the entire world."[8]

Furthermore, if all efforts had failed and no one had been saved, the task was nevertheless required, for effort is measured, not success. Still, with little staff and less money, the Orthodox activists managed to save tens of thousands of lives. There is little doubt that had more money been available, many more tens of thousands of Jewish lives could have been saved.

After the war, Rabbi Silver stated: "I can say for myself and all my friends and colleagues in the leadership of the Vaad Hatzalah and also for the whole community of Orthodox Rabbis that:

> ... our hands did not spill this blood that could have been saved and was not ... Within the limits of our possibilities, we neglected no direct or indirect line of communication nor any legal or illegal ways of rescuing our brethren in Europe. More than once did we enter into doubtful deals or dubious action the moment we saw any prospect or opportunity at all of saving Jewish lives."[9]

The reference implicit in Rabbi Silver's statement is *Deuteronomy* 21:1-9, which requires the community to accept responsibility for any loss of Jewish life that could have been prevented. "If one be found slain in the land which *Hashem* your G-d has given you ... and it be not known who has smitten him, then your elders and judges shall go forth ... and declare: 'Our

---

* By "Torah" is meant both Written Scriptures and Oral or Talmudic Law or Tradition.

hands have not shed this blood.' " This above all is the context in which Orthodox efforts must be judged.

This book is divided into two parts. Part I traces the development of Orthodox rescue organizations and the social and religious factors that paved their way. It also analyzes the Jewish perspective that motivated the Orthodox, their search for cooperation and their lonely individualistic road when cooperation proved unfeasible. Part II presents personal portraits of the individuals involved, material often based on reminiscences of rescue activists. In some cases, previously published sketches by other authors have been translated and edited especially for this volume.

Preface: Four Episodes

I. Irving Bunim and The Shabbos Ride

T WAS A SHABBOS AFTERNOON sometime in January 1941, and I was sitting at the Sabbath table having dinner with my wife (of blessed memory). Suddenly, the tranquility of the Sabbath atmosphere was shattered. The unthinkable happened; a cab drove up, and out leaped two prominent rabbis with whom I was acquainted: Rabbi Boruch Kaplan and Rabbi Alexander Linchner (now head of Jerusalem's Boys Town). It was virtually unthinkable for two such devout Jews to be traveling on the Sabbath unless the matter was one of life and death.

"And so indeed it was. 'Mr. Bunim,' they declared in compelling tones, 'we have been sent by Rabbi Shraga Feivel Mendlowitz (Dean of Mesivta Torah Vodaath), Rabbi Moshe Feinstein (Dean of Mesivta Tifereth Jerusalem), and Rabbi Shlomo Heiman (Associate Dean, Mesivta Torah Vodaath),' as impressive a group as you could muster. 'You must go immediately to Brooklyn,' they continued, 'and raise a riot among the Jewish community. Tell them that the Jews who escaped to Russia were given notice that within thirty days they must leave the country or they will become permanent residents and will never be allowed to leave.* Great sums of money are needed immediately to provide for their transportation and other expenses. We must act now to save as many as we can.'

---

* Russian-occupied Lithuania. Russia gave the Jewish refugees from Poland an "opportunity" to opt for Soviet citizenship — or else.

"The very fact of our traveling on the sacred Sabbath instilled in us a holy fervor and we proceeded in a cab driven by a gentile driver. When we arrived at each of the homes we were to visit on our fundraising mission everyone became extremely excited. They wanted to know if we were putting on an act — could it be one great practical joke? However, when they realized that we were in dead earnest and that every moment could mean a life, they responded generously. In a short time we raised the necessary $50,000.

"That night we contacted the Joint, which had the money in its Lithuanian account. We gave them the money in the U.S. and then used their account to help arrange for the transportation of several hundred rabbis from Russian-occupied Lithuania. In this way, the great sages Rabbi Aaron Kotler and Rabbi Reuven Grozovsky (both now of blessed memory) were rescued. First they were brought from Russia to Japan and in mid-1941 they made it to the United States."

II. The Rabbis and the Treasury Secretary

It was the spring of 1944, and millions of Jews had already been murdered by the Nazis. One small avenue of escape was the use of "bogus" Latin American papers, from countries such as Paraguay, Salvador, etc., which the Nazis, for their own reason, recognized as valid. A group of about 240 Jewish holders of such papers had been sent from Poland to a detention camp in France near the town of Vittel.[2]

WORD SUDDENLY GOT OUT that for some reason the Swiss and Spanish representatives no longer were willing to serve as the

Latin American Papers protecting powers for these holders of Latin American documents. Recha Sternbuch, the Swiss representative of the Vaad Hatzalah, the Orthodox rescue committee, quickly alerted Rabbi Abraham Kalmanowitz of Vaad Hatzalah (rabbis' rescue committee) and Yaakov Rosenheim, president of World Agudath Israel, urging them to do everything in their power to convince the State Department and the War Refugee Board (the governmental agency established in January 1944 by President Roosevelt for the rescue of European Jewry) to pressure the Latin American governments to officially recognize these bogus papers. This would, in turn, pressure the Nazis to continue to provide special protection for the Jewish holders of these papers.

The following episode, derived from the *Morgenthau Diaries*, provides a glimpse into the methods applied by the rabbis in their quest to save Jewish lives, and the impact they had on some government officials.

Although the emotion, the tears and the quivering voices are missing from the printed pages of these dialogues, much of the drama, nevertheless, comes through by implication and reading between the lines. The sad truth is that Judge Samuel Rosenman, FDR's Jewish confidant, promised the rabbis to get in touch with the State Department and to use his influence to prod them into action. Yet, as soon as the rabbis left his office he phoned Morgenthau to tell him that this problem belonged to the WRB, not him. He was too busy for particularist Jewish concerns.[3]

MORGENTHAU THEN GREETED THE RABBIS and asked who would be their spokesman. The eldest, the patriarchal Rabbi Kalmanowitz, in his broken English made the opening plea:

"Do the Utmost"

Coming to you Mr. Secretary about saving the lives of the Jewish. We have a question from two thousand two hundred and thirty-eight interned people in the camps of Vittel and Tittmoning.

We received yesterday [April 5] by cable that every inmate there is in danger of life and death.

We come to the office of Mr. Pehle, and Mr. Pehle, I know very well, in the four or six weeks or less that he is working very hard to save the lives ... Mr. Lesser, Miss Hodel and Mr. DuBois, who are willing to work day and night for the saving — I know very well and I recognize — the saving has not come. I don't know about the blame. I think the blame is in the State Department. There is every danger not only for the lives of the two thousand two hundred and thirty-eight people, but for three and a half million people. We have not very much help.*

Please Mr. Secretary do the utmost that you can do to save them, every one.[4]

Then, as Morgenthau related to Secretary of State Cordell Hull, "the rabbis broke down and cried here in my office, and we had quite a time."[5]

Obviously, Rabbi Kalmanowitz's plea was an emotionally laden entreaty that somewhat unnerved the cool, WASP-like exterior of the Jewish Secretary of the Treasury, since the latter responded, "Now, look, you get upset and you get me upset, and I

---

* The 2,238 referred to the inmates of several camps possessing Latin American papers, including the 238 in Vittel.

can't do anything either."[6]

Unfazed, the Jewish sage went on to explain the problem of the delay in the cables which were to have brought the recognition of the validity of the Latin American papers, declaring:

> I know Mr. Lesser and [Miss] Hodel and [Mr.] DuBois have at hand three cables that must go yesterday, and the cables are not going; one cable to Spain, one cable to the Swiss, one cable to the South American countries. You know very well, the less cables you have to send through the State Department ...[7]

Evidently, his message got through to Morgenthau, for unlike Judge Rosenman, he decided then and there to goad State into getting out those cables. Moreover, Morgenthau insisted that he take the "strongest position [and] ask the Swiss Government as the intervening power to insist with the Germans that these passports be recognized."[8]

HE THEN PHONED Secretary of State Cordell Hull but only reached his secretary [Brown] who was not too familiar with the issue. When
Bureaucratic Delay he tried to shake off Morgenthau by assuring him that he'll pass the message along, and when Brown said that he'll call back, Morgenthau replied, "Well, either you or Mr. Hull call me back ... and I'll just sit here and wait until I hear from you."[9]

The obviously concerned rabbis, impatient with the bureaucratic delay, bore down on the Jewish Secretary of the Treasury, who thus acted immediately, encouraged by both Pehle and DuBois. Within an hour, with the rabbis waiting outside, Morgenthau finally got Hull on the phone. With an unusual sense of urgency, Morgenthau explained the problem and demanded that Hull's assistant George Warren come over that night to settle the matter of the cables that were supposed to have been sent by mid-March, adding, "I'll wait till he comes."[10] That very evening the matter was settled, a fact Morgenthau was quite proud of.[11]

The next morning, April 7, with a sense of accomplishment and a fairly accurate assessment, he noted that:

> ... nothing has pleased me more than being able to get the State Department to send out this cable in regard to Camp Vittel. It just shows that if we put enough heat in the right place it can be done, and believe me, we have put plenty of heat on Mr. Hull proper ...
>
> When these things are out and nothing happens, they must ask themselves, "Well, after all, what is all this fighting for?" So

the fact that the March 16 cable went — of course in the room I can say it is a tragedy it didn't go on March 16. Most likely two hundred and fifty people have been murdered because it didn't go out on the 16th of March.[12]

Then, quite inadvertently, Morgenthau touched upon the real reason he and the WRB put the heat on State, when he added:

I made up my mind last night, and I told these people [i.e., rabbis] I would stay here until it did go. I did stay here with the help of you people, and with the result that people over there who were opposed to the thing — evidently Mr. Hull, although I haven't spoken to him since last night ... But the results were good. I just made up my mind I would stick it out ...[13]

Morgenthau not only pinpointed the culprit in the State Department who probably held up the cables, he also raised his omnipresent fears — of antisemitism, pointing out:

Well, it turned out it wasn't the last word, and he most likely can say again as he did once before, "It is that damned Jew in the Treasury" who overruled him. He said it once before, and now most likely he will say, "G-d-damned Jew." It is a badge of honor.[14]

Still, revealing the same naive trust in the President as did most Jews, he preferred to lay the blame on the State Department instead:

It is unfortunate that such people exist in Mr. Roosevelt's administration, and they should be gotten rid of, but Mr. Hull doesn't seem to want to get rid of them ...[15]

Concluding in a lighter vein, Morgenthau regaled his staff with the story of how:

... I called up this Rabbi [i.e., Kalmanowitz] and wanted to thank him. After all it was a nice Passover present. He said, 'I want to wish you Mr. Morgenthau an Orthodox Passover.' [laughter] So I wish you all a very Orthodox Passover.[16]

What Rabbi Kalmanowitz undoubtedly must have said was the usual Jewish Passover greeting, "Have a *kosher* Passover," which the assimilated Morgenthau translated as an "Orthodox Passover."

The Rabbis' Persistence

THE RABBIS' PERSISTENCE, HOWEVER, did not stop at this point. That night, at 10 p.m., a tired Morgenthau was awakened by George Warren of State, who informed him about changes in the above cables, still trying to procrastinate by telling Rabbi Baruch Korff one thing and Morgenthau another. However, a surprised Morgenthau discovered that the audacious Korff had called up Hull directly, causing Miss Klotz to exclaim, "They [i.e., the rabbis] won't stop at anything." Adding on her own, "They're right."[17]

As he pointed out, Korff had no hesitancy in calling up Mr. Pehle at 2 a.m. on emergency matters — calling him "an angel to stand the pressure that we put on him." Nor did he hesitate to include in the pressure on State a disclosure to the famed columnist Drew Pearson, who wrote up its procrastinating tactics in his syndicated column.

When the astonished Morgenthau asked Korff, "Did you talk as forcefully as that?," the young rabbi answered:

> ... Oh, yes, Mr. Secretary ... When you feel in the heart and soul as I feel about it, there is no question whether Mr. Hull or Mr. Morgenthau or Mr. Roosevelt — human life is at stake.[18]

That the above and many more such conversations by the rabbis had a profound effect on the Jewish Treasury Secretary is evident from his response to Rabbi Korff. When the latter desired to thank him for his efforts, he said:

> ... I got so upset the other day that I have been physically ill until last night.

Noticing Rabbi Korff's concern, Morgenthau added:

> It is very unimportant, but I have been so moved by this thing. After all, I feel this thing very, very closely, and the tragedy is that these things don't happen in the same day. Maybe Mr. Hull will take more interest now.[19]

Unwilling to merely accept the assurance that a cable to be sent to the Latin American countries and Spain was now authorized by the Secretary of State himself, and aware that Ambassador Carleton Hayes in Spain was not very helpful in rescue matters, Rabbi Korff asked whether it was possible to call up the Ambassador directly as a follow-up to the cable. Morgenthau sympathized but suggested:

> ... Let the sympathetic DuBois write the cable in that manner [i.e., to act without delay]. You see it before it goes over. Write it that Mr. Hull is ordering Ambassador Hayes to see the proper authorities today — today is Monday — to the proper authorities on Tuesday and report back the same day ...[20]

Despite the fact that all these efforts were too late to save the 238 inmates of Vittel, they were not in vain. The eventual recognition of these phony Latin American papers by their governments and the acceptance by Spain and Switzerland of the protection for their holders meant that many thousands of Jews in Nazi-occupied countries were eventually able to survive as a result of the official recognition pressed by the State Department via the WRB and initiated by the few determined and dedicated Orthodox rabbis.

III. A Sefer Torah for Sale

It was some time in 1944. Rabbi Abraham Kalmanowitz had brought the desperate cables sent by Rabbi Michoel Ber Weissmandl, head of the Slovak Jewish underground, to Baltimore, in an attempt to arouse the Jewish community. An opportunity existed at the time to bring refugees from Poland across the border into the-then relatively safe Slovakia at $1,000 a head — an enormous sum at the time.

Rabbi Kalmanowitz went to see the Jewish leadership of Baltimore, the established Associated Jewish Charities, all the rabbinical organizations, etc. In emotional terms, as befitting the crisis, Rabbi Kalmanowitz sought to arouse this leadership into creating a special emergency campaign, in order to rescue as many Jews as possible.

After delivering his impassioned talk, the organized Jewish leadership had an opportunity to assess the situation. Most would neither believe Rabbi Kalmanowitz nor heed his call. Some dubbed him "hysterical" and prevaricator, while others said, "Let's not make waves, we can't do anything anyway." And so they voted to ignore the pleas.

A few of the more Orthodox rabbis, unwilling to stand idly by, decided to make their own emergency appeals. Rabbi Shimon Schwab, of the Congregation Shearith Israel, himself a refugee from Germany, made such an appeal on *Parshas Bo* (the weekly portion of the Torah reading for that week).

Standing up at the podium, Rabbi Schwab declared to the surprised congregation, "This is the most important speech of my life." Paraphrasing Rashi's comment on the words of *Moshe Rabbeinu* to Pharaoh, he thundered: "Why are we acting like poverty-stricken and lowly people in the face of this enormous need that has just arisen?" He went on to read the demands of Rabbi Weissmandl, that unless they respond immediately and with more than they can afford, they will be held accountable by heaven for the Torah's injunction of *Lo Sa'amod.*

The people did respond to the alarm. Straining their resources, many, especially the women, gave their personal jewelry. Rabbi Schwab told the congregation:

> As a refugee, I have no resources of my own, but I do have a small Torah scroll which I cherish dearly. It had been entrusted to me by the *parnasim* of the small town of Kleinurdlingen whom I served as a *rav*, but which, by 1936, no

longer had a *minyan*. The Talmud notes that one may not sell a *Sefer Torah* except for three important reasons: to enable one to study Torah, to get married and for questions involving *pikuach nefesh*. Today it is a question of *pikuach nefesh*, a matter of life and death. I hereby offer this treasure of mine for sale as my contribution to the appeal.

One of the congregation's trustees bought the the scroll for $1,000, and placed it in the ark, where it remains to this day. Despite the small size of the congregation, the appeal raised over $10,000, an immense sum, yet so pitifully small compared to the need.

IV. The Rabbi and the Children: Solomon Schonfeld to the Rescue[21]

It was the fall of 1938. Rabbi Dr. Solomon Schonfeld was a young rabbi of twenty-six who had taken over his late father's positions as rabbi of a small congregation and principal of a small day school — the first in England. News of the persecution of Jews in Germany and Austria began to filter in, especially the day after the terrible pogrom of *Kristallnacht* of November 9-10, 1938. This episode is based on an interview of Mr. Leo Schick, a witness to the event.

❧ ❧ ❧

Sitting in his modest office, Dr. Schonfeld could not settle down to his daily work. A sensitive man, he understood the full impact of the tragedy. He had thought that such things could only happen in the Middle Ages, not in our own age of progress. Here he sat, safe in his cozy room, while his fellow Jews on the other side of the Channel languished in concentration camps. What could he do to help them? He had no money. His father had never been money-minded. Whatever he had managed to save from his own modest salary he usually gave away when confronted with an emergency among his congregants. So the only thing left was compassion for his brethren, but this was clearly not enough.

DR. SCHONFELD'S THOUGHTS were interrupted by the sharp ring of the telephone. It was a Mr. Julius Steinfeld calling from Vienna.

An Urgent Phone Call (See Chapter 14b.) Dr. Schonfeld had talked to this man several times in Austria. Steinfeld, a courageous communal leader in Vienna, had been doing his utmost for his brethren in Austria without regard for his own safety. Briefly and carefully, so as not to run afoul of the censors, who he was sure were listening in on the telephone conversation, Mr. Steinfeld now told Dr. Schonfeld of hundreds of children whose parents had been arrested or killed in the pogrom and who were now left on their own. Could Dr. Schonfeld help them? His voice choked with emotion, Dr. Schonfeld told him he would try. A council of members of Dr. Schonfeld's congregation was hastily summoned to grapple with the problem. The gentlemen decided to raise enough money to bring over to England ten children for a start. Dr. Schonfeld left the meeting in a depressed mood. They didn't understand, these good men, that it would take weeks, even months to raise the large amount they thought would be necessary to care adequately for the children. Meanwhile, hunger, sickness and the threat of further pogroms would take a heavy toll. Ten children indeed!

Something much more drastic had to be done. But Rabbi Schonfeld at first did not dare spell out his plans to me. He was afraid he would be put into a strait-jacket. He knew his congregation; they were a well-fed, well-housed community. The troubles on the Continent still seemed very far away. Bombs and war appeared highly unlikely. Perhaps the people of the congregation were a little too complacent. After a sleepless night, mulling everything over again and again, Dr. Schonfeld went to the British Home Office.

THE IMPRESSIVE FIGURE of a handsome six-footer with gleaming eyes and a winning smile gained ready access to one important **A Bold** official. Dr. Schonfeld told the official what had **Plan** happened in Austria. This, of course, was no news to that gentleman. He, too, had read the newspapers. Then Dr. Schonfeld unfolded the details as he himself saw them, and reported what Mr. Steinfeld had told him on the telephone. The official muttered that he was very sorry but there was nothing he could do to help. Then, for the first time, Dr. Schonfeld revealed his plan. He said he wanted to bring 300 Jewish children from Vienna to London and care for them personally. The British official was stunned. How could one rabbi provide for so many children, to house, feed and clothe them? Dr. Schonfeld told him he had neighbors who would be willing to help; he personally would guarantee with whatever assets he himself possessed that the children would not become burdens to the British government. All that was necessary was that the children should be given permission to come to England.

The British official sized up his petitioner with growing admiration. A young man, not yet thirty years old, with a pure soul, a good heart and a tremendous will to help others. Could he send this man away? Would he ever be able to sleep peacefully again if he said "No" now? Thinking of his own children, his own home, he would have been ready to give his approval. But his duties as an official of the British Government forced him to hold back. "Tell me, Rabbi, where will you put the children to sleep the first night they are here?" he asked.

Dr. Schonfeld fell silent, but suddenly he had an inspiration. "I have two schools of which I am principal. I will empty the school buildings. I will house the children there," he replied.

"I want to see for myself where there is room for 300 children in your school," said the man behind the desk.

The rabbi and the British government official went out together, hailed a taxi and drove off to North London. Before the eyes of the startled pupils, the two men measured the length and width of each classroom. They began to figure in terms of so many children and so many square feet. It would have been barely enough, but there was one large room which could not be used. It had to be left clear as a dining room for the students. Forty children would still be without shelter. "Well," said the official, "in view of the circumstances, I can give you passports for only 260 children." But the official had not reckoned with Rabbi Schonfeld. "I own the house in which I live," the rabbi said, "I will empty that out, too, in order to make room for the children." Back Dr. Schonfeld went, the government official in tow, to his private home. Again, the yardstick came out. Defeated by the overwhelming humanity of this man, the official diffidently asked Dr. Schonfeld where he himself would sleep. Dr. Schonfeld took him upstairs to a tiny room in the attic filled with bric-a-brac. "I can sleep here," he said. The official had tears in his eyes as he shook the rabbi's hand and asked him to submit the names of the children to whom he should issue the permits to enter England.

Immediately, in the presence of the official, Rabbi Schonfeld telephoned the leaders of Vienna's Jewish community. He asked them to draw up a list of names and admonished them to see to it that the children on this list would be ready to travel as soon as possible. Two days later he was back at the Home Office with all the data about the children. A passport official began to prepare the individual papers. He was only halfway through when it was closing time at the office. He told Dr. Schonfeld to come back the next day;

he would finish the remaining passports then. But on being reminded of the joy which these papers would bring to 300 families in Europe, this kind man disregarded closing time and worked on the papers until midnight. Then he helped Dr. Schonfeld pack the papers and carry them to the post office to speed them on their way to Austria.

NOW THAT THE FIRST STEP had been taken, the real worries began. On an urgent call from Dr. Schonfeld early in the morning, **Housing** his friends assembled at his home. He told them what **Three** he had done and asked them to help him. A search **Hundred** for beds began. The local Boy Scout troop had a sufficient number of beds and blankets at their summer camp. They were only too willing to lend them for such a purpose. Several trucks were sent out to the scout camp to bring these, plus many dishes and large pots and pans which were necessary to cook for the refugees. Meanwhile, a cable reported that the children had left Vienna. Then disaster struck. A blizzard, the heaviest in eight years, blanketed London and the schools were snow-bound. But this did not deter Dr. Schonfeld. Together with a group of youngsters he went out with shovels to clear the way for the trucks that would bring the refugee children. This accomplished, the school and his own home ready for the children, he hurried to the port of Harwich to greet his 300 new charges.

What he saw moved him deeply. Here were ragged, starved, frightened youngsters, the remains of once-proud families. He shepherded them into the hired trucks to bring them to their new shelters. Neighbors were waiting there. Everyone was willing and ready to help feed and wash the children and put them to bed on this, their first night in their new country. The rabbi was close to exhaustion, but he stayed on duty until all the children had been settled. Only after that did he go home for his first good night's sleep in a week. Entering his house, he heard a little six-year-old refugee girl crying for her mother. He took the child in his arms, talked to her about her new country and promised to bring her mommy to join her soon. Then Dr. Schonfeld went up to his attic chamber for a well-earned rest.

WHAT INSPIRED THIS ORTHODOX LEADERSHIP, *roshei yeshivah* and laymen and women alike, to act differently than the vast

What Inspired Them? majority of Jews in the free world? What motivated this politically and financially insignificant segment of world Jewry and its network in different parts of the world, to battle the Jewish Establishment and indifferent Allied governments alike? And why were these least likely candidates for militant action in the forefront?

Only a historical analysis of the classic Jewish approach to rescue and concern of one Jew for his fellow Jew and the changed perspectives wrought by the rise of secular Jewish ideologies at the end of the nineteenth and the early part of the twentieth centuries can provide the answers. Such an analysis is presented for the first time.

CHAPTER ONE

Pikuach Nefesh:
The Jewish Foreign Policy

R ABBI MICHOEL BER WEISSMANDL, *rosh yeshivah*, son-in-law of Rabbi Shmuel Dovid Unger (the leader of Slovak Jewry and head of the Yeshivah of Nitra), was the true genius of

Genius of Rescue rescue. Weissmandl headed the Slovak Jewish Underground, called the Working Group, with Gisi Fleischmann, a distant relative. He was the personification of the Torah's perspective of rescue.

He began working on relief and rescue in 1938, but by 1942 almost three-fourths of Slovakia's 80,000 Jews had been deported. When he learned that year that Dieter Wisliceny (Adolf Eichmann's assistant for Jewish Affairs in Slovakia) had agreed to exempt a Jew from deportation in exchange for a bribe, Weissmandl negotiated with Wisliceny, through a Jewish intermediary, for the ransom of the remaining 25,000 Jews for US $50,000. (See Chapter 15b.) Weissmandl then sought to broaden the ransom plan to include all the Jews under Nazi control. The Europa Plan, as the result of his negotiations with Wisliceny came to be called, would have halted all deportations in Axis territory in exchange for two million dollars, to be paid in installments of $200,000. Most of the money would have to come from American Jewry. The plan failed because the Jewish organizations doubted it would work and were unwilling to buck the Allied governments' strong aversion to sending money to an enemy with whom they were at war. That the plan was proposed by an Orthodox rabbi made it doubly suspect to the Jewish Establishment. Smaller ransom plans followed, however, in 1944-45, and were responsible for the rescue of thousands of Jewish lives. (See Chap. 7.)

In his history of the Joint during the Holocaust, Yehudah Bauer noted the dismal response of world Jewry to Rabbi Weissmandl's pleas and wondered whether a "Jewish foreign policy" — one based on the assumption that "the saving of Jews [was] a priority, while yet not denying the first necessity of winning the war" — might have served collective Jewish interests better than what actually occurred during the Holocaust.[1] That was essentially what Rabbi Weissmandl had been calling for, and what had been standard Jewish policy for 2,000 years. Bauer sums up by saying, "The time was not yet ripe for such a revolution in political outlook."[2] The irony is that what the secular Jewish world needed was not a revolution but a counter-revolution, one that reverted to the Torah traditions of *pikuach nefesh* and *hatzalos nefashos* (the preservation of life) epitomized by Rabbi Weissmandl — principles that had united the differing voices of Orthodox Jewish leaders throughout the Diaspora.

PIKUACH NEFESH IS INTIMATED in the Scriptures, is enlarged upon in the Talmud, is also codified in Jewish law, and has thousands

Pikuach Nefesh of years of Diasporan precedent behind it. Since the Torah commands that saving life takes precedence over virtually all other activities, a practice such as *pidyon shevuyim* (ransoming captives) based on the concept of *arevus* (the responsibility of one Jew for another) became commonplace, even where no immediate danger was present.

Torah literature is replete with thoughts on the sanctity of life. In the Mishnah, Jews are instructed to remember that "every person bears the Divine image and every person was created unique and irreplaceable. Therefore everyone can say, 'for my sake was the world created.' "[3] Rabbi Akiva raised the Biblical dictum to "love your neighbor as yourself" into a cardinal principle of Judaism.[4] The Talmud asks, "From where do we know that if you see your friend drowning or in danger from wild animals or robbers that you are required to rescue him even if you have to spend money [to hire someone to do the job]?" And answers, Scripture states, 'Do not stand idly by while your neighbor's blood is being shed.' "[5] Some authorities even go so far as to say that one is required to put oneself in danger if there is the opportunity to stop — or even kill —

someone who is pursuing another person for the purpose of murder or rape.[6]

For the Jew, the sanctity of life should take precedence over all else, even the Sabbath except for certain restrictions involving idol worship, murder, and adultery.[7] The Torah commands: "Ye shall keep My statutes and My ordinances, which if a man do he shall live by them."[8] Thus, according to the Talmud, if an action involves saving life, the transgression of Torah law — or any other — is not only permitted but commanded, so that "he shall live by [the commandments] and not die" as a result of fulfilling them. Virtually nothing stands in the way of *pikuach nefesh*, the preservation of life.

If *pikuach nefesh* is the philosophy behind lifesaving efforts, *pidyon shevuyim* is often the means by which lives are saved when Jews have been captured or unjustly imprisoned. According to Maimonides, *pidyon shevuyim* takes precedence over every other form of charity.[9] Maimonides even notes the halachic hierarchies in ransom activities, including the place of women over men, and scholars over kings.[10] In stressing the significance of this *mitzvah*, he states:

> The redemption of captives has precedence over the feeding and clothing of the poor, and there is no commandment as great as that of redeeming captives, for the captive is among the hungry, thirsty and naked, and lives in constant danger. He who closes his eye to an opportunity of redemption violates [several positive and negative commandments].[11]

To that, Rabbi Joseph Colon (known as the *Maharik*) added, "Unnecessary delay in ransoming a captive is as great a sin as murder."[12]

PIDYON SHEVUYIM AS A PROGRAM for action is reinforced by the obligation of *arevus*, the brother's-keeper concept that has always

A Jew was Never Alone

been as much a part of Jewish identity as the Sabbath, Yom Kippur, and *kashruth*.[13] Both gave Jews great strength during their Diaspora history. Both concepts permitted Jewish merchants to travel long and dangerous routes in the early Middle Ages, a time when most Europeans lived and died within a few square miles. "Thus a Jew," one historian of this period writes,

> was never alone, never friendless or abandoned, never without the full and active protection of all the Jews living within a considerable radius of whatever place he happened to be in at

the time. Even when he was hundreds of miles from his home town, he was practically surrounded by devoted brothers."[14]

Jews literally paid fortunes to ransom fellow Jews from Mediterranean pirates and Tartars and Cossacks. In 1487, Spanish Jews led by Chief Rabbi Abraham Senior paid the enormous sum of 27,000 florins to ransom 1,000 Jews in Malaga. In seventeenth-century Venice, there was a special Jewish ransom society — with a branch in Hamburg — dedicated to ransom whenever and wherever necessary and supported by membership dues and export duties on all goods shipped to Jewish merchants in the east. A sixteenth-century French traveler in the Balkans and Asia professed to be amazed that "the Jews were so united among themselves that they never permitted one of their people to remain in servitude."[15]

AT THE CENTER OF JEWISH RESCUE was the *shtadlan*, or intercessor, a noted lay or rabbinic leader and often an important

The Shtadlan

financier. Usually a man of great persuasiveness and resources, the *shtadlan* worked with outside authorities to reverse anti-Jewish policies on behalf of individuals, communities, even entire regions. As such, the *shtadlan* was the Jewish community's foreign minister, one who bargained under difficult circumstances and from a position of weakness.

Perhaps the most famous *shtadlan* of Moslem Spain was Rabbi Shmuel Hanagid, a great Talmudist and poet, vizier to the king and commander of his armies. Yet for all his secular honors, Rabbi Shmuel saw himself primarily as his community's *shtadlan*. In the time of the Holy Roman Empire, the recognized *shtadlan* was Joselman of Rosheim who, living in Germany in the 15th and 16th centuries, defended the Jews against a variety of accusations, including ritual murder, and was given the title Commander of all Jewry by Emperor Maximilian.[16]

Often the *shtadlan* had high standing at the ruling courts of Europe. In the seventeenth and eighteenth centuries, for example, many *shtadlanim* were royal bankers, so-called "court Jews." Some, such as Joseph Suess Oppenheimer, were killed working for their fellow Jews. Others, such as Moses Montefiore in England and Baron Hertz Ginzburg in Russia in the nineteenth century, were esteemed in both the Jewish and secular worlds. While many *shtadlanim* used a variety of methods to achieve their ends, virtually all of them considered ransom and bribery their most effective weapons.[17]

By the 19th century, however, Jewish emancipation and the rise of secular Jewry meant the decline of the individual *shtadlan* and the rise of "civic defense organizations." The Board of Deputies of British Jews, founded in 1760, the French *Alliance Israelite* (1860), the American Jewish Committee (1906), and the American Jewish Congress (1918) were all created to protect Jews and their civil rights. The more observant segments of the Jewish community continued to rely on the *shtadlan*. Some were outstanding scholars, such as Rabbi Nachum of Grodno (1812-1897), Rabbi Yitzchok Elchonon Spector in Kovno (1817-1896), and, in pre-World War II Poland, Rabbi Avrohom Perlmutter, and Rabbi Aaron Lewin, although elected members of the Polish parliament acted in a similar way.[18]

IN THIS CENTURY, between the two world wars, secularist Jewish parties arose in most of Eastern and Central Europe. There were

New Era of "Jewish Politics" Began

Marxists, socialist Bundists, and Zionists both socialist and liberal. A new era of "Jewish politics" began. The secularists were taken with the visions of freedom and equality promised by emancipation. Part of the price they were willing to pay was the discarding of much of Jewish traditions and the Torah way of life. They would "normalize" Jews and Jewish life by becoming more and more like their gentile neighbors. Having lost their Jewish sense of honor and dignity, they adopted the gentile's code of honor instead. This meant that all the indignities that Jews had endured for centuries could no longer be tolerated. While the Orthodox Jew could slough off the insults of the physically superior non-Jew and still retain his dignity, in spite of outward obeisance, the secularist was no longer psychologically protected from the inferior position the Russian or Pole or any other gentile ruler placed him in. Equality and rights would now be demanded, rather than pleaded for. Physical combat, or even dying for the "honor" of one's country, the highest expression of the romantic Polish code, now became part of the secular Jewish posture.[19]

For the Orthodox, during the period between the two world wars, for example, survival was much more important than a heroic but futile battle. The secularists viewed such an attitude as cowardice. The Orthodox never presumed full equality with the Poles and did not try to impose this concept on their unwilling Polish neighbors. They simply tried to gain as many rights as possible and to retain their religious way of life, though they were not always successful.[20]

THE RADICAL SECULAR JEWISH IDEOLOGIES viewed the political
arena in post-World War I Poland in terms of confrontation politics,

Secularists Deplore Shtadlonus stressing unrealistic *demands* of Jewish nationalist *rights* in a way that antagonized the Polish nationalists. Yitzchok Grynbaum, the dynamic Zionist leader and member of the Polish
parliament, who espoused confrontation politics, "epitomized the
new style in Jewish politics and became the most popular Jewish
leader in Poland." As the historian Celia Heller noted, "The
secularists deplored the humble Orthodox practice of *shtadlonus*,
which stressed accommodation, patriotism, and loyalty, and
emphasized only 'religious' demands."[21]

Unlike Agudath Israel, which had no hesitation in dealing with
the Pilsudski government or with even the fascist Sanacja regime,
the new "honorable" Jewish politics of the secularists did not allow
for negotiations with such virulent extremist antisemites — or worse
— fascists. Says the historian Celia Heller, new politics encouraged
"extreme factionalism and emphasis on ideology, [and] did not
encourage much flexibility in negotiations, since for Grynbaum, for
example, the idea of negotiations with an avowedly antisemitic
government was an anathema."[22]

Furthermore, while Agudah unofficially continued to use old-
fashioned Jewish diplomacy in modern Poland, the secular proponents of the "honorable and proud stand against the antisemites"
shunned the traditional weapons of ransom and bribery and other
illegal means of rescue as "repugnant and demeaning."[23]

These acquired characteristics were not merely part and parcel
of the secular Jewish ideologies in Europe, which tried to fashion a
new Jew from the *golus Yid*, but were accepted as readily by the
assimilationist, western liberal Jews, who presumed full equality
with their neighbors in the western countries.[24]

BETWEEN THE TWO WORLD WARS, (non-Zionist) Orthodox Jews
and the traditional methods of *shtadlonus* were represented in

Jewish Pride and Dignity Poland primarily by the Agudath Israel World Organization. Founded in 1912 as a counter-poise to the Zionist and socialist Jewish forces,
the Agudah entered the political arena in Poland and the Baltic states
in a spirit of pragmatic accommodation with authorities. The Agudah determined its policies by the vote of its members not by ideological line — unlike the Bundists and Zionists, whose independent
opposition aggravated the Poles' antisemitic tendencies.[25]

Was the secular Jewish representative a more proud Jew than his Orthodox counterpart? Not at all. In fact, the Agudah's role as *shtadlan* was praised by M.A. Hartglass, a Zionist and assimilationist who hardly considered himself an ally of Orthodox Jews. The Agudah representative, he wrote:

> behaved toward the Polish Ministers with such dignity and Jewish pride, spoke so courageously to them, that I never would have expected this from a member of the Agudah ... Unfortunately, not all our Jewish representatives were able to behave with such courage when dealing with non-Jews. Yes, they managed to be very brave and extremist when they spoke in the Jewish Caucus, they managed to speak sharply and even aggressively in the Diet when they spoke for the benefit of the press. But in person with a *goy* they became so subservient that it was simply impossible to recognize them.[26]

It is important to note as well that while settlement of Eretz Israel (as distinct from advocacy for a secular political state) was part of the Agudah's program from its creation, and especially during the 1930's, its focus was always on Jewish rights and activities in all the countries where Jews lived. During the Holocaust local Agudah branches, individual Agudists, and virtually any Orthodox Jews living in such free countries as Switzerland, England, Turkey and Sweden, all served as vital links in a world-wide relief and rescue network.

Moreover, another source of friction between Agudah and the Zionists was the tiny quota of six percent of all certificates for immigration to Palestine, assigned to Agudah by the Jewish Agency even during the twenties. This greatly reduced the number of those Orthodox Jews, Agudists and non Agudists (except for Mizrachi), who sought *aliya* during the interbellum period.

What is more important for the tragic era of the Holocaust is that the Orthodox leadership — whether in Poland, Palestine or the U.S. — never lost their sense of traditional Jewish diplomacy, or *shtadlonus* based on *arevus* and *pikuach nefesh*. Therefore, they never relinquished their primary weapons of bribery, ransom, or the use of illegal methods as a means of assuring the survival of the Jewish people. In contrast, secularist Jews of all varieties, whether assimilated or members of the various secular Jewish ideologies, lost these key weapons at a time when they could have been most effective. This was true of the Jewish leadership in the free world as well as in Europe.

CHAPTER TWO
Pikuach Nefesh in Action

MUCH OF THE HOLOCAUST cannot be understood unless one is aware of this basic premise of the priority of *pikuach nefesh* — one that so far has escaped all the historians of the Holocaust. It is therefore no surprise that sooner or later the proponents of traditional Jewish diplomacy had to clash with those espousing the secularist viewpoints. Both the Jewish nationalist and leftist parties in Poland termed the Torah view — concern for lives over concern for honor — weak, as did the Jewish Joint Boycott Council in the United States. (See Chapter 7A.) And the Agudah's accommodationist policy, dictated by a superior enemy and commanded in the Torah, led to accusations of Uncle Tomism and *mayofisnikes*.[1] Additionally, such concepts as dying in battle for personal or ethnic honor were invoked, both of which are foreign to Jewish thought and tradition.[2]*

---

* What is important to remember is the fact that unless the fate of a Torah way of life is involved, the Torah does not demand suicidal resistance. Otherwise, when merely social, political or economic reasons are involved, alternative weapons were used in the Diaspora. In fact, even during the destruction of the Second Temple, Rabbi Yochanan ben Zakkai pointed to the proper Torah approach in the struggle with Rome. Since the Romans, unlike the Syrian Greeks, did not seek to impose restrictions on a Torah existence, he felt it imperative to make peace with the Romans. He thereby assured the future of the Jewish people by requesting the protection from the Romans for the city of Yavneh and its scholars. This was in sharp contrast to the zealots (Bar Yona) who fought bravely, but foolishly, for political liberty.

IN MANY PLACES, and especially in Eastern Europe, the Jewish use of non-violent resistance was mistakenly judged as weakness and

Weakness or Non-Violent Resistance? subservience. While not relishing violence, the Jew did not fear death any more than his Polish neighbor. It was a matter of Torah priorities. Martyrdom — for *Kiddush Hashem* (the sanctification of G-d's Name) — was one thing; but for all other issues the dictum that "you shall live by them" took precedence.[3]

Whereas in the political arena the secularists demanded equality and rights from non-Jews, their rejection of traditional Jewish thinking left them no basis for demanding assistance from fellow Jews in an emergency. In contrast, the Orthodox rescue activists, who never demanded rights or equality from non-Jews, and assumed a common "language" and outlook on life in the Torah concepts, could and did cajole, threaten, and make demands on fellow Jews when help failed to arrive.[4]

The pleas to save Slovakian Jewry sent by Rabbis Unger and Weissmandl from the Nitra Yeshivah, or from the Underground headquarters in Bratislava, were all based on *pikuach nefesh*, not some secularist rationale, and Hungarian and Swiss Jewish leaders refused to transfer funds illegally for that purpose. The obligation on every Jew to save life was used to great effect in the United States by such Vaad Hatzalah activists as Rabbi Abraham Kalmanowitz and Rabbi Eliezer Silver, for their fundraising appeals. The contributions of the Orthodox were greatly disproportionate to their numbers and economic resources.

The response of the assimilationist and secular Jewish community was proportionately weaker. Appeals to them were based on pity, on the "conscience of the world", on Zionist or nationalist feelings or, in the case of the Bund, on an alleged solidarity with the Polish workers.*

AT WORST, funds were raised or distributed according to a philosophy of "business as usual," the monies coming in a purely

Business as Usual organizational or bureaucratic manner. Dr. Joseph Schwartz, for example, was chairman of the Joint's Committee in Europe and was a most sympathetic

---

* For example, as late as May Day 1944, after the decimation of most of Polish Jewry, the Bund had not lost its indestructible faith in the Polish worker and humanity, proclaiming: "In keeping with our glorious tradition, we are bound to the working people of Poland and other lands through our common destiny in common struggle against our common enemy for our common ideals of liberty. These ideals are today the slogans and the postulates of our common labor holiday the First of May.[4]

and concerned individual. Yet, with conditions at the beginning of the war in the Pacific for most of the 17,000 refugees in Shanghai getting worse every day, he was unwilling to commit the Joint's guarantee for the repayment of loans after the war beyond a six-month budget for the refugee community. Naturally, this severely limited the Joint's local representative's ability to borrow the necessary relief funds to keep the refugees from starving.

In defending his action, Dr. Schwartz said that "the six months already far exceeded the 'normal' two-month budgetary commitment."[5] The Shanghai problem is more haunting because the question — what would happen to the refugees *after* the six-month deadline — was not even considered by Jewry's foremost relief organization, despite the fact that it was indeed posed by the United States government.

Only if one understands the concept of a Jewish foreign policy can one appreciate not merely the course of rescue by the Orthodox, but the difference in approach between the Orthodox and the secular Jews. Of course, exceptions did exist, many due to the ideological factors discussed, but essentially the approach to rescue by the Orthodox leadership differed considerably from that of the rest. This was both its strength and its weakness.

ITS WEAKNESS RESULTED FROM the fact that Orthodox Jewry in general, and rabbis and rabbinical students in particular, were considered backward, reactionary obstacles to the

Orthodox Rabbis Considered Backward
many messianic utopias espoused by the secularists. They were also considered by the secularists to be unassimilable and surely the most impractical members of the human race. Therefore, their rescue suggestions and activities were usually suspect. At best, this hostility towards, and suspicion of the Orthodox rescue activists, caused their reports of rescue opportunities to go unnoticed, resulting in tragic delays. This made greater cooperation unfeasible. For example, when the ransom plans for Slovakian Jewry, and later for all incarcerated Jews, were proposed by Rabbi Weissmandl, members of the Zionist organizations, reform rabbis and adherents of Marxist ideologies found it difficult to believe that a rabbi, Orthodox to boot, should have anything worthwhile and practical to contribute. Gisi Fleischmann, Rabbi Weissmandl's co-leader of the Slovak-Jewish underground, and others, for instance, had to try to convince the socialist-controlled Vaad Hahatzalah of the Jewish Agency in Istanbul that Weissmandl

was 100% reliable and important to listen to.[6]

In his classic, unfinished memoirs, *Min Hametzar*, Rabbi Weissmandl recalled one such instance when he opened a letter sent by the *Moetza* in Istanbul (the local rescue committee of Vaad Hahatzalah of the Jewish Agency) to Moshe Dachs, a socialist-Zionist member of his underground "Working Group." In it a member of the *Moetza* inquired about the veracity of a letter it had received from an Orthodox rabbi [i.e., Weissmandl] "who has a notion about saving all the Jews from deportation — and we *don't believe any Orthodox Jew.*" That's why they asked Moshe Dachs, one of their own, if there was any substance to this rabbi's words and then they would believe him.

Dachs responded to his skeptical friends in Turkey that:

> Should you have heard any negative rumors re this [rabbi's] letter, from any source unknown to us, we assure you with the full weight of our responsibility, that that which was written by the rabbis [Weissmandl and Armin Frieder] as well as that which we write, are but hundred percent in accord with reality. ... We want you to believe our words ...[7]

This letter was signed by Moshe Dachs, Gisi Fleischmann and Oscar Neumann, the three Zionist members of the Working Group.

RUDOLPH KASTNER, the representative of the Jewish Agency in Budapest and leader of a very small group of Zionists in Budapest,

Kastner's Canard who wrested leadership of Hungarian Jewry from the Orthodox Philip Freudiger, tried to convince Slovak SS chief Wisliceny that only the Joint and the Zionists, and not the rabbis, were reliable and had the power to deal with "world Jewry."[8]

He repeated this canard at a later stage of negotiations with Himmler at the end of 1944 when he refused Sternbuch's plea to cooperate in a common stand vis-a-vis the Nazis for last-minute rescue of the several hundred thousand survivors of the camps.[9]

The strength of the Orthodox was their Torah-impelled commitment to rescue as a top priority which mandated the use of bribery, ransom, and willingness to go the illegal route, as the key weapons of the Jewish foreign policy. These did not exist to the same degree for most other groups.

It was the Torah-based commitment that impelled Rabbi Weissmandl, the chief exponent of Jewish foreign policy, to use ransom and illegality as his prime weapons, whereas even the members of his Working Group concentrated much of their efforts and money on gathering guns for an eventual uprising of Slovak Jews. It was only Rabbi Weissmandl who could make his "demands" on the Orthodox Jews everywhere, especially in Budapest, to secure the necessary second $25,000 to ransom Slovak Jewry when his and Gisi Fleischmann's personal appeals to the Zionist and assimilationist groups in Budapest failed to produce the money. Weissmandl's ransom plans saved Slovak Jews for two years but the premature uprising of the Slovak peasants along with the Jews proved to be a disaster for most of the surviving Jews who were then deported to Auschwitz.[10]

It was also Weissmandl's genius that originated the idea of bombing the railroad lines to Auschwitz, but it was his persistence in pressing this means of rescue that went far beyond the attempts by the other members of his underground. Likewise, it was the same "foreign policy" that propelled Reb Shloime Stern, Rabbi Weissmandl's aide, to bribe all the couriers that carried hundreds of Weissmandl's messages to the free world. Similarly, Stern had the Slovak rail workers on a constant "payroll" to ascertain the latest information on train movements and deportations.[11]

PIKUACH NEFESH AND *AREVUS* generated a sense of urgency which is manifest not merely in all of Weissmandl's cables and

Pikuach Nefesh messages but in almost all of the cables, messages and appeals made by Orthodox rescue activists throughout the world. It was this sense of urgency that among other things made Sternbuch's cable concerning the mass murder of Polish Jews to Rosenheim differ significantly from the Riegner cable sent several days earlier to Stephen S. Wise. (See Chap. 7B.)

First, they sent it illegally via the pouch of the Polish Government-in-exile, as well as through regular channels, then they made a direct phone call to Rabbi Kalmanowitz to confirm it. Moreover, their tone of horror and urgency and interest in letting the world know differed markedly from the cold, clinical Riegner cable, with its equivocation and no mention of spreading the word elsewhere.

The reception which the Orthodox in New York accorded this cable also contrasts greatly with the response of Stephen S. Wise and his close collaborators and friends in the World Jewish Congress, the Zionist Organization and members of the Roosevelt inner circle.

We can clearly see the workings of *pikuach nefesh* in almost all the rescue activities of the Orthodox. Dr. Yaakov Griffel, for example, who represented Agudath Israel in Istanbul, in the Moetza of the Vaad Hahatzalah of the Jewish Agency, placed his bed in the office so that he should never miss any message or lose even an hour of rescue.[12] Mrs. Renee Reichmann in Tangier (Spanish Morocco), a housewife like that great Swiss rescue activist Recha Sternbuch, was impelled — not by any organization — to send packages to the ghettos and then to the camps. What moved her was simply the dictates of *pikuach nefesh*. The Joint representative in Tangier proved somewhat helpful to her in providing her with some funds. But it was only after seeing the successful operation elaborately and painstakingly built up by herself and her family that he decided to help. It was Mrs. Reichmann who kept in touch with the various camps, with Vaad Hatzalah and especially Recha Sternbuch and her husband, Yitzchok, in Switzerland, to obtain the latest information and find out the best opportunities for rescue. It was she who obtained the help of the American charge d'affairs in Tangier to help rescue children from Hungary in 1944, and it was she and her eldest daughter Eva who made a successful trip to Spain for help from Franco's fascist government and the Spanish Red Cross. (See Chap. 13D.)

It was the same Torah imperative that influenced Dr. Solomon Schonfeld, the rabbi of a small Orthodox community in London and student of Rabbi Weissmandl, to take matters into his own hands — to bypass all the organizations and successfully approach sympathetic members of the British government for help in rescuing thousands of people prior to and immediately after the war.

IT WAS *PIKUACH NEFESH* and *arevus* that made Rabbi Isaac Halevy Herzog, Chief Rabbi of Palestine and Mizrachi leader, go to

Chief Rabbi Herzog in Turkey

Turkey in February 1944 at the call of Yaakov Griffel, when rescue opportunities presented themselves. And it was the lack of this Torah-inspired duty for immediate rescue that made Ben Gurion refuse this same call, since his priority was *aliyah* rather than rescue. Only when the opportunity for *aliyah* from Rumania arose in September 1944 did Ben Gurion consider it important enough to make the trip to Istanbul. (See Chap. 13B.)

In the U.S., too, because rescue assumed the priority for the Orthodox that it did, they were ready to cooperate with anyone, regardless of ideology or viewpoint, on behalf of rescue. Except for the Revisionist-Zionist Peter Bergson group, all other Jewish organizations were not prepared to overcome their ideological barriers, even when much-needed unity could have achieved so much more. (See Chap. 5.)

THE ABOVE APPROACH, which was quite typical for most American Jews, reveals an organizational and bureaucratic mentality **Volunteers** that lacked the deep concerns and sacrifice that are demanded by the Torah's dictum of *pikuach nefesh* and the concept of *arevus*. For real sacrifice (obviously in America, a peaceful country, not under circumstances of occupied Europe [where many offered all sorts of sacrifices]), one must turn to some of the Orthodox rescue activists whose thinking and working did not take on the usual organizational approach. In addition to the *roshei yeshivah* and rabbis, laymen — such as Elimelech (Mike) Tress, Yitzchok Sternbuch, and Irving Bunim — were volunteers who gave up or neglected promising careers or flourishing businesses for rescue work — at a time when the wartime boom could have brought them considerable profits.

These and other Orthodox rescue activists were widely dissimilar men and women, from divergent backgrounds and certainly having distinct, and at times even incongruous, attitudes, reasons, and goals for themselves as well as their work. More important, though, were their similarities, for they had a sincere dedication to Torah, a true love for their fellow Jews, and a deep *mesiras nefesh*, a willingness to sacrifice all their possessions, and their lives, at times, to save Jews. They usually set aside political differences in order to work for a greater cause. The Vaad Hatzalah, for example, was comprised of yeshivah deans, European-born members of the Union of Orthodox Rabbis, and American-born members of such organizations as Young Israel, Agudath Israel, and Mizrachi. Rabbi Aaron Kotler, a key member of Vaad Hatzalah and spiritual head of Agudath Israel, set the tone for the unified Orthodox approach when he said that "no internal politics in deference to rescue work," a stand that in all likelihood brought the Zionist Mizrachi to the same table with numerous non- or anti-Zionist groups by mid-1941.[13]

UNLIKE THE PAID STAFFS of other organizations, the Orthodox rescue agents knew no time clocks. When a life could be saved, there **No Time-Clocks** was neither day nor night, Shabbos nor Yom Kippur, for literally nothing stood in the way of saving Jewish life. For some, in fact, rescue work became an obsessive duty rather than an assignment — which may explain the seemingly limitless energy and drive of men in their late 50's, 60's and 70's. Rabbi Kalmanowitz, for example, upon returning to New York from a full day's lobbying on Capitol Hill, would not hesitate to telephone his weary secretary, Rabbi Alex Weisfogel, at 3 a.m. and suggest — or *demand* — that they meet at the railroad station in two hours, so that they could be back in Washington at a particular congressman's office promptly at nine to try a fresh approach.[14]

A New York textile manufacturer and noted lay scholar named Irving Bunim was Vaad Hatzalah's volunteer chairman of the board — and during the latter part of World War II he ran the Vaad's office at 132 Nassau Street for a remarkably low $1,000 a month, including salaries and rent.[15] Vaad disbursements in the extremely hectic year 1944 were $1,135,000, but less than $60,000, or roughly five percent, went to fundraising and administrative costs.[16] Much of the Orthodox rescue work was done by volunteers who, motivated like their leaders by Torah law, performed their myriad duties with dedication and quiet efficiency. Some were businessmen with yeshivah backgrounds who gave time and money where needed, and performed all necessary tasks — such as securing affidavits that guaranteed support for an incoming refugee. That work, which often involved official examination of the bank records, was tiresome at best, and involved risk of arrest at worst, yet was vitally important because it could mean the difference between life and death for a Jew in Nazi Europe.[17]

The Orthodox businessmen provided other services as well, notably creating government contacts in Washington, making direct appeals for money, and carrying out numerous tasks both in the United States and abroad. Such men as Mike Tress or Irving Bunim were crucial because of their ability to work with American government officials. Other Agudah and Vaad volunteers provided other kinds of rescue and relief services. Frank Newman, for example, conducted on-the-spot inquiries about Jewish refugees in China and Japan before the Pearl Harbor attack; London's Harry Goodman made numerous wartime trips to Switzerland, Ireland, and other countries; Louis Septimus, Stephen Klein, and Herbert Tenzer made trips to postwar Europe to aid the survivors. Neither the Agudah nor Vaad Hatzalah could afford to send these men on such missions; instead, all trips and expenses were undertaken by each individual. In part, their dedication was due to the inspiration of Rabbi Aaron Kotler, Rabbi Gedaliah Schorr, and Mike Tress, who worked closely with these men, guiding their efforts on behalf of Jewry.[18]

Throughout the rescue and relief work, the rabbis and volunteers took great care not to make personal use of the rescue funds. Rabbi Kotler, for example, insisted on depositing his own money into the Vaad's account *before* permitting payment to be made for ship passage for a group which included his own future daughter-in-law.[19] In Switzerland, Yitzchok Sternbuch gave strict orders to Herman Landau, his secretary for rescue affairs, that Landau was to use the company telephone so as not to make any unnecessary use of the relief funds.[20]

It was not uncommon for Recha Sternbuch to remain awake entire nights in the woods or snowbound mountains on the Austrian-Swiss border to assure the safe arrival of refugees.[21]

THE HOMES OF Rabbi Solomon Schonfeld in London, the Sternbuchs in Montreux, and the Lehmanns in Stockholm became

**Activists'
Homes —
Refugee
Hotels**

virtual refugee hotels. Consider the disbelief of Rabbi Schonfeld's widowed mother, Rebbetzin Rochel Leah Schonfeld,* who returned to London from a 1938 trip to the United States only to find her house, which she shared with the unmarried rabbi, transformed into a home for refugee children. To her further surprise, her son had set up a bed for himself in the attic — and had left no place for his mother to sleep.[22]

There were long periods when Recha Sternbuch, Irving Bunim and Harry Goodman — to name but three were away from home for extended periods of time. The adult members of the various affected households could understand the importance of the *mitzvos* involved, but for the children things were somewhat more tangled. Often a child found it difficult to understand why a bedraggled stranger had to usurp his bed — and why he had to be accorded such personal service and respect.[23]

THE ORTHODOX ACTIVISTS' struggle was difficult, their tasks daunting, and their obstacles came from many arenas, from their

**The
Greatest
Disappointment**

fellow Jews, from recalcitrant and antisemitic bureaucrats, and often un-yielding government agencies in Slovakia and Switzerland, Great Britain and the United States.

---

* Her husband was Rabbi Dr. Avigdor (Victor) Schonfeld, founder of the first Jewish day school in England.

And the actions of Jews too often added to the frustration. Rabbi Weissmandl's single greatest disappointment, in fact, came not from the refusal of the Slovakian government or the Church or the free world to save Jews. Instead, it was when Jews refused to provide the money to ransom all the Jews under the Nazi heel. This frustration is evident in his cry to his fellow Jews:

> Brothers, children in Israel, have you all become insane? Don't you know in what hell we are living! For whom are you keeping your money? Do you really want to wait until we send a special messenger to plead with you, to give us what is coming to us? To you, all our pleas don't even seem to have the effect of a beggar at the door; after so much urging you have thrown pennies at our feet.[24]

Throughout the deportations of 12,000 Jews daily to Auschwitz and despite his own harrowing escape from an Auschwitz-bound train, Rabbi Weissmandl continued to send hundreds of cables and letters — most unanswered, each costing precious funds in bribes.[25]

Yet, the personal risks that Rabbi Weissmandl took while conducting his behind-the-lines rescue work were not singular, for many Jews and non-Jews risked their lives to get people out of Nazi Europe. They had nothing to lose since their own fate was sealed. Yet the actions of those who placed themselves in danger while living in peaceful, free countries is more startling for they had everything to lose and nothing immediately perceivable to gain. Switzerland's Recha Sternbuch, for example, did not permit her own 1939 arrest for helping refugees cross the border to deter her. In fact, when threatened by the Swiss government with long-term incarceration unless she gave the names of her contacts, Mrs. Sternbuch replied, "Even if I have to rot in jail for the rest of my life, I will not divulge these names."[26] Similarly, FBI threats did not deter Rabbi Kalmanowitz from illegally transferring money to Shanghai after the Pearl Harbor attack. "If I am arrested," he said, "and ever get out, I'll do it again. Lives are at stake."[27] They not only failed to receive the approval, let alone the praise, of the Jewish community, but usually had to do battle with them as well.

CHAPTER THREE
Influence of the Rabbis

SOME MEASURE OF THE IMPACT these few Orthodox rescue personalities had on both Jews and non-Jews is highlighted by a few incidents involving rescue attempts during the Holocaust (see Introduction). They were certainly not the average, well-meaning individuals, since such could hardly have had the tenacity to overcome the tremendous odds they faced in terms of opposition by both the Jewish Establishment and governmental indifference. Nor could they have impressed officials to bend, ignore or even change the rules, all in order that some hapless Jewish victims of Nazism by spared.

THE RABBIS AND THE LAYMEN and women were highly dedicated, inspired, farsighted individuals who felt the call to implement the

Dedicated, Inspired, and Untrained

Torah's dictum re *pikuach nefesh* and *arevus*. No obstacles, human, bureaucratic or legal, would stop them. One observer termed them guilty of "bulldozer tactics."[1]

A colleague said of Rabbi Weissmandl's ability to convince members of the underground Working Group of the feasibility of certain plans, "he was fully aware of the efficacy of his hypnotic spell."[2] Similarly, Recha Sternbuch held such sway over the papal nuncio in Switzerland that every time she entered the room he removed his large crucifix as a sign of respect for this Orthodox woman. And in England, the charismatic Rabbi Schonfeld charmed members of Parliament, leading churchmen, as well as the Jewish establishment, all to carry out his duties for the Jewish people.[3] Yet their undeniably strong personalities and superior intelligence were put to use only for what they believed to be an all-important cause — saving Jewish life.

Even more remarkable than their results is the fact that activists such as Rabbi Weissmandl, Rabbi Kalmanowitz, Recha Sternbuch and Rabbi Schonfeld were hardly trained diplomats. Instead, they were amateurs, inexperienced and academically unprepared for their new, sophisticated encounters. Yet their obvious belief in their cause, personal sincerity, and deep concern for their fellow Jews made up for a superficial lack of diplomatic polish. In mid-1941, for example, as tensions within the United States mounted just prior to the Pearl Harbor attack, the American government virtually closed the country to potential refugees — due in part to a fear of spies and other undesirables. Yet the Agudah was able to obtain dozens of visas for Polish refugees who were stranded in Japan. A measure of their success came in a remark made by the Joint representative in Shanghai who asked, "Whom have they got in Washington?"[4] Whom they had was Mike Tress, Rabbi Eliezer Silver and Rabbi Kalmanowitz's small, dedicated band of amateur diplomats.

RABBI KALMANOWITZ EVEN MOVED those who were initially opposed to rescue, such as Congressman Emanuel Celler. Too late,

The Old Rabbi on a Rock Celler himself realized, he awoke to his own situation, to being a member of a government which was unwilling to work to save Jews, to being a liberal Democrat who had placed too much faith in his President. In his memoir he recalled:

It is difficult to describe the sense of helplessness and frustration which seized one when streams of letters poured in from constituents asking for help for a sister, brother, mother, child caught up in the Nazi terror. There is one day which is marked out from all others during this period ... Into my office came an old rabbi ... everything about him, his hat which he didn't remove, his long black coat and patriarchal beard, the veined hands clutching a cane, these stand before me, even to this day. Trembling and enfeebled, he had traveled from Brooklyn to Washington to talk to his Congressman. Not once did he seem conscious of his tears as he pleaded, "Don't you see; can't you see; won't you see that there are millions — millions —

being killed? Can't we save some of them? Can't you, Mr. Congressman, do something?"

"Do something!" I had talked and written to President Roosevelt ... The President's response was not very encouraging, and that of the rest of the bureaucracy was not much better ...

I tried to tell [the rabbi], too, that I was convinced that these officials of the State and Treasury Department wanted to do something. I believed this. But the rabbi kept interrupting, striking his cane on the floor of the office. "If six million cattle had been slaughtered," he cried, "there would have been greater interest. A way would have been found. These are people," he said. "People."

I dreamed about him that night. The old rabbi stood on a rock in the ocean, and hordes of people fought through the water to get to that rock. And the people turned into cattle and back again to people. I was on shore, held by a rope which somebody was pulling back."[5]

It is not easy to overstate Rabbi Kalmanowitz' appeal, for influenced by this great Orthodox activist, Congressman Celler became the prime mover in the successful transfer of the Shanghai yeshivah after the war at a time when Allied transports were busy transporting troops home across the Pacific and space on board ship was at a premium.[6]

ONE SINGULAR ORTHODOX VICTORY was their influence on the conversion of Treasury Secretary Henry Morgenthau, Jr., from a

Treasury Secretary Morgenthau passive observer of Jewish genocide to a concerned, active governmental leader and spokesman. In stark contrast to many other influential American Jews, both in and out of government, only Morgenthau was willing to put his official position and social standing in jeopardy on behalf of his fellow Jews. It was largely his singular and sustained demand for help — one instigated in part by his three humanitarian non-Jewish assistants — which was an important factor in the creation of the War Refugee Board (WRB) in January 1944.[7] Despite its notable inadequacies, the WRB was the American government's sole response to the death and displacement of millions of human beings.[8]

Initially, as we have seen, Morgenthau complained of the emotional pressure he felt while dealing with the Orthodox activists. "You get upset," he told the rabbis, "and that upsets me" — a very different reaction from the one he felt when dealing with other

Jewish representatives. Yet unemotional approaches were ultimately ineffective. For example, when Joint representatives went to the State Department to request permission to send money to Japanese-occupied Shanghai, they said, "We were not a pressuring organization and never used pressure methods in our work. [Government officials] said they realized this and appreciated it very much." The Joint representatives left the meeting "with the feeling that there was very little hope of securing permission to arrange this transaction."[9] Yet Dr. Joseph Schwartz, head of the Joint's European office, later admitted to this author that what eventually convinced the State Department to permit monetary transfers to Shanghai was "an old rabbi with a long white beard" — Rabbi Kalmanowitz.[10]

ANOTHER TIME, when Rabbi Kalmanowitz went to Washington to plead for the Mirrer Yeshivah, he arrived in the office of John Pehle, **Let's Go** head of the War Refugee Board, late in the day and **Now** just as Pehle was preparing to leave. "Don't worry, Rabbi," Pehle said, "I'll take it up with my boss [Treasury Secretary Morgenthau] the first thing in the morning. So why don't you sleep on it?"

"Sleep on it?" the white-bearded rabbi bristled. "Who can sleep at a time like this? I'll wait here until morning." Then Rabbi Kalmanowitz quietly settled into a chair next to Pehle's desk and began reading his ever-present *sefer*.

"But, Rabbi," Pehle protested, not knowing how to remove the elderly man, "you'll be disturbing the cleaning ladies."

"Don't worry," Rabbi Kalmanowitz answered tranquilly, "I won't get in their way." Then he sat back, obviously ready to spend the night if necessary.

Pehle then understood the lesson the rabbi was teaching, that rescue was not ordinary business. "O.K., Rabbi," he said a bit sheepishly, "you win. Let's go to Mr. Morgenthau right now and settle the matter."[11]

THIS EPISODE INVOLVED one small segment of a long complicated affair focusing on the American scene. The Orthodox rabbis had **No One** previously pleaded with members of the War Refugee **Believed** Board to approve a license to send nearly one million **Him** dollars to Switzerland for the Sternbuch-Musy negotiations with Himmler. The arrival of 1,210 Jews on February 7, 1944 from Theresienstadt dispelled the almost universal skepticism about the Musy negotiations voiced by Roswell McClelland and other members of the War Refugee Board. As General William O'Dwyer, the last chairman of the War Refugee Board, noted at an important meeting on February 28, 1944:

> ... The Vaad Hahatzalah [sic] succeeded in getting twelve hundred and fifty [sic] people across the line [into Switzerland] about two weeks ago. They had a man in Switzerland named Sternbuch who had been saying right along that through his friendship and work with Musy, the Swiss, [sic] that he could arrange to have people taken out of the land [of Germany] in large numbers and frequently, *and no one believed him*, apparently, but the twelve hundred and fifty [sic] came ...[12]

O'Dwyer continued to review the circumstances in preparation for a meeting and in making a final decision about sending the money to Switzerland.

> ... it so happened that between the time that they [i.e., the rabbis] got the money and came to us for the license that we had some official communications from Switzerland [especially McClelland] that there was something about the arrangements between Musy and Himmler and the generals under Himmler that might indicate ransom ...[13]

After much research into the facts, O'Dwyer continued, information came to the effect that "the Germans wanted to let these people out anyhow, and that it didn't look like ransom." O'Dwyer, like his WRB colleague Josiah E. Du Bois Jr., looked at the action in a more humanitarian fashion than did John Pehle. O'Dwyer then came to the crux of the problem:

> ... Now, the question of whether or not the money would be paid to Musy or how it would be paid to him was not the question before us. The question was would we say in a cable to Sternbuch, "You can't have the money," or would we say to him, 'You can have the money, but it must be under our control until we tell you to let it go." ...[14]

O'Dwyer felt positively about the entire matter, and

> ... recommended that the license be granted to send this money to Switzerland in the name of Sternbuch and McClelland ... if we were to say, "You can't have the money," without having all the facts, that ... have the effect of stopping the passage of people through the lines to safety. We might very well, by doing it that way, have defeated the purpose for which this organization was set up ...[15]

This, of course, was in contrast to the completely negative response of McClelland, the Board's man in Switzerland who, upon the request of the WRB to look into the possibilities of rescue responded typically:

> On his return Musy intimated to the Sternbuchs that if a fund of from ten to twenty million Swiss francs were placed at his disposal he would be able to "arrange" [inference being by buying them out] the exit from Germany of a considerable number of Jews. In view of Musy's extremely questionable reputation here in Switzerland (he is generally spoken of as the potential Swiss quisling) and the vagueness and unreliability of this whole "scheme,' I cannot recommend that it be supported by the [WR] Board.[16]

Back in the U.S., expressing an obvious fear of the steady pressure and growing influence of the rabbis, Pehle continued:

> I would guess that once the money is sent there would be tremendous pressure [by the rabbis] for the actual release of the money so that the issue will have to be faced.

Pehle made Morgenthau aware of the criticism faced by the War Refugee Board from the State Department and the British government among others, when he noted:

> This license and the sending of this money ... all the critics of this thing are waiting for it to let loose a blast ...

Such critics will argue against the United States having any kind of a dealing involving Himmler and his Swiss fascist friend, Musy, particularly in view of the very negative reaction by McClelland, who was of the same legalist mind as Saly Mayer.

> The sending of the money takes you in with the Musy-Himmler negotiations, because that is what this money and this whole thing is a part of. Now we are dealing with a guy — Musy — nobody trusts. We don't now what the deal is and we don't know why the money is being sent, and I am raising a question whether as Secretary of the Treasury you ought to take the position that this money should be sent.[17]

Pehle had little doubt about the potential rescue of enormous proportions that such negotiations would likely yield. As he put it, "I don't think much of a case has to be had to show this will actually save lives ... but the case [re its legality] is dubious to say the least ..." Yet, he cannot shake loose the thought, not of the numerous lives at stake, but of the consequences to the Board, should the license not be cleared. Therefore he said, "I think it should be cleared. There will be criticism either way you act."[18]

Yet, in effect, he had to admit the growing influence of the few old rabbis and *roshei yeshivah* within government circles in general and the War Refugee Board in particular, when he acknowledged,

"If the money doesn't go, the rabbis are going to tear the town loose ..."[19] [emphasis added]

EVEN THOUGH BOTH STRATEGY and tactics differed, the Orthodox activists' Torah-motivated efforts hardly went unnoticed

Different Tactics — even by those with whom they disagreed. A few years earlier, during a near-frenzied rush of activity to save the yeshivah students in Russian-occupied Lithuania, for example, the Joint mentioned to its fundraisers that they were "in constant touch — literally day and night seven days a week — with leaders of the rabbinic groups."[20] Unfortunately, the Vaad's efforts were not matched by the Joint, given general opposition toward bringing in hundreds of yeshivah students into the U.S. (See Chap. 4.)

Rabbi Weissmandl, operating in the worst conditions imaginable, had such an enormous workload that he slept only two or three hours a night. He faced many difficulties, not the least of which was the fact that his beard and obvious Jewish identity resulted in numerous beatings. Yet he not only headed the Jewish underground (called, with characteristic Jewish understatement, the Working Group), he also traveled clandestinely all over Slovakia to raise money for the Jews deported to Poland, formulated his plans and, using intermediaries, bargained with Dieter Wisliceny, a key aide of arch-murderer Eichmann, first for the ransom of Slovakian, then all European Jews. In May 1944, he also arranged for previously bribed diplomatic couriers to alert the entire world to the slaughter then increasing in Auschwitz at an alarming rate.[21]

Yet, at the end of a week's negotiations he usually returned for the Sabbath to Nitra, where he taught Torah in his father-in-law's yeshivah. In the midst of his frenetic activity, Rabbi Weissmandl suffered a heart attack — an illness which he did not permit to interfere with his work.[22] And even when he was forced to hide, he still sent out his pleas for the Allies to bomb both the rail lines leading to Auschwitz and the death camp itself.

THIS DEDICATION WAS MANIFEST in perhaps a minor but interesting fashion on the other side of the Atlantic. One of Rabbi

Rabbis Close the Yeshivahs Weissmandl's negotiations in 1944 had come down to $250 for every Jew brought across the border to Slovakia. In America, the rabbis responded by closing yeshivos and sending the children into the streets and subways to collect whatever they could. Within several days, many of the youngsters collected more than $100 each in nickels and pennies from passersby — at that time an amount more than a worker's three-week salary. While the amount of money raised was important, the closing of the yeshivos was significant per se. The Talmud states that even when the Messiah comes, children will not stop learning — even for the reconstruction of the Holy Temple.[23] At the same time, the Agudah raised $72,000 in private parlor meetings and solicitations by volunteers in schools, synagogues, and factories.[24] In one New York factory, all the workers gave an entire day's wages to the campaign. Some families sacrificed $500 or $1,000 — then enormous sums — borrowing on future earnings to do so.[25] Both these actions indicate the importance placed on Rabbi Weissmandl's efforts and on rescue work. Sadly, there was no parallel effort whatsoever in the secular Jewish community, despite their greater numbers and vastly superior resources.

CHAPTER FOUR
Orthodox Jews, Unorthodox Approach: Ideology at Work

UNLESS ONE IS AWARE what motivated these men over forty years ago, it is impossible to understand or appreciate their decisions and their actions. It is surely wrong to rationalize what they did on present standards or to accuse them of poor judgment or worse, from hindsight. Neither would do justice to great men who lived in a world sharply different than ours and who tried to serve the needs of *Klal Yisroel* as they saw them.

IT IS IMPORTANT TO REVIEW some aspects of modern Jewish history in order to appreciate the change it wrought in the Jewish community. A major turning point in the history of Judaism was the French Revolution, when Jews were accorded unheard-of civil rights. Yet freedom carried a hidden price — the mixture of secular ideologies with Jewish thought, which often obscured or supplanted traditional Jewish practices and values. While in the abstract emancipation and certain aspects of the Enlightenment were as good for the Jews as they were for the world at large, their infusion of the concepts of rationalism, universalism, assimilation and secularism for the previous medieval-structured society in general and a Torah-dominated way of life for Jews in particular, seduced Jews away from their sense of uniqueness and from the framework of Torah. Quickly, then, Jewish attitudes

Aftermath of The French Revolution

changed from gratitude for new freedoms to a desire *not* to stand out, to assimilate. At that time there were also many great thinkers, Rousseau in the 18th century, and Marx a century later among them, who through their faith in human nature and progress promised utopias of all sorts. For secular Jewish leaders who believed in these dreams, the world could be saved, society could be redeemed — and Torah was simply discarded.

Far-sighted Jews, especially the Torah scholars, were not taken in by slogans like secularism and the brotherhood of man. Yet for most of the Jews who fell to the enticements of the Enlightenment, assimilation became an ideology. The Jew, then, owed allegiance to the country in which he lived, not to Torah or a larger Jewish group. What's more, the Jew now believed in the larger, secular order, and any disquieting aspects such as antisemitism could be explained as medieval relics, or something irrational, soon to be discarded in a modern, rational world order. Religion, then, became a form of social club, to be used to further one's lot in society. Therefore, it was with a great willingness that many Jews indulged in the ultimate form of assimilation — they converted, something so abhorrent to their own ancestors that they much preferred death — while those who remained Jewish sought easier, less obtrusive ways of maintaining ties.

ONE OF THESE MEANS of entering into the spirit of the modern age of emancipation during the 19th century and the equality or hope of equality it held out was provided by Reform

Reform Eliminated Jewish Distinctiveness Judaism, which eliminated almost every vestige of Jewish distinctiveness. It became preoccupied with the need to prove the worthiness of Jews and Judaism to the western world. It provided, at first, the German Jews and later their counterparts across the Atlantic with a means of integrating into society with precious little to make one stand out as a Jew, except "religion" as viewed from the narrow, Christian perspective. The Talmud, or Oral Law, was chucked as a useless product of its times and all "practical" *mitzvos*, rituals and traditions along with it. Hebrew was discarded for most prayers and the longing for the Messiah and the return to *Eretz Yisrael* were omitted from the *siddur* and the mind. Services were usually switched to the Christian Sunday. Most rituals, even the *bar mitzvahs*, were seen as embarrassing relics of the dark medieval era.

The concept of "chosen people" was changed to that of a

universal mission, whereby Jews would embody the so-called moral and ethical portions of the Scriptures by leading exemplary ethical lives and by participating in many of the social causes and movements substituting for the "practical" *mitzvos*. That is why one finds to this day the greatest concentration of Jews in all sorts of social causes such as racial equality, labor, women's movements, etc. — all with a distinct universal flavor but of no particularist Jewish interest. Many American Jews expressed their penchant for social causes in their dreams of a socialist society, though by the second generation the vast majority viewed the milder form of a welfare state, the goal of modern liberalism, as their secular religion.

THE REFORM JEWS considered themselves as equal citizens of the country they resided in and no longer a distinct people with nothing

"The People of Israel No Longer Live" more than loose, sentimental religious (in the Christian sense) ties with Jews throughout the world, except *Eretz Israel*. The peoplehood of *Klal Yisroel* was replaced by a universal faith, as Abraham Geiger, pioneer of German reform, put it in his revised prayerbook:

> The people of Israel no longer live ... It has been transformed into a community of faith ... Hebrew no longer lives ... The present heap of ruins, Jerusalem, is for us, at best, a poetic and melancholy memory, but no nourishment for the spirit. No exaltation and no hope are associated with it ...[1]

To this the American reform movement added, "America is our Zion and Washington our Jerusalem."

Ambassador Henry Morgenthau Sr., father of the Jewish Treasury Secretary under President Roosevelt, encapsuled the American Reform assimilationist philosophy that feared any manifestation of singling out Jews as a separate people, when he declared:

> We have fought our way through to liberty, equality and fraternity ... No one shall rob us of these gains ... We Jews of America have found America to be our Zion ... I am an American.[2]

Zionism was rejected as a major obstacle to assimilation with the fear of the question of dual loyalty a pervading theme among the Reform. This philosophy, however, did not preclude financial support for their co-religionists in trouble everywhere, though the loose bonds that very tenuously held German Jews to those in India, Palestine, or Italy were no longer the former unity of *Klal Yisroel.*

Expressing the fears of the charge of dual loyalty, Geiger's son Ludwig, a professor at the University of Berlin, went so far in his condemnation of Zionism as to say, "The German government would be fully justified in canceling the citizenship of any German Jew who is a member of the Zionist Organization."[3]

However, a few of the American Reform clergy, Dr. Stephen S. Wise the most outstanding, did not reject Zionism or Jewish nationalism. Following the philosophy of Justice Louis Brandeis, an early leader of American Zionism, Wise saw the upbuilding of a model welfare state with social justice by European Jews seeking a haven from antisemitism as a very American thing to do. This social experiment was no less American than encouraging a welfare state on a broader scale in the U.S. For him both ventures translated prophetic Judaism into reality.[4]

In America, virtually from the beginning, general social freedom was so seductive that assimilation went on virtually unabated for nearly a century. Equality was taken for granted, and economic opportunities were unprecedented. It was no accident, then, that by the end of the nineteenth century, with the arrival of East European masses, millions of European Jews saw America as the *goldene medina*, the golden land, and there was little but praise for the concept — and practice — of the Melting Pot. In fact, the first group of Jews in America that had come from Spain and Portugal via Brazil in 1654 was so entranced by the philosophy of the Enlightenment and the American Revolution that in two hundred years their identity all but disappeared. The German Jews of *Our Crowd** began to reach unprecedented levels of affluence in the 1870's and '80's — and with their riches they became decreasingly Jewish and increasingly patriotic Americans of Mosaic persuasion.

IN 1933, when Franklin Delano Roosevelt took office, American Jews felt as if history was marching with them. To those Jews who believed in their secular liberal faith, it

For the Jewish Liberals the Messiah had Come

seemed as if the Messiah had come. Jews not only admired the New Deal, they also helped build it. Two principal architects, for example, were Felix Frankfurter, appointed to the Supreme Court after a term as a Presidential advisor, and Benjamin V. Cohen, a Frankfurter protege

---

* This refers to the popular semi-fictitous book by Stephen Birmingham about the financially successful German-Jewish element of the latter part of the nineteenth and early part of the twentieth centuries.

from Harvard. Other highly trusted New Deal Jews included Treasury Secretary Henry Morgenthau, Commerce Secretary David Niles, Judge Samuel Rosenman, financier Bernard Baruch, Supreme Court Justice Louis Brandeis, New York Governor Herbert Lehman, and union leaders Sidney Hillman and David Dubinsky. All of them shared the same heady goal and faith of the liberal, to reshape American society into a welfare state.[5]

One root of the Jewish espousal of Roosevelt, and of the superpatriotism of much of American Jewry, was the clear insecurity of many socially and politically prominent Jews who feared that a mass influx of refugees would disturb their image — and serve as grist for such notorious, inflammatory antisemites as Father Charles E. Coughlin.

To their mind, the Jew was not an alien as long as he was an American. The alien, instead, was the European Jew, especially the Orthodox, undesirable because unassimilable and a threat to social aspirations. As such, secular American Jews sought to keep European Jews out of the country — or at best out of sight — on the spurious grounds that they were protecting American Jewry from incipient antisemitism, which the Orthodox supposedly brought on by their distinctive customs and dress. This attitude was nowhere more pronounced than in Walter Lippmann, the dean of American political analysts and a great liberal humanitarian who also epitomized the insecure, assimilated Jew who consciously ignored the plight of his fellow Jews during the Holocaust. Lippmann even tried to lay a portion of the blame on the Jewish victims themselves, on their distinctive Jewish appearance.[6]

LACKING THE OPTIMISTIC LEGACY of the Enlightenment, which assured secular Jews that antisemitism was only a medieval holdover

The Orthodox Could React Pragmatically of religious fanaticism that would soon disappear in a rational, liberal world, the Orthodox knew differently. They knew that no matter how rapidly Jews discarded their distinctive heritage and assimilated into the broader society, it would not disappear quickly. Thus they were much more capable of reacting pragmatically. Instead of trying to rid the world, or even one country of this irrational disease by spending millions on education, pamphlets, and inter-faith dialogues, or to bring down Hitler by means of a boycott, they merely applied their millennia-old technique of Jewish diplomacy to save as many Jews as possible under the most adverse conditions.

Typical of the assimilationists' insecurity of being identified with the "alien," especially the Orthodox, is evident from this event in Cincinnati in mid-1940 during the week of Sukkos, as reported by a participant, Rabbi Asher Rand. In a tongue-in-cheek article about the convention of Agudath Israel in Cincinnati, Ohio, center for the American Reform Jewry, Rand noted:

> What an amazing event occurred here in Cincinnati. This city, the citadel and mother for the confused, the Reform in America, was conquered at the hands of the zealots of Agudath Israel. This is not just any Agudah, but exactly as the name implies [comprised of zealots]. A fear gripped the Reform leaders and laymen when they discovered that Orthodox Jews deliberated about coming here to Cincinnati, and they fled the city, or else they hid out in every nook and cranny.[7]

The writer goes on to describe his impressions of this capital of American Reform Judaism:

> For the whole week of the convention I searched with candles, in the nooks and crannies, but I was unable to meet even one — they disappeared like water. Here's what happened ... Two days before the convention they phoned its chairman about the amazing thing that suddenly occurred [and said,] 'Listen! and your hair will stand up! Jews with beards and *payos* and dressed in silk wander about the streets of the city.' Therefore, a Reform official, the "guardian [against] anti-semitism," was curious as to the solution to this puzzle. "Why did the Orthodox select this city for their convention? Aren't these [Orthodox] afraid that they will create antisemitism not only here but throughout the land?"[8]

What disturbed the guardian against antisemites even more was the fact that:

> Once you chose to convene in the capital and fortress of modernism, how did you allow that all the general press should write complete pages about every detail ... Are you out to make fun of and embarrass all of Jewry? ... [9]

Worst of all:

> How did you dare to put up a *sukkah* in the center of the town in full daylight, and prepare your meals there and sing and dance so that the entire city is amazed.[10]

The writer further noted that as a result, all on their own, most Jews "left the city in anger and shame."

The writer put the caller at ease by telling him that:

> Heaven forbid, neither the *payos* nor the silk clothing will create antisemitism ... After traversing the entire city no one stared nor lifted a finger. On the contrary ... Everyone came to

greet the holy rabbis ... I saw how the newspapermen approached many of the bearded gentlemen with respect and requested their blessings.[11]

A Deeper Conflict

CONTRARY TO A HIGHLY SUPERFICIAL READING proposed by some historians, the Orthodox-assimilationist battles over fundraising and rescue had their basis not merely in competing political ideas. The antagonists themselves realized that their differences were profound and hardly limited to a response to Nazism. An editorial in the August 1944 issue of *Liberal Judaism*, then the official publication of the Reform movement, recognized that the ongoing skirmishes between the two groups masked a deeper conflict, that of the leadership and future direction of American Jewry. In fact, the Reform leaders correctly perceived a long-term threat to their own long-held control of American Jewish leadership. Among other factors, nothing summarized their dilemma more than the arrival of numerous charismatic Orthodox leaders during the war.

> ... Jewish Orthodoxy is now sounding a new note of belligerence. It has declared war against Conservatism and particularly against Reform. The change is due, chiefly, to the recent immigration of strictly Orthodox rabbis from Europe during the last decade. These men, *unaccustomed to American conditions*, look with horror at the types of Judaism they find in America ... and recently they have begun to protest against the prominent position of leadership held by Reform rabbis in many national and international Jewish organizations.
>
> When Orthodox Judaism in America will develop men like Abba Hillel Silver, Stephen S. Wise, James G. Heller, Jonah B. Wise and a host of others, will members of its rabbinate be called to the leadership of great Jewish organizations. *You cannot demand leadership. You must earn it.*[12] [emphasis in original]

Liberal Judaism makes a valid point. At the time of the Second World War, Orthodox Jewry was by and large an insignificant factor in American Jewry.

Propelling Torah-Judaism to Prominence

AT THE END OF THE DEPRESSION, Orthodox Jewry was hardly in the economic, social or political position to undertake any major relief or rescue activity whatsoever. In fact, the vast majority of American Jews who could reasonably be called Orthodox were in the working class, for whom $20 a week in

1939, or $40 in 1942, was considered a salary sufficient for raising a family. In general, too, the leaders of the Orthodox community were reticent and reserved — the result of a personal feeling of inferiority vis-a-vis the economically and politically influential secularist Jewish Establishment. Yet, after seven years of work for the greater Jewish cause, particularly after mid-1943, their transformation was as astounding as it was previously unexpected — propelling, in effect, Torah Judaism to national and international prominence. The circumstances of rescue and the Holocaust forced the Orthodox Jews to break through those social, political, psychological and ideological barriers that were previously considered insurmountable. Saving lives and adhering to Torah law caused them to confront the totality of American-Jewish life — and to become stronger as a result. In 1943, for example, when the Jewish Establishment had all but given up on European Jewry, the Orthodox looked at the power vacuum and set to work. Although the numbers saved are few in comparison to Holocaust victims, the Orthodox victory was enormous — considering the speed of the genocidal program, the stumbling blocks of Jewish antipathy, bureaucratic footdragging, legalistic obstructions, and Allied indifference. The thousands who were rescued — of all levels of observance — would surely have perished were it not for this unprecedented and extraordinary effort.

This fashioning of a new ad hoc leadership by *roshei yeshivah* and allied laymen and women for rescue laid the groundwork for the amazing renaissance of Torah and right-wing Orthodoxy during the postwar era.

Unlike the assimilationists who mistakenly let others create their bargaining strategies, the Orthodox retained their old weapons in dealing with the enemy. Because they were not bound, as the assimilationists were, by a rigid adherence to the law, doctrinaire political views, or considerations about their own position as staunch American citizens, they were much more flexible. For the assimilationists, their country and its laws — and often its leader — came first even at the expense of the existence of European Jewry. Therefore, the Joint, still controlled during World War II by the assimilated German Jews of *Our Crowd*, refused to contravene American law for any Jewish cause, however tragic, if illegality was involved. In 1939, for example, the Joint refused to feed Polish refugees in Lithuania simply because they had crossed the border illegally.[13] As late as 1944-45, when the stakes in Jewish lives were far higher, neither the Joint nor any other American-Jewish organizations was willing to chance any suspicion of their loyalty and buck the legal barriers to rescue. (See Chap. 3.)

MOREOVER, THE AMERICAN JEWS' FEAR of being identified with newly arrived refugees, particularly the very Orthodox ones, was

"A Foreign Sickly Weed" merely a manifestation of their own insecurity in American society in which they claimed an equal share. And because the secularists' assumption that the unassimilable, old-fashioned, caftaned Orthodox Jew "creates" antisemitism by virtue of clinging to his religious customs and traditions, the entire Jewish Establishment were loathe to push for the admission of 2,800 yeshivah students from Poland in 1940, as one of their leaders noted, for "social and other reasons."[14] Dr. Joseph Tenenbaum in this polemic phrased it more crudely when he wrote about some of the great talmudic sages that had made it to this country in the spring of 1941:

> It is to be deplored that the Agudas [sic] Israel of America, a sickly weed transplanted from foreign soil to the liberal American environment, should continue to poison the atmosphere without regard for the consequences to the entire Jewish people.[15]

Of significance is Tenenbaum's exposition of a major component of the secularist-Zionist perspective, which accepted the Pole's code of honor on the battlefield and sacrifice for the nation, and which had its reflections during the Holocaust. Tenenbaum exclaimed to the Orthodox, "There are times when bringing sacrifices are more important than even our own lives. Now we are living in a period such as that." He then asked rhetorically, "Are the Jewish people different from other nations? Is the Jewish sacrifice to be of lesser importance than the Gentile sacrifice?" In this theme song, reiterated time and time again by Ben Gurion's supporters in Palestine, England, the U.S. and elsewhere, the idea was that only through sacrifice will the nation be born. Yitzchok Ben Zvi, Israel's second president, wrote, "In blood and fire Judea fell — and in blood and fire it will rise again."[16]

ALTHOUGH THE ORIGINAL CONTEXT of Greenberg's poem* does not bear any direct relation to the concept of sacrifices on behalf of

---

* The Zionist poet Uri Zvi Greenberg expressed this concept of the sacrifices to be made in the process of reclaiming *Eretz Yisrael*, in the following terms:
  And I say land is not acquired by money
  And with the spade one also digs and buries the dead
  And I say land is conquered with blood
  And only the land is conquered with blood ...

Chapter 4: ORTHODOX JEWS, UNORTHODOX APPROACH / *51*

Zionist Concept of Sacrifice the state, its terminology became popular during World War II in most Zionist-ideological circles, especially those supporting Ben Gurion's world-wide campaign on behalf of a postwar Jewish state that was to be *the* solution to the Jewish problem.

This was the response given by the Zionists to Rabbi Solomon Schonfeld when they opposed his 1943 rescue motion in Parliament, which would have granted Jews temporary refuge [or papers testifying to this] in any of the British dominions and territories, but specifically excluding Palestine. The Zionists killed the motion rather than permit its passage without Palestine. As Rabbi Schonfeld recalled, the Zionist argument ran, "Every nation has had its dead in the fight for its homeland — the sufferers under Hitler are our dead in our fight."[17]

The presumption was that after the war, when Jews would come to the UN to request a Jewish state in Palestine, they will be asked about the sacrifices they offered for such a goal.

Nor was this a theoretical position only; it held tragic consequences. Rabbi Weissmandl speaks of a message from Nathan Schwalb (the Swiss representative of Hechalutz). Rabbi Weissmandl and Gisi Fleischmann used him as a major contact for all their messages to the Zionist groups and the Jewish Agency. Schwalb's letter was written in 1942 in response to Weissmandl's plea to ransom the remaining 25,000 Jews in Slovakia. The letter was written in Latin letters but it took a while for Rabbi Weissmandl to realize that the message was really in Hebrew. When he understood its implications he kept staring at it — he noted — until all the letters became etched deeply into his memory, something he could never forget. The contents, translated freely, read:

> You [in Slovakia] must remember that eventually the Allies will win. And following victory, the world will again be divided just like after World War I. This would be the first step. Now, when the war is over, we must take all measures to assure the creation of a state, and steps have already been taken toward this end. As for the cries reaching us, we must know that all nations, members of the United Nations* are making tremendous sacrifices, and if we don't bring sacrifices with what right do we have to "come to the table" after the War, when they will divide up the countries? It is foolish, even *chutzpah*, on our part to ask the nations that are spilling their blood, that they should give us permission to bring their [i.e., American]

---

* The term "United Nations" was used in a popular sense throughout World War II despite the fact that the organization by that name was first created in 1945.

money to their enemies' country to protect our blood — because *rak b'dam tihje lanu haarez* [sic] [for only with blood will we have a land]. This is as far as matters in general are concerned. As far as you, members of the group, are concerned, *atem tajlo* [sic] [you go on a walk or hike, a code word for escape] and for this purpose I am preparing to send you money illegally via this messenger.[18]

In short, it spells out the Zionist concept of sacrifices to be made on behalf of a postwar state, sacrifices including the Jewish victims of the Holocaust.

WEISSMANDL, TOTALLY IMBUED with a Torah perspective, working with mostly secularist Jews, and fully immersed in the rescue of **Weissmandl's** every single Jew, found it difficult to **Response** comprehend the stark implications of this letter and the Zionist policy behind it.

He then showed and read and reread it to all his colleagues in the Underground, mostly Zionists themselves, especially Gisi Fleischmann, who were also shocked by this.[19] Weissmandl was particularly shocked to read that it was a crime to permit the illegal entry of money into enemy territory; that it was preferable to sacrifice the countless number of Jews on behalf of the state. And yet, Schwalb had no hesitancy in sending money illegally for the chosen few (Zionist leaders).

Weissmandl's logical response to this Zionist notion of "blood for the land" was:

> If it is really true that everything has a price and if this blood [of all the Jewish victims] is the price for the land — then for whom will the land be — even their distorted vision will realize this awesome problem ... If there does not exist a nation without a land, then surely there can exist no land without a people — and where will the living Jewish nation come from, if not from Europe.[20]

The great-hearted Rabbi Weissmandl was unaware that the Socialist-Zionists, including those in Schwalb's movement, did not envision an ingathering of all the Jews or even most. Rather, *Eretz Yisrael* was to be a relatively small, model socialist state, with little concern for what will happen to the Jews of the *golus*. This negative view toward most of the world's Jews outside of Israel is known as *shlilat hagalut* or "Negation of the Exile."*

---

* This harsh view has been only partially mitigated in Israel after the 1973 Yom Kippur War.

THE ASSIMILATIONISTS FOLLOWED all the laws of the United States and Great Britain, even if they were inimical to the survival of

The Letter of the Law European Jewry. One of the worst during the Second World War was the Anglo-American Trading With the Enemy Act, which in accord with the war effort prohibited communication with, and any transfer of funds, food, or surplus, to anyone in occupied territories. There is no doubt that this law was passed with all good intentions, and indeed helped the Allied war effort, but it also prevented Jews from feeding their starving brothers in the Warsaw Ghetto in 1941.[21]

As Yehudah Bauer writes, the policy and philosophy of the Joint were enunciated as early as September 1939, by James N. Rosenberg, on behalf of its Executive Committee, in a letter to the entire organization, in which he pointed out that "our course must be to lean over backward," to avoid engaging in any relief work that might infringe the country's laws. He foresaw "frightfully difficult problems" in determining whether JDC was doing anything that might aid the belligerents. "We must not and cannot let our desire to help suffering cause us to lose our moorings. Our rule must be, 'When in doubt, ask the State Department.' " Moreover, Bauer noted, "His words appear to echo the stand taken by the AJC [American Jewish Committee] which after all was the political organization of JDC's leadership."[22]

This was so not only during the period of declared neutrality during 1939-1941 by President Roosevelt, but was followed to the T throughout the world even after America's entry into the war. Not even the steady revelations of the Nazi genocide and mass murder would change this stance by the Joint, although the Joint was not different than most American-Jewish organizations.

A case in point is that of the approximately 18,000 Jews stranded in Japanese-occupied Shanghai. After the Pearl Harbor attack, the Joint cut off all relief funds to Shanghai and severed communication with its representative, despite the fact that 8,000 of the Shanghai Jews were virtually destitute and wholly dependent on the Joint. The premise was that "we, as an American organization, cannot be involved in anything that has the remotest color of trading with the enemy."[23] The Joint continued this policy even after an American Treasury Department official, M.L. Hoffman, realizing the plight of the refugees, strongly hinted that the Joint send "unauthorized" cables to Shanghai.[24]

THE JOINT RESPONDED SIMILARLY in Europe, where the ills ranged from malnutrition to mass murder. One example: it withheld

The Law vs. Malnutrition and Murder funds for the "illegal" flight of thousands of Jews from Vichy, France, to Spain between April 1943 and May 1944.[25] But while the Joint did nothing that would break the law, the Orthodox activists had no illusions that adhering to the Trading With the Enemy Act, regardless of circumstances, would benefit any endangered Jew whether in Nazi-occupied Europe or Japanese-occupied Shanghai. Rabbi Abraham Kalmanowitz of Vaad Hatzalah, for example, transferred money illegally and sent numerous messages — via the Polish pouch, the International Red Cross routes in neutral Switzerland — to send money to the Sternbuchs for rescue, or to feed the refugees of the Mirrer Yeshivah, stranded in Shanghai.[26]

Rabbi Kalmanowitz was rewarded for his efforts by arrest threats from the FBI. He persevered, and by the end of 1943 it was he who finally convinced the American government, through Treasury Secretary Henry Morgenthau, to permit the legal transfer of funds to enemy-occupied areas in Europe or Shanghai — a victory that occurred before the establishment of the War Refugee Board. As we have seen, even Dr. Joseph Schwartz, then the head of the Joint, had to admit that it was the Orthodox leaders generally, and Rabbi Kalmanowitz specifically, who were primarily responsible for the change in United States policy.[27]

Similarly, in early 1945, when food was needed in Switzerland to feed incoming groups of liberated Theresienstadt survivors — 1,210 Jewish lives saved through negotiations instituted by the Sternbuchs and Vaad Hatzalah — legalistic resistance came from Herbert Lehman, a leading assimilationist Jew and head of the United Nations Relief and Rehabilitation Administration (UNRRA). Lehman was asked for the food, a request he refused on the grounds that Switzerland was not a member of UNRRA and therefore could not receive such shipments.[28]*

YET, ONE MUST NOT ATTRIBUTE the assimilationists' refusal to sanction extra-legal rescue with a lack of personal decency and

---

* Rabbi Aaron Kotler, Rabbi Kalmanowitz, and Irving Bunim got the food shipments delivered anyway. They met with Lehman's legal advisor, a Jew named Abe Feller, and he managed to work out a deal with Gen. William O'Dwyer, the last head of the War Refugee Board; the food went from the American Red Cross via the International Red Cross to the Swiss Red Cross.[29]

Super-Patriotic Thinking

compassion. Senator* Lehman supported dozens of distant relatives from Europe for several years.[30] The issue wasn't kindness but rather, the assimilationists' fear of jeopardizing their status as equal members of society and the resulting need to constantly prove their patriotism.

In Switzerland, rescue efforts faced other problems, among them the similar patriotic thinking of Saly Mayer, the Joint representative. Mayer, unfortunately, let his assimilationist loyalty to Switzerland and fears of overburdening the small Swiss Jewish community and of an antisemitic backlash stand in the way of his duty toward the higher moral law of the Torah and the survival of the Jewish people. Early in the war, for example, Mayer helped ship illegal Jewish refugees back to France,[31] and he was responsible for the arrest of Recha Sternbuch, the rescue activist, as well as the deposing of the Sternbuch's sympathetic co-worker, Police Captain Grueninger.[32] In 1942, he refused to listen to Rabbi Weissmandl's plea for $25,000 (US) for ransom. Mayer was clear in his reasoning: "There is presently no legal possibility to send even one penny, because our organization's money was contributed from America, and there is a law there forbidding the sending of money to enemy countries. We have no desire to bypass laws." What encouraged him in his obstinacy was the fact that his position was endorsed by Swiss representatives of the Jewish Agency, the World Jewish Congress and the American representative of the War Refugee Board.[33]

Even in Hungary, soon to be swallowed whole by the Nazis, only the Orthodox community answered Rabbi Weissmandl's plea for funds, though even they did so reluctantly. The powerful, financially secure Neolog (Hungarian-Reform) Jewry stood on patriotism and refused to provide illegal funds "to commit such a grave sin against the government." They soon had second thoughts. As Rabbi Weissmandl tells us, "When German troops entered Hungary in 1944, Samuel Stern, the president of the Budapest [Reform] community, admitted his mistake and expressed profound regret for not having sent help in time to Slovak Jewry."[34]

Insecurity Dictated Response

THE UNSTINTING PATRIOTISM of the assimilationist Jewish establishment is epitomized by Dr. Marcus Ehrenpreis, Chief Rabbi of Sweden. A former secretary to Theodore Herzl, a prolific author, one of the pioneers of modern Hebrew literature, Dr. Ehrenpreis had been a staunch Zionist while a young rabbi in Bulgaria.

---

* He became senator of New York State in 1949

When he went to Sweden, however, which had a total Jewish population of roughly 7,000, Rabbi Ehrenpreis abandoned Zionism for Reform Judaism and became highly influential both in Jewish and non-Jewish circles. Furthermore, since there was no formal separation of church and state in Sweden at that time, Ehrenpreis as Chief Rabbi had great potential power as a leader in Swedish relief and rescue work for Jews.[35] Tragically, however, Ehrenpreis let his typical assimilationist insecurity dictate his political responses to the Holocaust, and so generally refrained from helping the Jewish cause, even stifling publicity that would have led to rescue efforts. When, for example, Yitzchok Grynbaum of the Jewish Agency's Vaad Hahatzalah in Jerusalem wanted Ehrenpreis' verification of an August, 1942 report concerning the murder of Warsaw Jews, Ehrenpreis was simply "unwilling to make any effort to find out."[36] Yitzchok Sternbuch, on the other hand, passed the same report on to Yaakov Rosenheim in the U.S. and thereby alerted Jewry — and the world.[37]

NOWHERE WAS THE DIVISION between traditional and "modern" Jewish behavior more sharply rendered than over the issue of **Official Venality** ransom, smuggling, or other "illegal" rescue efforts. The patriotic Jewish organizations followed their governments and ignored Jewish history and condemned such vital tactics even when the fate of the Jewish people was at stake. In 1939, the passenger ship *St. Louis* and 900 passengers were turned back from Havana harbor because the Joint refused to pay a ransom of one million dollars, an amount equal to one-eighth of its annual income. As happened so often throughout the Holocaust, the Joint changed course — but too late for these hapless passengers. As Yehudah Bauer, the official historian of the Joint, put it, the Joint "had never agreed to pay ransom to unscrupulous operators for innocent human beings," although he admits that "Cuban officials had to be bribed.[38] Cuba remained one of the havens throughout the period, largely because of the venality of its officials."[39] Evidently, the secularists' condemnation of venality overrode the concern for Jewish lives. Rabbi Weissmandl and the other Orthodox rescue activists were the very antithesis of such a *Weltanschauung*. Ransom, bribery and all other means, legal or illegal, were their primary weapons for the rescue of endangered Jews.

In some ways, throughout the entire Holocaust period, the Nazis and others proved themselves no different from other barbarians who have intruded darkly into Jewish history. They were vicious, violent, murderous antisemites who swore eternal hatred for Jews with greater technical means and efficiency — but were at times ready to offer Jews as human chattels for sale and saw no contradiction in their position. This was especially true of SS Chief Heinrich Himmler. There was much action that could have been taken if Jews had gone beyond personal or ideological considerations. From 1940-1942, for example, on a very minor scale, Herbert Kruskal, former assistant to Jacob Rosenheim in Germany, set up a special World Agudah office in Nazi-occupied Holland and sent thousands of pounds of flour for bread as well as for matzos via Belgium to Cracow and other Polish ghettos, often using the German Red Cross as a courier.[40] Yet in 1942, when George Mandel-Mantello, the Jewish Secretary-General of El Salvador in Switzerland, suggested sending trainloads of Swiss food and medicine into Poland, the Joint's Saly Mayer refused to commit such "unlawful" acts.[41] Such considerations, however, did not deter Meier Raphael Springer in London or Renee Reichmann in Tangier from sending food packages directly into the concentration camps — with the assistance of the London-based Czech government-in-exile and the Spanish Red Cross respectively.[42]

MUC.I OF THE RESCUE accomplishments could not have occurred without the Orthodox activists' illegal use of the Polish diplomatic cable, a service obtained by Recha Sternbuch. If nothing else, the cable and its codes were invaluable in creating direct transmissions between Switzerland and New York without interference from Allied censors.[43] Yet Saly Mayer of the Joint and the rest of the Jewish Establishment refused to use the cable, and when the Polish government-in-exile suggested that it send $5,000 or $10,000 to the Shanghai refugees via diplomatic pouch, the Joint turned the offer down on "patriotic" grounds.[44] In fact, of all the Jewish groups that knew about the refugees stranded in China, only Vaad Hatzalah maintained contact and continued financial support.

Rescue and Relief vs. Legalities

Again and again, Orthodox activists put relief and rescue before legal considerations — and often before their own personal safety. Recha Sternbuch, perhaps the single most influential activist in unoccupied Europe, cared little for Swiss regulations against smuggling Jews over the border from France.[45] At one point, in 1944, Roswell McClelland, the American representative of the War Refugee Board in Switzerland, aware that the Sternbuchs paid bribes and ransoms, warned them that their tactics might result in an American blacklist and the arrest of their aide, Hugo Donnenbaum, a refugee in Switzerland. The Sternbuchs told Mr. McClelland that his blacklist was of very little importance and the threat of arrest did not deter Mr. Donnenbaum either.[46]

What was illegality in the face of certain death? In 1941, Rabbi Shimon Kalish, the Admor of Amshenov in Kobe, Japan, had no hesitation counseling refugees to make the best use of their few Curacaoan visas by illegally creating entire "artificial" families, since a whole family could utilize a single transit visa. Similarly, the Agudah and its many sponsors had no compunctions about using the same bank account more than once to prove that refugees had the requisite financial standing to emigrate.[47]

WITHOUT THE SUSTAINED USE of illegal tactics, a high percentage of those saved would also have perished. Thousands survived the ghettos of Poland and Budapest because of **Mantello's Salvadoran Citizenship Papers** counterfeit Latin American passports or citizenship papers provided by several rescue activists, notably George Mandel-Mantello, who personally issued thousands of Salvadoran documents. Many holders of these documents were spared because they were detained in such camps as Vittel in France, as well as the privileged sector of Bergen-Belsen. And in 1944-45, thousands of others, along with those carrying forged copies, were saved in the so-called "protected" ghetto of Budapest by diplomats Raoul Wallenberg of Sweden and Charles Lutz of Switzerland. The use of these Latin American papers was initiated by Yitzchok Sternbuch and Yisroel C. Eis in early 1942. A Zionist historian of the Holocaust, Nathan Eck, who himself made use of them, notes that they were extremely helpful.

> Reports of the special treatment afforded by the German authorities to aliens were speedily and widely circulated. The happy holders of foreign citizenship papers informed the relatives and friends who had helped furnish them with the requisite documents of this favorable attitude. These reports had very important consequences, especially in Agudas [sic] Israel circles in Switzerland. These circles were the first to endeavor to transmit foreign passports to the German-occupied countries as a means of protection against the anti-Jewish measures adopted by the Germans. They had no qualms whatever about utilizing this means of rescuing Jews, despite

the fact that because of its doubtful legality other elements might have balked at it.[48]

Eck says that in the Warsaw Ghetto, as early as 1942, the Sternbuchs were known to be sending Latin American papers, and he echoes Orthodoxy's point that successful actions had an influential effect on others:

> Ultimately even statesmen and high church dignitaries did not recoil from using "doubtful" methods in the work of rescue. For example, the Pope ... the War Refugee Board ... too boasts in its final report of supplying counterfeit documents to victims of persecution.[49]

The initial cost of these papers was at least 400 SF, a high price when $25 a week was considered a good salary, and rose as high as 3,000 SF. Yet once Mantello began to mass-produce his Salvadoran papers by the thousands and sent them without charge to Jews in occupied Poland, Slovakia, Holland, Belgium, France and Hungary, the price dropped drastically. For this work, he employed a staff of ten, including the wife and children of Matthieu Muller, long-time head of the French Agudath Israel.[50]

IRONICALLY, SOME OF THE Latin papers were traded by Jews and Gestapo agents, within sight of the burning Warsaw Ghetto. In June

Queen Wilhelmina's Help 1943 some families escaped the Ghetto's fires, via sewer and ditch, reaching the Hotel Polski, the sole place in Warsaw proper that Jews were permitted. The hotel, also known as the document exchange, hosted a busy traffic in papers, and although not all possessors of the papers survived, many did.[51] This was due in no small measure to the leaders of the Agudah and Vaad Hatzalah, who persuaded the American State Department to pressure the Latin American governments in turn to pressure the Germans into recognizing the validity of the documents.[52] This campaign of "persuasion" had no little help from Queen Wilhelmina of Holland, who was spurred on by Rabbi Tuvia Lewenstein, the former Chief Rabbi of Holland. Rabbi Lewenstein was under the influence of Mantello and Muller.[53]

By the end of the war, as a result of Rabbi Weissmandl's early and persistent efforts, ransom became somewhat more palatable to the assimilationists. Three independent negotiations were underway with SS Chief Heinrich Himmler to ransom Europe's remaining Jews. Recha Sternbuch and Dr. Jean-Marie Musy (former Swiss president) pursued their own paths, but Rudolph Kastner and Saly

Mayer of the Joint, Hillel Storch and Norbert Masur of the World Jewish Congress and Felix Kersten, Himmler's humanitarian masseur, were also bargaining cash-for-Jews. And the early example of the Agudah sending food packages was also repeated by a representative of the World Jewish Congress in Switzerland during the war.[54]

Perhaps the Orthodox activists were successful because they did not have to cope with the secularists' largest stumbling blocks: their faith in humanity's progress and their insecurity in a society that pressured Jews to be like everyone else. With no such insecurities or doctrinaire ideological blinders to confuse them, the Torah-oriented activists could take a more pragmatic approach to the Nazis and use whatever means that were available, however illegal or unpleasant. The Sternbuchs frequently quoted an old Yiddish adage, *as men darf dem ganef nemt men ihm arup fun di tliya.* (If you need the thief, you even take him down from the gallows.)[55]

THE ASSIMILATIONISTS WEREN'T the only Jews whose ideology was a deterrent to rescue. Tragically, the Zionists, especially the **Ben Gurion's** Socialist-Zionists controlling the Jewish Agen-**Zionists** cy, headed by Ben Gurion, were even more difficult. This was in part because of their rigid **Deter Rescue** anti-Torah and anti-*golus* beliefs, but mainly because, as we have seen, under Ben Gurion's orchestration, the Jewish Agency and its policy makers in the U.S. and elsewhere concentrated on the formation of a postwar state to the virtual exclusion of almost everything else. In contrast, even the assimilationists, as represented by the American Jewish Committee and its financial arm, the Joint Distribution Committee, frequently cooperated with the Orthodox or other groups on a humanitarian basis when rescue did not impinge on their ideological stand.[56]

For the Zionists, only a Jewish state would solve the "Jewish question," especially antisemitism, which was predicated upon the fact that Jews were homeless for 2,000 years, always guests in other countries, without a home of their own. Rescue per se, where Palestine was not involved, was simply not part of the lexicon. Such rescue was denigrated as "palliative, philanthropic and unproductive."[57]

The controlling Socialist-Zionists limited their interest for settlers to the young, the ideologically indoctrinated and the agriculturally trained potential *kibbutzniks* and *chalutzim.* The most undesirable immigrants or refugees in their eyes were the Orthodox (reactionary bourgeois) and the most "unproductive" of all, the yeshivah student. For the Socialist-Zionists the dream of a state was not the "ingathering of all the tribes," which became the post-state policy, but that of a small model socialist state, a "light unto the nations."

THIS POLICY OF A HIGHLY SELECT form of immigration or better, *aliya*, is manifest in the letter sent by Henry Montor, head of UJA,

Selectivity of Immigration

in February 1940, in reference to the unrestricted illegal immigration fostered by the Revisionists. He noted that:

... "selectivity" is an inescapable factor in dealing with the problem of immigration to Palestine. By "selectivity" is meant the choice of young men and women who are trained in Europe for *productive purposes* ... [emph. added, quotes in original][58]

Only on this basis is it possible to understand the policies of the Jewish Agency during the Holocaust and its American followers in the U.S. and elsewhere. Naturally, where the Zionists were split between the followers of Ben Gurion, such as Dr. Abba Hillel Silver, and opponents such as Dr. Wise, who refused to pressure the White House even for a Zionist state, the results were not as predictable.

On the other hand, the Orthodox had no problem in cooperating with the Revisionists on rescue, whether in Vienna, Bratislava, Istanbul, Zurich or New York, as described by this author elsewhere. The Revisionist-Zionists lacked the intense hatred the Socialist-Zionists had of Torah Jewry and desired to bring in as many Jews as possible to Palestine.

Moreover, the conflict between the Jewish Agency and the Joint which competed for the millions raised by the United Jewish Appeal was also highly detrimental to rescue. The Jewish Agency accused the Joint of pouring its funds into a sieve, while the Joint was defended by the Jewish *Daily Forward*, which noted that, "it thanked G-d for having created the *Yehudim*, for 'if the Zionists would have been the leaders of the JDC, the Jews of Europe would not have received a single cent; all the money would have gone for Zionist purposes.' "[59]

What is important about the control of the Jewish Agency by Ben Gurion and his way of thinking during the Holocaust is the fact that the Jewish Agency was given a monopoly on the lifesaving certificates by the British Mandate Government. One could not enter Palestine without such a certificate unless one obtained the "capitalist visas," which were given to anyone who had a bank account of about $5,000 — a fortune at the time — or the special approval of the British Government.[60] In other words, the Jewish Agency controlled the entry of all the world's Jews to *Eretz Yisrael*, and Agudath Israel as well as any and all non-party Orthodox Jews were confined to six percent of the certificates. Even this six percent quota was frequently not allotted. After the 1939 White Paper, the British limited entry to 15,000 people per year, or 75,000 for a five-year period ending in mid-1944.

ANOTHER EXAMPLE: IN HUNGARY in 1944 the Zionists were but a tiny minority and the Orthodox a much larger proportion. Moshe **Only for** Krausz, the Zionist head of the Budapest **Registered** *Palaestina Amt*, which distributed these valuable certificates, admitted to this author that in all the **Zionists** years he never gave any certificate to anyone not a registered Zionist. Only once did he make such an exception, when he gave one to a *melamed* (elementary school Hebrew teacher) and his seven children, all of whom spoke Hebrew.[61]

This Zionist posture was manifest early in the Nazi period. Although the new order posed new dangers to thousands of German Jews, the Jewish Agency, then under control of the Marxist-Zionists, offered certificates only to young, agriculturally oriented Jews. Lewis Strauss, in his memoirs, recalls that Chaim Weizmann "was allotting his scant allowance of entry permits for months ahead to people who are Zionists but who are under no pressure of any sort, whereas we are swamped by poor souls who have no place to go and who can't get one of his permits."[62]

This lack of concern for endangered Jews caused Weizmann to boycott the 1938 Evian Conference, called by President Roosevelt and attended by thirty nations concerned with the Jewish refugee problem, because Palestine had been omitted from the agenda. As historian Yoav Gelber saw it, "The fight on the Jewish front for the Zionist solution removed the Zionists and the *Yishuv* [the Jewish settlement in Palestine], even before the war, from rescue attempts and strategies not connected to *Eretz Yisrael*."[63]

The Zionists' extremely restrictive Palestinocentric view, which concerned itself only with a certain territory and a small segment of the Jewish people, was highly detrimental to Jewish rescue. This was especially so in view of the fact that the Jewish Agency claimed to speak for all world Jewry.

COMPARE FOR A MOMENT THE ATTITUDE toward rescue by two activists during the crucial years of 1938-1939, when only the Jews

Children's Lives vs. People's History

of Germany and Austria were considered in danger. On the one side was Rabbi Solomon Schonfeld of London, who made personal visits to Berlin and Vienna in 1938 and who obtained specially created permits from the British Government to extricate many hundreds of children to safety in Britain. As we have seen, he even lodged them in his school and home, in order to get them out as quickly as possible. On the other side was the contemporary statement of Ben Gurion as noted by a historian:

> If I knew that it would be possible to save all the children in Germany by bringing them over to England, and only half of them by transporting them to *Eretz Yisrael*, then I would opt for the second alternative. For we must weigh not only the life of these children, but also the history of the People of Israel.[64]

With these words he highlighted the Zionist concept of a long-range solution, i.e., a postwar state, as opposed to immediate rescue, a Torah-based concept, termed derisively "philanthropic."

This priority for long-range settlement of Palestine over immediate rescue is manifest in even greater starkness and tragedy in the close to an hour-long conversation Chaim Weizmann had with President Roosevelt in June 1943. This was at least eight months after the revelation of the murder of two million Jews by the Nazis. In both sets of minutes of this meeting, Weizmann talked solely about his Zionist goals of a postwar state. Not one word was spoken about the tragedy of the Holocaust, the possibility and need to do something about it.[65]

Thus, while Weizmann pressed for slowly building up Palestine through selective *aliya*, "Cow by cow, dunam by dunam," Ben Gurion devised a strategy for achieving American Jewish support for a postwar Jewish state. This same philosophy had its impact on American Zionists as well, with tragic results for rescue efforts in the U.S. For example, Cincinnati's Rabbi Abba Hillel Silver, one of America's foremost Zionists, a brilliant orator and a major supporter of Ben Gurion, reasoned that just as World War I brought the Balfour Declaration, the conclusion of World War II would bring about a Jewish state — but only if Zionists acted quickly and American Jewry brought pressure on the government. His program was duly endorsed by the Jewish Agency in Palestine in November, 1942, and steadfastly maintained throughout the war, despite the growing number of cables confirming the mass murder of Europe's Jews. There were Zionists, such as Mizrachi's Dr. Zev Gold, who argued for both the state and rescue, but they were dismissed by Dr. Nahum Goldmann, who said that manpower was limited and that the campaign for the Jewish state took precedence.[66]

DR. STEPHEN S. WISE, American Jewry's foremost Jewish leader, stood fully neither in the Zionist nor in the assimilationist camps.

Dr. Stephen S. Wise

His singular personality was forged by several competing ideologies.

Wise was a stirring advocate for Reform Judaism as well as American Zionism, and the liberalism of Franklin D. Roosevelt. Like millions of other American Jews, he encountered undreamt-of freedom and economic opportunity in this country, and clung not to Torah and its "foreign policy," but instead to the more popular ideology, the secular religion, of liberalism. It was precisely this ideological difference that brought about the acrimonious relationship between the Orthodox activists and the other two American Jewish branches, the assimilationists and the Zionist Establishment as to both the strategy and tactics (of rescue) during the Holocaust.

Although Wise may have seemed to act in conflicting ways, there was a hierarchy to his priorities. First was his position as the foremost proponent of liberalism, having been in the vanguard of every liberal and progressive legislation for over a half century. He was also a Reform rabbi with its assimilationist tendencies, its worship of a narrowly conceived view of what was Americanism and espousal of the melting pot theory of integration. Although Wise was a leading American Zionist as well, he was a far more vocal proponent of the secular faith of liberalism with its particularist commitment to his own people, always subsumed to the larger social masses. In this he had been influenced by the Social Gospel Movement espoused by several liberal Protestant groups in the late 19th century and furthered the tendency to spread the prophetic message into concrete social activism, as the essence of Judaism. In a six-decade career, he was the champion not only of American Jews, but of America as well. An almost omnipresent activist, he co-founded the NAACP, worked with the American Civil Liberties Union, supported women's suffrage, organized labor, and the general civic good. Simply stated, Wise epitomized much of American Jewry at the time; having lost the observance of his fathers, he transformed traditional religious zeal into social action.[67]

FOR HIM, AMERICA WAS HIS REAL ZION, a point he made manifestly clear to the Zionist-sponsored American Jewish

FDR — The American "Messiah" Conference as he thundered, "We are Americans, first, last, and all the time. Nothing else that we are, whether by faith or race or fate, qualifies our Americanism," a creed he openly professed and repeated throughout his lifetime.[68] To Wise, who believed in the superiority of America and its way of life above all else, and whose Judaism was translated into the faith of secular liberalism's primary goal of social and economic equality as epitomized by the welfare state, the election of Franklin Roosevelt seemed like the coming of the Messiah. To Wise, Roosevelt and his New Deal therefore represented the highest ideals of Judaism, a real opportunity to transform America into a just society. Hence, Wise's support of the man and the New Deal was sincere and complete, a religious adherence to the tenets of secular liberalism.[69]

Wise's priorities and actions then followed logically. If Roosevelt were indeed the American Messiah, then as a committed American Jew, Wise's own task was to assist the President, nurture him, support his programs, and above all, protect him from anyone who might hinder or prevent the reconstruction of America. Anything — or anyone — that might conceivably disturb Roosevelt's mission was to be thwarted at all costs, including criticism, which was to be avoided. Even Jewish suffering was never permitted to interfere with the President's program. In September, 1940, for example, when the State Department was hampering the flow of Emergency Visitors' Visas to Jewish refugees in Nazi France and Soviet Lithuania, Wise sprang to his President's defense, saying that the Administration feared an influx of radicals who might embarrass the President during the coming election. "Cruel as I might seem," he wrote, "his re-election is so much more important for *everything that is worthwhile* and that counts more than the admission of a few people, however imminent their peril," [emphasis added] "worthwhile" referring to his vision of the welfare state.[70]

IN A LITTLE-KNOWN INCIDENT OF 1940-1941, Wise showed not only his concern for protecting the President, but also his

"Unassimilable" Talmudists assimilationist tendencies which found it so difficult for him to identify with the European refugees in general and the "unassimilable" East European talmudic students in particular. It is also illustrative of the misunderstanding of events during the

Holocaust even by historians of that period.

This involved the combined efforts of Agudah and Vaad Hatzalah to bring out of Russian-occupied Lithuania the few yeshivos that managed to flee Poland after its invasion by Germany on September 1, 1939. Fully aware of their own political and numerical insignificance, the Agudah and the Vaad tried to get the American Jewish Establishment, i.e., the Joint, the American Jewish Congress and Dr. Wise, to use their influence in obtaining special above-quota visas known as Emergency Visitors' Visas.[71]

This unique idea had its origin in a project initiated by the Jewish Labor Committee after the fall of France to rescue political refugees, i.e., leading Jewish and non-Jewish labor leaders, intellectuals, artists, writers, etc. who were in danger from the Nazis. Assisted by William Green, president of the AFL, the Jewish Labor Committee presented lists of such endangered political refugees to the State Department which, under political pressure, approved it. These were above-quota visas, ostensibly granted by the President on an emergency basis to "visitors" of the 1939-1940 World's Fair in New York. The program was administered by the President's Advisory Committee, headed by the sympathetic James G. McDonald. In all, over 2,500 such visas were issued, of which the Jewish Labor Committee obtained about half. The World Jewish Congress submitted its list of about one hundred key Zionist leaders and the Orthodox had desired to include thirty yeshivos, with about 2,800 talmudic scholars, the cream of Polish scholarship, under this program, which had no numerical ceiling.[72]

The Agudah and the Vaad approached Stephen Wise and other leaders of the Jewish Establishment at a conference held on August 15, at which the latter concluded that it would be inadvisable to press for the admission of so many yeshivah students because:

> There were *political and social and other implications* in regard to the possibility of securing sufficient visas for the admission of any appreciable number of these people to the United States, and the *feasibility from the public-relations angle* of attempting to transplant close to thirty such institutions in the United States, involving 3,000 to 4,000 persons, was one that had to be seriously considered with other major organizations. [emphasis added][73]

Moses Leavitt of the Joint clarifies the opposition to the entry of the yeshivos:

> It was his [Wise's] opinion that a few of them, perhaps three or five hundred, might be absorbed here ... but he did not

feel it was feasible to think in terms of resettling a large number in this country, and *he disadvised the use of pressure on the Administration in connection with the issuance of visas.* [emph. added][74]

Anachronistic Rationalization

EPHRAIM ZUROFF ATTEMPTS TO RATIONALIZE the refusal by the Joint as being a question of "tremendous technical and financial problems." Yehudah Bauer added,

> The Zionist movement, the Joint, in fact all the Jewish organizations except for the Rescue Committee of Rabbis [Vaad Hatzalah] were not prepared to deal with this case due to the anxiety lest it increase the anti-Semitism then widespread in the U.S.[75]

In a later work Bauer gave the additional rationalization which became his theme in distinguishing between the Joint's (especially Saly Mayer's) concern for the *klal* and the Orthodox narrow particularist concerns. Discussing the speech Wise gave in declining to push for the entry of these thirty yeshivos, Bauer anachronistically and ironically rationalized the refusal as: "He [Wise] might perhaps have argued, as Saly Mayer was to do later in the war, that *all Jews are equal* and that *no elite group could demand preference.*"[76] Bauer's analogy to Mayer's views is correct, but for quite different reasons. As we have seen, the problem of absorbing these yeshivah students had nothing to do with the ability of American Jewry to absorb and even fully support the huge number of 2,800 or even 4,000 refugees. Nor were there "tremendous technical and financial problems," where an interest in saving these Jews was concerned. When *pikuach nefesh* was involved in getting the yeshivah students out of Russian-occupied Lithuania, Rabbi Aaron Kotler ruled with Rabbi Shlomo Heiman that one had to travel on the Sabbath to collect the necessary $50,000 immediately, which was accomplished, as we have seen, with the help of Irving Bunim.[77]

Nor, as we have pointed out, was there any real physical danger of antisemitism increasing because of the arrival of these several thousand talmudic students. Did they really expect an outbreak of pogroms because of the arrival of the yeshivos? Wise, Leavitt and others rationalized the refusal as "political and social and other reasons," which implied antisemitism, but these are obviously not the real reasons. It was not the European physical antisemitism but the fear of being identified by Americans with these most Orthodox, and therefore most unassimilable, Jews that assimilated American

Jews feared to bring in. These secularist Jews twisted their own insecurity within American society into a public facade of antisemitism, as one can see in the terms, *social, political and other reasons.* Their presence, it was feared, would prevent them from joining certain clubs or schools.[78] The underlying reason for the refusal to help the Jews of Eastern Europe and the yeshivah students was the widespread notion that such outwardly different Jews would increase American antisemitism — indeed, that antisemitism itself was fostered by the "unassimilable, ethnic Jew, who retained his different Old World mode of dress and culture."[79]

The negative view of Orthodox Jews in general and these yeshivah students in particular was also part and parcel of American Jewry's superiority complex towards Jews of the "Old Country." In turn, this attitude simply reflected Americans' condescending view of European civilization in general. Moreover, the refusal to help the yeshivah students was not affected by the Joint's policy of evenhanded distribution of funds — or by the quotas on Emergency Visitors' Visas. Each group, including the American Jewish Congress, made out its own list — but most went for secular intellectuals and Zionists.[80] In addition to Wise's insecurity was his penchant for not desiring to pressure the President, especially during an election year.

We see in these few examples, amplified elsewhere by this author, how ideology played such a crucial role as a deterrent to rescue at a time when it was readily possible.

CHAPTER FIVE

Cooperation and Ideology

THROUGHOUT THE HOLOCAUST, the Orthodox activists usually set aside narrow partisanship to work for all endangered Jews. We will see (Chap. 7B) how Rabbi Kalmanowitz and Yaakov Rosenheim were responsible for the first united effort by all of American Jewry in the fall of 1942, following the arrival of the Sternbuch cable. It was the Orthodox together with the Jewish Labor Committee that tried, albeit unsuccessfully, to maintain the Joint Emergency Committee (JEC) in 1943, comprised of all major American-Jewish organizations, which was dissolved by Wise. Likewise, even after the breakup of the JEC by Stephen Wise in the fall of 1943, and throughout the war, the Orthodox worked with any group, whether the American Jewish Committee, the World Jewish Congress, the Bergson Group or the Jewish Labor Committee in order to achieve success in any and all rescue schemes proposed.

WHILE EACH OF THESE GROUPS had its ideological limits of cooperation — the Zionists insisting on the inclusion of Palestine as

Cooperation Limited by Compunction

an issue; the Jewish Labor Committee, on excluding communists or the Bergson Group; the American Jewish Committee, as well as the others, taking a legalistic stance toward rescue methods and the exclusion of the political issue of Palestine — the Orthodox had no such compunctions. One needs no better picture than to see the aged long-bearded sage Rabbi Abraham

Kalmanowitz with the bare-headed atheist Jacob Pat of the Jewish Labor Committee, walking together in the garment center to collect money to send to Rabbi Weissmandl for the rescue of Polish refugees into Slovakia.[1]

The Orthodox groups worked for rescue all over the free world. Even those groups which normally had little to do with Orthodox Jews found that cooperation was to their benefit. In the Jewish Agency's Vaad Hahatzalah operating out of Turkey, for example, even the Marxists had high praise for men such as Rabbi Weissmandl and Dr. Yaakov Griffel.[2]

Similarly in England, after the December 1942 publication of the Riegner and Sternbuch cables, Rabbi Dr. Solomon Schonfeld, head of the Chief Rabbi's Religious Emergency Council (which worked closely with Vaad Hatzalah and Agudath Israel), organized a broad-based, largely non-Jewish coalition called the National Committee for Rescue from Nazi Terror, led by Lady Eleanor Rathbone.

Back in the U.S. the Orthodox activists were the sole Jewish representatives willing to join the Bergson Group in the 1943 call for what later became the Rabbis' March on Washington.[3] Peter Bergson,* a Revisionist-Zionist, and a member of its military arm, the Irgun Zvai Leumi, came to America in 1940 to raise funds for a Jewish army in Palestine. But when he learned of the Nazi exterminations from Wise's press conference in November 1942, he turned his attention to rescue. The Bergson Group was reviled by almost every segment of American Jewry for their radical approach to rescue. Their provocative advertisements and rhetoric angered the Roosevelt camp and the non-Revisionist Zionists, especially Stephen Wise, who considered them fascists or worse. The Bergson Group was considered a pariah by the Jewish Establishment due to its ideology of Revisionist Zionism (considered fascist by the socialist-Zionists) and its flamboyant press releases and provocative ads in the American newspapers. While most Zionists worked behind the scenes to scuttle the Bergson Resolution on rescue in Congress (which eventually led to the creation of the War Refugee Board), major Jewish organizations such as the Joint and the American Jewish Congress refused to become involved. (See Chap. 7D.) The Orthodox, however, pushed for its passage — and once President Roosevelt established the War Refugee Board, virtually every Jewish organization came forward to take credit.[4]

---

* His real name was Hillel Kook, a nephew of Palestine's first Chief Rabbi Avraham I. Kook.

THROUGHOUT THIS PERIOD, the Orthodox activists were less interested in credit than action, and they would forge any alliance,

Mayer's and McClelland's Rescue Work

work with any person or party, who would aid their cause. The Sternbuchs, for example, had no compunctions about working with the fascist Jean-Marie Musy in their ransom negotiations with Himmler. In fact, the Vaad even pressured them to cooperate with Saly Mayer as well, despite the fact that he had thwarted their work many times before. In a letter of October 26, 1944, to Sternbuch via Roswell McClelland, the WRB's representative in Switzerland, the Vaad implored Sternbuch, "Please try to coordinate with Mayer and McClelland last-minute action for the rescue of this pitiful remnant in the hands of the Germans. Spare no money." The Sternbuchs pleaded with the Vaad not to force them to work with Mayer and the Joint, for "the morbid anti-religious conviction and seeming patriotism of [Mayer] are a hindrance for any collaboration."[5]

The Sternbuchs had good grounds for their position. That summer, because Saly Mayer refused to put up funds to buy the 40 tractors which the Nazis had demanded as ransom, the so-called Kastner Train with 1,684 Hungarian Jews bound originally from Budapest to Spain was rerouted to Bergen-Belsen instead of going to Switzerland.[6] Mayer disapproved of ransom and besides, since the request for the rescue of the train passengers had come from Rabbi Weissmandl, Freudiger and Sternbuch, he assumed that the passengers would all be Orthodox Jews and rabbis and he did not think that they should be prime candidates for rescue. "Captains," he is said to have said to WRB representative, Roswell McClelland, "should go down with their ships."[7] Six weeks later, Mayer finally sent sufficient funds to make a deposit on the tractors — roughly 400,000 francs — but only after intense pressure from the Joint in New York. This pressure had been generated by the War Refugee Board, itself hounded by the rabbis of the Vaad. Tragically, the delay by Mayer was responsible for the sending of the train to Bergen-Belsen for six months instead of to Switzerland.[8]

Herman Landau, executive director of the Sternbuchs' HIJEFS* rescue organization, had informed Mayer on July 5, 1944 that the Kastner rescue did not merely involve Orthodox Jews, but Mayer

---

* HIJEFS was the acronym of the rescue organization created by Recha Sternbuch in 1941 which in English means, *Relief Committee for Assistance to Refugees in Shanghai*. When its scope broadened in 1943, its name and acronym were changed to *Relief Committee for Assistance to Refugees Abroad*.

did not listen. "I know what to do," he said, "[because] a Sternbuch action is surely a particularist one." Landau, frustrated with his inability to convince Mayer, asked pointedly, "Why don't you talk directly with the Sternbuchs?"[9] Throughout it all, of course, Mayer tried to emphasize that his party alone was interested in the *klal* — in all Jews — and not in an *einzelsach*, a distinguishable group.[10]

YET THE STERNBUCHS, like other Orthodox activists, would not only work with anyone, they would also go to great lengths not to

Relationships: Actual vs. Official

antagonize any potential ally. The Sternbuchs knew full well War Refugee Board (WRB) representative Roswell McClelland's obstructionist policies toward rescue, yet they deliberately spoke of him as helpful and cooperative in their public cables to the WRB and the Vaad when using official channels. Via the secret Polish diplomatic cable, however, they sent the truth to the Vaad. Thus, on July 5, 1944, Yitzchok Sternbuch sent a sanitized account of the Kastner Train negotiations via the official cable. "We are having the best relation through Mr. McClelland and this gentleman grants us, as all Jewish organizations, his best help willingly ... He understands our particular interests that we have and that we are working for him and we are acting always in a harmonious way with him ... [sic]"[11]

The truth, however, was quite different than what had been prepared for government eyes. At another time, and using the Polish Embassy cable, Yitzchok Sternbuch told the Vaad that "some of the money is used for bribery to rescue people. It is impossible to discuss this with McClelland."[12]

Recha Sternbuch knew that this rescue effort to get Polish refugees across the border into then relatively safe Slovakia would require bribery and ransom, and worked to make the negotiations acceptable to McClelland — "I am the very last person who would want to see these scoundrels get a single cent. But it is an urgent necessity ..."[13] McClelland responded by threatening to blacklist the Sternbuchs if they continued to pay ransom.[14]

Despite this sorry record, though, later, during the Musy negotiations, when the Vaad asked Yitzchok Sternbuch to cooperate with the Joint because they couldn't finance the rescue efforts by themselves, he complied, and immediately got in touch with Mayer, Kastner, as well as Dr. Joseph Schwartz, head of the European Joint. Sternbuch pleaded with each of them to cooperate on this crucial venture, for only through such joint efforts could the greatest number of lives be saved. All three refused to work with the Orthodox faction, a decision which had tragic results.[15]

THESE SAME IDEOLOGICAL BLINDERS prevented Jews in the socialist, assimilationist, and liberal camps from participating in **Non-Orthodox** other rescue opportunities. The Nazis had, **Reject Ransom** in fact, been willing to allow Jews to leave **Opportunities** Germany from the outset under a variety of plans. Most, including the early Schacht-Rublee Plans of 1938-39, and even earlier, from 1933 on, were ransom oriented, if in no other way than to utilize part of the Jews' assets to finance so-called orderly emigration. For example, as a *New York Times* headline of December 19, 1938 pointed out, "Nazi Ransom Plan is Rejected here: Joint Boycott Council Votes for Intensification of Drive Against German Goods: Failure of 'Barter' Seen." Dr. Tenenbaum declared, "Refugees Do Not Seek Freedom at the Cost of Dishonor," adding, "no Jewish refugee will accept freedom at the cost of dishonor and national disgrace."[16]

There was thus substantial opposition by Jews of the free world to this mode of emigration — with notable exceptions, including the *Haavarah* plan between Germany and the Jewish Agency, which permitted the well-off German Jews to take out part of their fortunes in German goods with them into Palestine. Even this method, which brought more than 60,000 Jews to Palestine, met with objections by some segments of Palestinian as well as American Jewries, especially from those like Wise and the World Jewish Congress and Abba Hillel Silver who were against it on the grounds that it broke the Jewish Boycott of Nazi Germany. "We hold in abhorrence," Wise wrote, "any Jew, whether in or out of Palestine, who undertakes to make commercial arrangements with the Nazi government for any reason whatsoever."[17]

SPAIN UNDER GENERAL FRANCO, although fascist and an ally of Nazi Germany, was also a haven of sorts for Jews. Indeed, according **Spanish** to one estimate, roughly 100,000 Jews found **Assistance** sanctuary in Spain for brief periods or used **Under-Utilized** well-traveled routes to freedom through Spain or Portugal. Ironically, the government headed by Franco, who was universally condemned by the free world, permitted Jews access to Spain from occupied France and, among others, protected over 1,200 Jewish children in Nazi-occupied Hungary in 1944, through the intercession of Mrs. Renee Reichmann and even authorized the Spanish Red Cross to pay the postage for the thousands of food packages she sent into the concentration camps.[18] Sadly, however, so many more Jews *could* have made use of Spain as a haven or at least as a way-station, had they been more willing to accept that route. As Haim Avni, the authoritative historian of Spain and the Jews, has noted,

> The image of Franco's regime in the eyes of the public and press in *Eretz Yisrael*, and especially in the eyes of the socialist elements in the *yishuv*, should also be remembered. It is likely that they never imagined that help or shelter could be expected from that quarter.[19]

Unfortunately, the Joint decided *not* to finance an illegal escape route from France through Spain during the key period of April 1943 to May 1944, despite the fact that it was successfully used by thousands of escaping Jews.[20] Switzerland, on the other hand, hailed as a bastion of democracy, sealed its borders and turned back thousands of Jews — at least 150,000 by Recha Sternbuch's estimate. Indeed, the problem was so acute that it was common knowledge in France that unless one had small children, Switzerland was not even worth the effort.[21]

THE STORIES OF ideological barriers to rescue are as varied as they are tragic. One 1942 plan, for example, proposed by Angelo Donati, **Italian** an Italian Jew and a Sternbuch ally, called for **Rescue** transferring 50,000 Jews from Italian-occupied Nice in southern France to Italy proper. By and large, **Rebuffed** Jews were well treated by Mussolini's fascist government in Italy — and especially by Italian soldiers and civilians as well — and Donati wanted to take advantage of the different political climate across the border.[22] Although Donati's plan was a sound one, and he worked closely with Italian Inspector General Guido Lospinoso in charge of Jewish affairs in southern France, Donati failed because, as the historian Lucien Steinberg wrote, "The Jewish communists [in occupied France] opposed the idea because they considered Italy an enemy country and an occupier like Germany, and because from an ideological point of view they could not trust fascists."[23]

IDEOLOGY WAS AN OBSTACLE when yet another escape route presented itself — Japan. After the Evian Conference in the summer

Japanese Welcome Mat of 1938, when the world effectively announced it would not accept large numbers of refugee Jews, and after *Kristallnacht* in November of the same year, when Nazis attacked Jewish homes, businesses, and synagogues, there were only two places open for immediate emigration: Trujillo's Dominican Republic and Shanghai, the latter a Chinese port city of four million, including 100,000 Japanese and Occidentals.[24] At that time, Japan occupied parts of the Shanghai International Settlement and permitted more than 17,000 Austrian and German Jews to enter and reside there. Just prior to the Pearl Harbor attack in late 1941, but after restrictions to further immigration were enacted, the Japanese — allies of Germany and purveyors of Nazi anti-Jewish propaganda — let in an additional 1,000 Polish refugees, including roughly 500 yeshivah students, conveniently routing them southward through Japan.[25]

Japan was willing to let these Polish Jews travel through it to Shanghai for a number of reasons. In December 1938, the highly secret Five Ministers Council created Japan's pro-Jewish policy because of their mistaken idea that "Jewish power" controlled the West, notably England and the United States. This idea was hardly original with the Japanese, of course, having appeared first in *The Protocols of the Elders of Zion* and other antisemitic tracts, which numerous Japanese military and government officials accepted as true. Yet the Japanese had little experience with Jews — and less with western expulsions of this supposedly powerful group. Instead of putting Jews at arm's length, then, the Japanese welcomed them because they might be able to use their supposed influence on behalf of Japanese causes, including its much-heralded plans for an "East Asia Co-Prosperity Sphere," whereby Japan would lead East Asia out of the European sphere of influence into a purely Asian state of political and economic independence. It is easy to follow the Japanese logic, especially in view of their perception of the prominence of such American Jews as Treasury Secretary Morgenthau, presidential speechwriter Samuel Rosenman, Stephen Wise, as well as financier Jacob Schiff, chairman of Kuhn, Loeb and Company, who had floated the Japanese loans in the Russo-Japanese War of 1904-05.

In line, then, with their own pragmatic, pro-Jewish policy, the Japanese not only opened up Shanghai to Jews, they went so far as to sponsor three annual "Far Eastern Conferences" on Jewish Communities in 1937-39. Delegates came from eight East Asian-

Jewish communities, made up largely of Russian Jews who had fled the October 1917 Bolshevik Revolution to resettle in Manchuria, China, and Japan. Zionism was encouraged and Betar Zionists in uniform served as honorary guards, and top Japanese military officials spoke of the friendship between the two peoples. It was hoped that the newly arrived Jews would somehow influence President Roosevelt to soften the stringent anti-Japan stance he adopted after the 1931 invasion of Manchuria. Further, it seemed reasonable to the Japanese that Jewish bankers would be so grateful that they would lend two or three billion dollars to help industrialize Manchuria — a sparsely populated area where several hundred thousand highly skilled German Jews could easily settle and make it into another Palestine.

AT THE TIME, the stateless Russian Jews had no idea what lay behind Japan's generous policy, but they were grateful for their **Wise** hospitality and did fulfill one Japanese hope by **Saw it** passing on the message to fellow Jews in America. **Differently** In 1938, for example, they sent Lew Zikman as a representative to see Cyrus Adler, president of the American Jewish Committee, and Stephen Wise, president of the American Jewish Congress. Zikman requested the opportunity to speak at the Congress' convention the following year, a request which Wise denied, declaring:

> I think it is wholly vicious for Jews to give support to Japan, as truly Fascist a nation as Germany or Italy. I do not wish to discuss the matter any further and I deeply deplore whatever your reasons may be that you are trying to secure support for Japan from Jews. I promise you that everything I can do to thwart your plans, I will do. You are doing a great disservice to the Jewish people.[26]

Desperate, Zikman replied the next day.

> In the name of the 15,000 Jews in the Far East, I implore you to think of us; not to throw upon us the waves of disaster and not to take upon yourself the responsibilities of any consequences where there might be at least the minimum hopes for betterment of our situation.[27]

Yet that appeal — and a further one — went unanswered.[28]

CHAPTER SIX

Not Giving Up

MONG THE MANY NAGGING ISSUES presented by the Holocaust is the seeming passivity of the Jews in the free West regarding the genocide in the East — especially after the details became well known. Raul Hilberg, for example, noted nearly thirty years ago that Henry Monsky, president of B'nai Brith, sent a letter to thirty-four organizations on January 6, 1943, stating that:

> American Jewry, which will be required in large measure to assume the responsibility of representing the interests of our people at the Victory Peace Conference, must be ready to voice the judgment of American Jews along with that of other Jewish communities of the free countries with respect to the postwar status of Jews and the upbuilding of a Jewish Palestine.[1]

Hilberg then offered a glimpse of the general American-Jewish attitude at the time:

> In this letter no warning to the Germans is proposed, no scheme to put an end to the destruction process is suggested; the destruction of the European Jews is not even mentioned. The European Jews are already given up, and all thoughts turn to postwar salvage ... The paralysis was complete.[2]

SIMILARLY, YEHUDA BAUER in his brief survey "The Holocaust and American Jewry" expands upon this same theme, but attributes

Postwar Planning Takes Precedence it further to all Jews in the West — including Palestine. First, he notes, the Jews had to internalize the terrible information coming from Europe but even then, he adds, they could not act because they "suffered from an absolute powerlessness."[3] Finally, Bauer concludes that the Jews simply gave up.[4] "The Joint," he adds, "likewise was also involved — just like all the other major agencies — in postwar planning."[5]

The Joint was hardly alone. The American Jewish Committee, then a powerful force in the non-Zionist Jewish Establishment and led at that time by the monied German Jews, also turned away from Europe. Naomi Cohen, that organization's own historian, writes that for the AJC:

> There were no longer any possibilities for independent maneuvering or rescue operations. Even when news of Hitler's 'Final Solution' leaked out to the Western world, American Jewish organizations could only appeal to their government and hope that the Allied military campaign would include measures to save the doomed Jewish population of Europe.[6]
>
> The Committee's activities on other fronts compensated for its enforced idleness on the European scene ... In anticipation of postwar reconstruction, it invested heavily in a research institute ...[7]

Generally, then, and especially after the failure of the Allied Bermuda Conference of April 1943 to propose any concrete measures to rescue Jews, most of American Jewry accepted what amounted to the official verdict of the United States that

> there was really nothing one could do to help Jews under Nazi rule except to win the war quickly ... Nothing that might hamper the war effort, including any rescue plan that diverted means and manpower from the pursuit of victory, could be justified.[8]

The reaction was equally pessimistic on the other side of the Atlantic in Great Britain, and an inescapable feeling of impotence marked the reaction of Palestinian Jewry as well.[9]

BAUER PROVIDES THE KEY to the activities of the American Jewish community in his discussion of the differences between **Basic Morality** information, internalized knowledge, and action. While some others did — or perhaps felt — nothing, the Orthodox activists said, in effect, that internalization took place when the news began to hurt sufficiently so that action became a necessity — regardless of the possible consequences. In this case, however, the actual decision to act comes only after an individual Jew feels *personally* liable for the life of his fellow Jews. Setting aside such humanist notions as universal ethics or basic morality, Bauer's conclusion is an apt one. "In the end," he writes, "beyond political and religious convictions, it was basic morality that counted."[10]

Yet both abandoning hope and choosing inaction are paths which cut directly against the Torah demand that Jews "do not stand idly by when thy brother's blood is shed."[11] As we have noted earlier, the Orthodox efforts differed from others because they believed that each Jew is *obligated* to try to save the life of even a single other Jew — even if he thinks beforehand that most or even all his efforts will be wasted. So whereas the secular Jewish organizations protested that they could not affect any substantive rescue action, and could not work against their country's war effort, the Orthodox activists said they could not "stand idly by." Where the others spoke only of defeat, the Orthodox had no choice. They were commanded to try — regardless of result, regardless of realism, faced with Allied condemnation and American ostracism.

Unfortunately, not all the Orthodox Jews in the free world understood these issues clearly, and then marshalled their forces effectively and acted intelligently and quickly. The ransom of untold thousands of Jews was a unique opportunity in 1943-44, but pitifully few of Rabbi Weissmandl's plans ever came to fruition, in some measure due to confusion and to the fact that Orthodox groups had neither the fiscal resources of the Joint nor the political power of the American Jewish Congress.

In the fall of 1943, for example, there was an opportunity to rescue thousands of Jews from Poland and Hungary into the still relatively safe Slovakia. Rabbi Weissmandl requested one million dollars for this project but Sternbuch was only able to send him $100,000.[12] Again, even the Orthodox failed to press sufficiently hard and fast.

The Joint's Reluctant Help

LATER, DURING THE MUSY-HIMMLER negotiations of February 1945, initiated by Recha Sternbuch, which brought about the release of 1,210 Theresienstadt inmates, the Nazis demanded one million dollars to begin bi-weekly releases of all remaining concentration camp detainees. The Orthodox groups felt powerless to raise such money, having just raised and spent more than one million dollars for rescue the previous year. And even if they did have access to such funds, the Orthodox groups would not have been able to raise such an amount in the few weeks provided. They had only been able to raise $100,000 in an emergency campaign. Again they asked the Joint for help, this time in the form of a loan, and again the Joint refused because ransom was unacceptable.[13] Only after the Vaad's Irving Bunim — and several important Orthodox contributors — brought intense pressure to bear on the Joint did they finally grant the loan.[14]

Yet even when the Joint finally did act, it did so in a way that ultimately hindered the very rescue effort it was supposedly helping. The most effective route for the money was through illegal channels to Switzerland; instead, the Joint insisted on sending the funds through the War Refugee Board, creating a virtually impossible restriction because the War Refugee Board and especially Roswell McClelland, the WRB representative in Switzerland, would not countenance ransom or the slightest resemblance to it. And when the attempt failed, almost all funds allocated for ransom had to be returned to the Joint.[15] Despite the need for food in the camps and the Sternbuchs' attempts to ship it to the inmates, McClelland and the JDC insisted on taking back almost all the money and thereby missed an opportunity to keep many more thousands alive in the camps during the last few weeks of the war.[16]

THE ORTHODOX ACTIVISTS attempted to work with the Jewish Establishment throughout the period, yet their struggle for

Fruitless Struggle cooperation was ultimately fruitless. The few instances where the Jewish groups attempted to work together, whether in the ad hoc subcommittee established after the arrival of the Sternbuch cable in September 1942 or in the March 1943 establishment of the more formal Joint Emergency Committee, proved to be more of a hindrance than a help to the Orthodox activists. Although some, notably Recha Sternbuch, felt from the outset that the Orthodox groups should work alone, the American-Orthodox Jewish leadership stuck valiantly to a more cooperative course, only realizing later how much greater their gains might have been had not a sizeable portion of their energies been siphoned off in trying to enlist aid from their fellow Jews. It was, in fact, only after constant prodding by Rabbi Weissmandl in late 1943 that the Orthodox activists jettisoned thoughts of a united Jewry and began working alone or with selected allies such as Peter Bergson or the Jewish Labor Committee. And despite the satisfactions of some successes after striking out on their own, the Orthodox groups continued to feel the sting of lost opportunities due to a lack of political and financial power — or insufficient strength to mobilize even their own small resources.

THE VIRTUAL TORRENT of articles published in the Jewish press in 1943-44 by Dr. Isaac Lewin of the Agudath Israel World **Isaac** Organization reflects the continued concern of **Lewin's** Orthodoxy, their feelings of helplessness, the **Articles** difficulty of their fight — and fears of defeat.[17] The ill-fated American Jewish Conference of August 1943, which quickly degenerated into a Zionist-dominated attempt to establish a postwar Jewish state, drew a characteristically sharp response. "It is insufficient," Lewin wrote, "to concern ourselves with Jews only after the War."[18] Further, he recognized what he termed "the passive attitude of American Jewry," for conferences of that sort were far more suited to times of peace than during a "life and death struggle." In fact, Lewin stated flatly in February 1943 that:

> in order to achieve the postwar status of Jewry and to struggle for *Eretz Yisrael* on their behalf — there must first of all remain Jews, some Jews left in Europe, since all this work is intended on their behalf.[19]

Similarly, in a front-page editorial entitled *Mir Alarmiren!* (We raise the alarm!) which appeared in *Die Yiddishe Shtimme* (The Jewish Voice), Agudath Israel's monthly Yiddish newspaper, Dr. Lewin demanded real action to save Europe's Jews while decrying the dissolution of the Emergency Committee for European Jewish Affairs and indicting Stephen Wise for wanting publicity instead of results. In its conclusion he wrote, "We raise the alarm! The world is going under! Do not remain silent! Our blood is flowing! Rescue must come!"[20] Lewin further pleaded that "Every day plays a role. Every day countless Jewish lives are consumed. And whoever is able to do something about it and does not, shares the responsibility of this great catastrophe. More than relief is required," the editorial reminded, "there is a real need for a united Jewish effort to achieve the necessary political power."[21]

A few months later, in an article headed, "Do Not Despair," Lewin again pleaded against the overpowering feelings of helplessness which engulfed the Jewish community.[22] He repeated the theme once more in "We Dare Not Give Up On Our Brethren in Poland," written in July 1943. "It appears as if American Jewry has totally given up hope on its European brethren ... All is lost anyhow, there is nothing one can do." Dr. Lewin warns American Jewry however, "We dare not slumber — it is still possible to save innumerable Jews."[23] Further calls for uplifted spirits and concerted action followed. "There *are* ways," he wrote, "to make a halt to the slaughter of Jews in occupied countries!"[24] "There *are*," he added of the Jews trapped in Transnistria (Rumania), "possibilities of helping the Jews in Europe."[25]

Lewin did not stop beseeching individuals specifically and Jews generally to *act* for those trapped in Europe. In November 1943, for example, he published "Rescue Opportunities For Jews That Are Being Neglected," an article that appeared concurrently with a Bergson group-Vaad Hatzalah resolution on rescue then brought before Congress demanding a separate governmental agency devoted to the rescue of European Jewry.[26] In December of that year, when there was a chance to save many Hungarian and Slovakian Jews, but not enough money, Lewin again alerted Jews with his article: "The Clock Strikes Twelve."[27] In January 1944, just prior to the establishment of the War Refugee Board, Lewin deplored the fact that organizations followed "politics as usual" and refused to unite to save Jews. In an article called "How Long Will Politics Be Played With Jewish Blood" he called for the reestablishment of the Joint Emergency Committee.[28] And, when the situation did not improve even after the creation of the War Refugee Board, Lewin published, "Concerning Jewish Unity and the War Refugee Board," where he concluded, *"It is possible and there must be created a Jewish unity for the rescue of our dying brothers!"*[29] And but a month later he wrote, "One *can* save Jews, one merely needs the means."[30]

Such concern and sense of urgency was sadly lacking among the vast majority of American Jewry.

CHAPTER SEVEN

Survey of the Orthodox Rescue Activities During the Holocaust

A. FOOD TO THE GHETTOS

IN 1940-41 JEWS THROUGHOUT the world, even those in the ghettos, believed that the Nazis meant to kill them passively, through starvation and disease. From inside Poland's ghettos the world heard the plaintive cry: "Send us food! Don't let us die of hunger, we and our little ones behind the gates of the infernal ghetto."[1] At the time, food shipments were still possible, and relatives and friends, Jewish and non-Jewish companies and organizations such as the Joint regularly sent food packages into occupied Poland. The Agudah, too, began to send food to rabbis, scholars, and other Orthodox Jews. Such was their success that they offered to send packages for $5.25 to anyone, regardless of background or politics.[2]

The route was easy. Using the simple device of a money transfer, the Agudah had a Jew named Deutsch mail the packages from Belgrade to Poland while it deposited the money in his account in the U.S. At the end of April 1941, after the invasion of Yugoslavia, new arrangements were made, with the packages going out from Portugal.[3] The system continued to work well, so well, in fact, that 2,000-4,000 food packages arrived monthly, each documented by a return receipt. The Joint was impressed by such efficiency and asked for the Agudah's help in sending matzohs into Poland for *Pesach*, 1941.[4]

THIS DIDN'T LAST LONG. The Joint Boycott Council, then under the chairmanship of Dr. Joseph Tenenbaum, was pressing to

The Flow of Food is Stopped exclude German goods from the United States, and to prevent any materials from being sent to Germany and occupied territories. The Joint Boycott Council had been organized in 1936 by the American Jewish Congress and the Jewish Labor Committee with the hope of bringing down the Nazi regime — or at least inflicting substantial damage on it. Following a call by the State Department some time in mid-1941, which was prompted by the British ambassador, the Council soon began pressuring all Jewish organizations and export firms to cease sending food to Polish Jews. Dr. Nahum Goldmann recalled that a State Department representative telephoned this request to the American Jewish Congress, saying that shipments were "against the interests of the Allies, especially Britain and France." Later Dr. Goldmann noted that:

> Since the call came from the State Department we were in no position to question its authority. We were all shook up by this news. The first to tell us to cease immediately was Dr. Wise, who was himself a favorite of the American Government ... I recall that conversation he had with me. Wise explained: "[This shipping of packages] is a great humanitarian activity, and one must help. However, since there is a danger that the Germans will utilize it for their benefit, it is incumbent upon us to stop [it], especially for the benefit of Britain." Thereby he also influenced Dr. Tenenbaum to halt the Joint action. From that day on we ceased sending packages. True, there were organizations that were not ready to follow dictates of the American Government, such as Agudath Israel ... But in the end it stopped.[5]

By that summer, 1941, while the United States was still a neutral country, all the organizations and firms had agreed to the boycott save for Agudath Israel, which felt that "feeding our unfortunate brothers and sisters in Poland is a clear-cut instance of [not standing idly by while their blood is being spilled]."[6] It further argued that the "thousands of heartrending cries for help are far more important and authoritative [than the Boycott Council]."[7]

The Agudah's position found little or no support. Most vehement was Boycott Council chairman Tenenbaum, who wrote:

> Many are of the opinion that England cannot decide what is good for the interest of the Jewish people and what is not. To which we reply that this question is not only to the interest of the Jewish people but to the world at large, with which the interest of the Jewish people must be in accord. Everything against the war interest of England is against the interest of the Jewish people.
>
> *We dare not do anything now, as a nation or as an organization, which would awaken those slightly stilled cries that we are only for ourselves. The British interests are our interests. The American interest is our interest.*
>
> Smuggled letters sent to this country reveal that packages received in Nazi-controlled countries only add misery to injury. If one receives a five-dollar package, the receiver must pay five dollars additional before the package is delivered to him. Many packages before being delivered are pilfered and only delivered in part, while others never reach their destination.
>
> *If only a small portion of the food sent to these quarters does reach its source, is it worth it? Is it a good idea to help fill the Nazi coffers with food and money?* [emphasis added]

Tenenbaum was particularly annoyed at Agudath Israel:

> The bad effects of this example can be seen in the replies which we received from private companies, which say that since the Agudas [sic] Israel of America is continuing to send packages, they feel justified in starting to send packages to Nazi-occupied territories.[8]

DR. TENENBAUM EVEN PICKETED the Agudah's New York City offices at 673 Broadway — Jews picketing Jews for sending food **Jews** packages to Jews starving in ghettos. The picketing **Picket** continued for weeks, yet the Agudah refused to relent. The Jewish press picked up the issue. Most papers sided **Jews** with the Joint Boycott Committee, although the Agudah argued that the issue should be resolved not through editorials but by an impartial arbitration board. The Boycott Committee refused. The Agudah demanded proof that the goods were being pilfered or that feeding impoverished Jews aided the Nazi cause. The Agudah asked why there were no similar British objections to shiploads of American grain sent to the civilian populations of occupied Greece and Yugoslavia. And, the Agudah asked, was this not a parallel to Britain's own request during World War I that food be shipped to

Jews in Palestine — an action which violated its own blockade of Turkish-occupied territory? The Agudah knew quite well, of course, that the earlier World War I move came for political and not humanitarian reasons. The British then had wished to curry favor with Zionist and American interests. In 1941 there was no such lever.[9]

The dispute became more heated. The Boycott Council brought personal invective into play against the Agudah and its halachic authorities. "It is to be deplored that the Agudas [sic] Israel of America, a sickly weed transplanted from foreign soil to the liberal American environment, should continue to poison the atmosphere without regard for the consequences to the entire Jewish people."[10] Nor did the committee spare Rabbi Aaron Kotler and other newly arrived Torah sages, calling them "Jewish-Polish refugees, recent arrivals in this land of freedom and opportunity, who, though they speak of Torah and prayer with pious glances, yet a dollar is a dollar."[11] Throughout, only the Union of Orthodox Rabbis of the United States and Canada backed the Agudah's stand, publicly stating that "it sees no crime in the work of saving Jewish lives from hunger." They added, "We believe in the talmudic teaching, 'He who saves one life is considered to have saved the whole world.' "[12]

The Boycott Committee's characterization of the Agudah and its Torah scholars as foreign elements and refugees are but one manifestation of the negative attitude toward both the Orthodox leadership and the "alien" observant Jews of Eastern Europe. As Dr. Tenenbaum saw it, the issue came down to one of selfishness — or universalism and self-sacrifice. "There are times when bringing sacrifices are more important than even our own lives. Now we are living in a period such as that. Are the Jewish people different from other nations? Is the Jewish Sacrifice to be of lesser importance than the Gentile Sacrifice?"[13]

Misplaced Priorities

THE PATHOS OF THIS SITUATION is that neither Dr. Tenenbaum nor Stephen Wise nor any of the Boycott's other Jewish leaders were ignorant or wicked individuals insensitive to Jewish suffering. Much the opposite was the case, for Dr. Tenenbaum himself, as president of the Federation of Polish Jews, had sent numerous packages to Poland. What was crucial, however, was these leaders' perceptions of what was important for the greater Jewish community and where its priorities lay. While the Orthodox leaders identified more closely with their dying brethren overseas, the secular establishment saw themselves as loyal Americans first — and acted accordingly.

Agudath Israel's staunch resistance in the face of steady picketing brought more condemnation from Dr. Tenenbaum, who wrote that "... after three weeks of continuous picketing, the Agudas [sic] Israel of America still continues in the sorry role of being the only organization breaking the British blockade and Jewish solidarity."[14] He concluded that "under no circumstances will the Joint Boycott Council permit single organizations to subsidize the Hitler regime under the guise of helping the [Polish] Jewish organization [sic], whether through ignorance or lack of conscience."[15] Matters did not end there, for a Boycott Council report led directly to intervention by Lord Halifax, the British Ambassador to the United States, who brought an implicit threat to arrest Jewish refugees in Britain. Faced with a terrible situation — the closure of a vital exit point out of Nazi Europe — the Agudah finally — and reluctantly — stopped its food shipments just prior to the entry of the U.S. into the war on December 7, 1941.[16]

An interesting juxtaposition of war-relief work by large numbers of Jewish organizations will further highlight the secular Jews' emphasis on the universal in contrast to the particularist Jewish needs.

IN MID-1941, Dr. Israel Goldstein, chairman of the Jewish Section of the Interfaith Committee for Aid to the Democracies in **Food** Cooperation with the British War Relief Society, a **Rich in** group created just prior to the picketing of the Agudah, **Irony** pleaded with the American rabbinate and all Jewish organizations to solicit funds to help the civilian population of Great Britain, particularly "the victims of bomb-shattered cities, children's homes for children who have been orphaned as a result of air attacks and other forms of civilian aid."[17] It is a double irony that his letter appeared at a time when Jews fought with each other over food for their own people, and that the letter went to all Jewish clergy. The letterhead bore the names Abba Hillel Silver and Stephen S. Wise, and the text said in part that "the sentiment of American Jews for the cause of Great Britain ... is unanimous in consonance with the prevailing sentiment of all Americans." Dr. Goldstein also reported that his appeal had the support of a "score of national organizations, religious, fraternal, social, philanthropic, Zionist and non-Zionist."[18]

How far secular Jews had strayed from the classic Jewish

position on *arevus* is highlighted by an important historical precedent involving a "Jewish Boycott." There, too, the case called for a logical, and surely an emotional response, by Jews in a position to revenge themselves upon the perpetrators of crimes against their fellow Jews. The halachic decision by the rabbis, however, ruled against any boycott that might prove harmful to Jews.

The episode occurred during that sorry period when the Inquisition reared its ugly head throughout Catholic-dominated Europe. Twenty-four Marranos had been burned at the stake during 1556-1557 in Ancona, Italy, then under papal rule, for the crime of desiring to return to or retain their ancestral faith. This cruelty naturally aroused the concern of the large and powerful Jewish community of Turkey, led by Joseph, Duke of Naxos, who was vizier to the Sultan, and his aunt, the influential Donna Gracia, themselves former Marranos. In fact, most of the community was comprised of refugees who had found a haven in Turkey following their expulsion from Spain in 1492.

In an attempt to avenge themselves against Ancona, the Turkish Jews planned to use their economic clout and divert their considerable commerce from that city to the nearby duchy of Pisaro, competitors of the papal states. The Pope, upon learning of this plan, threatened the Jews of Ancona with dire consequences, and they, in turn, pleaded with their fellow Jews in Turkey to cancel the planned economic boycott of Ancona. Naturally such an issue was posed to the Rabbi of the major synagogue in Constantinople, Rabbi Joshua Soncino, of the well-known printing family.

His decision, endorsed by two other eminent contemporary authorities, is found in his work of responsa, entitled *Nachla L'Yehoshua*. Aside from complicated related matters discussed by this author elsewhere, Rabbi Joshua Soncino made clear his basic halachic premise that since the boycott would be detrimental to the welfare of the Jews of Ancona, the perpetrators of the boycott would be guilty of *shefichas domim* (shedding of blood).[18a]

All this cannot be properly understood unless one is aware of the historical forces that splintered world Jewry into numerous secular ideological movements which rejected the millenia-old Torah concepts discussed above. (See Chap. 1.)

B. THE STERNBUCH CABLE:

THIS NEXT EPISODE in the rescue activities of the Orthodox was a major event from every angle despite the attempt by most historians

News of the Holocaust Reaches American Jewry

of the Holocaust to either ignore it or denigrate it. Part of the reason for this is of course ideological, since some secularist Jewish historians, still find it difficult to credit the Orthodox with doing things, or working in a manner that accomplished much in the field of rescue. It would prove even more difficult to absorb the fact it was the Sternbuchs in conjunction with the American Agudath Israel and Vaad Hatzalah that were actually responsible for the news of the Holocaust to reach the large masses of American Jewry.[19] And it was these same "particularist" Orthodox who were responsible for the first and sole attempt at unifying *all* of American Jewry on behalf of rescue.

It is most interesting to juxtapose the series of three major cables in 1942 with breakthroughs about the Nazis' determination to murder all Jews in occupied Europe. What impact did they have on the American-Jewish leadership and what finally instigated some movement toward a united front on behalf of rescue? While the facts per se have been mostly made public, they have not been fully understood even by historians of the Holocaust.

The first news of major proportions was a report from Poland by members of the Jewish underground belonging to the Jewish Bund (socialist party) which reached America in June 1942. In unequivocal terms, this report, known as the Bund Report, detailed the mass slaughter of about 700,000 Polish Jews and the Nazi plans to murder the rest. As Yehuda Bauer has already pointed out, this report was not properly absorbed and very little reaction by American Jews took place.[20]

The second, even more shattering news, detailed in specific but equivocal terms the Nazi plans to exterminate almost four million Jews. This was found in the so-called Riegner cable of August 28, 1942, sent to Stephen S. Wise.[21] Wise did not publicize it among American Jewish leaders, but only among his few close friends. Instead, he sent it to the State Department for verification. He surely did not view the Riegner cable as confirmation of the earlier Bund Report.[22]

The third cable, the one sent by Yitzchok Sternbuch, arrived five days later in Washington at the Polish Embassy which relayed it to the Orthodox rabbis in New York. It recounted, in unequivocal terms, the deportation of 100,000 Jews from Warsaw to the death camps and the plan to kill the rest of the Jews. The Orthodox, however, though unaware of the other "supporting" Riegner cable, pressured Wise into making a major effort to unite American Jewry behind rescue efforts.[23] Let us examine the arrival of the Sternbuch and Riegner cables a little more closely.

ON SEPTEMBER 2, 1942, a cable detailing the deportation and extermination of 100,000 Warsaw Jews was sent by Yitzchok Sternbuch **The** in Switzerland to Yaakov Rosenheim in New York **Sternbuch** via the Polish Embassy's confidential pouch. Rosenheim was president of the World Agudath **Cable** Israel, an international organization of Orthodox Jews founded in Poland in 1912.[24] Warning that the same fate faced Jews throughout the Nazi-occupied countries, Sternbuch described how Jewish bodies were being used to make soap and fertilizer for German industry and begged Rosenheim to:

> Do whatever you can to cause an American reaction to halt these persecutions STOP Do whatever you can to produce such a reaction stirring up statesmen the press and the community STOP Inform Wise Silver Lubavicer Einstein Klatzkin Goldmann Mann and others.[25]*

By 9 p.m. on September 3, the day he received the cable, Rosenheim had sent its details to President Roosevelt and begun to notify the individuals mentioned. He asked Roosevelt to get all neutral states to express their moral indignation and proposed retaliatory Allied action against Germany to halt the massacres.[26] To assure the arrival of his grim message, that same day Sternbuch in Switzerland personally telephoned Rabbi Kalmanowitz of the Vaad Hatzalah in New York.[27] Shortly afterward, a third copy of the cable reached Rosenheim via the normal channels from the U.S. Legation in Bern, Switzerland.[28]

At Rosenheim's request, Dr. Isaac Lewin in New York, the Orthodox's liaison to the Polish Government-in-Exile in London, asked the Polish Embassy to set up an appointment with Roosevelt through the State Department. But that effort was unsuccessful and Roosevelt never responded to Rosenheim's cable. FDR forwarded it to the State Department three weeks later. In late September, Thomas Mann publicized the contents of the Sternbuch cable over the BBC in London. He was the only one mentioned in the cable who

---

* Those referred to were Rabbi Stephen S. Wise, president of the American and World Jewish Congresses; Abba Hillel Silver, chairman of United Palestine Appeal; J.J. Schneerson, the Hassidic Rebbe of Lubavitch; Albert Einstein; Jacob Klatzkin, philosopher; Nahum Goldmann, Jewish Agency representative in the U.S.; and Thomas Mann, a German novelist and the only non-Jew on the list.

followed through on that particular plea for help.[29]

ON AUGUST 28, nearly a week before Sternbuch's message was delivered by cable and phone, Dr. Stephen S. Wise received a cable **The** from Dr. Gerhard Riegner, the World Jewish **Riegner** Congress' man in Switzerland. Though less graphic and more equivocal than Sternbuch's, its message was **Cable** the same:

> Received alarming report that in Fuehrer's headquarters plan ... under consideration according to which all Jews in countries ... controlled by Germany number 3½-4 million should after deportation and concentration in the East be exterminated at one blow to resolve once and for all the Jewish question in Europe STOP The action reported planned for autumn methods under discussion including prussic acid STOP *We transmit information with all reservation as exactitude cannot be confirmed* STOP Informant stated to have close connections with highest German authorities and his reports generally speaking reliable.[30] [emph. added]

As we have seen, Dr. Wise did not contact anyone outside his inner circle. In fact, the Orthodox leadership did not find out about the Riegner cable until after the war.[31]

Rabbi Kalmanowitz received a copy of the Sternbuch cable from Rosenheim on September 3 and called Dr. Wise to tell him its message and request a meeting. The next day, Dr. Wise met with Kalmanowitz, Rosenheim, and Rabbis Aaron Kotler and Eliezer Silver, two Vaad leaders, at the Lower East Side office of the Union of Orthodox Rabbis. Also present at that heated debate on priorities were Aryeh Tartakower and Aryeh L. Kubowitzki, assistants to Dr. Wise.[32]

DR. WISE WAS FINALLY PERSUADED, as the foremost leader of American Jewry, to call a meeting of the heads of thirty-four **Wise** American-Jewish organizations. At that meeting, on September 6 at the World Jewish Congress office in **Orders** New York, the leadership of the entire American- **Silence** Jewish community was officially made aware for the first time of the charges of Nazi genocide against the Jews.[33]

To the assembled leaders, Dr. Wise quoted from Sternbuch's cable, but made no mention of Riegner's. Over protests, he imposed an oath of silence on those present, to be lifted only if Sternbuch's report was confirmed by the State Department. Dr. Wise also accused the Orthodox of spreading *greulmaerchen* (atrocity tales).[34]

It is quite obvious that Rabbi Wise, and a few of his close associates, as well as the State Department, should have considered the three cables, including the two unequivocal ones from the Bund and Sternbuch, as confirming each other, but they chose not to. In fact, due to his penchant for not wishing to disturb the President, Wise prevented others from drawing this same logical conclusion by suppressing the existence of the Riegner cable. The only reason why the American Jewish leadership was informed of the Sternbuch cable was the persistence of the Orthodox rabbis, especially Rabbi Abraham Kalmanowitz, otherwise it would have shared the same fate of silence.

EVEN WITH THEIR LIMITED KNOWLEDGE, the Orthodox tried to breach the oath of silence but did not have enough influence. All

Orthodox Breach Oath of Silence

they could do was vent their frustration in *Die Yiddishe Shtimme*, the Agudah's house organ. In the November 1942 issue, Dr. Lewin bemoaned his inability to get other Jewish organizations to go public with the news from Europe:

This information which arrived on September 3 demanded unequivocally: Raise a storm, because what is happening now has never been heard of! The first duty of the Jewish leadership was to alarm and publicize. We Jews have no other weapons other than the "Voice of Jacob." Our history has taught us that the stirring up of the [Jewish] camp has frequently brought about means to halt the catastrophe.[35]

At the September 6 meeting called by Dr. Wise at the behest of the Orthodox, an ad hoc committee was formed. By the end of the year, its efforts had yielded the following results:

— At a press conference on November 24, following verification and new information from the State Department, Dr. Wise made the first public announcement of the murder of more than two million Jews.

— December 2 was declared a world-wide fast day for Jews by the Chief Rabbi of Palestine, Isaac Halevy Herzog.

— On December 8 the committee met with Roosevelt.

— On December 17 the Allies condemned the Nazis for murdering Jews.

This was the first time during the war that Allied statesmen publicly referred to Jewish victims as Jews and not as political refugees. (This condemnation was to become the basis of the "crimes against humanity" charge against the Nazis at the Nuremburg Trials.)[36]

THE STERNBUCHS had kept the documentation coming. Gerhard Riegner, who had sent the August 28 cable to Dr. Wise,

Sternbuch Letters Confirm Riegner Cable acknowledged two letters from Warsaw addressed to "friends in St. Gallen, Switzerland" as major substantiation of the charges against the Nazis (the "friends" can now be identified as the Sternbuchs[37]); the State Department also accepted these letters as substantiation and used them to verify the Riegner cable.[38]

Besides notifying the Agudah, the Vaad, and Riegner, the Sternbuchs informed the American ambassador in Bern, Saly Mayer of the Joint Distribution Committee, and other Jewish leaders in Switzerland. Riegner also sent the information he received, and copies of the Sternbuch letters, to the American embassy for confirmation.[39]

After it met with Roosevelt in December, the ad hoc committee representing the thirty-four organizations was disbanded by Dr. Wise, over strong protests, on the grounds that it had served its purpose. But the Orthodox, the Jewish Labor Committee, and the American Jewish Committee continued to press for unity on rescue as atrocity cables kept coming in from Europe. In March they finally prevailed, with the formation of the Joint Emergency Committee on European Jewish Affairs. The JEC consisted of the eight major American Jewish organizations, four Zionist and four non-Zionist, and focused solely on rescue.[40]

C. BREAKING UP REAL UNITY

Meanwhile, a parallel series of meetings was going on that sought the unity of American Jewry behind a different goal. They were held in response to David Ben Gurion's maximalist call for a Jewish state in Palestine. When his Biltmore Resolution, as it came to be called, passed in May of 1942, Ben Gurion had succeeded in swinging American Zionists behind him.[41]

With that mandate in hand, Ben Gurion devised a three-step strategy: achieve American Jewish unity in favor of abrogating the British White Paper that limited Jewish immigration to Palestine (75,000 for a five-year period or 15,000 annually, ending in May

1944); achieve the same unity in favor of a postwar Jewish state; use that unity to gain the support of the U.S. government for both goals.[42] Ben Gurion's long-range goals proved more appealing than immediate rescue, and it is worth taking a close look at how unity for rescue died.

PURSUANT TO BEN GURION'S STRATEGY, Nahum Goldmann of the Jewish Agency and other Zionist leaders arranged for Henry

Rescue Not on the Agenda
Monsky of B'nai Brith to call a conference in Pittsburgh in January 1943, whose purpose was to plan for a meeting that summer of the major American-Jewish organizations. The topics of the main meeting would be postwar reconstruction in Europe and establishment of a Jewish homeland in Palestine. Rescue was not on the agenda.[43] As Rabbi Lewin recalled:

> ... at the Pittsburgh Assembly, which laid the basis for the American Jewish Assembly, I proposed that it should preoccupy itself with rescue work for European Jewry. It was then that the chairman, Monsky, declared that he can't even permit a vote on this issue, because the assembly was called for a different purpose.[44]

The non-Zionist American Jewish Committee and Jewish Labor Committee stayed away from the Pittsburgh planning session. Thus, the agenda there for the upcoming conference for the summer was heavily weighted toward the Zionists. In fact, as Nahum Goldmann put it: "It was the mistake of their life ... because with them absent, we took over the real leadership."[45]

Lewin, representing the Orthodox, continued to insist that rescue be on the August agenda and finally prevailed, when it became clear that such a move would bring the American Jewish Committee and the Jewish Labor Committee to the August proceedings. Lewin's persistence during the drafting of the agenda's language also helped persuade those two groups to attend. ("Homeland" — the moderate Zionist term — was used instead of "commonwealth" — the maximalist term which would denote a Jewish "state.")[46] In his report on the Pittsburgh planning session, Rosenheim of the Agudah noted:

> ... we did our best to urge this [American Jewish] Committee to participate in the assembly ... The chief condition was that *no majority vote of the coming assembly could bind the single organization in the matter of principal* [sic]. [emphasis in original][47]

Judge Proskauer of the American Jewish Committee was chosen co-chairman of the August meeting, along with Dr. Wise and Henry Monsky. After achieving this support for rescue, however, the Orthodox chose not to take part in August because the Zionist leadership had broken its promise to give equal voice to each of the major groups. For example, they were allotted only one fourth the number of delegates they had been promised. They realized sooner than either the Jewish Labor Committee or the American Jewish Committee, that this conference was to become a forum for the Zionist goals, with the rescue on the bottom of the list of priorities.[48]

ON AUGUST 29, Monsky opened the proceedings in New York of what was now called the American Jewish Conference* by stressing

American Jewish Conference unity and citing the prayer: "How good and beautiful it is for brothers to dwell together." It was a futile hope. Abba Hillel Silver, head of the United Palestine Appeal and co-chairman of AZEC (American Zionist Emergency Committee), promptly torpedoed the compromise among the non-Zionists, moderates and maximalist Zionists.[49] In a speech that night that was not on the agenda, Silver reiterated Ben Gurion's philosophy in thundering terms:

> There is but one solution for that national homelessness which is the source ... of our national tragedy ... that is a national home ... We cannot truly rescue the Jews of Europe unless we have free immigration to Palestine ... If we surrender our national and historic claim to Palestine and rely solely on the refugee philanthropic appeal, we shall lose our case, as well as do violence to the historic hopes of our people.[50]

Silver tackled the unity issue head-on:

> I am for unity in Israel, for the realization of the total program of Jewish life: relief, rescue, reconstruction, and the national restoration in Palestine. I am not for unity on a fragment of the program for a fragment of the program is a betrayal of the rest of the program and a tragic futility besides.[51]

One observer wrote that Silver's speech:

> ... carefully timed and placed ... aroused the hall to an emotional delirium such as I have rarely witnessed. The whole audience stood on its feet — yes, all but Rabbis Wise and Heller ... the Hatikvah finally brought them to their feet ... I venture

---

* The American Jewish Conference, born at these proceedings, continued to exist as an organization by that name after the proceedings ended.

to say that not one in the audience will "return" [to Zion], including those that did not sing the American National Anthem.[52]

Judge Proskauer of the American Jewish Committee vehemently protested Silver's speech, accusing him of undermining the unity of the conference:[53]

> Nobody expects a Jewish state now, nobody wants it now ... There are those who are not identified with Zionists but who want to help in the building of Palestine, yet they believe that it is a grievous error to ask for statehood now. That is why I say to you, let us have unity.[54]

ONE SPEAKER, representing the Reform Union of American Hebrew Congregations, came closer to the Orthodox view, when he **The Immediate** tried to make the audience understand that **Problem** not only was the agreed-to compromise by the Zionists necessary, as the American Jewish Committee had sought, but he contradicted Silver's very thesis. He noted:

> The *immediate problem*, ladies and gentlemen, is *rescue;* and I don't care what else you say — that is the immediate problem and that is the problem that we should be concerned with. [emphasis added][55]

An editorial about the "Conference" in the *Orthodox Tribune* (house organ of Agudath Israel Youth) of July-August 1943 commented likewise:

> As history records the virtual extermination of the Jews of Europe, the ears of those of us who are spiritually attuned to the harrowing misery of our people can almost hear the piercing cry of four million human souls pleading for *immediate action* to save them from an almost inevitable fate. In spite of the urgency of the hour, the leaders of the "Conference" have declared it fit to focus the eyes of the world only upon *postwar* problems of European Jewry, without pausing to think that every tick of the clock beats out the dirge of Jews whom no planning will ever again help. Because of the fanfare revolving about the "Conference," its leaders have totally neglected any effort or thought of the rescue of our stricken brethren.
>
> To what extent will these leaders spend countless hours wrangling over beautifully-worded resolutions about postwar problems of European Jewry, if, G-d forbid, no European Jewry remain?

The editorial goes on to exhort Orthodox Jewry to immediate action.

> *Now is the time to speak!* With the Jewish masses being
> continuously misled by the press and a heavy publicity barrage,
> Orthodox Jewry must rise to the height of the occasion and *let
> its voice be heard.* Orthodoxy must assert itself with vigor and
> decisiveness as the spokesman for *Klal Yisroel,* the Jewish
> people. [emphasis in the original][56]

Obviously, such sentiments seemed pallid compared to the golden solution provided in Abba Hillel Silver's speech.

So the American Jewish Committee pulled out, and not long after, for ideological reasons, the Jewish Labor Committee did too, leaving the Conference completely Zionist oriented. The Orthodox then proposed that the non-Zionist organizations establish their own rescue front, but even that attempt at partial unity on the subject was rejected.[57]

AT THE CONFERENCE, Dr. Wise tried to get all rescue efforts placed under his own control. He had been forced to form a **Wise's Goal: Protect Roosevelt** conference rescue committee, but he did not give it any funding or authority of its own, even preventing it from passing resolutions without approval by the three conference chairmen. Then he tried to bring the Joint Emergency Committee under the new conference committee, but that move was voted down.[58]

His efforts were reminiscent of his dissolution of the ad hoc rescue committee in December 1942. They also shed light on his subsequent engineering of a shift to the Zionists within the Joint Emergency Committee, which thereupon went out of business (on November 5, 1943).[59] In all these actions, Dr. Wise's goal was, in his own words, to protect President Roosevelt from the "wild men of the [JEC] Committee" and to maintain Zionist priorities.[60] During the debate on dissolving the JEC, he never responded to this question by Isaiah Minkoff of the Jewish Labor Committee:

> Why shouldn't the question of rescue be left with this
> Committee [the JEC], which includes all the organizations
> concerned with the problem, instead of creating a special rescue
> committee? The question should not be whether one must for
> reasons of principle or prestige support the Conference but
> what is better for the rescue of European Jews.[61]

RABBI KALMANOWITZ REMINDED the members of JEC that: when terrible news was received from Europe, it was the Union of

Zionists Break Up Real Unity Orthodox Rabbis which took the first initiative to invite all groups on behalf of rescue ... In these catastrophic times it would be very damaging to disintegrate the united front of all organizations. Because then there will appear before the government not one single voice but many.

Dr. Lewin added that "to dissolve [the JEC] was a crime because the rescue work will become even more divided and decrease still further any chances for success."[62]

Neither of these Orthodox rescue activists, of course, had any idea that the Zionists with a single-minded determination were out to push for a totally different approach to rescue — that of a post-war solution.

With hindsight, of course, what seemed a tragic breakdown of a seemingly united Jewish front turned out to have been the best thing that happened, as far as rescue was concerned. Since most of the members of the JEC were motivated by the powerful twin ideological forces of Zionism and assimilation, there is no way that the Orthodox could have made the JEC adopt immediate rescue as its top priority. At best, they might have been able to push for a little here and a little there, which happened even following the breakup of JEC. The Orthodox did manage to cooperate with individual organizations such as the American Jewish Committee or Jewish Labor Committee for specific rescue schemes until the end of the war. However, were the JEC to have remained viable, it would at best have dragged the heels of the Orthodox and anyone else sincerely interested in immediate rescue.

WITH THE DEMISE OF the JEC — the last unified rescue front — it became clear to the Orthodox that, given the deep ideological

Weissmandl Cables Prod Orthodox conflicts between groups with widely differing levels of priority, they could no longer waste time chasing a dream: unity for rescue. In the fall of 1943, prodded by desperate cables from Rabbi Weissmandl, they began rescue attempts on a broader scale, using their small international network with Rabbi Weissmandl at its center.[63]

D. THE RABBIS MARCH ON WASHINGTON:
The Sole Public Demonstration on Behalf of Rescue

The Orthodox, now outside the pale, and not part of the American Jewish Conference, joined hands with the Bergson Group to effect rescue.[64] And in order to pressure the U.S. government into creating a separate agency on rescue, Bergson organized a march of Orthodox rabbis on Washington.[65]

ON OCTOBER 6, 1943 (8 Tishri), the day before Yom Kippur eve, 400 Orthodox rabbis, dressed in their long, dark traditional garb,

The Pre-Yom Kippur March
marched from the Capitol to the White House. To encourage participation in the march, the *Yiddishe Shtimme* had printed a full-page appeal which said, "The silence of the world when an entire people is being murdered is a crime in which all who tolerate it are equally guilty."[66]

The march was led by Rabbis Eliezer Silver and Abraham Kalmanowitz of the Vaad, and Bergson. Roosevelt absented himself on the advice of his closest Jewish advisors, Wise and Judge Rosenman. As an FDR aide later noted:

> ... he [Rosenman] had tried — admittedly without success — to keep the horde from storming Washington. [He] said the leading Jews of his acquaintance opposed this march on the Capitol.[67]

That same day, Nahum Goldmann of the Jewish Agency and Wise met with Judge Rosenman to discuss abrogation of the White Paper, a move the American Jewish Conference had voted for the previous month. They also complained to Rosenman about Bergson's provocative newspaper ads.[68]

The response to the march was strong and gratifying. The Senate sent the rabbis' petition to a special commission, which resulted in a Senate bill to take immediate steps for rescue. The rabbis met with Vice President Henry Wallace, House Speaker Sam Rayburn, and a delegation from Congress. The result was public hearings on rescue in the House and Senate.[69]

THE HEARINGS FOCUSED on Bergson's proposal for a separate government agency devoted solely to the rescue of European Jewry.

Inject Palestine and Harm Refugees
The concept came from a suggestion by Rabbi Solomon Schonfeld.[70] All mention of Palestine as a refuge for Jews was omitted. As Rep. Will Rogers Jr., a sponsor of Bergson's appeal, noted:

> This resolution was specifically drawn up to eliminate Palestine. Any time you inject that into the refugee situation, it reacts to the harm of the refugees.[71]

Dr. Wise testified against the rescue resolution on the grounds that Palestine was the appropriate refuge. "The one thing that arrested our thought," he said, "was that no provision was made urging England to keep the doors of Palestine open."[72] In contrast, Chief Rabbi Isaac Halevy Herzog of Palestine sent a cable supporting the Bergson Resolution in which he prayed "that the greatest success crown you and your colleagues USA supreme effort to rescue the remnant of Israel." His cable did not mention Palestine.[73]*

Meanwhile, at the direction of Dr. Abba Hillel Silver, the American Jewish Conference was lobbying unsuccessfully for congressional action on its resolution to create a Jewish state as a long-term response to the Holocaust.[75]

At the hearings on November 26, Breckenridge Long, the Assistant Secretary of State in charge of immigration presented grossly inflated figures on the number of immigrants and rescue effected with American help.[75a] The uproar caused by his blatantly distorted testimony added to the pressure on Roosevelt. With an election year looming, the cumulative impact of the rabbis' march, the hearings, and the Long incident was particularly telling.[76]

The atmosphere thus created enabled three non-Jewish aides of Secretary of the Treasury Henry Morgenthau, Jr., to prepare — and persuade their boss to submit on January 17, 1944 — Morgenthau's famous Personal Report to the President. The result was the creation, by presidential order, of the War Refugee Board five days later. Many leaders of American Jewry had called the rabbis' march a failure, and it is true that the WRB, the march's primary achievement, had many shortcomings. But as one scholar put it:

> The War Refugee Board was a unique case of humanitarian and moral considerations superseding political and utilitarian arguments in the midst of a terrible war.[77]

Furthermore, the Board was the only U.S. government body that did any rescuing. As Professor David Wyman has pointed out, it was responsible for the rescue of more than 100,000 Jews.[78]

Except for its administrative expenses, the War Refugee Board never provided funds for rescue; money from American Jewish

---

* In reality, however, Wise objected to the rescue resolution even were it to contain reference to Palestine, since his main concern was to prevent undue Jewish pressure on the President. This is made obvious from the fact that for this very reason Wise objected to the Palestine resolution put forth by Silver in 1944, although it concentrated solely on a postwar state in Palestine. He rejected Abba Hillel Silver's suggestion of bringing persuasive influence ... to bear upon the Administration ..." As he explained to President Roosevelt, "From the beginning ... we did not wish under any circumstances to proceed [with the Palestine resolution] unless we had your full approval."[74]

organizations was channeled through it. During 1944, for example, when Hungarian Jewry was being deported, the giant, broad-spectrum Joint Distribution Committee, still run by the wealthy German-Jewish elite, supplied more than $15 million. The Orthodox, by far the poorest segment of American Jewry, contributed more than $1 million. The Jewish Labor Committee sent through about $300,000 as did the World Jewish Congress. At the same time, the Zionist leadership, headed by Abba Hillel Silver, spent $500,000 lobbying in vain for its Palestine resolution.[79]

E. VITTEL AND THE LATIN AMERICAN PAPERS

During the war, Vittel, a detention center in France, held about 240 Jews who possessed bogus papers issued by Latin American consuls, most of them based in Switzerland. These papers protected their owners from the full thrust of the Nazis' fury. The Nazis ignored the dubious provenance of these papers, since these Jews were a potential bargaining chip in negotiations for Germans in Allied territory. Besides Vittel, there were privileged holding areas at several other concentration camps, including Bergen-Belsen.[80] Thousands of these Latin American documents — and many more than that were forged — also protected Jews in occupied countries who were not in camps.[81]

This development came about because Yitzchok Sternbuch discovered in 1941 that a holder of Latin American papers was given special treatment in Warsaw. Through Dr. Kuhl at the Polish Embassy, Sternbuch and Yisroel Chaim Eis, another Agudist leader and rescue activist, were able to buy papers from the Paraguayan consul. Hundreds of these reached Jews in occupied lands. Others then began to emulate Sternbuch, among them Dr. Abraham Silberschein, an official of the World Jewish Congress who founded RELICO, a relief organization in Switzerland for Polish Jews.[82]

THE DOCUMENTS COST between 400 and 3,000 Swiss francs each, a veritable fortune at the time. But in 1942, when George Mandel-

Mantello's Papers Gratis Mantello became Secretary-General of the Salvadoran consulate in Bern, the price was drastically reduced. Mantello, a Rumanian businessman who was a Revisionist-Zionist and an Orthodox Jew, produced Salvadoran citizenship papers gratis by the thousands. They were issued to anyone who could provide an address of a Jew in occupied territory. Later, Mantello sent thousands of authorized blank forms behind the lines. As John

Winant, the American Ambassador to Britain, wrote: "Only the consul of El Salvador has acted from purely humanitarian motives."[83] Some still purchased Paraguayan and other papers under the mistaken notion that they provided more protection than the Salvador citizenship papers.[84]

For some unknown reason, the Swiss authorities were made aware of these dubious papers. As a result, the Germans, through the Swiss Embassy in Berlin, threatened to withdraw the protection these papers represented unless the Latin American countries confirmed the documents.

Interestingly enough, as Dr. Hillel Seidman, one of the few survivors of Vittel, pointed out, while the Swiss representative (as "protector" of the interests of many of the Latin American countries to Germany) periodically checked into the welfare of the inmates of Vittel, he was extremely unsympathetic to the plight of the holders of these bogus papers. This was in sharp contrast to his Spanish counterpart who was most accommodating. The latter constantly tried to stall the Nazi efforts to disqualify these papers, while the former eagerly pressed for the Nazis to withdraw their recognition.[85]

Desperate pleas from Vittel were sent to Sternbuch, who contacted the Orthodox in America. As we have seen, Rabbis Abraham Kalmanowitz and Shabse Frankel immediately traveled to Washington, though it was Passover, and met with Secretary of State Cordell Hull and Treasury Secretary Morgenthau to get help in persuading the Latin countries to recognize the papers. At Kalmanowitz's request, the major American Jewish organizations helped him press this point with the government.[86]

That effort was successful, but recognition of the documents came too late for most of the Vittel Jews. In May and June of 1944, despite diplomatic efforts, two transports took most of those inmates to Auschwitz, Recha Sternbuch's parents among them. But thousands of holders of these papers were saved, particularly in Budapest later in 1944, when Raoul Wallenberg of Sweden and Charles Lutz of the Swiss consulate succeeded in placing them into "protected houses."[87]

Monsignor Bernardini, Papal Nuncio

AT THE BEHEST OF Recha Sternbuch, the papal nuncio in Switzerland, Monsignor Bernardini, was very helpful in convincing Latin American and Spanish diplomats there to accept the bogus citizenship papers.

Fillippe Bernardini, another "righteous Gentile," became a pivotal character in the rescue drama. As dean of the diplomatic corps, he wielded a powerful moral influence on the Swiss authorities, and his courier system throughout occupied Europe proved invaluable to the rescue effort. Kuhl and the Sternbuchs brought him together with other Jewish organizations, which made use of his services for rescue.[88] It was Bernardini who, in mid-1944, persuaded the Swiss to halt their policy of *refoulement* (shipping illegally entered refugees back into Nazi hands) on the Italian-Swiss border.[89]

In contrast, to the end of the war, Roswell McClelland, the War Refugee Board's representative in Switzerland, was unsympathetic to the use of bogus papers. His attitude reinforced the legalistic stance of Saly Mayer, the Joint Distribution Committee's man in Switzerland, who would have nothing to do with the Vittel affair.

F. THE AUSCHWITZ PROTOCOLS
AND PLEAS TO BOMB AUSCHWITZ

In April 1944, two escapees from Auschwitz, Rudolph Vrba and Alfred Wetzler, arrived in Slovakia, just after the Nazis moved into Hungary. They had been at Auschwitz since the beginning, working in the administrative offices, which collected data on every aspect of the extermination process. They made their way to the Slovakian Jewish Underground, headed by Rabbi Michoel Ber Weissmandl and Mrs. Gisi Fleischmann.[90]

VRBA AND WETZLER warned that Auschwitz was being enlarged to accommodate Hungary's Jews and, under questioning by the **Weissmandl's** Underground, provided a thirty-three-page statistical report on the camp's operations that **Plea to Bomb** became known as the Auschwitz Protocols. **Auschwitz** Weissmandl sent out a condensed Hebrew version to all Jewish groups in Hungary and Switzerland. On May 16, the day after the Hungarian deportations to Auschwitz started, he began sending out his famous plea to bomb the camp, especially the rail lines carrying 12,000 Jews there a day. He pointed out that these rail lines were also being used to transport military personnel and material.[91]

Among the recipients of Weissmandl's plea was Dr. Yaakov Griffel, the Agudah representative in the *Moetza*, the Jewish Agency rescue committee in Istanbul. Through the U.S. ambassador to Turkey, Griffel notified the War Refugee Board in the U.S.

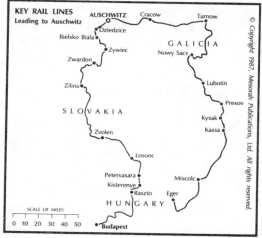

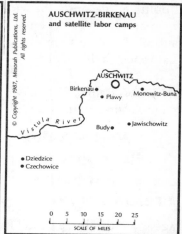

Weissmandl's message also went to at least four people in Switzerland: Nathan Schwalb of Hechalutz, a Marxist-Zionist youth pioneering organization; Saly Mayer of the JDC; the World Jewish Congress representative; and the Sternbuchs.[92]

The Sternbuchs, who received the cable and decoded it on May 20, a Friday, traveled to Bern on the Sabbath to see Dr. Kuhl, who went with them late that night to the homes of the military attachés of the American, British, and Russian embassies. The attachés were sympathetic but could not sway their governments. The specific British response was that bombing was done for strategic, not humanitarian, reasons. Sternbuch asked that the message be sent to the Vaad via the U.S. diplomatic pouch.[93]

Day after day, as desperate cables from Weissmandl reached Sternbuch, he forwarded them to Roswell McClelland of the WRB but never heard from the Vaad Hatzalah. Finally, in mid-June, Sternbuch sent the bombing plea via the Polish diplomatic pouch. It was the first the Vaad had heard of it. From then until October, Rosenheim and Kalmanowitz pleaded with the WRB and the U.S. government to bomb Auschwitz, but got nowhere. On June 22, Sternbuch wrote McClelland asking why he had not received a response from the United States. McClelland never answered.[94]

An early Hungarian translation of the complete Protocols was given to Rudolph Kastner, the Jewish Agency representative in Budapest, who had been negotiating with the Nazis on Weissmandl's plan to ransom Hungarian Jewry. Kastner was supposed to deliver it to Admiral Horthy, the regent of Hungary, but did not do so. Likewise, as Kastner himself noted, for dubious "political reasons" the *Moetza* in Istanbul and in Jerusalem decided to maintain silence on this matter. At the same time Griffel had submitted Weissmandl's pleas to the U.S. Ambassador to Turkey, Laurence Steinhardt.[95]

IN CONTRAST, ON JUNE 21, Mantello, the Salvadoran Secretary-General in Switzerland, received from Budapest a copy of the complete Protocols with a report on the deportations from Hungary to date and a plea to do something. Within five days, Mantello arranged with Walter Garrett, a British intelligence officer who was head of the British Exchange Telegraph, a news agency, to have the Protocols condensed into four cables, authenticated in an attached letter signed by four leading Swiss theologians including Karl Barth, and sent to foreign-press offices in Switzerland. (See Chap. 11F.) Within two weeks the story, spelling out the murder of 1,715,000 Jews, was published in more than 500 Swiss newspapers. Both Kastner and Saly Mayer attempted, unsuccessfully, to silence Mantello's publicity for the Auschwitz Protocols.[96]

World-Wide Response to Mantello's Press Campaign

The world-wide response was immediate and powerful. On June 26, U.S. Secretary of State Hull issued a warning to Hungary's Admiral Horthy, as did Anthony Eden of Britain. King Gustav V of Sweden sent a personal protest to Horthy and dispatched Raoul Wallenberg on his mercy mission to Budapest. The Pope also sent a note to Horthy. For the first time, the International Red Cross took an active interest in saving Jews, as did the Swiss government.[97]

As a result of the world-wide response to Mantello's campaign and despite Nazi pressure, Horthy stopped the Hungarian deportations by July 8. While smaller forced marches and other methods of extermination occurred thereafter, the Nazis could no longer ship tens of thousands of Jews a day out of Hungary with impunity. Thanks also to the safe houses provided by Sweden's Wallenberg and Charles Lutz, the Swiss consul in Budapest, more than a hundred thousand Jews ultimately were spared in the capital. But over 400,000 Hungarian Jews died at Auschwitz in the two months between Weissmandl's plea and Horthy's action.[98]

G. THE KASTNER TRANSPORT

In June of 1944, when Joel Brand was arrested by the British and failed to return from Istanbul, the Nazis were ready to break off the Weissmandl negotiations to ransom more than half a million Hungarian Jews for 10,000 trucks. But Kastner, who had also been working on that deal, convinced Eichmann to exclude the Orthodox Philip Freudiger from the negotiations, and to allow 750 Hungarian Zionists with Palestine certificates to leave by special train for a neutral country. In addition, Kastner placed several hundred friends and relatives from Cluj on the train.[99]

Seats were also sold to wealthy Jews and converts to Christianity to defray the cost of the transport. Philip Freudiger, head of the Budapest Orthodox community and the original middleman in Weissmandl's Hungarian negotiations with the Nazis, paid the Gestapo to get eighty of the Orthodox Jews aboard — notables and their families — including the rabbis of Satmar and Debrecin and Rabbi Jonathan Steif. In all, 1,684 Jews were on the train, including 450 inmates from a nearby labor camp, who climbed aboard during a stop.[100]

Some two million dollars was paid to get all 1,684 aboard, but Eichmann was also willing to transfer 18,000-20,000 Jews to Austria, to be kept as potential hostages in negotiations with the Allies. And until the Nazis received some positive reaction to the broader deal with Joel Brand, they refused to allow the train to leave Budapest.[101]

AT THAT POINT, to keep the negotiations going, Weissmandl let Freudiger know that 250 trucks were available in Switzerland for

Revive Negotiations with the Gestapo

trade. Since the Nazis had expressed interest in establishing contact with the U.S. Jews, the message was signed by Ferdinand Roth, Weissmandl's fictitious representative of American Jewry. The news of the 250 trucks made a "very favorable impression ... with the Gestapo chief in Budapest." Further, this same Gestapo man declared, "Not one of the 40,000 Jews whose emigration to Palestine is now being planned will be allowed to depart from Hungary unless tractors are secured for them."[102]

Freudiger contacted Sternbuch and asked for 750,000SF ($187,500) to pay for forty tractors, not trucks, as a down payment on the 1,684 lives. Sternbuch cabled back that he had only 150,000SF on hand, and asked Saly Mayer to provide the balance from JDC funds. Mayer, however, as legalistic as ever, refused to pay what was obviously ransom.[103]

Moreover, Mayer informed McClelland that Sternbuch was about to close a deal with the Nazis, and McClelland threatened Hugo Donnenbaum with arrest for dealing with the enemy in heavy equipment. Donnenbaum, a refugee businessman in Switzerland and an Orthodox Jew, was the Hungarian contact for the Vaad Hatzalah. Sternbuch was warned that if he persisted in violating the Trading With the Enemy Act, he'd be blacklisted by the U.S.[104]

But Sternbuch was used to harassment by authorities for his rescue activities. His wife Recha had even been arrested in 1939 for illegally helping Jewish refugees across the Swiss border.[105] He and Donnenbaum went ahead, obtained a letter of credit for 150,000SF and showed it to the Nazis, who agreed, in late July, to continue the negotiations. Meanwhile, the train of 1,684 Jews had been moved from Budapest to Bergen-Belsen in Germany. On August 21, as a result of the letter of credit, 318 of the 1,684 were released and allowed to travel to Switzerland. The names of the 318 were sent to Sternbuch, who sent them on to Saly Mayer.[106]

At McClelland's insistence, Mayer replaced Sternbuch in the negotiations with the Nazis on August 21,[107] thereby drastically changing the purpose of those talks. Mayer was not interested in release, only in keeping the Nazis talking until the war ended. As the assimilationist leader of the Jewish community in Switzerland, he was concerned primarily about creating a "Jewish question" which he assumed would follow an influx of Jewish refugees. In other words, he and other "real" Swiss Jews would be lumped and identified together with the "unassimilated" despised East European-Jewish refugees. He didn't want Jews flooding his country.[108]

CONSTANT PRODDING BY THE VAAD on the JDC and the WRB in the United States got them to pressure Mayer into paying for the tractors. As Morgenthau noted at the time, "The

"The Rabbis Put Heavy Pressure On Us" rabbis put heavy pressure on us because Mayer won't help rescue 1,200 rabbis."[109]

Mayer made several payments between September 1944 and January 1945. At the same time, he and Kastner were also trying to keep the talks on ransoming all of European Jewry going, at one point brandishing a bogus cable (created by Kastner) claiming that five million Swiss francs were available for that purpose. The combination of those negotiations and the tractor payments resulted, in December 1944, in the release of the remaining 1,366 members of the Hungarian transport at Bergen-Belsen.[110]

Both Weissmandl and Sternbuch were convinced that had the money been available when Mayer was asked for it, the train would have gone directly to Switzerland, without the five-month stopover in Bergen-Belsen. In any event, it was Weissmandl's offer of trucks through Freudiger and Sternbuch that kept those negotiations going.[111]

In fact, this rescue effort by the Orthodox eventually saved approximately 20,000 Jews. Leland Harrison, the U.S. minister to Switzerland, spelled it out in a cable to the WRB on August 11:

> ... the affair of the forty tractors which Sternbuch brought to our attention ... was part of the deal [that Gyula] Link [an Orthodox merchant] with Freudiger of the Orthodox group at Budapest negotiated and relayed to Sternbuch ... on the basis of these offers the Gestapo in Budapest refrained from sending to Auschwitz ... the following groups totaling 17,290 souls ... 1,690 [actually 1,684] ... sent later to the camp of Bergen-Belsen ... approximately 15,000 [actually closer to 18,000] ... sent to an unknown destination in Austria to be kept "on ice" ... and 600 persons ... still confined in Budapest.[112]

Harrison's view was confirmed by Kastner himself, no friend of the Orthodox. By October, Sternbuch could tell Vaad Hatzalah, via the secret Polish cable, that:

> the Gestapo declared that they were satisfied that the rest of the tractors were placed at their disposal, which had been demanded two months earlier. The Gestapo is preparing to send the rest of the Hungarian Jews on Bergen-Belsen transport to Switzerland ...

Then came the crucial point:

> There are still larger sums ... which we deposited for tractors in Swiss banks. We still are unable to inform McClelland about this.

This explains why Mayer, under leverage by the Joint, which in turn was pressured by the War Refugee Board under the Vaad's influence, finally provided the money for the tractors to assure that the negotiations continue with the Gestapo. And also why neither Sternbuch nor Mayer could discuss the payment for these crucial tractors with the unsympathetic McClelland.[113]

H. THE STERNBUCH-MUSY-HIMMLER NEGOTIATIONS

The Sternbuch-Musy negotiations lasted more than eight months, from September 1944 until the last days of the war. They stemmed from Recha Sternbuch's search for the two transports that had been taken out of Vittel. In the process she discovered that Dr. Jean-Marie Musy, a former president of Switzerland, had secured the freedom of a Jewish couple for 10,000SF. Musy, a fascist who published a pro-Nazi newspaper called *La Jeune*, was also a long-time friend of Himmler's.[114]

AFTER SEVERAL MEETINGS with Musy, Mrs. Sternbuch decided to try for the release of all Jews. Musy cabled Himmler, who agreed to

The Deal a deal in principle. On October 20, with his son Benoit as driver, Musy, a man close to seventy, traveled to Berlin in a Mercedes bought for him by the Sternbuchs, who also provided 60,000SF in cash, 500,000SF in checks, and 200 liters of precious gasoline.[115]

Sternbuch's confidential cable to the Vaad following Musy's return is instructive on the cross-currents within the rescue forces:

> After ... negotiations with Himmler our representative notified us of the possibility to evacuate 300,000 Jews ... for ... 20,000,000 (20 million) SF STOP Such evacuations could be accomplished in groups of 15,000 monthly ... the money to be deposited in Swiss bank in ... rates of 1,000,000SF after arranging the evacuation of each group STOP In principle we have accepted this proposition STOP Our representative is a very influential and important personality STOP
>
> We beg you not to demand any collaboration from us with the Joint STOP We did so at your request in the case of Hungarian Jews [the Kastner transport, most of whose passengers were still in Bergen-Belsen awaiting payment for the tractors] and the result was catastrophic as attested in the sixteen-page document from the Neutraer Rav [i.e., Weissmandl] STOP Morbid anti-religious convictions and seeming patriotism of the Swiss representative of the Joint [Mayer] is a hindrance for any collaboration with him STOP The Swiss and American authorities favor him because he rarely troubles these officials STOP
>
> We confirm you by oath that immediate decision be forthcoming exclusively addressed to us for utilizing this only remaining opportunity for rescue of a great number of Jews STOP At this moment we are in need only of your cable agreement ... through the American Embassy ... STOP We beg you to dispatch further cables ... in the usual fashion [i.e., the Polish diplomatic pouch][116]

Musy was able to reduce the US $5 million ransom price (twenty million SF) to US $1 million. For Himmler, this amount was just a guarantee that Musy and the "rabbi Jews," as he called the

Sternbuchs, were serious. The more important consideration for him, which Musy stressed, was that Germany's image, badly tarnished by the publicity of the Auschwitz Protocols engendered by Mantello's press campaign four months earlier, be restored — especially since it was losing the war.[117]

HAVING ALREADY RAISED more than one million dollars in 1944, however, the Vaad could only muster $100,000 this time; so it urged

No Cooperation by the Joint Sternbuch to work with Mayer and pressured the WRB and the JDC in New York to release money for the Sternbuchs' use. But Mayer preferred his own negotiations with the Nazis and refused to have anything to do with Musy's. In December 1944 when Kastner, Dr. Joseph Schwartz, head of the European JDC and Mayer's boss, and Mayer's Gestapo contacts were all in Switzerland, Sternbuch tried again. Mayer and Schwartz refused any cooperation.

The Sternbuchs then turned to Kastner, who was still involved in Mayer's negotiations. Kastner admitted that Mayer was just trying to keep the Nazis talking, but he refused to break with him, even when the Sternbuchs offered him use of the Polish diplomatic pouch so he could bypass McClelland and Mayer in telling the United States about Mayer's stalling.[118]

The Sternbuchs even offered to turn the entire negotiations over to the JDC if it would stop stalling and bring Jews out. But at best Mayer was willing only to give the money to the International Red Cross and have them take over administration of the concentration camps at the war's end, thus keeping the inmates in the camps.[119]

BY MID-JANUARY 1945, Himmler became tired of Mayer's stalling and his constant refrain that the "rabbis" were powerless and only

Limited Success the JDC had influence with America. So he broke off those talks and concentrated on the ones with Musy, with their promise of improved public relations. One result was the release on February 7 of 1,210 inmates from Theresienstadt, a camp in Czechoslovakia.[120]

Five days before, the Sternbuchs had cabled the Vaad in New York:

> It is imperative following the release of the first train that five or six major American newspapers declare that in this

respect Germany was very favorably inclined ... Should you fail, then don't expect another train.[121]

Through the efforts of the Vaad and the Agudah, several major papers published the story, including *The Times, The Sun,* and *The Herald Tribune* in New York. A similar effort with the Swiss press by Dr. Reuven Hecht, Sternbuch's colleague, was even more successful.[122]

The favorable publicity angered Mayer, who told Kurt Becher, his Gestapo liaison with Himmler: "This is *eine furchtbare Schweinerei* (a horribly filthy thing). The press is full of Himmler-Musey [sic] and Muesy-Himmler [sic]."[123] Soon stories appeared in socialist papers in Switzerland criticizing the ransom of the Theresienstadt group. They cited the original ransom price of 20,000,000SF, assailed Sternbuch for using a fascist (Musy) as his negotiator, and said Musy was involved for personal enrichment. An international radio broadcast at the time also implied that the deal involved asylum for 250 Nazis.[124]

THESE STORIES WERE PICKED UP by the Swiss office of the PALCOR News Agency, which sent them out to Jewish papers in

"You Have Herr Saly Mayer to Thank"

other countries. PALCOR's Swiss office was run by Nathan Schwalb, a close friend of Mayer's and someone McClelland thought highly of. One headline read, "We Do Not Want Any Favors From Germany." In another it noted, "Himmler is getting a good price for every released Jew."[125]

Sternbuch cabled New York, Istanbul, and London for help in getting PALCOR to put a stop to it, but the damage was done. A second transport — 1,200 more inmates from Theresienstadt and 800 from Bergen-Belsen — was ready, scheduled to leave two weeks after the first one, but it never did. General Ernst Kaltenbrunner, chief of Reich security and a competitor to Gen. Schellenberg, showed Hitler the critical articles from the Swiss socialist press. Kaltenbrunner had gotten them from Becher, Mayer's Gestapo liaison. Hitler, enraged, ordered that "not a single Jew should be allowed to leave Germany."[126]

Musy went to Berlin at Sternbuch's request to find out why the second transport was delayed. The answer he got was succinct. "It was explained to me in Berlin last week," he wrote Sternbuch, "if no trains of Jews from the German camps arrived in Switzerland, you have Herr Saly Mayer to thank."[127]

IN THE UNITED STATES, after the first Theresienstadt transport was released, the Vaad again asked the Joint Distribution Committee **Another** to lend it, not give, the one million dollars the **McClelland** Musy-Himmler deal required to ransom the rest of the Jews in the camps.[128] **Obstruction** But by JDC rules, the money had to be channeled through the War Refugee Board, and McClelland, who still refused to pay ransom. Even though 1,210 inmates had just been released, he agreed with Mayer that the Jews should be kept in the camps under the International Red Cross (IRC). Yet in May, in the last days of the war, when Sternbuch asked for $200,000 of the JDC million to send food into the camps, McClelland refused on the grounds that the funds were for rescue, not for "food relief during the post-hostilities period in Europe."[129]

STILL, THE STERNBUCHS CONTINUED their negotiations with Himmler, through Musy, during the last hellish weeks of the **Safe Transfer** Holocaust. Of major concern was the safe **of Concentration** transfer of the concentration camps to the Allies. In October 1944, the Vaad had **Camps** gotten wind of Nazi plans to exterminate every last Jew. General Eisenhower issued a warning that had some effect, but elements of the Gestapo, especially Kaltenbrunner, regarded killing Jews as the first priority. In the camps there were rumors of troops with flame-throwers standing by outside to destroy all life and all evidence of Nazi crimes.[130]

Benoit Musy made several trips to Berlin by himself to negotiate the peaceful camp transfers with his Himmler contact, General Walter Schellenberg. He also visited the camps at Theresienstadt, Ravensbrueck, Mauthausen, Bergen-Belsen, and Buchenwald to assure cooperation. On April 8, in Berlin, Himmler, who had agreed to stop the killing in the camps, demanded assurance that the guards wouldn't be shot on the spot but would be tried as members of the Wehrmacht as long as they wore Wehrmacht uniforms. At Sternbuch's request, McClelland sent this message to Washington, which quickly agreed.[131]

But the Himmler-Kaltenbrunner and Himmler-Schellenberg elements of the Nazi leadership were working at cross-purposes. Benoit Musy reported seeing a document that called for forced marches by prisoners to keep them away from the advancing Allies. So the senior Musy and Recha Sternbuch crossed into Nazi-occupied Austria to see their Gestapo contacts and Benoit returned to Berlin. Schellenberg immediately warned all camp commanders, who generally heeded the Hitler-Kaltenbrunner line, not to disobey Himmler's orders. As a result, a forced march from Buchenwald was halted, and Mauthausen, Bergen-Belsen, Theresienstadt, and Buchenwald, all of which Benoit had visited, were turned over to the Allies relatively intact.[132]

Musy Sr.'s negotiations with Carl J. Burckhardt of the International Red Cross (IRC) by the end of January 1945 helped pave the way for the first inspections of the camps by the IRC. It also prepared the ground for the later negotiations with the Nazis by Count Bernardotte of the Swedish Red Cross and Kaltenbrunner's meeting with the IRC in March 1945. Young Musy also negotiated the safe evacuation of Ravensbrueck — almost 14,000 women, 2,000 of whom were Jewish. Schellenberg, who had been in contact with Sweden's Count Bernadotte since the first Theresienstadt transport was released February 7, allowed most of them to go to Sweden. Benoit Musy went on to Stockholm to continue negotiations with the help of Felix Kersten, Himmler's masseur, and Hillel Storch and Norbert Masur of the World Jewish Congress.[133]

Thus, while the plan to release all inmates failed at least in part through obstruction, one camp was evacuated and four others were handed over to the Allies virtually without incident, thanks to the Sternbuch-Musy efforts. One person rescued through these efforts was Weissmandl, who reached Switzerland in April with sixty-nine other Jews. He had escaped from a train bound for Auschwitz and had been hiding in Slovakian bunkers until the senior Musy negotiated the release of his group. The Vittel deportees Recha Sternbuch had been searching for, including her parents, all died at Auschwitz.[134]

CHAPTER EIGHT

If ...

CONTRARY TO SOME CLAIMS that little could have been done to save Europe's captive Jews, the record indicates that an enormous amount was accomplished by a few committed activists, **Something** and that so many more would have been spared if **Could Have** there had been different people in key positions **Been Done** — or different attitudes at key times. Such non-Jews as Wallenberg in Budapest, Bernardini in Switzerland, and Sugihara in Kovno made a great difference in the rescue of many thousands of Jews. Nor could anyone dismiss such Jewish giants of rescue as Rabbi Weissmandl, George Mandel-Mantello, and Recha Sternbuch.

Yet it is also possible to point to those Jews and non-Jews who were in the wrong place at the wrong time. Switzerland's Saly Mayer, for example, was in a crucial position. Yet, he not only refused to embrace the cause of rescue, he actively thwarted it. The actions of both Treasury Secretary Morgenthau and Ambassador Steinhardt, on the other hand, show that changes in attitudes were possible — but only if the right persons were influential. Unfortunately, no one could have induced such a change in the legalistic Mayer, in part because Roswell McClelland, America's representative to the War Refugee Board in Switzerland, was someone whose outlook merely served to confirm Mayer's, not to change it.

Although the reason for McClelland's tenure in Switzerland was ostensibly rescue, he was hardly a Wallenberg — in energy, spirit, or dedication. In Budapest, by contrast, the Swedish diplomat not only welcomed papers of dubious legality such as the Salvadoran and other Latin American documents, but he actively encouraged further forgery and proliferation. For example, he provided Mr. Samuel Frey, an Orthodox rescue activist in Budapest, with the Swedish Embassy's stationery and stamp, to use in making up additional Swedish papers of protection. McClelland, on the other hand, would not permit the use of any bogus papers regardless of their value in saving lives. He went so far as to openly discourage Salvadoran diplomat George Mandel-Mantello from distributing authentic papers issued with the approval of the Salvador Embassy.

As but one more example, while McClelland cabled brief versions of the Auschwitz Protocols to Washington in June 1944, it took until mid-October before he would transmit the full report. And even then his tone was negative. "In the main," he wrote, "I personally feel that [while] the handling of such material ... cannot be considered as a positive contribution to the real relief or rescue activities it does constitute a tragic side to the whole problem."[1] In fact, the entire document, which had an enormous impact on Morgenthau, and American Jews in general, also contained Rabbi Weissmandl's plea to bomb Auschwitz. And where McClelland delayed, the Board demanded action.

MCCLELLAND'S NEGATIVE ATTITUDE toward the Sternbuchs is nowhere made more clear than in a marginal note he made on a 1944

McClelland's Negative Attitude Sternbuch letter to the Vaad repeating Rabbi Weissmandl's plea that "thousands of Jews in enemy-occupied countries could be saved if large sums of money could be made available."[2]

McClelland added, "typical Sternbuch allegation."[3]

Similar negative comments by McClelland were added to the following four additional desperate attempts at rescue:

A. July 1944: Weissmandl cable: "... prima ware ['top-grade goods,' i.e., the so-called 1,200 rabbis] to enemy unless letter of credit to bank in 24 hours." (McClelland's comment in the margin before forwarding it to Mayer: "Teleg, from the Holy Men! Rec'd 7/20/44 *Old Pressure Game!*" [emphasis added]

B. July 4, 1944: Weissmandl cable: "Deportations from Hungary to Poland [Auschwitz] irreversible [sic] unless your firm [Mayer] puts up one million Swiss franc letter of credit [for the tractors]." McClelland in margin: "*typical.*" [emphasis added]

C. Nov. 28, 1944: WRB message to McClelland urging cooperation with Sternbuch and quoting his plea "that thousands of Jews ... could be saved." McClelland repeated in the margin: "*typical Sternbuch allegation.*" [emphasis added]

D. In a confidential message to the Vaad (7/13/44), Sternbuch wrote: "... part of the money is used for bribes in order to rescue people. It is impossible for us to discuss such things with McClelland." In the letter, which inspired the "bribery" remark, Recha Sternbuch tried to explain that: "I am the very last person who would want to see those [Nazi] scoundrels get a single cent. But it is an urgent necessity, no matter how hard it is for us ... we are in an awful situation and we have to suffer all that, if we care to save the life of people ...[4]

McClelland's negative attitude involving rescue was not merely directed at the Sternbuchs and other Orthodox rescue activists. It was manifest as well in his cavalier attitude toward rescue of Jews in general or even relieving their misery somewhat. This is borne out, among other examples, from his response to a relatively minor request by the Sternbuchs in September 1944.

As a result of Mantello's effective press campaign, the International Red Cross was finally willing to facilitate the sending of food and clothing to the starving inmates of the concentration camps. Nevertheless, in response to Sternbuch's request to send such packages to Theresienstadt, Bergen-Belsen and Birkenau, the IRC presented bureaucratic obstacles which would hinder such relief anywhere from three to four weeks. The Sternbuchs then asked McClelland to use the prestige and power of the WRB and the US to pressure the IRC into expediting the shipping of the vital supplies to the hapless victims of Nazism, stressing the fact that "these inmates are totally exhausted, so that every day's delay is injurious."[5]

INSTEAD OF RUSHING to fulfill his charge of aiding and abetting rescue, McClelland showed his cold indifference. On the margin of

McClelland's Cold Indifference

the letter as well as in his official response to the Sternbuchs, he noted:

I do not feel that the circumstances at Theresienstadt are so critical that it will not be possible for you to tolerate the three to four weeks' time required by the Joint Commission [of the IRC] to procure the supplies you wish to buy.[6]

He neatly omitted Birkenau and Bergen-Belsen from his reply, leaving only Theresienstadt. While it is true that the conditions in the latter camp were milder relative to the others, it was still a place where most inmates were hungry most of the time. And even this request took him over a week to answer.[7]

Both Mayer and McClelland supported the cruel Swiss policy of *refoulement*, of sealing the borders against illegal refugees and returning all but the very young or old to the Germans. (Actually, the Swiss had two policies: asylum was given to so-called political refugees. Racial refugees — primarily Jews — were subject to *refoulement*.) McClelland and Recha Sternbuch had a strong disagreement over this policy in June-July 1944, when 10,000-12,000 Jews were being transported daily to Auschwitz and when George Mandel-Mantello's anti-Auschwitz press campaign in the Swiss press was in full swing. The United States, Sweden, and the Vatican responded quickly, causing Hungary's Admiral Horthy to halt the deportations by July 8. It was a crucial time, for thousands of Jews from Hungary, Czechoslovakia, and France could still be saved — and the Sternbuchs seized the moment to try to have the Swiss government change its *refoulement* policy. In fact, the initial reason for *refoulement* was a Swiss fear of Nazi invasion, which had no longer been valid for years.

This battle had to be fought under cover, though, for many of the *refoulement* regulations were not published — because the Swiss did not wish to be known as a people who sent refugees back to their death. (Outside Switzerland, only the refugees crowding near the borders knew the truth and went to Fascist Spain, where they would not be turned over to the Nazis.) Recha Sternbuch wrote to McClelland and suggested that the American government pressure the Swiss into easing the regulations, especially when the danger of a Nazi invasion seemed nil. She added, too, that the Swiss could learn a great deal from the Swedes, who had opened their borders to all refugees and unlike the Swiss allowed them not only to move freely but also to work. "I am surely ready to expend much effort," she said, "and to make no distinction between day and night. It was six years ago that I learned to appreciate the refugee problem — in a St. Gallen jail experience."[8]

MCCLELLAND, UNMOVED, suggested that if Recha Sternbuch felt that way, then Sweden might be a better place for her to live than

Recha Sternbuch's Reply

Switzerland. "I do not believe," she replied in her letter,

that I should have to leave my mother country for the past thirty-five years for Sweden, just because I disagree with some aspects such as the laws of *refoulement* and believe that much more should be done for these unfortunate ones. All this involves neither personal ambitions nor any search for improving my lot elsewhere. It concerns a broader, general question. For this very reason I consider it my duty to remain here, where I could contribute to an improvement, however modest.

However ... one is no better Swiss or American merely by total agreement with the actions of each and every department of the country. Nor is one, by the same virtue, a worse citizen for dissatisfaction with any one of these. The good Swiss foundation is based upon free and open criticism, as long as it remains within its constitutional limits, and pursued by legal means.

I can only assure you that my views coincide with those of Switzerland's greatest personalities. We frequently heard their voices in the national assembly and lately from private authoritative sources as well.[9]

FURTHER, SHE CONTRASTED her own stand with that of Swiss patriots such as Saly Mayer who put the country's secular laws

Refoulement is the Real Danger

before those of the Torah:

I have much greater respect for the [true] Swiss mentality than those who keep silent or demand ... *refoulement.* That is why I raise my voice in opposition to actions that besmirch the good Swiss reputation ... It is quite paradoxical, on the one hand, to sacrifice large sums of American money to rescue individual families, while on the other, watch passively at what is occurring at the border. The number of those turned back is irrelevant. Surely the enemy has murdered most of these. Somewhere there are those still hidden who would brave the danger in enemy territory, if they did not have to contend with the additional danger at the Swiss border. It is through *refoulement* that the real danger accosts the refugees.

There is an abundance of proof. The Swiss authorities need no such proof, since they are fully aware of these objectionable facts. These are not actions that have to be proved, because they are not unjust according to the law. These actions conducted at the borders are performed in accordance with the regulations of the federal alien-office, that we wanted to abolish.

After so many years of *refoulement* it is high time to give thought [to abolishing it]. Most people did not want to believe in the Hungarian deportations, and the daily figure of 12,000 people when we received the cable after the first deportations. There were numerous individuals who did not believe in Hitler's determination to exterminate, despite his open declarations to this effect ...

There is still another voice, which must be heard, the voice of G-d, who asks, 'Where is your brother?' [Appealing to McClelland's Quaker background, she mentioned a few of his historical heroes.] Were one to ask this of John Fox or William Penn, they would surely find no means in the world sufficiently vigorous to stand up for the rights of these unfortunate ones ...

I therefore repeat my request ... to interest yourself in these aforementioned matters in order to carry out the immediate abolition of the different regulations for crossing the border.[10]

HOW DIFFERENT EVENTS would assuredly have been if the man receiving Recha Sternbuch's sincere humanitarian pleas in her **What if ...?** letters had not been the staunchly legalistic Roswell McClelland, a Quaker who helped Jewish children in France but who neither encouraged Saly Mayer to help the refugees nor brought any American pressure on the Swiss to alter *refoulement.* How different if Recha Sternbuch's pleas had gone to Wallenberg, or at least to Polish Ambassador Lados, who gave her the illegal use of his Embassy's diplomatic cable. Or to Papal Nuncio Fillippe Bernardini, who in fact did use his influence to stop the practice of *refoulement* on the Swiss-Italian border. So few people did so much. What if there had been different people in different places at different times? How many more Jews would have been saved!

PART II:
PERSONALITY PORTRAITS

CHAPTER NINE

The United States

A. INTRODUCTION

THERE WAS NO SUBSTANTIVE refugee problem until 1938, when the Nazi annexation of Austria (the *Anschluss*) and *Kristallnacht* caused thousands of Jews to flee German-held lands.

New Deal — "Jew Deal" America, however, could hardly be considered a sanctuary: This was a country still deep in the worst economic depression in its history, with jobs at a premium and anti-alienism a fairly common component of the existing climate of the day. Antisemitism seemed pervasive, nowhere more so than on Father Coughlin's weekly radio broadcasts, which featured a serialization of *The Protocols of the Elders of Zion.*

At the same time, however, Jews were making unprecedented inroads into the highest reaches of the federal government. As President Franklin Roosevelt sought the advice and goodwill of organized labor, for example, such powerful leaders as Sidney Hillman and David Dubinsky, of the clothing trades, found a ready ear in the White House. So many Jews came from academia and elsewhere to make Roosevelt's New Deal work that the derisive term "Jew Deal" had at least some truth to it. The leading figures, by position or influence with FDR, were: New York Governor Herbert Lehmann, Supreme Court Justice Felix Frankfurter, Judge Samuel Rosenman, financier Bernard Baruch, David Niles, and of course Treasury Secretary Henry Morgenthau Jr. Had all this potential Jewish political power been put to use, especially during the important election year 1943-1944, to aid the Jewish cause in

Europe, it might have made a crucial difference in the lives of millions.

Yet, throughout the war the American-Jewish Establishment maintained its ties with Roosevelt in part by concentrating on domestic antisemitism and future plans for Palestine — the postwar cure-all, it was hoped, for the refugee problem. As Judd L. Teller observed, for American Zionists it was easy:

> ... to mobilize protests against British policy in Palestine, exercises in public indignation that kept the movement afloat and the names of its leaders in American headlines. There was nothing daring about protesting against a foreign government, nor about soliciting statements denouncing Britain from congressmen and senators who were delighted to accommodate their Jewish constituents.

The sole domestic target was the State Department:

> ... against whose policies they habitually appealed to the White House, thus conveying the impression that all diplomatic policy that was unsympathetic to their cause had been formulated without even the President's knowledge, let alone his consent. This myth made political life easier for them since their protests involved no risk.[1]

Indeed, as a matter of policy, *The New York Times*, the bastion of assimilationist perspective, rarely printed any Jewish news whatsoever, reserving its meager coverage primarily for items pertaining to antisemitism. Behind this policy lay the publisher's basic philosophy that "*The New York Times* does not wish to be thought of as a 'Jewish newspaper.' "[2] Throughout the Holocaust period, in fact, most of the news from Europe — including that from unimpeachable sources — was not published in the *Times* or was given very inadequate coverage. In one instance, the verified account on July 7, 1944 of the death of two million Jews rated only a short article on page 10. This same news made front-page headlines in several hundred Swiss newspapers as a result of the press campaign instigated by the Jewish Secretary General of El Salvador. (See Chap. 11E.)

HOW UNLIKELY, THEN, that in this climate two small, virtually unknown Orthodox organizations produced giants of rescue, a **Agudath Israel and Vaad Hatzalah** handful of leaders previously known only to the Torah world who became welcome in top government circles and whose opinions had to be considered before any official action was taken. These groups which rose from obscurity before the war into major forces for rescue by 1944 were Agudath Israel and Vaad Hatzalah.

It is a sad footnote to American-Jewish priorities of the period that in 1944 the relatively tiny Vaad was second only to the immense and powerful Joint among all American-Jewish organizations in funds spent for rescue — more than $1,135,000 to the Joint's $15 million. Groups like the American Jewish Congress and the Jewish Labor Committee — larger, richer, more established, and far more powerful than the Vaad — together spent only two-thirds of the Vaad's budget for rescue, while spending an equal amount fighting antisemitism at home.[3]

In the U.S., neither Agudath Israel nor Vaad Hatzalah were involved during the early years of the Jewish anti-Nazi Boycott, simply because they did not yet exist. Only in 1938 did Zeirei Agudath Israel, Agudath Israel's Youth Division, under the leadership of Elimelech ("Mike") Tress, begin work on refugee matters and immigration. Vaad Hatzalah, the rabbis' rescue committee (originally called *Vaad Hahatzalah Emergency Committee for War Torn Yeshivoth*), was founded in the fall of 1939 by Rabbi Eliezer Silver under the auspices of the Union of Orthodox Rabbis of the United States and Canada *(Agudas Harabonim)*. Its purpose was to rescue the yeshivos that fled Poland to Lithuania. That same year, as some of the more mature members of Agudath Israel arrived in the United States, a branch of Agudath Israel of America was begun.[4]

Both Vaad Hatzalah and Agudah in all its three branches (the World Organization, Agudath Israel of America and the Agudah Youth Division) were essentially volunteer organizations, with a few individuals and secretaries the only paid help. They had something of a common leadership, though a separation of sorts was maintained.

For example, Rabbi Eliezer Silver, the founder of Vaad Hatzalah, was simultaneously president of Agudath Israel of America, while Yaakov ("Jacob") Rosenheim, president of World Agudath Israel and Elimelech Tress, head of the Agudah Youth Division,* were lay leaders of the Vaad. Rabbi Aaron Kotler, head of Agudah's Council of Torah Sages and the greatest talmudic scholar to immigrate to the U.S., was one of the three principal leaders of the Vaad Hatzalah along with Rabbi Abraham Kalmanowitz and Rabbi Silver.

---

* The latter had come into existence in the U.S. already in 1922, and Jacob Rosenheim's unit began operation in the U.S. first in early 1941, after he arrived in the U.S. from England.

Dr. Isaac Lewin

Tress' Youth Division concentrated on visas, affidavits and other immigration matters for Torah scholars who were the concern of the Vaad Hatzalah,* and for other Orthodox Jews. But any Jew seeking help, regardless of political or religious orientation, could get it. World Agudath Israel, headed by Yaakov Rosenheim, concentrated on political action. Rosenheim's key aide, and a very important rescue activist in his own right, was Dr. Isaac Lewin, the well-known historian and Agudah leader. He not only served as the lone "Voice of Jacob" to warn Jews not to give up and not to be pessimistic about helping their unfortunate brethren in Nazi-occupied Europe, but acted upon it as well.

Furthermore, he played a crucial role as the intermediary between the Orthodox and the Polish Government-in-Exile both in Washington as well as in London and Bern. All messages sent via the secret Polish pouch were sent first to Washington which in turn relayed the crucial dispatches to Dr. Lewin. He not only conveyed the communication, whether from the Sternbuchs in Switzerland, Griffel in Turkey or Harry Goodman in London, to Rosenheim and the Roshei Yeshivah, he personally epitomized the dedication and urgency behind those messages. Moreover, his very good relations with the Polish diplomats in Washington helped form a strategically useful cooperative effort between the Polish Government and the

---

* Vaad Hatzalah concentrated on raising funds for rescue, at first for the yeshivah students in Lithuania, later in Shanghai and eventually for rescue in general.

Orthodox in their common attempts to deal with the catastrophic events in Europe.

Dr. Isaac Lewin usually represented the Orthodox at meetings on rescue matters with the Jewish organizations.[5]

BOTH AGUDAH AND VAAD HATZALAH developed independent political connections, particularly after the changing of focus to the

Independent Political Contacts

rescue of all Jews, in the latter part of 1943. Some, such as Rabbi Eliezer Silver, had established contact with Republican Senator Robert Taft of Ohio, Rabbi Silver's home state. Mr. Rosenheim had the ear of James McDonald, former High Commissioner for Refugees, who resigned this post in 1935 in protest against the League of Nations' poor record in this area. Rabbi Kalmanowitz also made contact with the Democratic Senator Robert Wagner from New York, while Rabbi Herbert S. Goldstein, an Agudist, brought in his congregant, Congressman Sol Bloom, for assistance in refugee matters.[6]

They often worked both sides of the political aisle on the same issue, Rabbi Kalmanowitz utilizing his Democratic contacts, Rabbi Silver his Republicans, including the influential Senator Robert Taft.[7]

Following the standard procedure among Orthodox rescue activists, the two rabbis cooperated with anyone whom they felt might benefit their cause. One particularly helpful group was the Jewish Labor Committee, an organization representing leftists, secular Jews in the "Jewish" trade unions. Not only did the JLC join in delegations to government officials, but they were also extremely helpful in fundraising efforts. Unfortunately, though, the Jewish Labor Committee and the Bergson group were virtually alone in their willingness to cooperate with the Vaad on most rescue matters. Other Jewish organizations, for various reasons, as we have seen, either did not recognize the true nature of events in Europe, did not wish to compromise their autonomy, or only wanted to focus on postwar planning.

IT ALL STARTED FOLLOWING *KRISTALLNACHT* in 1938: the pleas were as clear as they were heartbreaking. Hundreds of letters

Agudath Israel

came from Orthodox Jews in Germany and Austria begging for help — and the Youth Division of Agudath Israel of America, under the leadership of Tress, quickly organized a Refugee and Immigration Division at the

Agudah's new 616 Bedford Avenue headquarters in the Williamsburg section of Brooklyn. The building served a dual function; not only was it the center for planning rescue activities, it was also a dormitory which housed newly arrived refugees.[8]

The operation was staffed largely by Agudah members, and graduates and students of yeshivos — amateurs, in the best and most idealistic sense of the word. Despite their relative lack of experience with either the planning or the practical ends of this sort of operation, they quickly became formidable experts in the field. The rescue staffers became specialists in the technical end of immigration and pioneered the use of collective affidavits — those assurances of support from organizations rather than individuals applied to more than one potential refugee. Indeed, their work proved of enormous value, not only in 1938, but during and after the war as well.[9] In most areas of rescue work, the Agudah worked closely with Vaad Hatzalah, which in turn specialized in raising the large sums of money required for rescue.

In time, the Agudah activists learned key lobbying techniques, and widened their once-narrow circle of political friends and allies in Washington. The relationships they formed helped them secure outside-quota visas for such special interest groups as yeshivah students and rabbinic or community leaders.

In the early days of rescue, from 1938 prior to the German invasion of Russia in June 1941, the main problem for Jews was not getting out of Germany and Austria; instead, it was finding a willing host country. Jews could leave with relatively little difficulty — *if* they had a place to go. At that time, the central requirement for entry into the United States, for example, was either fitting into a pre-set quota (not too generous for Germany and Austria; suffocating for Eastern Europe), or having a visa and an affidavit of support. The latter, unfortunately, was extremely difficult to obtain because Europe-based American consuls generally applied a strict interpretation of the "public charge" clause in the immigration law. Simply stated, this required an American sponsor to have $5,000 or more in a bank account, a then-enormous sum which would indicate that the immigrant would not become a public charge. (At that time $20 a week was a decent salary.) Eventually, thousands of affidavits were secured by Agudath Israel and used to rescue Jews from Nazi and postwar Europe.[10]

It was, of course, Rabbi Kotler who stressed unity in rescue above all, and therefore it is more than a little interesting to note that at this time Rabbi Eliezer Silver was president of both Agudath Israel and Vaad Hatzalah.

PRIOR TO THE SECOND WORLD WAR, most of the larger yeshivos in Eastern Europe, especially in Poland and Lithuania, maintained
Vaad Hatzalah fundraising offices in America. With the onset of the war, the yeshivos were disbanded, transatlantic contacts were broken, and many students were left without funds, food, clothing — in some cases even without a place to live. These bleak circumstances caused the American yeshivah representatives and support organizations to pool their talents and their funds to form a single relief agency, the Vaad Hatzalah, which was initially charged with the task of relocating the stricken yeshivos[11]. Yet, within several years, the Vaad's focus shifted from mere relocation to all-out rescue of a people who were being systematically destroyed.

WHEN THE EUROPEAN-BORN ORTHODOX leaders succeeded in penetrating official indifference and antisemitism, it was rarely
Irving Bunim and Vaad Hatzalah without the help of their highly capable English-speaking Orthodox assistants. Often they acted merely as interpreters; at other times they did more, serving to bridge the intellectual and cultural gaps between two highly different worlds, between talmudic scholars and American bureaucrats. Among the most effective of these highly important go-betweens was Irving Bunim, a successful businessman, a founder, pillar and chairman of the board of Vaad Hatzalah. He frequently went to Washington with Rabbi Kotler, to see and influence Treasury Secretary Henry Morgenthau Jr. and other government officials. Indeed, Bunim was in the forefront of every aspect of the rescue movement, an inveterate and highly successful fund-raiser for Vaad Hatzalah, and was one of the most active proponents of vocal and visible protest. His philosophy was to take action — then face the consequences — to save Jewish lives.

It was his close association with Rabbi Aaron Kotler, since the latter's arrival in the United States in 1941, that helped propel Bunim into becoming the singular most prominent lay leader of the Orthodox Jewish community during and especially after the Second World War. He was a pioneer leader and spokesman for Young Israel for six decades, using his influence to bring in this major Orthodox body as an active member of Vaad Hatzalah. He was simultaneously president of Yeshiva Rabbi Jacob Joseph, on the Board of Torah Umesorah (the Orthodox Day School Movement), the Lakewood Kollel and the Chinuch Atzmai school system in Israel, among others.[12]

AMONG THE MORE SPECTACULAR feats of World War II was the escape of thousands of Polish Jews from Lithuania. In 1940-41,

Vaad Hatzalah and the Soviet Union

2,000 Polish refugees, including some 500 yeshivah students, used so-called Dutch "Curacao visas" which, along with Russian exit-visas and Japanese transit-visas, enabled them to leave Russian-occupied Lithuania for Japan. As we have seen in the story of the "Shabbos Ride," Vaad Hatzalah came through with the enormous sum of $50,000 at the crucial moment to finance this flight of Torah scholars to East Asia. At the time, of course, they were not at all certain that they were doing the right thing.[13] After all, requesting an *exit-visa* from the Soviet Union on the basis of an *end-visa** from Curacao placed them in a position not unlike that of contemporary Refuseniks: they could have been considered traitors by the Soviet Union because of their request to leave and sent to internal exile in Siberia. Indeed, Jews of Lemberg (Lvov), in Soviet-occupied Poland, had been sent to Siberia in 1939 when they rejected offers of Soviet citizenship and attempted to return to the German sector of their country. So this Curacaoan escape route was fraught with potential dangers, which caused many to object to its use. At that time, as well, the full fury of the Final Solution had yet to be unleashed, so it was unclear who posed the greater threat, the Nazis or the NKVD,** the Soviet secret police with their spies, informers, and portfolios full of trumped-up charges. Moreover, their memories were colored by the German-occupation during World War I, when the Germans were the humane ones and the Russians were the barbarians. Yet, with the prodding by Rabbi Shimon Kalish, the Rebbe of Amshenov, and Zorach Wahrhaftig (the Mizrachi leader and later Israel's Minister of Religion), the holders of the "Curacaon visas" went ahead, across Russia and Siberia, to Vladivostok, then to Kobe, Japan, finally to Shanghai. Few, in all likelihood, realized their good fortune in being

---

* An "end visa" is granted by a country willing to accept one as an immigrant. In contrast, a "transit-visa" merely allows temporary stay in a country on the way to a permanent destination.

** The predecessors to the present KGB.

shipped through Siberia in 1941, just a few months prior to the war with Germany.*[14]

B. SIBERIA, TASHKENT, SAMARKAND:
The Vaad Hatzalah and
three unlikely havens for Polish refugees[1]

OF ALL THE REMARKABLE STORIES to emerge from the Holocaust, the Siberian incarceration of more than 400,000 Jews is certainly one

The NKVD of the most unlikely. Indeed, the nearly half-million Jews who by 1939 had fled east from Poland into then-neutral Lithuania felt that they had left tyranny behind — only to be incorporated into the Soviet Union by the advancing Russian army. Quickly, the Jews were singled out by the NKVD and sent for hard labor in Siberia, the vast, inhospitable Asiatic wasteland. The NKVD, according to their standing policy, rounded up those whom they felt to be the most suspect among the newly captured; yeshivah students and Torah scholars topped the list, 3,000 perhaps of the 3,500 whom the Vaad had previously tried to rescue from Lithuania.[2] Yet, what at first seemed a certain tragedy was soon after rendered a victory, for with the help of Vaad Hatzalah's global-aid network and the assistance of the Joint, thousands of these Jews, including numerous Torah scholars, were saved.

Normally, of course, reports are not circulated about so-called exiles in Siberia, but due to the Soviet Union's concerted attempt to garner support from the western democracies during the war, news began to leak out in June 1941 about the conditions and whereabouts of the "exiled" Jews. From that point until the following December, all that was known was the existence of this group — no direct communication was permitted. After America's entry into the war, however, and the official alliance of the United States and the Soviet Union, the Vaad Hatzalah established what could indeed be considered a direct lifeline with the Siberian captives.

Further, as a result of the Sikorski-Stalin Polish-Russian Agreement of August 12, 1941, many of the Polish Jews, including the yeshivah students, were granted a kind of amnesty and were

---

* It is worth mentioning, as well, that following the invasion of Russia by the Nazis, roughly 400,000 Jews were sent to Siberia to stay, and that tens of thousands of them died of starvation, the climate, or forced labor. The majority, however, survived, due to some extent to the help of Vaad Hatzalah. Among the survivors were many Torah scholars and yeshivah students who, after the War, helped revitalize Judaism in the United States and elsewhere.

taken from Siberian labor camps to the somewhat more inhabitable areas of Tashkent and Samarkand in Asiatic Russia. Once there, the yeshivah students originally from Radin and Kletzk were among the first to contact Jewish agencies in the United States for aid — a particularly poignant request, to be sure, for the Vaad, for Kletzk was Rabbi Aaron Kotler's own yeshivah, which he left only in order to continue his own important rescue work. "Out of Siberia," the cable to Rabbi Kotler read, "arrived at Samarkand ... cable money."[3]

A SEPARATE CABLE, sent to Rabbi Reuven Grozovsky, Rosh of the Mesivta Torah Vodaath in Brooklyn, hinted at the students' new living conditions.

A Coded Message

Dear friend E. Reuven. Your cable arrived wherein you inquire about Isaac's children [i.e., the students of the yeshivah]. I only know [of the whereabouts] of some, not all. I know about eighty that traveled with us, eleven of whom have already gone to their [departed] father R. Boruch Baer [Levovitz, of blessed memory] [i.e., they have already died]. It could be that they are better off than we ... We feel fine. Our friend *Raav* [Hunger] is our frequent guest ... We received 6,000 rubles and 1060 rubles. I sent these to acquaintances whose addresses we know. We beg of you, send packages via *Eretz Israel*. We eagerly anticipate your packages and letters.

We just completed the *Yahrzeit* of our father the *Gaon* Yitzchak Charkover of blessed memory, who died of hunger and cold. Now we are again orphaned, from our mother, the daughter of the Dean of the yeshivah R. Naftoli [Tropp] of blessed memory ... Save us ... How long can we hold out! ...[4]

The Vaad took immediate steps to alleviate these problems, channeling efforts in a number of different directions. While, for example, most of the relief funds originated in the United States, they were actually distributed from Jerusalem — simply because the route through Teheran to the Soviet Union was more workable. Prior to America's entry into the war, many Jews supported the work of the Federation of Polish Jews and sent relief packages to the Polish ghettos. After America's entry into the war, however, fewer Jews sent packages, thereby shifting more of the burden onto the Vaad Hatzalah to keep the aid flowing into the heart of the Soviet Union. At that point the two countries were officially allies; direct communication was possible, and therefore a steady flow of food staples, used clothing, medicine (including saccharin, for example, which proved invaluable for barter), matzohs, and money went regularly to 3,000 or so internal exiles, who in turn shared the relief goods with others. (Verifying names was itself an enormous chore, and Chief Rabbi Herzog in Jerusalem helped in no small way.)[5]

THERE WERE SEVERAL ORGANIZATIONS through which packages and money were sent from the United States, including the

Other Helpful Organizations

American Red Cross and the Russian War Relief, a particularly popular charity, due in part to the work of the United Jewish War Effort. The Jewish Labor Committee was helpful once again in enabling the Vaad to send the food packages to Siberia. It utilized its good connections with the Russian government to develop channels for the shipment of such packages. These channels were frequently utilized by the Vaad along with others, to make the maximum use of all ways to alleviate the plight of their fellow Jews in Siberia and Tashkent.[6]

In London, as well, the Polish government-in-exile helped with both cable communications and direct subsidies. All told, roughly 12,000 packages a month went from America to the Siberian Jews, and 700 more from Jerusalem via Teheran, the latter often containing scarce household goods, which again could be sold or bartered for more vital items.[7]

Still, relief was at best only a stopgap, an interim way of maintaining the captives until they could be evacuated or rescued. Attempts were made — with the help of General Sikorski and others — to get the Jews out, or at least have some reclassified, such as the rabbinical students, into what were known as spiritual guides. Yet except for a very small number, who went to Israel by the soft route through Teheran, most of the Polish Jews had to suffer their Siberian exile until the Vaad was able to work for their release after the war was over.

C. RABBI ABRAHAM KALMANOWITZ[1]

RABBI ABRAHAM KALMANOWITZ ARRIVED in the United States from Lithuania (via Sweden), in April 1940, and quickly emerged as

Most Dynamic Rescue Activist one of the key figures in the Vaad's wartime efforts. He had been rabbi in Poland and president of the Mirrer Yeshivah. At first Rabbi Kalmanowitz's efforts centered around his own institution, the Mirrer Yeshivah, working with his associates and Agudath Israel to secure affidavits — from a wide variety of sources — for the endangered students. Because until June of that year Lithuania was still a free state, communication was relatively easy and available, and under Rabbi Kalmanowitz's direction telegrams poured out to anyone who might rescue a *yeshivah bochur* by sponsoring entry into America. Many, however, refused to help; some could not believe that threatened events would take place, others feared financial or social burdens, although funds earmarked for each refugee's support had already been guaranteed by the Vaad, the Joint, or other organizations.

Yet like so many other rescue giants, Rabbi Kalmanowitz was hardly one to give up. He literally worked around the clock on additional methods and new solutions — once, in fact, as we have noted, Rabbi Kalmanowitz called Rabbi Alex Weisfogel, his secretary, at three in the morning to discuss a new thought. ("He ate, slept and breathed only rescue, rescue, rescue," Rabbi Weisfogel has said.) The two men agreed to meet at Penn Station in four hours, where they boarded a train for Philadelphia. Later that day, at the Labor Department, the federal agency responsible for issuing visas, they tried to gain as many additional lifesaving scraps of paper as they could.

The Vaad, under Rabbi Kalmanowitz's guidance, never turned away any Jew in need of assistance, either for himself or for relatives and friends. One reason, of course, that Rabbi Kalmanowitz had such a reputation was because — unlike many others — he never allowed legal niceties to stand in the way of getting results. Like Rabbi Kotler, Rabbi Kalmanowitz set aside any partisan differences in the cause of rescue. Indeed, after a particularly beneficial conference, he once said to Reform leader Dr. Stephen S. Wise, "I hope that one day you will see the light. G-d bless you, and may you keep up this great work. It's a great *mitzvah.*" For Rabbi Kalmanowitz, as for Rabbi Kotler and others, saving lives was *the mitzvah,* one which took precedence over all others.

Unlike Rabbi Kotler, who was calmer and more pensive, Rabbi Kalmanowitz, along with Rabbi Eliezer Silver, was emotional, forceful and quick to act, moving almost instantly when rescue was at stake.

He would often cry himself and move a congregation to tears. Yet Rabbi Kalmanowitz's highly visible public and private emotional displays were often put to good use. For it was his well-nigh unique ability to affect people — from individuals to large gatherings — that earned him the reputation of Orthodoxy's best fundraiser, a term granted him out of respect for his sincere emotional pleas.

His dedication was so profound that there were personality clashes within the Vaad when Rabbi Kalmanowitz's considerable zeal was mistaken for aggressiveness. One point of contention, for example, was his oft-stated opinion that he would rather deal with a non-Jewish government official than a Jewish one. Sadly, of course, he had learned that non-Jews tended to show more respect to European-bred rabbis than did assimilated American Jews.

RABBI KALMANOWITZ'S HEARTFELT RESPONSE to events in Europe often led other men to their own singular accomplishments.

Heartfelt Response For example, Yitzchok Sternbuch, Rabbi Kalmanowitz's main European contact (see Chap. 11C), called with a horrible and unimaginable, yet completely verified story out of Warsaw. A lone Jew had escaped from the Polish ghetto and managed to get into Switzerland, to Sternbuch's headquarters. There he told his hosts that the Nazis had built a factory which rendered the bodies of their Jewish victims into soap. At first, they did not want to believe him, but when he supplied the name of the German officer in charge, and the address of the factory, they were convinced. The next question was could Rabbi Kalmanowitz convince President Roosevelt to intervene?

Rabbi Kalmanowitz reacted by fainting in the middle of the trans-Atlantic conversation. When he recovered he immediately contacted many Jewish leaders who might be able to influence Roosevelt, among them Stephen Wise, Nachum Goldmann, chairman of the executive board of the World Jewish Congress and representative of the Jewish Agency, and Henry Monsky of B'nai B'rith. Two days later, a delegation of prominent Jews, including Rabbi Kalmanowitz and Irving Bunim, held a meeting with Treasury Secretary Henry Morgenthau, where Rabbi Kalmanowitz's great eloquence was put to good use. Morgenthau himself immediately called Under Secretary of State Sumner Welles requesting that he set up a meeting with Secretary of State Cordell Hull — so that they in turn could arrange for a meeting with President Roosevelt. Welles dutifully called and reported back that Hull had balked, saying that he was too busy with other matters to get involved. Morgenthau angrily retorted that if this matter wasn't urgent enough to merit a Cabinet member's meeting with the President, then the Secretary of State could have his resignation the next morning. That message, fortunately, was clear, and the meeting took place. The results were, however, only partially successful. After the initial meeting with Roosevelt, and a later one on December 8, the Allies on December 17, 1942 issued what was to be their sole proclamation of condemnation specifically mentioning Jewish victims. (See Chap. 7B.)

AS WAS THE CASE with other Orthodox activists, Rabbi Kalmanowitz's tireless efforts were the result of his belief that G-d **His** had given him the opportunity to perform the great *mitzvah* of saving Jewish lives. The requirements of **Singular** rescue also caused Rabbi Kalmanowitz and others to **Goal** violate the Sabbath a number of times, when lives were at stake. On one Friday afternoon, for example, Rabbi Kalmanowitz discovered that a list of potential immigrants that he and others were preparing had to be delivered to the Philadelphia-based Department of Justice by the next morning or the opportunity would be lost. Although the work was difficult — for Rabbi Kalmanowitz had to labor with foreign names whose difficult spelling had to be changed to make them intelligible to American officials and evaluate who stood the best chance of meeting government requirements — they continued, until nearly sundown. Then, seeing the hour, Rabbi Weisfogel called a halt to their work, asking who could return the next night to finish the job. Rabbi Kalmanowitz pointedly reminded everyone present that saving Jewish lives is a Torah precept that took precedence over the Sabbath. He simply demanded that the list be finished that Friday night in time to be taken to Philadelphia and avoid any delay.

It seemed to his assistants and close associates that Rabbi Kalmanowitz was constantly in meetings, in his own office, at the Vaad, in Irving Bunim's home or office. Often, they discussed rescue policy and fundraising, large campaigns or particular strategies to be employed with the Federal Government. When, for example, a matter was before the War Refugee Board, one fairly standard question was whether the Vaad should appeal directly to the Vice President — and risk antagonizing the Board members.

It was an oft-asked question: how could they exert influence in one area without antagonizing another faction? A standard Vaad policy had to be created, and then constantly re-evaluated by the men who knew Washington best, Rabbi Kalmanowitz and Rabbi Silver.

And Rabbi Kalmanowitz, and others at the Vaad, understood political realities, understood that others would often have to get the credit for something they actually accomplished and yet they were willing to forgo the credit. Because, unlike others, the Vaad members had the single goal — rescue: everything else was secondary.

ONCE, FOR EXAMPLE, IN THE SPRING of 1944, following the German occupation of Hungary and the ghettoization of most of its **Lives Over Mere Buildings** Jews, Rabbi Kalmanowitz heard that a Vatican-inspired conference was about to begin concerning saving the city of Rome by declaring it an "Open City." Rabbi Kalmanowitz immediately contacted Lawrence S. Lesser, assistant director of the War Refugee Board, who in turn wrote a memo to John Pehle quoting Rabbi Kalmanowitz and pointing out "the higher value of human lives and dignity" over mere buildings. Lesser then asked the Board, "whether it is not possible to put saving the lives of the Jews and other persecuted people on the agenda of that conference."[2]

Rabbi Kalmanowitz was among the most vocal Orthodox leaders in favor of Rabbi Weissmandl's plan of bombing Auschwitz and the rail lines leading to it in an attempt to halt the mass murder of 12,000 Jews a day. From the time the Vaad Hatzalah received the first such message from Yitzchok Sternbuch in early June 1944, until September of that year, Rabbi Kalmanowitz did not cease in his efforts to have the Allies take action on this clearly humanitarian request. He continued as long as he could. As Professor David Wyman noted:

> At the beginning of September, pressure built once more on the War Refugee Board for bombing rail lines, this time the lines between Auschwitz and Budapest, where the last large enclave of Hungarian Jews was threatened with deportation. These entreaties came from the Orthodox rescue committee in New York. Rabbi Abraham Kalmanowitz, anxious for the appeal to reach the WRB as soon as possible, placed a night phone call to Benjamin Akzin, who relayed the plea to Pehle the next day. Akzin took advantage of the opportunity to spell out to Pehle, in polite terms, his dissatisfaction with the inaction of the War Department regarding the bombing requests ... But the Board did not move on the appeal.[3]

In this, as in other important rescue and relief causes, Rabbi Kalmanowitz and the other Orthodox activists were — despite their great efforts — ultimately unsuccessful. Yet even in their failure there was a kind of victory, for if nothing else they impressed the government officials with whom they worked with the quality of their commitment and the level of their understanding. These ideas were, in fact, articulated by John W. Pehle, at a dinner honoring the War Refugee Board in December 1945, when he gave a rare tribute to a remarkable Jewish leader.

> Nor could I permit this occasion to pass without a few words, however inadequate, about my friend, Rabbi Kalmanowitz. No one in government or out of it was more devoted to our lifesaving mission. His hard work, his earnestness, and his enduring faith were an ever present inspiration to us all.
>
> Rabbi Kalmanowitz, you and I could reminisce for hours, if not for days, about the many harrowing problems we shared together. Life and death hung in the balance, and frequently there was no solution but to wait. Yes, to wait and see what the next move of a cruel, relentless and soulless enemy would be. I know the sleepless nights and the troubled days you and your colleagues lived through. We shared them with you. We shared your anxiety when those mysterious and secret negotiations in

Switzerland seemed to be taking a turn for the worse and when news from the Rabbi of Neutra [sic] omened ill for the persecuted in Slovakia and Hungary. But we exulted together when, as the result of the united efforts of all participating in this noble work, precious lives were saved — when the escape route through Romania became a reality — when food parcels from Tangier reached Theresienstadt and Bergen-Belsen — and when the Apostolic delegate informed us of the Vatican's forceful message to Dr. Tiso.[4]

D. RABBI ELIEZER SILVER[1]

Rabbi Kalmanowitz was hardly alone among the leaders of the Vaad Hatzalah in either intelligence, spirit, or dedication. One man stood as his virtual equal in all areas, except perhaps in patience and *halachah*, where his encyclopedic knowledge marked him a renowned master. Rabbi Silver was probably the leading European-trained Orthodox rabbi in the U.S. He was a talmudic scholar par excellence, and served as a rabbi in the U.S. ever since 1907. In 1939 he was to become president of Agudath Israel as well as a long-time member of the presidium of the Union of Orthodox rabbis. Yet despite their differences in style, Rabbi Silver and Rabbi Kalmanowitz worked together, traveling all over the U.S. and Canada in tireless fundraising efforts, leading numerous delegations to Washington, exerting immeasurable influence on countless government officials and committees, scouring every resource available for visas and passports and means of support, all for the relief and rescue of Europe's Jews.

During the war, Rabbi Silver also served in another important capacity, as the primary contact between Vaad Hatzalah and Agudath Israel and the non-Establishment Peter Bergson group. Indeed, Bergson thought so highly of Rabbi Silver that he had the rabbi serve as a member on the national executive board of his Emergency Committee to Save the Jewish People of Europe. Rabbi Silver, like all the other Orthodox rescue leaders, had no compunctions whatsoever about working with Bergson, the brilliant, vocal leader of the Irgunists. Although their eventual goals were entirely different, both Bergson and Rabbi Silver had the same immediate aim: rescue.

In all likelihood, it was Irving Bunim who introduced Rabbi Silver to Bergson, a man whom Bunim had known and supported because of Bunim's approval of their rescue of Jews from Europe to Palestine since the thirties. Bergson, at that time, along with Yitzchok Ben-Ami and Samuel Merlin had been seeking money to fund their illegal immigration route from Vienna to Palestine, and Bunim was the lone Jewish businessman to support them. With Bunim's help he had also pressured Young Israel to help their rescue efforts.[2] When the war broke out in Europe, and escape routes to Palestine became increasingly difficult to use, they shifted their efforts to promoting a Jewish army to fight for Palestine. Yet Bergson changed back to rescue in November 1942, after he read newspaper accounts of the murder of more than two million Jews.[3] Shortly thereafter, in mid-1943, after the collapse of both the Bermuda Conference and the American Jewish Conference, Bergson began to work with Rabbi Silver and the Vaad, publicizing the truth about events in Europe.[4] Among other victories, the rabbis' march on Washington in October 1943 came about in part because of their cooperation.

Like all the major Orthodox rescue activists, Rabbi Silver affected the lives of people with whom he worked, not only sparking new Torah insights, but also leaving indelible memories of dedication and commitment. One such account is by Dr. Isaac Lewin, himself a leading rescue participant.[5]

> Rabbi Silver was not merely the head of Vaad Hatzalah, he personified *hatzalah* — rescue itself. He lived and breathed rescue. To say that he displayed extraordinary zeal on behalf of

rescue does not begin to convey the depth of his dedication. He gave his entire being for rescue: his time, his money, himself. He spent virtually every waking moment upon the sacred task of rescue, he created through sheer willpower and backbreaking toil the necessary connections to effect the goal of rescue. Thus he was able to open the doors of the highest government offices in Washington (which were always receptive to him, thanks to his friendship with Senator Robert Taft of Ohio).* He personally gathered huge sums of money, stormed the sessions of the Jewish organizations, demanding, cajoling and forcefully presented the case that not a moment or opportunity be lost to save a Jew.

At the same time, he always remembered his role as a rabbi, representing the majesty of a Torah nation. He never lost sight of this noble legacy and responsibility which was thrust upon him. His zeal derived from the awareness that leadership is to be used for Torah Jewry, and he cherished and nurtured this awesome responsibility. At a time of crisis, when Jewish blood flowed in Europe, he feared no one. With pride and courage he got up to demand our right to live.

Before my eyes there is the image of the scene, where we stood on the steps of the Capitol in Washington, D.C. Hundreds of rabbis had participated in the March on Washington just before Yom Kippur of 1943. Addressing the Vice President of the United States (President Roosevelt conveniently absented himself) in the name of Orthodox Jewry, Rabbi Silver demanded help for the Jews who were being systematically murdered in Europe. At that moment one felt he could hear a leaf descend from a tree, so deafening the silence. The ring of Rabbi Silver's voice resounded throughout the area in front of Congress. The voice was that of the recognized representative of Orthodox Jewry.

I participated with Rabbi Silver in another rescue march. This was already after the war, when we visited the Displaced Persons (DP) Camps of the Jewish survivors in Germany and Austria. It was no longer a matter of grave peril from the Nazi murderers. But it was a crucial effort at the rescue of the survivors from slow disintegration. Jews suffered terribly from near-destitution and scrambled frantically towards freedom, towards a new life. Here, Rabbi Silver revealed his "golden heart." I recall innumerable scenes where, in order to help alleviate the immediate daily needs of the unfortunates he

---

* Rabbi Silver had gotten to know and appreciate Robert Taft's humanitarian approach decades earlier when as a lawyer Taft supported Rabbi Silver's construction of a *mikvah* in Cincinnati. [ed.]

visited, he gave away everything he had on his person without any reckoning. We came into the refugee camps, which were surrounded by barbed wire, and saw what was happening: shortages of food and clothing, and Jews begging for help. Rabbi Silver could not waste a moment. He immediately organized relief and paid for it from his own pocket. Naturally, his money soon ran out, but that did not deter him. He borrowed money from wherever he could. Wherever there was a Jew with ready cash, he was brought to Rabbi Silver. He wrote out notes to repay these loans in the United States. With this money he not only helped to minimize the daily problems, but he also rebuilt Orthodox Judaism, opening Talmud Torahs for children, supporting *Kashrus*, establishing *mikvaos* (ritualariums) and provided generous support for the marrying off of poor girls.

For a long while after returning from Germany he was unable to clear all his debts. A seemingly endless stream of Jews came to America with his signed promissory notes which Rabbi Silver honored through blood and sweat — always looking for ways to repay the loans he had obtained for relief actions on behalf of the survivors.

Thus, the man who had raised and handled millions on behalf of his fellow Jews passed away without a penny in his bank account. Yet the spiritual legacy he left of rescue remains one of the most inspiring of that era and will always be treasured in the bank account housing good deeds for *Klal Yisroel.*

E. RABBI AARON KOTLER[1]

FOR ALL THE GREATNESS of the others in matters of rescue, however, there can be little doubt that the most influential figure of

Foremost Talmudic Scholar in the U.S. the age — for Agudath Israel, Vaad Hatzalah, and indeed for American Orthodoxy in general — was Rabbi Aaron Kotler, who arrived in America Passover eve 1941.

Rabbi Aaron Kotler was perhaps the foremost talmudic scholar ever to live in the United States. Yet he was no cloistered Torah sage who allowed the world's problems to pass by unheeded. Not only was Rabbi Kotler the acknowledged leader of the movement to establish American Torah centers along European models, he was also a giant in the Orthodox-led rescue effort, both during and after the war. Given the hours and complexities that rescue effort alone involved, it would have proven too demanding for any one of lesser talents or energy. Yet Rabbi Kotler performed his duties with the admirable dedication and humanity for which he was justly renowned. As dean, for example, of the famed yeshivah in Kletzk, Poland, Rabbi Kotler was known not only as a brilliant lecturer, but also as a man who cared for his students' smallest needs — down to their meals and clothing.

By 1941, life in Lithuania (occupied by Russia since mid-1940), where Rabbi Kotler had gone in the mid-1920's, had become so perilous that he was forced to emigrate to the United States. The decision, however, was hardly an easy one, for he had to leave his students, and the institution he had administered for fifteen years, since the departure of his father-in-law, Rabbi Isser Zalman Meltzer, for Jerusalem in 1925. Rabbi Kotler made the decision to go not, however, out of a sense of his own safety — he had been on the ruling communists' subversive list for twenty years because of his work at what was then known as the Slutzker Yeshiva. Instead, Rabbi Kotler considered what would be best for the entire Jewish community, and decided that he would be able to do the greatest good if his base of operations were in free America rather than in occupied Europe. What's more, several difficult sessions with the NKVD had also convinced him that yeshivos had no future in Eastern Europe. The solution — which he and others sadly realized too late — was to evacuate everyone as soon as possible.

NOT SURPRISINGLY, RABBI KOTLER'S heartfelt anguish at leaving his yeshivah is clear in a talk to the Agudas Horabonim (Union of Orthodox Rabbis) in New York City, given shortly after he arrived.

Father of Sons

I am the father of sons who are wandering aimlessly from one place of exile to another, totally abandoned, forsaken. It is my responsibility and yours to save them ... I cannot even describe to you the bitterness and pain we felt upon my departure ... The one consolation lay in the hope that I would be able to find some help ...[2]

The trip had been arduous — he came by rail through the Soviet Union, then by boat from Kobe, Japan, finally reaching San Francisco Passover eve, 1941. During the intermediate days of Passover he took the train to New York, where he was joyously greeted at Pennsylvania Station by a reception committee made up of prominent rabbis and hundreds of yeshivah students. Rabbi Kotler responded in character: he ignored the festivities made in his honor and inquired about additional efforts made on behalf of those who had been left behind. Then he gave the crowd — and by extension all American Jews — clear marching orders.

On the other side of the ocean our brothers are waiting for our help. Only you, the Jews of America, are able to help them. Do it now! Save them! I did not come to this country to save myself but rather so that with your help we could save our brothers and the centers of Torah learning.[3]

Rabbi Kotler finished by outlining his plans for transferring the yeshivos of Europe to the United States, then defied the myriad pessimists, both Orthodox and non-Orthodox, who felt that yeshivahs could never really take hold in *treife* America, by giving a firm and compelling prophecy: "There *is*," he said, "a future for Torah in America."⁴ He was right. For with his own arrival in America, Rabbi Kotler began a new era in American Judaism, and became a major factor in transforming a politically weak, almost moribund Orthodoxy into a dynamic, growing force of yeshivos, *kollels*, and Bais Yaakovs, institutions virtually unthinkable forty years ago.⁵

Yet, in the spring of 1941, when Rabbi Kotler arrived, the future was hardly his chief concern, for there was the immediate problem that millions of Jewish lives were at stake in Europe. So great, in fact, was Rabbi Kotler's identification with the suffering Jews of Europe, that those who visited his house invariably remarked on the air of mourning, on the fact that except on the Sabbath *Rebbetzin* Kotler denied herself meat, coffee, and tea.` While the suffering in Europe continued, the entire Kotler family could not enjoy itself.⁶

AND RABBI KOTLER ISSUED ANOTHER *psak* at the time, this one directing all Jews to set aside partisan differences, to stop all political

Setting Aside Differences bickering, and unite instead in the holy cause of rescue. Because of Rabbi Kotler's unique stature, his total dedication, optimism and boundless energy, and his ability to inspire American laymen such as Irving Bunim to translate his dreams into the American vernacular, he succeeded where others failed, and was indeed able to bring together disparate factions of the Jewish community for concerted efforts. The Vaad Hatzalah, for example, worked well and efficiently because of Rabbi Kotler's ability to smooth over such political rough spots; and that group's extended relationship with Agudath Israel was also aided to a large degree by his leadership. As we have seen, it was Rabbi Kotler, who in his desire for full cooperation of all Jews toward rescue, was the primary catalyst for getting Mizrachi to join Vaad Hatzalah in 1941. It was he, too, who pressed for a compromise on the resolution read during the rabbis' march on Washington which included, through Mizrachi's insistence, the demand that the "Allies open the gates to Palestine," even though R' Aaron had opposed this demand as being counterproductive when working for rescue. For this reason, at the Congressional hearings on rescue following the rabbis' march, the demand was intentionally omitted by the Bergson group in conjunction with Vaad Hatzalah. And Rabbi Kotler, of course, followed his own *psak* too; he subordinated his own feeling with regard to secular Jewish ideologies to work with anyone who might be able to help — including Dr. Stephen Wise, a renowned proponent of Reform. Predictably, Rabbi Kotler was criticized by some overzealous Orthodox for meeting with Wise, yet he shrugged such reprobation aside. "I would prostrate myself before the Pope," he said, "if I knew it would help to save even the fingernail of one Jewish child!"[7]

For this same reason, although he had been closely connected with Agudath Israel in Europe, and even more so in the United States after the war, Rabbi Kotler did not promote this relation with Agudath Israel during the years that he was closely associated with Vaad Hatzalah in rescue work.[8]

Before Rabbi Kotler could be effective, however, he had the unenviable task of changing the American view of the Torah sage from that of a *batlan* — a naive parasite who understood little about the world — to a committed, knowledgeable man of action. After a while — and bewilderingly, for ill-informed American Jews as well as Washington officials — there were long-bearded, caftan-clad rabbis who were both articulate and well versed in economics, strategies, and international politics who dealt with authorities in a thoroughly professional manner.

IN ONE INCIDENT, RABBI KOTLER showed an astute understanding of Franklin Roosevelt, a man whom most Jews

Selecting the Proper Channels supposed to be the great supporter of Jewish causes. In 1944, Dr. Isaac Lewin brought a report to the Vaad indicating that the Nazis were separating Jewish prisoners of war from all others, with murder as their obvious intent. Though ill at the time, Rabbi Kotler assembled a delegation and led it to Washington that same night. Along the way they prepared a memorandum for the President, which read in part that "after 2,000 years of murdering innocent men, women and children of our people, it is sad that this is now being carried out with prisoners of war as well." Yet when Rabbi Kotler saw the message he immediately vetoed its use, wisely telling his colleagues to "beware of this statement. If President Roosevelt sees that this has been done for 2,000 years, he will say, 'Let it be done for another year.' This line," he added, "can do more harm than good."

Then, astutely and incisively, the Torah scholar suggested a better use for their data. First, he had the improper statement struck from the document. Then, it was sent *not* to Roosevelt, but instead through David Niles, the secretary to Roosevelt, who happened to be Jewish, to General Eisenhower. Eisenhower, as the rabbis had hoped, took immediate action by going on radio and announcing that such a plan would be considered "the greatest transgression of international law." The German separation program stopped.[9]

In the winter of 1944-1945 at the time of the Musy-Himmler negotiations, Rabbi Kotler traveled to Washington with Irving Bunim to see Treasury Secretary Morgenthau about the on-going effort. The Vaad had borrowed nearly $1 million in ransom money from the Joint — but it had to be cleared officially before the Joint would permit its use. The government's position, however, was clear and was simply repeated by Morgenthau. "Ransom?" he retorted. "Exchange? We cannot allow any transaction of this sort."

Irving Bunim translated Morgenthau's statement to Rabbi Kotler, who naturally became upset. "Does the Secretary feel," Rabbi Kotler said angrily, "that perhaps he would lose his position? Then tell Mr. Morgenthau that the life of one solitary Jew is worth more than all the positions in Washington."

Morgenthau, of course, felt Rabbi Kotler's anger, and pushed Mr. Bunim for a translation. "Tell the rabbi," the Secretary responded, speaking to his aide but facing Rabbi Kotler, "I am a Jew and I am willing not only to give up my position but my life to save my people." With his characteristic acumen, then, the rabbi's harsh words got the desired results and as we have seen, Morgenthau eventually approved the license for sending the million dollars.[10]

RABBI KOTLER'S EFFORTS WERE THOROUGH and unstinting, as in the case of the several thousand Polish yeshivah people who, after

Intellect and Emotion

hard labor in Siberia, were allowed in 1942 to go to Samarkand and Tashkent in Central Russia. It was Rabbi Kotler who, despite an eighty-percent loss in buying power on the exchange by the Russians of such monies, insisted that American relief funds be sent directly and immediately to those needy Jews. Rabbi Kotler was not concerned that a high percentage of the money would be lost through the unfair fiscal policies of the Soviet Union. He felt that it was important to save Jewish lives and get *something* to desperately needy Jews until slower-traveling packages could arrive. In this action, and in all others, he was a unique combination of intellect and emotion, of pragmatic, concerned action for the benefit of Torah and *Klal Yisroel.*

F. IRVING BUNIM AND THE VAAD HATZALAH:
An Autobiographical Retrospect[1]

MY INVOLVEMENT WITH RESCUE began as early as 1936, when the impending doom portended by events in Europe spurred some in the Orthodox Jewish community into action. Throughout Jewish religious circles, tremendous efforts were undertaken to obtain affidavits for European Jews to immigrate to America. Unfortunately, the immigration laws were such as to make it very difficult for us to bring our brethren into the United States. There were strict racist-inspired quotas governing the numbers of each nationality, and their percentages were based on how many members were in the United States in 1900. Thus, Eastern European Jews had a very tiny quota.

Initial Involvement — Affidavits

"Nevertheless, undaunted, we did the best we could, getting affidavits of support for as many Jews as possible. Movements were started in Young Israel and other Orthodox organizations to obtain support for more of these affidavits and many were secured. I personally made out several hundred of these affidavits, committing myself to the fact that these people would be supported. Sometimes, we had to deposit $600 per person in escrow to prove to the government that we had cash available in case it should be needed.

"Of course, since every action we took could have an effect on the saving of a life, we had an obligation to use every means — financial, the use of political influence, and even what would otherwise be duplicity — in our sacred work.

"A STRIKING EXAMPLE OF THE NEED, in those fateful days, to take a strong, even obstinate stand on the side of saving lives is

The Story of Rabbi Farber
illustrated by the story of Rabbi Joseph Farber. The founder of *Yeshivat Heichal Hatalmud* in Tel Aviv, Rabbi Farber, who had previously been a *rosh* [dean of] *Yeshivah* in Slobodka, was in America in 1939 to collect funds for his institution. He had forgotten to obtain a return visa to Palestine, and under British law one had to show that he was a capitalist with at least a $5,000 bank account, in order to enter on a "Capitalist" Certificate. I made a deposit in a savings account in Rabbi Farber's name, and he took the bankbook to the British consul. The fact of the money before his eyes was not sufficient to the consul, and he demanded, 'Where did you get this money?' Rabbi Farber, keeping his wits about him, replied, 'I have received this from Irving Bunim through a business transaction.' The consul thereupon demanded to see the proof of the transaction in the form of business papers.

"Luckily, my former partner, Isidor Farber, had just gone to *Eretz Israel*, leaving with me some contracts I had made out to him. The Consul did not realize that Joseph Farber was not Isidor Farber and accepted the business papers as they were. According to procedure, he then sent him to the Zionist office at 105 Fifth Avenue to get a slip of paper authorizing his visa [certificate].

"At this office, Rabbi Farber met Dr. [Joseph] Tenenbaum, a major Zionist leader, who was rather surprised that a rabbi would indeed have such a huge sum as $5,000. The rabbi, assuming that a representative of such an office would be sympathetic to such a harmless ruse in the face of dire need, told Dr. Tenenbaum the truth about our deception. Dr. Tenenbaum was enraged at this revelation and declared self-righteously, 'This is the government — we do not allow such phony tricks. You are not getting a visa.'[37]

"Rabbi Farber came back to me crying. His family was in Poland, he had to go to *Eretz Yisroel* to work on getting them out. Hitler was about to enter Poland and his efforts were their only hope. At this grave news, I decided that immediate drastic action had to be taken. I called up Leo Gelman (president of Mizrachi), Ephraim Kaplan (a famous writer on the *Jewish Morning Journal*), and A.

Goldberg (a leading Zionist) and invited them for supper that Thursday night.

"When we were all gathered together, I told them with the utmost conviction, 'Tomorrow, Friday, at 12 noon, I am going to the Zionist office at 105 Fifth Avenue, which has a large window on the first floor. I will have a stone in my pocket, and if Rabbi Farber has not received his visa I will break that window.' Gelman asked me if I was really serious, and I replied with gravity, 'I swear by my share in *Olam Haba* (the World to Come).' They all asked pointedly, 'But what will you accomplish?' To which I replied, 'Beware, you are dealing with a crazy man. The police will undoubtedly come to arrest me and then I will tell them exactly why I was compelled to break that window. American Jewry will then rise up in revulsion and revolt against you.' And so I ended my emotional speech and they left.

"At 12 noon that Friday, Rabbi Farber called me, his very tone communicating joy. 'Mr. Bunim, *Mazel Tov*.' he declared, 'they gave me my visa and now I can go to Eretz Israel and get my family out of Poland. He left me that very Sunday and thank G-d met his family in Paris and succeeded in bringing them all to *Eretz Yisroel*.

"AFTER THE WAR, IN 1945, a new period and aspect of rescue began, as we turned out attention to getting the Jews we had earlier

From Russia to Kobe to Shanghai to ...

saved from Russia out of Shanghai, where they had been sent via Kobe, Japan.[2] The questions and problems were once again international, and Rabbi Kotler, Rabbi Kalmanowitz and I went to Dean Acheson, then Secretary of State, and told him the entire story of our plight. We explained to him that our schools in America had no teachers, our synagogues had no rabbis, and the Jewish holidays were approaching in the most bleak and somber of ways to the Jewish people.

"We cried and pleaded; we begged and cajoled. 'If you grant us visas for these 600 people,' we told the Secretary, 'your name will be written in letters of gold in Jewish history.' We explained that in Jewish tradition, scholars and rabbis are the lifeblood of the nation, and we told him of the saying of our sages *(Mechilta: Yisro)*: 'Moses was as important, by himself, as all the 600,000 men who went out of Egypt with him.' We continued our plea, 'Imagine, Mr. Secretary, how valuable these men are to us. They will help to bring G-d's word to this country.'

"The Secretary of State then called in his assistant, Cyrus

Vance (later Secretary of State under President Carter), and ordered him, 'Forget the red tape. Get boats, get secretarial help, get whatever you need, but get them out fast. Skip the physical exams and spare no effort!' This they did, and many prominent rabbis came here from Shanghai as a result of that fateful meeting.

"A FASCINATING VIGNETTE — a glimpse into the mind of a *gadol*, a true sage of Israel — came to light following that meeting. As **To Avoid** Chairman of the Board of the Rescue Committee, I **Suspicion** was prepared at that time to send the money needed by cable to bring over our brethren in Shanghai. Suddenly, the secretary made me wait. About ten minutes later, he allowed me to proceed. 'What happened?' I asked, not able to imagine what had delayed the cable, since all was in order. 'Rabbi Kotler,' he replied, 'was holding it back. There is a girl named Rischel among the evacuees, and the rabbi believes she will become his son's bride. He did not want it to appear in any way as if she was receiving special treatment, so he paid her fees himself and only then allowed the cable to go out.'

"Such was the dedication and self-sacrifice of those giants of Torah and goodness — Rabbi Aaron Kotler, Rabbi Eliezer Silver, Rabbi Mordechai Gordon, Rabbi Abraham Kalmanowitz, Rabbi Mendel Zaks and others. They not only raised the funds so crucial to Vaad Hatzalah, but also infused hope and life into the weary pulse of the Jewish nation.

"TOWARD THE END OF THE WAR, when we completed the well-known Musy ransom deal with Himmler to free over 1,200 Jews **The Bridge** from Theresienstadt concentration camp, a new **is Burning** roadblock appeared. It seems that at that point [end of 1944, beginning of 1945] Switzerland was willing to accept as many Jews as we could send them. The head of the government even came to greet the first transport from Theresienstadt and was very sympathetic. Unfortunately, from a practical standpoint, there was not much they could do because they did not have enough food to go around.

"Realizing the extreme urgency of every moment, we ran to various people and agencies and appealed to anyone with any power at all. William O'Dwyer, then head of the War Refugee Board [succeeding John Pehle] and later Mayor of the City of New York, was very helpful and introduced us to Governor Herbert Lehman, who was also the head of the UNRRA (United Nations Relief and

Rehabilitation Administration). Governor Lehman was very moved by our appeals and cried genuinely. However, he too felt that he could do nothing because Switzerland was not a member of the United Nations.

"Rebuffed at every turn, I went to Abraham Feller, legal advisor to Governor Lehman, and beseeched him, 'The Brooklyn Bridge is burning. Manhattan says, 'Let Brooklyn save it''; Brooklyn says, ''Let Manhattan save it.'' Meanwhile the bridge is burning down.' My words seemed to have an effect, and by 11 a.m. the next morning Mr. Feller had arranged everything.

"EVEN AFTER THE WAR, THERE WERE MANY problems involving rescue. In Prague, for example, where Vaad Hatzalah was directed **300** by Rabbi Victor Vorhand, three hundred **"Convention"** Jewish men were stranded and wanted to get **Delegates** out. A ruse was devised in order to save their lives, by setting up a convention of Agudath Israel, to be held in the United States with the three hundred men as delegates. Mr. Haring wanted to know why we had so many delegates from one city, but we explained that in actuality they were from Rumania, Poland, Hungary, and other places.

"Of course, the unfortunate souls overstayed their official welcome and had to leave. We sent to the head of the Immigration Department, to try to get them permanent visas. I showed him the list of people and a Hebrew book.

"I began to plead for the immigrants with the knowledge that the United States at that time was very worried about the slow spread of communism. 'These people, I began, have written an entire book explicating the Tenth Commandment — Thou Shalt Not Covet. The essence of this commandment is a true understanding of the laws of personal rights and property.' I used the commentary of Ibn Ezra, 'The wording of the Commandment is 'Thou shalt not covet the next man's house, his wife, and his property.' Just as a pauper would not think of marrying a princess since she is so far beyond his reach, so must man consider anything which belongs to his neighbor far beyond his reach, so that he will not even consider or concern himself with obtaining it.'

"THESE INCIDENTS ILLUSTRATE THE FACT that literally a handful of dedicated people were able to accomplish what might

A Handful of Dedicated People normally have needed a staff of hundreds of thousands. If it were not for these wonderful people, very little would have been accomplished. Our formal facilities at Vaad Hatzalah were minimal, with a $250-a-month office at 132 Nassau Street. In 1944, at the height of our activities, our entire budget was $1,000 per week. Rabbi Karlinsky, the head man, was getting $150, Pinchas Shoen $125, and Lee Stein $110; plus two salaried secretaries. The rest of the work was done by volunteers."

❦   ❦   ❦

PERHAPS A MOST FITTING TRIBUTE to Vaad Hatzalah — and all the Orthodox rescue personalities as well — is found in the words of **Ingenuity** John Pehle, head of the War Refugee Board. After the war he assessed the role of Vaad Hatzalah in words that until now have not found an echo in the writing of Holocaust historians. This holds doubly true for some big "authorities" who pooh-poohed the very idea of the special rescue efforts by individuals such as Rabbi Kalmanowitz and others.

Pehle wrote:

> The Vaad Hatzalah may not have had available to it the largest sums for rescue and relief; it may not have had the greatest impact on public opinion; but for imaginative and constructive ideas, for courageous programs, for ingenuity and singleness of purpose, your organization need bow to none. General Eisenhower's stern warning to the German people on his entry onto German soil not to molest those in concentration camps had its origin in a suggestion made by you. Your persistent efforts to bring relief to the refugee group in Shanghai, to the victims of oppression in Slovakia, Poland, Hungary and elsewhere testify to the fervor with which you fought to save precious lives. Under almost insurmountable difficulties you devised a program to finance underground means of bringing endangered Jews from Poland across the Carpathians to the safety that Hungary afforded early in 1944. Significantly enough, this program was approved by this Government on January 22, 1944, the very day that the late President Roosevelt created the War Refugee Board. Later, when Hungary was occupied by the Germans, your plans and projects were directed to securing safer places of refuge. Your assistance reached deep into Bohemia itself and brought release from Theresienstadt to many.[3]

The Vaad had good lineage. It was inspired by Rabbi Chaim

Ozer Grodzenski, of Vilna; was founded by his student, Rabbi Eliezer Silver, along with members of Agudas Horabonim and was led by deans of several prominent yeshivos. In September 1939, immediately after the Nazi invasion of Poland, a meeting of the Union of Orthodox Rabbis formally took up the issue of the future ⁓f the yeshivah students who had fled to Vilna, in Lithuania.[13] Rabbi ⁓⁓ver was joined at the helm of Vaad Hatzalah by Rabbi Abraham N⁓ ⁓anowitz in 1940 and Rabbi Aaron Kotler in mid-1941. Under their joint leadership, the Vaad expanded greatly — eventually increasing its scope of rescue from Torah scholars to all of European Jewry. Simply stated, Vaad Hatzalah was the second half of the Orthodox rescue team.

G. ELIMELECH "MIKE" TRESS
AND THE ZEIREI AGUDATH ISRAEL GROUP[1]

THE ZEIREI AGUDATH ISRAEL youth organization played a major role in American rescue operations. The twenty-six-year old **Young Volunteers** American-born Elimelech Tress, known to all as "Mike," assumed its leadership in 1937, and led a group of young volunteers in a tireless rescue campaign throughout the war years. While there is still no formal history of those successful rescue activities, Dr. Gershon Kranzler,[2] one of Tress' young followers during those years, has written a detailed, highly personal remembrance from that period of Mike Tress from which we cite the following few passages:

THROUGHOUT THE PERIOD OF 1938 until Pearl Harbor in December 1941, Mike Tress and his Zeirei (youth) group worked virtually **Mike's** without stop, using hard-won visas and affidavits to save Jews. Along the way, he had to learn the legal **Mentors** technicalities of immigration procedures, and had to form a reliable network of political allies. He didn't do it alone — few do, of course — and Tress was fortunate enough to learn from two men. The first was Dr. Leo Jung, rabbi of Manhattan's West Side Jewish Center since 1921.[3]

The second was Meir Shenkolewski, a long-time member of the World Agudah executive board who had settled in the United States in the early 1930's. After working for some time with Rabbi Jung on the immmigration problem, Shenkolewski made the first of what turned out to be a number of highly important political contacts in Washington, that of James McDonald, an energetic philo-Semite and a former League of Nations High Commissioner for Refugees. In due course, these highly important contacts were made available to Tress and Rabbi Kalmanowitz.[4]

There were several other figures who helped transform Tress, an American-born youth leader, into one of the foremost catalysts for Orthodox relief and rescue efforts in Europe, and one of the major architects of Agudath Israel. Certainly to be counted prominently on the list were Rabbi Gedaliah Schorr, soon to be named dean of the Mesivta Torah Vodaath, and a spiritual guide to Zeirei and the Agudah itself. In 1938, when the rescue efforts began in earnest, Rabbi Schorr had just returned from a year's study with Rabbi Aaron Kotler in Kletzk, Poland, and his dedication to help other Jews inspired Tress and countless others ...

Yet perhaps a stronger and more pervasive influence came from the world-renowned sage, Rabbi Elchonon Wasserman, whose extended 1938-1939 visit on behalf of his yeshivah in Baranovich, Poland, gave many young men both the direction and incentive toward a lifetime of service for the Jewish community.

... In 1938, at the Stoliner Rebbe's home on Rodney Street in Williamsburg ... Rabbi Elchonon Wasserman came to visit us on urgent business. It was he who started us off, comforted us, encouraged us, warned us of the great challenges ahead, gave us his blessing. Afterwards, we accompanied him to the boat on which he set sail for the long journey back to his yeshivah in Poland, never to return ... Reb Elchonon blessed us and told Mike that the fate of the Torah world was in his hands ...

Rabbi Shraga Feivel Mendlowitz, dean of Torah Vodaath and pioneer of Torah education in the United States, also inspired Tress and others to work for the greater good of the Jewish community. Moreover, Rabbi Mendlowitz also introduced Tress to his yeshivah's financial supporters, who proved to be invaluable in helping to perform the *mitzvah* of rescue ...

Another ... influence was a young Agudist named David Turkel, who came as an eyewitness from Vienna. He served as a personal emissary of Rabbi Yaakov Teitelbaum, and detailed the increasingly worsening conditions for Jews under the new Nazi rule.[5]

THE ZEIREI GROUP OPERATED out of a "dusty, dingy, but grand old building at 616 Bedford Avenue in the heart of Williamsburg,"

616 Bedford Avenue which was even then a major Orthodox community in Brooklyn.

Tress set up the initial operation by donating his own desk and typewriter. The operation grew rapidly to encompass a staff of almost fifty, busy with rescue work in those badly overcrowded quarters. The Zeirei volunteers begged and borrowed the money to keep the operation going, to come up with the modest salaries for the secretaries, and postage to send thousands of air-mail letters around the world which were vital to the rescue effort. Tress gave up a business career to devote full time to the rescue work. He even spent his own savings and sold his stocks in order to finance Zeirei rescue operations.

Gershon Kranzler recounts many touching personal examples of those hectic days. He describes how these mostly teenage Zeirei volunteers, from the Jewish neighborhoods of the Bronx, Brownsville and the Lower East Side, learned quickly "to become public speakers, experts on affidavits and international diplomatic regulations." They canvassed friends, business associates, customers, suppliers and entire neighborhoods to provide needed goods and services and lifesaving contributions. They also spread the terrible truth about the relentless mass murder of European Jewry.

The group succeeded despite all obstacles in bringing many European Jews to the United States. Once they arrived, the Zeirei group helped provide for their physical, spiritual, and financial needs. After Tress married, it was not uncommon for ten or more newly arrived immigrants to eat in his home. Tress eventually established a separate department in the organization to set up many of these new immigrants in their own businesses. For others, the group arranged for lodging complete with borrowed or donated furniture, linens, pots and pans. The volunteers often dug into their own pockets to provide food, clothes and medicine. They arranged for the younger immigrants to continue their interrupted yeshivah educations, and jobs for the older ones.

In emotional terms, Kranzler reminisced about one refugee from Shanghai, who acknowledged Mike's rescue efforts after the war.

> Remember the evening you and a group of your *chaverim* each one a Torah scholar, arrived in the U.S.? You came to our downtown office, into the midst of an executive meeting, threw down your raincoat and ran over to the smiling young man pointed out to you as Mike Tress. Tears in your gentle eyes, you embraced him, then each one of us. Then you made a brief but memorable speech on behalf of your many rescued *chaverim*, describing the love of one's fellow Jew and kindness of the group of young men that Mike headed.

Many of these immigrants have gone on to great success and prominence in the Orthodox community today, but, according to Gershon Kranzler, they all fondly recall the selfless assistance provided by Tress and his volunteers. Some, in utter desperation, successfully turned to Tress' group for help to save family and loved ones still trapped in Europe. In a number of cases Zeirei succeeded when all other rescue attempts failed.

Tress and his group nursed the new arrivals back to health when they were sick, and provided them with the bare necessities of life until they could establish themselves in their new country. Tress and other volunteers opened their homes and their hearts to the immigrants who "arrived strangers in a new and hostile world, hurt, lonely, full of traumas that no psychiatrist could cure."

THE ZEIREI GROUP DEVELOPED its own rescue specialists. Before Pearl Harbor, Frank Newman traveled to Kobe, Japan, to arrange

Mike's "Chaverim" visas and transportation for hundreds of escaped Lithuanian Torah scholars. Rabbi Perr of Jamaica, Queens, compiled lists of Torah scholars to be submitted to the U.S. State Department for Emergency Visitor Visas, or to Latin American diplomats for end visas to their countries.

At first it was just Mike and the *chaverim*. But gradually Mike widened the circle of those who worked for him and for whom he worked. Soon that circle was even to include Hassidic *rebbes*: the sainted Boyaner, the Kapitshenitzer, the old and the young Novominsker, the Modzitzer, the Stropkover — from the least known to the most famous, the Satmarer and the Lubavitcher — they all worked with Mike and treated him with a respect they accorded to few "Amerikaners ..."

The most famous names of the yeshivah world were Mike's most intimate co-workers: Horav Aaron Kotler, Horav Reuven Grozovsky, Horav Elya Meir Bloch, Horav Motel Katz, Horav Kalmanowitz ...

There was Rabbi Eliezer Silver, who commuted by plane from one corner of the world to the next to help organize our rescue work. There was Mr. Feivel Mendlowitz, the great mentor and molder of generations of Torah scholars, who opened for us the doors to outstanding community leaders who were his personal *chassidim*.

All were spurred on to great efforts by the reports from Europe. One example was a stirring speech by Rav Schorr one Saturday morning early in 1944 at the Zeirei synagogue at 616 Bedford Avenue.

A cable [from Rabbi Weissmandl] had arrived just before the reading of the *haftorah;* * he stepped in front of the *bimah*** and beat his fist on it. With tears streaming down his face — which caused tears to stream down our own faces ... he cried: "How dare we follow our own personal pursuits at a time like this? Where is your conscience? Jewish lives can be bought for money, and you think of your jobs, careers? You have the heart to sit and learn when every moment it may be too late?"

That was all we needed. At Rav Schorr's and Mike's appeal, yeshivos, day schools for boys and girls everywhere were closed. Some of these youngsters manned the telephones for seventy-two hours. Others organized hundreds of teams of boys who searched the streets for money with spread-out tablecloths, not mere *pushkes*. The subways, apartment houses and housing projects resounded with the music of the appeals our children made everywhere. They attended every meeting of any Jewish organization, from the tip of the Lower East Side to Washington Heights and the Bronx, in a ceaseless effort to raise ever-growing amounts.

---

* The section from the Prophets read in conjunction with the weekly portion of the Torah.

** The platform from which the Torah was read.

THE MANY SUBSTANTIAL RESCUE accomplishments of Tress and his dedicated volunteers contrasts vividly with the paralysis and **Accomplishments vs. Paralysis** timidity of the established international Jewish rescue and relief agencies, and the secular leadership of the era. These rich and powerful interests allowed themselves to be handcuffed by government regulations and bureaucrats, and sidetracked by partisan political considerations, while the singleminded efforts of a relative handful led by Tress and the Vaad Hatzalah saved many thousands by any means available.

The postwar era did not abate Mike's efforts on behalf of rescue or work for the *Klal*, at first in the DP camps, which he personally visited and helped to liquidate, as well as the assistance he provided for the refugees from the Hungarian Revolution of 1956 and the children from North Africa he helped bring over a few years later.

In the process of establishing an independent role for Zeirei (later a combined Agudah-Zeirei) in the arena of rescue, Tress cooperated with, but was no longer dependent upon, the powerful secular Jewish Establishment. As a result, he willy-nilly lay the groundwork not merely for a strong and dynamic postwar Agudath Israel, but he became simultaneously an important catalyst for the emergence of a strong, and even militant postwar Orthodoxy.

H. MOREINU YAAKOV (JACOB) ROSENHEIM

ONE OF THE FOUNDERS AND PRESIDENT of World Agudath
Israel, Jacob Rosenheim came in 1941 from England to the United

**Focal Point
of Rescue
Communication**

States, and helped to set up the offices of
the Agudath Israel World Organization an
additional arm of the Orthodox group. Not
only did Rosenheim provide much
experience and guidance in dealing with national figures and
organizations, he also served as a focal point for much of the rescue
cables coming in from Switzerland via the Polish diplomatic cable.
Rosenheim also served as a tireless liaison with other American-
Jewish groups, and brought to the table many of the rescue activities
he had worked on in Great Britain.

One of Orthodox Jewry's leading spokesmen since his election
as president of World Agudath Israel in 1923, Yaakov Rosenheim
continued this role during the Holocaust. At first he helped bring
German-Jewish refugees to England where he had fled in 1935,
working very closely with Harry A. Goodman, Secretary of World
Agudah, and Rabbi Solomon Schonfeld, the founder and head of
the Chief Rabbi's Religious Emergency Council. Rosenheim and
Goodman were both members of Rabbi Schonfeld's Adas
Synagogue in London's Stamford Hill.

Rosenheim had a direct hand in the creation of the Chief
Rabbi's Religious Emergency Council in 1938, which was an

effective rescue body before, during and after the war (see Chap. 10B) as well as the British Agudah, under Harry Goodman, and its rescue efforts within the Joint Jewish Committee in London.

When Rosenheim and his family arrived in the United States, he continued his rescue efforts and became spokesman for a growing American-Orthodox Jewry. Among the first problems he tackled was the dangerous practice of governments of lumping together "enemy aliens," i.e., non-Jewish citizens of Germany and later Japan, with "refugees from Hitler with German passports." In England, as Rosenheim knew, thousands of Jewish refugees were interned on the Isle of Man or sent to camps in Australia and Canada. As usual, where the State Department was not too sympathetic, Attorney General Biddle was more understanding. Fortunately, this problem never became a major one for Jews in the United States, but Rosenheim worked hard for those German and Austrian Jews from England who had been deported to Canada. Most of them were eventually released.[1] As soon as the early deportations of Jews from Germany and Austria to Poland began in November 1941, Rosenheim pushed for a plan that would enable thousands of Jews from these lands to leave Europe and stay on Ellis Island, where they would be held while their individual cases were processed. Unfortunately, America's entry into World War II the very next month sealed this small escape hatch. At the same time, Rosenheim fought to place an Orthodox Jew in the Polish Government-in-Exile in London, but the Socialist Bundists were too influential, and their man, Shmuel Zygelbojm, was selected instead. (Zygelbojm later committed suicide in the hope of drawing the world's attention to the annihilation of Polish Jewry.) In all his work, particularly since he was already in his seventies when he arrived in the United States, Rosenheim had the assistance of Dr. Isaac Lewin.

ROSENHEIM'S MOST IMPORTANT SINGLE rescue effort ended in failure. This attempt remained virtually unknown until Dr. Lewin

Dr. Isaac Lewin made historians aware of it. As we have seen (Chap. 7B), this involved the Sternbuch cable of September 3, 1942, which was sent to Rosenheim via the secret Polish pouch. In stark contrast to Stephen S. Wise, who sought to avoid "bothering" President Roosevelt with the Jewish tragedy, Rosenheim that same day sent a telegram to the President, along with the Sternbuch cable, concluding with the plea, "I dare in the name of World Orthodox Jewry propose for consideration apart from eventual other steps the arrangement by American initiative of a joint intervention of all the neutral states in Europe and America expressing their deep moral indignation."

We know now, through Dr. Lewin, who was then the representative of the Orthodox to the Polish Government-in-Exile in the United States that Roosevelt took no action. It took him three weeks before he even forwarded the cable to the State Department, and he never even responded to Rosenheim's plea.[2] As we have pointed out elsewhere, this seeming failure still produced a number of successes.

It was Rosenheim and Rabbi Kalmanowitz who sought to bring about unity among American-Jewish organizations after the pressure brought on Wise on Sept. 4, 1942. When later, Wise unilaterally dissolved the ad hoc Committee for European Jews, following his meeting with President Roosevelt on Dec. 2, 1942, it was Rosenheim who tried to keep at least the various Orthodox groups together to work on rescue independently. To this end he organized the *Vaad LePikuach Nefesh.* Although it was shortlived, the group sent a number of rescue proposals and met with Secretary of State Cordell Hull as well as the papal nuncio.

WHEN THE JOINT EMERGENCY Committee was formed in the spring of 1943, it was Rosenheim who got the Agudah and Vaad

Joining
Forces

Hatzalah to become active members.

In January 1943 Rosenheim, through his representative, Dr. Lewin, urged the Zionists' Pittsburgh Conference to put rescue on the agenda, "urging especially the moral duty not to forget imminent and present dangers for Jewish life and existence in Europe, for the sake of later concerns after the war."[3]

At Pittsburgh, Rosenheim and Lewin also pressed for compromises in language on the goals of the forthcoming American Jewish Conference, so that the non-Zionist American Jewish Committee and the socialist Jewish Labor Committee would be willing to participate. On the other hand, when the promises that had been made to Agudath Israel and Vaad Hatzalah for equal representation at this conference with the "big four" (the American Jewish Congress, the B'nai Brith, the American Jewish Committee, and the Jewish Labor Committee) were broken and they were assigned one-quarter as many seats, he pulled both groups out.[4]

In mid-1943, Rosenheim suggested that propaganda leaflets be dropped over Germany, informing the German people of the shameful acts the Nazi regime was perpetrating against their country, and their good name. At the very least, the Germans should not later claim "that they did not know anything." He wrote the text in a polished German. It was to have been signed by "the Germans in America." Dr. Lewin delivered Rosenheim's appeal to the State Department. In the Department's response, Mr. K. Travers, Chief of the Visa Division, told Lewin "that there were reservations against 'any class appeal'* along the line suggested ..."

Of greater practical import was Rosenheim's role in forging an independent rescue line for the Orthodox by the end of 1943. For a full year, ever since the arrival of the Sternbuch cable in the fall of 1942, Rosenheim and the *roshei yeshivah* in the Vaad Hatzalah had sought the unity of all of American Jewry for rescue. The relative helplessness of the Orthodox was as much a reason for that quest as the historic Jewish imperative of cooperation for the safety of the *Klal.*

Only after the Joint Emergency Committee was dissolved by Wise in the fall of 1943, and after Wise had tried to place any rescue efforts under the umbrella of the American Jewish Conference, where he could control them, did Rosenheim and the others come to realize that "thus ended the tragic story of American-Jewish cooperation in the matter of life-rescue for European Jewry."5

ONLY THEN, UNDER THE UNREMITTING pressure of the Weissmandl cables, which urged the use of the age-old methods of

Going it Alone ransom and bribery, and the realization that they were heading in the wrong direction — and that Zionist influence had succeeded in making a postwar Jewish state rather than rescue the top priority for American Jewry — did Rosenheim persuade the *roshei yeshivah* to go it alone.

Rosenheim now realized that they should have done this much earlier. "Our contacts ... with the State Department in Washington had to be more numerous than before ... No formal difficulties arose and the authority of our own organization to speak in the name of Orthodox Jewry all over the world was in no case challenged or denied."6

By January 1944, the Agudah was able to collect some $85,000 in nickels and dollars from private individuals, in homes and factories, which was sent to Sternbuch, "for the purpose of the European rescue work." In the next few months, an additional

---

* In the climate of opinion in the early 1940's, this phrase was a buzzword for singling out Jews for special treatment.

$50,000 was collected by Zeirei and World Agudah.[7]

However deficient were the results compared with the need — when millions were required to save hundreds of thousands in Slovakia, Rumania, Poland, and later Hungary — it was a major achievement for the small Orthodox community when compared with the potential of the other Jewish organizations. And despite his age and frailty, Rosenheim was involved in almost every rescue effort by Agudah and Vaad Hatzalah.

In January 1944 Rosenheim was responsible for having Yaakov Griffel made an official representative of the War Refugee Board in Istanbul along with Dr. Joseph Klarman and Ludwig (Lajos) Kastner. This arrangement made it possible for the Vaad and Agudah to use the free U.S. cables for sending funds and messages. It also gave Griffel greater prestige and freedom of action in his rescue work within the Vaad Hahatzalah of the Jewish Agency in Istanbul, which was controlled by the socialists who frequently hampered his rescue efforts.[8]

Rosenheim kept in close touch with Sternbuch in Switzerland and Griffel in Istanbul. Sternbuch frequently sent Rosenheim copies of his cables and letters to Vaad Hatzalah and kept him informed of Agudah matters in Switzerland. It was one of Sternbuch's cables to Rosenheim that prompted him with Rabbi Kalmanowitz to pressure the War Refugee Board and the State Department to bomb the rail lines to Auschwitz.[9]

ONE OF ROSENHEIM'S RESCUE EFFORTS in the Balkans involved obtaining the help of Laurence A. Steinhardt, the American **Ambassador** Ambassador to Turkey. At that time, in the fall **Laurence** of 1943, before the creation of the War **A. Steinhardt** Refugee Board, there was an opportunity for rescue of Jews from Poland who fled to Hungary and Rumania with Palestine Certificates and had the opportunity to get to Palestine via Turkey. At the time Turkey was not inclined to grant transit-visas to those Jews in occupied countries with Certificates who might or might not ever get to Palestine. Steinhardt's help was necessary to pressure Turkey to approve such measures.

It was Yom Kippur eve. Steinhardt had just returned to the U.S. from Ankara, Turkey, and Rosenheim had informed him that he would like to meet with him in order to discuss the refugee situation in the Balkans. The ambassador himself came to Rosenheim's apartment in midtown Manhattan which also housed the office of World Agudath Israel, and for several hours discussed the crucial issues at a meeting attended by Yaakov Rosenheim, Rabbi Dr. Leo Jung and Dr. Isaac Lewin. The great fear, as Dr. Lewin pointed out, was the fact that in any of the steps there would have to be some illegal operations, such as smuggling across borders, bribing officials, falsifying documents, sending American dollars into Nazi-occupied areas, etc. (Some of these, or at least aspects of these, were tolerated after the creation of the War Refugee Board in January 1944. This, however, was still in September 1943.)

To the pleasant surprise of the Agudah delegation, the American ambassador, who a few years earlier had been seen as highly assimilationist and a legalist with an anti-East European bias, now came to declare openly: "There is no law when it comes to rescue people. I personally stood by the Bulgarian border and accepted illegally smuggled Jewish children." In fact, this highly unexpected response left every one speechless, in view of the standard responses from Washington and what they expected from him.[10]

To the end of his life in 1965, Rosenheim continued to influence the perspectives of Agudath Israel onto the broader global needs of Klal Yisrael.

I. SANCTUARY U.S.A: LOUIS SEPTIMUS AND THE CAMP AT OSWEGO, N.Y.[1]

THE AMERICAN DETENTION CENTER for Jewish refugees was located at an abandoned army camp (Fort Ontario) near Oswego,

The American Detention Center

N.Y., a town on Lake Ontario 35 miles northwest of Syracuse. From the summer of 1944 on, it provided a temporary home for 982 non-quota survivors who had found themselves stranded in Allied-occupied Italy during the war. Mussolini had just fallen, and Jewish leaders in Rome got word to Agudath Israel that it was hazardous for them to remain. They could not return to their former homes and had no other place to go to. Nevertheless, it was imperative that they leave Rome immediately. Anarchy reigned, there was a shortage of food and the Italians were certainly not looking for another thousand mouths to feed.

Although Agudath Israel, with extremely limited resources, had been focusing on saving the neglected yeshivah communities, it contacted Presidential aides about the matter. A plan was formulated to send a warship to Italy to pick up the refugees; they would be brought to the U.S. ostensibly as prisoners of war — thus getting around the problem of quotas. Dr. Ruth Gruber, secretary to Harold Ickes, FDR's Secretary of the Interior, was chosen to accompany them, because as a speaker of many languages she would be able to communicate with them. Her biggest problem turned out to be persuading the refugees to board the ship; they tended to think it was just another trick of Hitler's ego to get them to the gas chambers. But with the help of Rabbi Moshe Tchechevel, the religious leader of the group, they were convinced that they were in friendly hands, and they came to the U.S. on the warship.[2]

Mike Tress handled communications for the project and did his best to keep the matter quiet, reasoning that if it were made public many complaints about non-quota entrance would follow — especially since Jews were concerned. For a month or so it was a well-kept secret. But then other Jewish organizations, without taking the trouble to consult with the organizations that had carried out this phenomenal feat of rescue, took steps that led to the operation being made public; soon the hush-hush operation became known and the remote corner of northern New York State swarmed with reporters and photographers. This was most tragic, for the Agudah had been assured that if the matter was kept quiet other such missions could be performed — with the cooperation of the government. But as it was, this first was also the last. No implication is being suggested here that the damage was caused maliciously. But to those who might have been rescued and weren't the effect was exactly the same as if it had been.

IN ADDITION TO HELPING ORCHESTRATE the rescue operation, Agudah and Young Israel saw to the religious needs of the new

Religious Needs of the Refugees community of Jews for the two years it was in existence. When weddings were celebrated, Dr. Isaac Lewin and I, who were in charge of administering the religious program, saw to it that there was a proper *chupah* and *kiddushin* (religious marriage); if there was a *bris* (circumcision), a *mohel* (ritual circumcisor) would be sent. A *mikvah* (ritualarium) was built with the cooperation of the field director, who was not Jewish.

We were warned that the local population of Oswego might not be friendly to Jewish refugees and we were therefore urged to buy all our supplies locally in order to build up good will with the townspeople. Therefore, even if the stores of Oswego did not have certain articles we needed, we placed our orders through them and paid whatever price they asked. The local residents soon began to visit the camp and chatted with the inhabitants through the fences and wires. We had been successful, it seemed, in dispelling their fear of "the aliens."

Since Fort Ontario was officially a prisoner-of-war camp, it was the government, of course, and not the Agudah, that was in charge of running it. Yet we, the Agudah, acted as the unofficial troubleshooters; when the government had a problem with the refugees we were immediately called in. There was, for instance, the matter of *kashrus* observance. Initially, only about twenty or so newcomers would eat the kosher food that was given them — the rest could not believe that, after the unspeakable horrors they had lived through, they would come to a place, be given any kind of food, let alone kosher. It took a lot of convincing on our part, but finally we gained their trust and they ate. At first, the Agudah paid for the special food; later the government assumed the cost.

THEN THERE WERE ARGUMENTS by the secularist Jewish organizations about education in the camp. The Joint Distribution Committee and the National Council of Jewish Women became involved, taking the position that no religious education should be permitted. There were even questions as to whether the *Shabbos* should be observed and whether kosher food should be served. At the meeting with them it was proposed that a vote be taken on the matter. I explained to them that one can't vote on whether or not to maintain the Sabbath and dietary laws: "These precepts have been our holy legacy for thousands of years — they're just not negotiable. Even if the non-religious win in a vote, will the others work on *shabbos*, will they eat *treif* (non-kosher)? No. These are religious issues," I continued, "the acceptance of which is not subject to mortal whim."

Joint and NCJW against Religious Education

I was very pleasantly surprised that a Reform rabbi representing the Council of Jewish Women who had been silent up to that point got up and sided with me. He said, "Septimus is right. We cannot impose our non-religious feelings on the religious Jews. We'll have to accommodate them." That's the way it was left. Agudath Israel with the help of Young Israel, provided for Jewish education and all other religious needs; concerning these matters, both Dr. Gruber and the camp director, Joseph Smart, were most helpful and deserve our everlasting thanks.

Yet, for all the benefits we could give these poor souls, the cold fact was that the camp in Oswego was a detention center. Within, the inhabitants roamed freely, but they were not allowed to leave. Although it was not guarded by the army, it was physically enclosed, and people needed special permission to get out, even to see a doctor. It was akin to getting off a plane in a country where one has no entry permit and must therefore be confined within an enclosure. Relatives of the refugees were not permitted to come in. The only outsiders allowed in were the official representatives of the organizations involved. The refugees were still technically prisoners of war, to be detained in the camp until a decision could be made as to their fate. (Eventually, after the war, all these 'prisoners' were released and given the option of remaining in the United States and becoming American citizens — which option most, of course, exercised.)

Among my most treasured momentos was a tiny *siddur* (prayerbook) which I obtained on my first day in Oswego (which was also the refugees' first day there). In my mind it is associated with a most poignant incident. An inmate who was there with his father saw me eating a meat sandwich; we, of the Agudah, had brought our own food. When this young man told me he hadn't had a substantial meal for a very long time, I gave him sandwiches for himself and his father. He thanked me profusely for this simple gift; then, suddenly, he concealed the food inside his shirt. In response to my query as to why he felt constrained to do so, he stated simply that he thought he might otherwise be killed by the guards or even fellow inmates for the food on the way back to the barracks.

Of course, no such danger existed but the incident illustrates the terror-filled state of mind under which these wretched souls had functioned and indeed are still functioning.

Later, he brought me this little *siddur*. He had copied it all in his own handwriting. I learned that back in Europe he had become an expert at forging exit-visas for refugees. He could not only duplicate signatures but even official markings. Every visa he crafted got past the authorities. He also wrote *siddurim* for his fellow refugees, but the Nazis would confiscate and destroy them. The *siddur* he insisted I take was the last he had left.

CHAPTER TEN

Great Britain

A. INTRODUCTION

THE FACE OF THE BRITISH LION turned completely eastward when it became clear how great the island-nation's dependence was on Arab oil. Prior to that realization, the Arabs had

Into Palestine — No
Into England — Yes

been treated as a virtually captive colonial people; afterwards, however, the British worked

diligently to appease Arab interests in order to protect their own. In 1939, for example, the British published the final and what quickly became known as the infamous White Paper, a statement of the new policy limiting the maximum number of immigrants to Palestine at 75,000 for the next five years. That decision rendered the ancient Jewish homeland almost off-limits to Jews, and at a time when it was needed more-than ever before.

However, Britain was willing to admit some Jews to their own home territory. Between 1933 and 1939, for example, she accepted more than 50,000 German and Austrian Jews, a record indicating, proportionately, a more relaxed immigration policy than, for example, that of the United States.

In Britain itself, there were various aid committees and groups, most notably the Central British Fund and the Council for German Jewry, the latter with headquarters in London. Later it became necessary to address the needs of the Orthodox refugees, especially those who arrived from Vienna in 1938-39, and to this end the Central British Fund organized several children's transports out of Germany and Austria — passage that included upkeep in Great Britain. Sadly, however, the *Kultusgemeinden*, the official Jewish communal bodies in Germany and Austria that selected the children, were controlled by assimilationists or secular Zionists, so that few observant children were chosen for the transport — despite the fact that the English Jews preferred more religiously oriented children.[1]

B. HARRY GOODMAN

OFTEN THE INITIAL CONTACT for those outside Britain — either offering help or seeking it — Harry Goodman was many things.

Initial Contact British born but related to a Swiss-German family, Goodman was a Torah-observant activist, but also a successful businessman, publisher and editor of the bilingual Anglo-Yiddish Jewish newspaper, *The Jewish Week* (later called *The Jewish Post*), and the political secretary of the World Agudath Israel.

Harry Goodman was also responsible for weekly broadcasts to Jews in occupied Europe via BBC sponsored by the British Government, to provide them with encouragement and faith. He wanted them to know that they had not been forgotten by world Jewry.

Goodman, like many in the United States, sought to unite the Jews in his country for rescue work, and to utilize his extensive contacts in British Jewish organizations for help. Thus, Goodman represented the World Agudah on many bodies, including the British Board of Deputies, the British Central Fund, and the so-called Joint Committee, which was made up of the Board of Deputies, the Jewish Agency, and the World Jewish Congress.

Exerting his own influence, then, Goodman helped institute the general follow-up to the food-package program, which had ceased by the end of 1941, and other programs. Although Goodman was often aided by his assistant Meir Raphael Springer, he sometimes spoke as the lone rescue voice in a vast congress of differing interests. While Rabbi Schonfeld (see below, section B), on the other hand, worked alone and therefore needed no consensus to act, he found it extremely useful to coordinate efforts with Harry Goodman as well as with other Agudists such as Yaakov Rosenheim (see chapter 9H) and Meir Springer (see below, section D). Indeed, because of the high visibility of these rescue activists, and their powerful influence in the British government, it proved helpful for important reports to be sent from Switzerland or Istanbul to London, where there was often some help available. For example, the plan to bomb Auschwitz was circulated widely in England; a great deal of pressure — albeit unsuccessful — was exerted in many directions by Harry Goodman and Rabbi Schonfeld. It is an interesting footnote to their failure that the request is generally remembered by the secularist historians as Chaim Weizmann's alone, with both the Orthodox source and pleas forgotten.[2]

There are numerous wartime stories about Harry Goodman, far too many, in fact, to chronicle here. Yet a few show not only his seemingly limitless energy in the rescue cause, but also the veritable magic that his name could work all over Europe. There was the cryptic message scrawled in the lining of a coat belonging to a British officer freed from Vittel detention camp in France. There was also his attempt to get help from the government of the Irish Free State in the release of 100, and later 500, children from occupied Europe — and to send food parcels via the Irish Red Cross.

When George Mandel-Mantello, the Jewish Secretary-General of El Salvador, proposed in Bern, Switzerland, his plan to settle Jews from Nazi Europe in Portuguese Angola, it was Harry Goodman he contacted in hopes of obtaining official British support.

Unfortunately neither the British nor the American government supported the plan, which had the full backing of the Portuguese government.[3]

ONE DAY, LATE IN 1944, a British army officer named Rand arrived in Dover, a British port on the English channel, as one of a group of **"Save the** exchange prisoners from the Vittel detention **Remnants of** camp in France. In the lining of his coat there was scrawled in German and Hebrew a series **Polish Jewry"** of messages and names, sent out by Dr. Hillel Seidman, a historian, author and journalist, who had been a fellow inmate of the officer in Vittel. Dr. Seidman had been rescued from the Warsaw Ghetto thanks to a Paraguayan passport obtained for him by the Sternbuchs. Among the names on Dr. Seidman's list was *Mr. Harry Goodman, 27 Lordship Park, London*, scrawled in large letters. Harry Goodman was well known to European Jews. Dr. Seidman's message included, in Hebrew, "Save the remnants of Polish Jewry," it read. "Don't delay, I am a lone survivor! ... The only hope is an exchange of German nationals in the Near East and Jews with Palestinian certificates ... sister Chana Horowitz-Seidman, Tel Aviv, and my cousin Anshel Fink, Brooklyn ... Get in touch with [Dr. Abraham] Silberschein [of the World Jewish Congress in Zurich] and [Dr. Ignacy] Schwarzbart [of the Polish Government-in-Exile in London] ... [Yisroel Chaim] Eis, Zurich ... [Yitzchok] Sternbuch, St. Gallen ...

The succeeding events were all but predictable. Harry Goodman could not respond to Dr. Seidman's pleas for two good reasons. The first was that the combination of his own prominence and the cryptic messages aroused the suspicions of Scotland Yard — so much so, in fact, that he was summoned and questioned. The second was that he himself was not sufficiently powerful or influential to convince the British government to take the actions necessary to save the endangered Jews. Notably, he was unable to effect what would perhaps have been an unusual* request — the exchange of Germans for Jews. One reason given at the time was that the British held but 1,000 Germans while the Nazis held far more Jews — and British subjects.

❧ ❧ ❧

---

* There was an exchange in 1942, of some Jews from Poland for Germans in Palestine. [Ed.]

The Irish Connection

Harry Goodman writes:

> I was in Dublin from May 3rd to May 6th [1943]. I went at
> the invitation of the Irish Government in order to discuss with
> the Minister of External Affairs a number of proposals resulting
> from several conversations I had had with Mr. J.P. Dulanty,
> High Commissioner for Ireland in London.
>
> Prior to my departure, I discussed these proposals with Dr.
> Feldman and Mr. Stein [two important communal and Zionist
> leaders] and left a copy with Mr. Brotman for Dr. Selig
> Brodetsky [Chairman of the British Board of Deputies]. I saw
> Mr. J.B. Walshe, [the British] Under Secretary of State for
> External Affairs. We went through the proposals and at his
> suggestion redrafted them in the following format.
>
> 1. The granting of a limited number of visas, say 100, to
> recommended individuals in regard to whom the Irish Consuls
> in Rome, Berlin and Vichy would approach the German or
> Italian authorities for their release. As and when the persons to
> whom visas are granted emigrate elsewhere further visas of a
> similar number would be issued.
>
> 2. The granting by the Irish Government of visas to enable
> individuals to come to neutral territory in regard to whom there
> is a reasonable hope of British, American or Palestine visas
> being granted.
>
> 3. The Bulgarian Government has agreed to release some
> 5,000 Jewish children, for whom the Palestine authorities have
> granted certificates. The transport facilities by rail from Bulgaria
> to Turkey are very small; and under these conditions it appears
> doubtful whether these children can all be moved. It is
> suggested that the Government of the Irish Free State (Eire)
> charter a boat in the Mediterranean to transport the children en
> bloc from Bulgaria to a Turkish or Palestine port. It is
> understood that the cooperation of both the Bulgarian and
> Palestine authorities would be available. The cost of the charter
> would not be a charge to the Government of Eire.
>
> 4. The Eire authorities might consider the possibility of
> receiving a limited number of child refugees, possibly orphans,
> who would be received at Jewish houses in Eire. The selection
> could be left to the Irish Red Cross Society delegation in Spain,
> in cooperation with the Joint Distribution Committee's
> representative in Lisbon.
>
> Prior to my departure I saw the papal nuncio [in Dublin],
> Dr. Pascal Robinson. We discussed the proposals; he assured
> me of his agreement; he undertook personally to support them
> to [President Eamon] De Valera, whom I had seen for a few

moments in the Dublin Parliament.

When I returned to London, Mr. Dulanty asked me to call to see him. The Dublin authorities had been in contact with him by telephone and he had already made inquiries with regard to chartering a boat. The International Red Cross had undertaken to arrange "security" [i.e., safe conduct]. I reaffirmed the cost of chartering the boat would be borne by the organizations interested.

Mr. Dulanty thought I should discuss these points with the Foreign Office [in London]. I saw Mr. A.W.G. Randall at the Foreign Office on May 13th [1943]. He stated that in general he thought there would be no objection to any of the proposals, a copy of which I left with him. In regard to the visas mentioned in items one and four, he expected that transit facilities through England would be made available, and possibly even shipping from Lisbon. I understand Mr. Kendall and Mr. Dulanty will meet to write out the proposals.

I also saw the Irish Red Cross and discussed with them:

(a) relief to Jewish refugees in Spain through the medical mission there;

(b) the sending of Irish food parcels to Poland;

(c) relief for the Polish Jewish refugees in Shanghai.

The negotiations in regard to these matters are proceeding.

16th May, 1943

[For various political reasons, this effort too remained unsuccessful. Ed.]

C. RABBI SCHONFELD AT WORK: A PERSONAL MEMOIR[1]

Introduction

AWARE OF THE GROWING PROBLEM, in 1938, Rabbi Dr. Solomon Schonfeld created the Chief Rabbi's Religious Emergency Council **Singlehandedly** for Austria and Germany (also known simply as the Chief Rabbi's Council) to place behind this rescue effort the official prestige and office of Britain's Chief Rabbi Joseph H. Hertz. In this endeavor, Rabbi Schonfeld received both inspiration and guidance from Rabbi Weissmandl who had been his teacher at the Yeshivah of Nitra and with whom he had devised a plan to relocate the entire yeshivah in Canada.[2] Rabbi Schonfeld also worked closely with Julius Steinfeld, who made several trips between Vienna and London to bring the latest news and lists of individuals to be rescued.[3] Except for one very modestly-paid executive secretary, himself a refugee from Vienna, and typists, Rabbi Schonfeld operated this British version of the Vaad Hatzalah virtually singlehandedly. He was able to inspire the Orthodox community of London to provide volunteers for numerous and often difficult tasks.

Then, using the network he had emplaced, including the Chief Rabbi's Council, Rabbi Schonfeld was able to secure separate Orthodox transports for children, older yeshivah students, and rabbis, all from Germany and Austria. Rabbi Schonfeld's excellent relations with numerous key officials in the British government as well as in Parliament did not hinder his efforts, of course. He was so successful that the British Home Office even issued special passes for the children he brought to England. Throughout Rabbi Schonfeld's ten-year rescue activity, which began in 1938 when he was only 26, he managed to save more than 3,700 children, adolescents, and adults in Central Europe before, during and after the Holocaust.[4]

The cause widened in both scope and support. Lady Eleanor Rathbone, MP, for example, helped Rabbi Schonfeld create the National Committee for Rescue from Nazi Terror, which was comprised primarily of non-Jewish notables, especially members of Parliament, who tried — and failed — to pass a Jewish rescue resolution. But, Rabbi Schonfeld's work was not limited to meeting and making plans with committees; he was personally involved with the physical and spiritual well-being of the thousands of individuals he rescued decades later. Some of the "Rabbi Schonfeld *Kinder,*" including England's current Chief Rabbi Sir Dr. Emmanuel Jacobovits, were to record their reminiscences of this remarkable man.[5]

Typical of Rabbi Schonfeld's work and the opposition even within his own ranks is an episode recalled by one of his aides. More than 300 children were rescued from Vienna and brought to Great Britain, and while their new living conditions were far from ideal — they slept on cots in the classrooms and hallway of the day school — the children were at least safe. One "well-meaning" member of Rabbi Schonfeld's own Rescue Committee, however, felt that the accommodations were inadequate and so informed the British Home Office, which in turn almost canceled the entire rescue project and was ready to send the children back. It was only Rabbi Schonfeld's own stature, and the force of his own personality, which prevented the British bureaucrats from sending the children back to Austria. At the next Committee meeting, Rabbi Schonfeld stood in the doorway looking for the man who had called the Home Office. When the man arrived, Rabbi Schonfeld shouted at him "*Moser* [informer], Out!" The man left the room and never returned.[6] [Ed.]

※　※　※

Marcus Retter recalled:

I FOUND OUT ABOUT RABBI SCHONFELD of London and the arrangements which he was making for refugee children from

Yeshivah Ohr Yisrael Austria. I was then seventeen years old, too old to apply for the Schonfeld children's transport, where the top age limit was sixteen. But I decided to contact Schonfeld directly to request my inclusion in a transport he was arranging for yeshivah *bachurim*. I had a younger brother and a younger sister, and felt that if I, the oldest son, succeeded in getting to England first, I would have a better chance of bringing the rest of the family. I began writing letters to Dr. Schonfeld in Hebrew, telling him about my background. I promised him that if he could get me to London I would do whatever he would wish me to do. Perhaps he needed a secretary to do Hebrew correspondence for him.

I wrote at least two dozen letters before an answer came from London. Shortly after the *Kristallnacht* pogrom of November 9-10, I received a carbon copy of a letter which Dr. Schonfeld had written to a Rabbi Hoffman in Palestine, telling him that he, Dr. Schonfeld, had taken an interest in the case of a young boy named Marcus Retter and would do for me whatever he possibly could. I did not know that the rabbi in Palestine might have helped me at the time, but for me the most important thing was to know that I had not been entirely abandoned to my fate.

I obtained my British visa early in February 1939. On March 5, I left Vienna by train, alone. I traveled through Germany and Belgium. The Nazis gave me no trouble, probably because I had a so-called "stateless" passport. I should add here that most of the yeshivah students in the "transport" from Vienna did not travel as a "unit," but alone, or in groups of three or four. They left Austria as individuals who happened to have been accepted as students at the Yeshivah Ohr Yisrael* in London. We had student visas, which meant that the British authorities expected us to return to our country of origin after we had completed our studies in England.

BUT IN ADDITION TO, AND SEPARATE FROM, the yeshivah students there was the *Kindertransport*, which took in about 250 to **The Kinder- transport** 300 children. These children left Austria as a group in March 1939. An earlier transport of about 300 children had left in December 1938. Thus, by the time I left Vienna for England as a yeshivah student, Dr. Schonfeld had already brought roughly 750 children and young people from Vienna to England.

---

* This yeshivah was "created" by Rabbi Schonfeld and staffed with refugee scholars with the express purpose of creating a medium for the rescue of youths between 16 and 21. [Ed.]

By that time Dr. Schonfeld had also begun to bring out religious teachers from Germany and Austria. They were in a particular plight because the London Jews were not especially eager to bring in more rabbis and Hebrew teachers. He requested the Home Office to grant permits to certain rabbis, teachers and Jewish scholars on the grounds that there was a shortage of "Jewish clergy" in England. Some of these individuals came from Germany — Berlin or Frankfurt — but most of them were from Vienna.

TWO OR THREE WEEKS AFTER my arrival in England, I visited Rabbi Schonfeld for the first time to thank him personally for all he

The Busiest Man under the Sun had done to bring me to England. I had a hard time finding Rabbi Schonfeld because he was the busiest man under the sun. He spent at least twenty hours a day on rescue work, trying to arrange transports to England, as well as to Canada and the United States for which transit visas through England would be required. Alas, these transatlantic transports never materialized. But Rabbi Schonfeld was a born optimist. He firmly believed that the group of students loosely organized under the Yeshivah Ohr Yisrael in London would automatically evolve into an established yeshivah in the pattern of the Etz Chaim Yeshivah, which had already existed in London for many years.

Rabbi Schonfeld was wrestling with a desperate shortage of funds for further rescue work. By that time he already had on his hands in England almost 1,000 refugees of all ages, for whom he had made himself personally responsible. He was still a young man, in his late 20's and unmarried. He was the spiritual leader of the Adas Yisroel Congregation, which was then a very small community with probably no more than 100 families. Most of the congregants were of German origin, but there were among them also quite a few native Englishmen. Rabbi Schonfeld was also the Presiding Rabbi of the Union of Orthodox Hebrew Congregations, which had been founded by his late father, Rabbi Dr. Victor Schonfeld, but this Union consisted of no more than twelve or fifteen *shtiblech* in London's East End, which belonged to the Adas Yisroel only for burial purposes and gave it no further financial support.

The relationship between Rabbi Schonfeld's Union and the Anglo-Jewish Establishment and the Chief Rabbinate was then the same as that between the "independent Orthodox" communities in Europe and the official *Kultusgemeinden*, the Jewish Establishment.

Just as the Union of Orthodox Hebrew Congregations under Rabbi Schonfeld's leadership considered itself independent of the Chief Rabbinate, so the Anglo-Jewish Establishment and its affiliated institutions refused to recognize Rabbi Schonfeld. They regarded him as the rabbi of a small group of ultra-Orthodox outsiders and "troublemakers" and would have nothing to do with him.

RABBI SCHONFELD, LIKE MR. STEINFELD and most of the Schiffshul-type of Viennese Agudists, was of Hungarian descent.

An Ungarisher Yid

His father had been born in a small village in Hungary; his mother, in Budapest. Although he had studied at the Yeshivah of Slobodka for less than a year, Rabbi Schonfeld knew little about Lithuanian Jewry; though British born, he considered himself an *"Ungarisher Yid."** Steinfeld, for his part, knew of Rabbi Schonfeld's family because Rabbi Schonfeld still had many relatives — mostly cousins of his mother's — living in Vienna, all of them Orthodox Jews and some of them affiliated with Agudath Israel.

Rabbi Schonfeld studied at the Yeshivah of Nitra for two years. His teacher there was Rabbi Michael Ber Weissmandl, who eventually was to become known for his underground rescue work during the Holocaust. In Nitra, Rabbi Schonfeld came completely under Rabbi Weissmandl's spell. Rabbi Weissmandl visited England several times before the outbreak of World War II and stayed at Rabbi Schonfeld's home. He came in 1936 and again in 1937 to do research on a Hebrew manuscript at the Bodleian Library in Oxford. On April 6, 1939 Rabbi Weissmandl came to England once again, this time on a rescue mission. He had compiled a list of 200 families from Nitra to bring over to Canada. The Canadian immigration offices had given him their approval.

Rabbi Schonfeld was to draw on the good will of the Archbishop of Canterbury, Dr. William Temple, in a heroic rescue effort during the war years. While this effort did not yield concrete results, it attests to Rabbi Schonfeld's originality of thought and vision. In December 1942, when the world first learned of the massacre of two million Jews in Europe, Rabbi Schonfeld inspired the founding of the Council of Rescue from Nazi Massacres, which in turn reached into the British Parliament to initiate a Parliamentary

---

* As a former student of the Yeshivah of Nitra, a bastion of Hungarian-style Orthodoxy in Slovakia, Rabbi Schonfeld had conceived a liking for the idea of "separatist" Orthodox communities after the pattern of Hungary and Slovakia, coupled with the *Austritt* ideology developed by Samson Raphael Hirsch in Germany. [Ed.]

Committee for Refugees supported by Dr. Temple and Miss Eleanor (later Lady Eleanor) Rathbone. Rabbi Schonfeld had known Lady Rathbone for some time through her work of educating the underprivileged and the handicapped.

In January 1943 Rabbi Schonfeld succeeded in enlisting the support of 277 members of Parliament for a resolution calling upon British dominions and possessions to offer a haven to Jews in Nazi Europe. This resolution was no empty gesture of sympathy because the Nazis at the time tended to give credence to documents or other evidence of foreign protection in the hands of Jews, even if it was patently impossible for the Jews to reach India or Canada. Had the resolution been passed, it would have encouraged satellite countries such as Rumania and Hungary, which were not as vicious in their Jew-hatred as the Nazi-occupied lands, at least to afford their Jews temporary protection from deportation.

TRAGICALLY, THE RESOLUTION WAS NEVER PASSED. Because of Britain's adamantly negative stance on the "Palestine problem," the

The Immediate vs. the Long-range document as drafted by its supporters in Parliament pointedly omitted Palestine from the list of British possessions that should open their doors to Jewish refugees. This omission incurred opposition from the Zionist Establishment, one of whose eminent spokesmen, Prof. Selig Brodetsky, was then President of the Board of Deputies of British Jews. The Zionist movement was committed to Jewish statehood in Palestine as a permanent, "long-range" solution to the "Jewish problem." It was dedicated to the proposition that true security for the Jews could not come from such stop gap palliatives as offers of "places of refuge" where Jews would still be in the minority and remain in danger of persecution. Rabbi Schonfeld and his supporters replied that the demand of the hour was not to hold out for long-range solutions to the Jewish problem but to take instant practical action for the immediate saving of Jewish lives, even if this had to be done through a Parliamentary resolution which ignored the most logical haven for the Jews — their homeland, *Eretz Yisrael*. As the debate continued and the Parliamentary proponents of the resolution found themselves drawn into the dispute, the resolution was shelved and nothing further came of it.

I have always associated three main character traits with Rabbi Schonfeld. First, he really enjoyed doing good. He was very human and therefore wanted to know that people appreciated what he had done, but he was not looking for tangible rewards. Certainly he never accepted financial compensation. He never had any money. Secondly, he never hesitated to speak candidly on behalf of what he called "undiluted" Judaism. He wanted to show that Orthodoxy counted, not as a "political" force but as an entity of like-minded people. In his view, every *ehrliche Yid*, every truly religious Jew, regardless of Jewish political affiliation, was important. His third outstanding trait was his love for his own "independent Orthodox" congregation, his "independent" network of schools, and his delight in seeing them grow.

HE CAME TO THE CONCLUSION THAT his rescue work would be greatly aided if he could obtain the official sanction of the Anglo-

The Chief Rabbi's Council

Jewish Establishment. To this end, some time in 1938, he approached Chief Rabbi Joseph H. Hertz, who, as distinct from the lay leadership of the United Synagogue in those days, was personally Orthodox in his religious observance and orientation, and asked him to join in the formation of what Rabbi Schonfeld originally called the Chief Rabbi's Religious Emergency Council for German and Austrian Jews. Rabbi Schonfeld, the "independent operator," was willing that the Chief Rabbi should be the chairman or presiding officer of this new body while he, Rabbi Schonfeld, would be content to be the activist behind the scenes. The Chief Rabbi agreed to this arrangement. Eventually the name of the new organization was shortened to "The Chief Rabbi's Religious Emergency Council" (or even "Chief Rabbi's Council").

Now, when Rabbi Schonfeld approached the British authorities for official permits, or went to Jewish communal leaders for financial or moral support, he was able to say, "I come before you as a representative of the Chief Rabbi's Religious Emergency Council." Chief Rabbi Hertz was able to work with Rabbi Schonfeld, who became his son-in-law in 1940, when he married his daughter Judith. Despite the sanction of the Chief Rabbinate, the Board of Deputies of British Jews and the Anglo-Jewish Establishment still did not accept Rabbi Schonfeld and did not approve of his rescue operations. But whenever these organizations said to the Chief Rabbi, "This is not an activity in which the Chief Rabbi should engage," Dr. Hertz would reply, "As Chief Rabbi I am supposed to care for the needs of Jewish religious teachers, scholars and clergy. Rabbi Schonfeld's activities come under this heading. This is not a communal matter but a religious matter, and when it comes to religious matters, no communal organization has the right to dictate to the Chief Rabbi. And remember, Chief Rabbis seldom die and never retire!"

DURING THE EARLY POSTWAR PERIOD, Rabbi Schonfeld was very much concerned that all orphaned Jewish children, boys and **Concern** girls, should be brought out of the countries **for Orphans** formerly occupied by the Nazis, particularly Poland. This included orphans who had been hidden in Gentile homes during the war, or who had spent the war years in orphanages, monasteries or convents.

Rabbi Schonfeld received a "block visa" for 1,000 Jewish children. Once again he gave a guarantee to the Home Office on behalf of the Chief Rabbi's Religious Emergency Council that these refugee children from Poland would not become public charges.

The refugee aid organizations of the Anglo-Jewish Establishment were still in existence. Their function was to raise funds; they were not intended to engage in any practical rescue activities, only to allocate money to groups actively engaged in rescue work. They were, however, not interested in bringing postwar Jewish DP's to England as permanent immigrants. They would have preferred Rabbi Schonfeld, or someone else, to take these children either to Palestine or to the United States.

Of course, Rabbi Schonfeld had to find a way of negotiating with the Polish authorities to permit the young survivors to leave Poland. Governments as a rule do not negotiate with private individuals, even if they are rabbis. There was in England at that time an organization known as COBRA (Council of British Relief Societies Abroad). This was a strictly non-Jewish organization, consisting primarily of Protestants. Although it was a private agency, it enjoyed the sanction of the British government. The Chief Rabbi's Religious Emergency Council therefore sought and managed to become a constituent of COBRA with the same standing as the Central British Fund and other refugee rehabilitation organizations. Under the flag of COBRA we, the staff of the Chief Rabbi's Religious Emergency Council, were even permitted to wear the uniform of the UNRRA (United Nations Relief and Rehabilitation Administration).

RABBI SCHONFELD ON HIS MISSIONS ABROAD wore a uniform which he himself had designed. It was a British army uniform

A New Uniform (which was very easy to obtain from the army) with the insignia of UNRRA, and underneath the letters CRREC (Chief Rabbi's Religious Emergency Council). I traveled in a similar uniform whenever I went on a mission to the DP camps. On the uniform cap we placed the Ten Commandments and a Star of David. We were regarded as military chaplains, but were not part of the Chaplain Corps.

The first children's transport to leave Poland after the War consisted of 1,000 children. The second, which I helped to organize, was smaller: it included only 500. The third transport, which left Poland early in 1947, consisted of 1,000 young refugees.

Once the refugee children from Poland arrived in England, of course, there was the problem of what to do with them. As with the children's transports of 1938 and 1939, Rabbi Schonfeld now too did not stop to think in advance how he would feed those youngsters. But times were different now. Most of the Orthodox Jews who had come to England as refugees before the outbreak of the war had already become established in England. They were making a living and had money, and they were grateful to Rabbi Schonfeld for having saved them. So, when he approached them and asked them to take in a refugee child from Poland, they could not say "no" to him. Before long, all the refugee children from Poland had been placed in Orthodox-Jewish homes. Even my wife and I (we were married in 1944) took a girl from Poland into our home.

D. AGUDAH LIFELINE: MEIR SPRINGER AND PACKAGES TO THE CONCENTRATION CAMPS[1]

As we have seen, despite the relentless, often overzealous censors, and other limitations placed on communication between the Allies and enemy countries by the Trading With the Enemy Act, a fairly accurate picture of what was happening in Eastern Europe began to seep out. Those fortunate few who managed to escape corroborated the reports received from Vatican couriers, and others, who smuggled back messages stating the unequivocal truth that murder — even by starvation — was virtually universal.

Like others who were highly motivated to act, Meir Raphael Springer, then chairman of the Federation of Czech Jews and secretary to Czech Foreign Minister Jan Masaryk, immediately devised a highly intricate plan for supplying food to camp inmates. First, he acquired individual names and the destination of various transports — rather easily accomplished by the Czech underground monitoring the early-morning German radio transmissions of intended camp arrivals. The list was then forwarded to the International Red Cross in Geneva with an outline for food shipments.

Yet, Springer shortly thereafter discovered what Goodman had, that Scotland Yard kept a close surveillance of any actions involving overseas accommodations. Springer's letter was intercepted, and he was placed under house arrest for allegedly counteracting the highly stringent economic boycott placed on Germany. Despite all objections and explanations to the contrary, Springer's efforts drew sharp criticism, particularly in light of the view that the Germans would naturally confiscate the packages and use the contents themselves. Undaunted, however, Springer contacted Masaryk, who assured him that he would help see the plan to fruition. Masaryk, in turn, took Springer's idea to Eduard Benes, president of the Czech Government-in-Exile, who not only gave his hearty approval but submitted it to Britain's Prime Minister Winston Churchill and Foreign Minister Anthony Eden and suggested a "trial run." The Czech Government would give the then-enormous sum of L60,000, or roughly $250,000, to initiate the project, which would ship packages from Czech embassies in Barcelona and Lisbon — two relatively neutral areas — directly to individual camp inmates. Springer made sure to include sardines and American cigarettes, two scarce items good for barter.

The first consignment of roughly 1,000 packages, from Spain and Portugal, was sent to several camps, particularly to Theresienstadt, because it was in Czech territory and obviously of interest to Masaryk. Gradually, again via Vatican and other diplomatic couriers, Springer and his organization received messages that the packages had been received and that their contents were being sold to the *kapos* (the camp's "block wardens"), the money going to buy staple food supplies for the inmates that lasted as long as two-and-a-half months. As a result, Springer redoubled his efforts and greatly enlarged the program. The Czech government, in turn, increased the grant from L60,000 to L200,000, and Masaryk added even more from the Polish and Dutch Governments-in-Exile.*

---

* Other nations, however, such as Switzerland, did not participate, for fear of violating their neutrality and fear of German reprisals. Spain, on the other hand, cooperated fully by helping Springer and Goodman save an untold number of lives. [Ed.]

CHAPTER ELEVEN

Switzerland

A. INTRODUCTION

WHEN THE NAZI EMPIRE stretched from the Atlantic past the borders of the Soviet Union, the small neutral country of Switzerland was literally surrounded — by Germany, occupied

Neutral Switzerland Closed to Jews
France, and fascist Italy. For most of the war years, there existed in Switzerland the real fear that Germany would indeed invade her for any one of a number of reasons. Jews, therefore, seeking asylum thought first of the nation known for centuries as a haven for refugees — and were disappointed. Jews were not welcome in Switzerland, due to its concern over possible Nazi reprisals, and the lesser but no less real problem of finding funds to support many thousands of refugees. Throughout the entire war less than ten percent of the roughly 250,000 refugees who made their way to or through Switzerland were Jewish.[1]

There were other factors as well. Antisemitism, for example, continued strong among certain Swiss. *Shechitah* (the ritual slaughter of cattle) had already been forbidden by law for so-called humanitarian reason since 1893; the "J" on passports — clearly branding the bearer as a Jew — was carried out in 1938 by the Nazis at the instigation of Dr. Heinrich Rothmund, head of the Swiss Alien Police. Rothmund had insisted on this tactic as a way to distinguish between so-called real Germans — who had free access across Swiss borders — and Jews, who were considered undesirable and therefore did not.[2] Rothmund's policy was one the Swiss stood by, for even according to Yehuda Bauer's ridiculously low and totally inaccurate estimate, "more than 5,000" Jews who had illegally crossed the border in the hopes of reaching a sanctuary were sent back. Recha Sternbuch, on the other hand, much more accurately, put the number closer to 150,000.[3]

Actually, the entire Swiss policy of *refoulement* (or "returning" refugees back into Nazi hands) was a strictly racial enactment alone since it distinguished between "political" and "racial" refugees. The latter, naturally, applied solely to Jews, with the Swiss accepting the Nazi racial definitions. Thus, deserters from Hitler's army were accepted while Jews fleeing from a fate in a concentration camp were returned across the border.

IN CONTRAST, FASCIST SPAIN under the dictator Francisco Franco, ostensibly an ally of Hitler, had a far better record. While only

Fascist Spain Open and Helpful several thousand Jews remained in Spain at any one time in dismal refugee camps, over 100,000 made their way through Spain and, via Portugal, eventually made their way to the west. Even during the worst period of 1943-45, when Switzerland's borders were closed to all Jews but the very young or very old, Spain's borders remained open. It may not have been easy to get across the snow-capped Pyrenees from France into Spain, and once across, life was not easy in the refugee camps, but getting across the Alps posed no less a hardship. Worse, once the journey was made safely, the vast majority were turned back, some as frequently as six and seven times. Even those permitted to remain, such as youngsters under sixteen or those over sixty, were placed in refugee camps as well, where life was no picnic either.[4]

Still, there were numerous people in Swiss society who fought antisemites in general and government policy in particular. In contrast to the spectre of Rothmund, there was also Paul Grueninger, the extremely humane Chief of Police in St. Gallen, who ultimately lost his position, as well as numerous anonymous people of all walks who helped the Sternbuchs smuggle in refugees illegally.[5] There were also the four Protestant theologians who openly fought to lift Swiss censorship of Nazi atrocity stories, and who in 1944 rallied Swiss public opinion behind them. (See Chap. 11E.)

ASIDE, THEN, FROM THE HOLOCAUST just across their borders, the situation in Switzerland itself caused Jews to be concerned — if

Assimilated Swiss Jews not over cautious. Many Swiss Jews, especially assimilationist Jews, like their coreligionists in Sweden, England and the U.S., feared the rise of a Jewish problem, i.e., the rise in antisemitism, including identification with so-called foreigners as well as economic competition from the refugees. The community, then, roughly 19,000 at best, was for a host of understandable reasons not eager to lobby for and then absorb a literal flood of impoverished refugees. Their attitude was no different from the less than 5,000-member native Jewish community in Shanghai which, with the assistance of the major American-Jewish organizations and the Allied governments, in the same period of 1938-39, pressed for restrictions to additional immigration in the face of the increasing influx of many thousands of Jewish refugees — despite the fact that the Jews had nowhere else to go.[6] The virtually negative feelings toward rescue made matters all the more difficult for the Orthodox activists who sought to bring as many Jews as possible into safety in Switzerland.

DESPITE ITS NEGATIVE ATTITUDE towards rescue work, Switzerland was extremely useful as a kind of listening post and

Communication Center communications center: it was vital for both receiving and transmitting fresh information about events in occupied Europe. As such, all the major Jewish organizations — the Jewish Agency, the Joint, Hechalutz, and the World Jewish Congress, among others — used Switzerland to monitor the situation.[7]

Switzerland was the initial transmission point for most of the information, plans, and pleas of Rabbi Weissmandl and other rescue activists. Weissmandl's underground gathered data and statistics, and charted rail movements, then bribed couriers to carry it into Switzerland, hoping of course for support — financial and otherwise — to combat the Nazis.[8] He depended on people like Zurich's Yisroel Chaim Eis, an Agudah activist, writer, and businessman who, up until his death in 1943, worked independently as well as with the Sternbuchs in a number of ways, including shipping food packages into the ghettos and using illegal Latin American passports.

Unfortunately, however, there was no coordinated effort in Switzerland to utilize the remarkable potential for relief and rescue. The sole attempt at unity among the representatives of the various

Jewish organizations in Switzerland was undertaken by the Jewish Secretary-General of the El Salvadoran Consulate, George Mandel-Mantello. His efforts proved futile because of ideological and personality clashes, which proved stronger than a common desire for rescue per se.

In Bern, the circle of Orthodox activists welcomed the arrival from Palestine of Dr. Reuven Hecht, a Revisionist-Zionist like Mantello, who eventually emigrated from Switzerland to Palestine. Beginning in 1937, Hecht worked for illegal immigration of Czech and Austrian Jews into Palestine — and from the outset of the war supplied vital information on Jewish conditions to Sam Woods, the American Economic Attache in Bern and a highly placed intelligence officer with close ties to Secretary of State Cordell Hull. It was in fact Woods who suggested that Hecht coordinate with the Sternbuchs since, as he put it, "they are the only ones who are doing anything."[9]

Woods overstated the case a bit, of course, because there were others, including Yisroel Chaim Eis or Franzi Goldschmidt who also worked hard, kept endless hours, used legal as well as illegal methods, and risked arrest for rescue, though they simply could not compare in results. Others sent out messages about Jewish destruction; the Orthodox activists gave their homes, their funds and themselves. The Torah teaches: "do not separate yourself from the community of Israel," and most of the Orthodox activists took this dictum literally.

AMONG THE MOST OUTSTANDING RESCUE ACTIVISTS based in a free country — was Recha Sternbuch.[10] She began her personal **HIJEFS** involvement in 1938 by smuggling more than 2,300 Jews across the Swiss border — many into other countries via Switzerland — rescue actions which resulted in her own arrest. Early in 1942 with the help of her husband Yitzchok, she founded HIJEFS (*Hilfsverein fuer Juedische Fluchtlinge in Shanghai*, or Rescue Committee for Jewish Refugees in Shanghai), which quickly became a vital link in the network for communication and money transfers to the yeshivos stranded in Shanghai.[11] Before the end of 1943, of course, all such monetary transactions were illegal by American law — a fact of life which hardly deterred the Sternbuchs from their work.

Indeed, HIJEFS did so well for the Jews of Shanghai that the organization — or the Sternbuch home, really — became the literal hub of virtually all Vaad Hatzalah work in Europe. The house itself, in fact, became a way station open at all hours to Jews escaping France, and later Italy; Polish and Slovakian Jews; Jews to and from Hungary depending on the politics of the day. To a limited extent, HIJEFS — or the Sternbuchs — sent food into the concentration camps using the International Red Cross, and also smuggled Latin American passports into Nazi-occupied areas. When, in the spring of 1944, the inmates of the Vittel detention camp were about to be deported despite holding South American papers, the Sternbuchs in Europe with the Orthodox in the U.S. worked desperately to save them — unfortunately to no avail. Later, they worked with former Swiss President Dr. Jean-Marie Musy, negotiating ransom terms with SS Chief Heinrich Himmler. In virtually all their work, the Sternbuchs were assisted by two non-Jews, Polish Ambassador Alexander Lados and papal nuncio Fillippe Bernardini.

When in 1943 the Vaad broadened its scope to include all rescue efforts, HIJEFS changed its purview as well, from an emphasis on Shanghai to one that included all occupied territories. At this time, too, various contacts were made through Dr. Yaakov (Jacob) Griffel based in Istanbul, and Philip Freudiger in Budapest, who were closer to the steadily worsening events in southeastern Europe — in Rumania, Bulgaria, and Hungary. At this time, for example, communiques from Rabbi Weissmandl often went from Slovakia through Hungary, to Turkey, and finally to Switzerland. Once in the hands of the Sternbuchs, the Polish cable sent them all over the world.[12] By 1944, the greater need — and opportunity — for rescue necessitated enlarging the original seven-member HIJEFS committee to include such men as Jacob Erlanger, a Swiss Jew with contacts in East Asia and Eastern Europe; Angelo Donnati, an Italian Jew responsible for Italy and the Italian-occupied sector of France; Hugo Donnenbaum, Sternbuch's contact man for Hungary; and Herman Landau, the man in charge of daily activities.[13] Moreover, Madame Renee Reichmann's successful efforts to send thousands of food packages from her home in Tangier to various concentration camps was supported by the Vaad Hatzalah through the Sternbuchs.

EIS AND THE STERNBUCHS STAND OUT among the Swiss Orthodox rescue activists, yet there were others who were

Other Activists enormously dedicated — and who can be credited with numerous accomplishments. Morris Rokowsky, for example, was a Zurich-based long-time Sternbuch friend who saved hundreds of Jews in the 1930's, prior to the outbreak of World War II. Similarly, Reb Boruch Meshulum Lebowitz, in Geneva, kept up a steady correspondence with Rabbi Weissmandl, his former Nitra classmate. Using couriers, he often sent money from the Sternbuchs to Rabbi Weissmandl.[14] Finally, much like Recha Sternbuch, Mrs. "Franzi" Goldschmidt specialized in saving those Jewish children who had been placed in non-Jewish institutions.

B. CHAIM YISROEL EIS[1]

THERE IS BEFORE ME A LETTER FROM WARSAW by Dr. Isaac Lewin[1] dated April 2, 1943, shortly before the heroic but tragic

Eis from Zurich uprising in the Warsaw Ghetto. This letter, which miraculously made its way out of hell, eventually reaching Dr. Yitzchok Lewin, was written by a woman outside the ghetto to someone in Switzerland and contains this plea: "Send for a package such as was sent by Eis from Zurich to his friends!"

"Eis from Zurich" — the very phrase became a symbol, representing rescue and solace. Neither in Warsaw nor in Switzerland did these words require any commentary; they were too well known. It is difficult to describe what this Swiss Jew did with his own limited means in the course of four years. The cost to him personally ran into tens of thousands of [Swiss] francs. Neglecting his business affairs, he spent days and nights seeking ways to provide relief to the Jewish victims of the Nazis.

Providing such relief was far from a routine matter. Fearing a German invasion, Switzerland was extremely concerned about maintaining its neutrality. Moreover, it did not have an abundance of food. For these reasons it forbade the export of food, even for relief purposes. So Chaim Eis and some friends made contact with a wholesale firm in Portugal, purchased 2,500 kilograms (about 5,000 pounds) of sardines for 10,000 Swiss francs, and sent them to the "Jewish Self-Help" organization in Cracow, Poland. That organization, in turn, exchanged these delicacies through the Nazi authorities for much larger amounts of flour and other staples.

Thousands of individuals received aid from R' Yisroel Chaim Eis on this and on other numerous occasions. In many cases he bestowed his life-saving generosity personally and directly. A letter dated August 4, 1942 states that he personally sent seventy food parcels to one of Warsaw's great Torah scholars, thereby saving not only the sage but the latter's entire family from starvation. This kindness and many other such deeds have been carefully documented and verified; together they comprise a most impressive record of rescue work.

Eis' correspondence with friends in the U.S. during the period of 1941-42 is filled with fiery indignation. In a letter dated May 28, 1942, he tells of receiving a communication from a friend in Warsaw who complained: "We are hungry. How can one eat while so many friends go hungry?" Then: "No one cares about us other than R' Yisroel Chaim Eis."

With his sharp, merciless pen he then turned to American Jewry and demanded, "Will you ever be able to bring the *egla arufa* offering?* Will you ever be able to say [as these leaders were required], 'Our hands have not shed this blood'?"

Yisroel Chaim Eis refused to accept excuses. "Where there is truly a will, one can always find a way," he maintained. "Everything in the world must be done in order to insure the immediate arrival of relief!"

And he was, of course, right. Others, when they acted at all, often took long, long months to get something accomplished. And those months were lost — together with thousands of our best.

How horrifying do his words strike us in a letter he sent during the intermediate days of Succos 5703 (September 30, 1942): "Were it not for the undue procrastination in the U.S. for sending relief

---

* Brought by the leaders of a community next to which there was found the body of a murdered innocent.

after they had already received permission from the government six months earlier, perhaps, then, they might have saved some people from extermination.*

All the necessary funds and means should have been made available to someone like R' Yisroel Chaim Eis so that thousands more could have been saved. However, one fact remains clear: much was lost due to neglect and apathy in the United States.

C. RECHA AND YITZCHOK STERNBUCH THE RESCUE TEAM PAR EXCELLENCE[1]

l. to r. Yitzchok Sternbuch, Dr. Isaac Lewin, Recha Sternbuch with a group of rescued children.

THE STORY IS HARDLY ATYPICAL. Recha Sternbuch had just dashed across the border from Switzerland into Nazi-occupied

To Bring Back My Brothers

France in a near-desperate attempt to take back roughly a dozen Jews who had crossed the border illegally and were being escorted back into France by Swiss police. A German guard stopped her, asked her identity, and demanded to know why she was there. Recha Sternbuch calmly showed him her Swiss passport and said, "I am here to bring back my brothers."

"But you're a Jewess," the soldier objected and, drawing a pistol, he told her to go back across the border. "I'll shoot," he added, pointing his gun directly at her.

Yet Recha Sternbuch was undaunted. Pointing to herself, she

---

* It is not clear what government permission Eis refers to, since Vaad Hatzalah, having had to contend with the Trading With the Enemy Act did not win its battle to legally send money to enemy-occupied territory until the end of 1943, months after his demise. [Ed.]

told him to "go ahead and shoot if you want to, but I will not leave without my brothers." The German, taken aback by such remarkable courage, put down his gun. The Swiss police had already departed and he allowed them all to return.

It is certainly an astounding feat of bravery, yet one not at all out of character for Recha Sternbuch, surely one of the single most influential rescue activists in the free world. The daughter of Rabbi Mordechai Rottenberg, chief rabbi of Antwerp prior to World War II and a member of the Council of Torah Sages of Agudath Israel, both she and her husband were brought up in the most Orthodox of homes. Although Yitzchok Sternbuch was raised in Switzerland, the family had deep roots in Russia. Their guests in Switzerland often included many prominent Torah scholars, including such luminaries as Rabbi Chaim Ozer Grodzensky and Rabbi Avraham I. Kook, Palestine's first chief rabbi.

It was Recha Sternbuch's initiative, charismatic personality, and extraordinary ideas that propelled the two of them into the forefront of rescue work for more than a decade, beginning in 1938 with the *Anschluss*, the German annexation of Austria. While Yitzchok Sternbuch was an important part of their operation, his wife was clearly the principal activist, theorist, and inspiration. There is little doubt that she was a brilliant woman — in her single days, she often delivered lectures to girls in Antwerp on Torah, for example, and freely entered into involved Torah and philosophical discussions with the many scholarly visitors to her home. But her real genius was manifest only after her fellow Jews were severely endangered.

In 1938, Dr. Heinrich Rothmund, Chief of the Swiss Alien Police, convinced the Germans to place a large red "J" on Jews' passports for ready identification — and then closed the border to all German and Austrian Jews. Rothmund, then, is more than a little responsible for Recha Sternbuch's initiation into rescue work, for he unwittingly presented her with her first major challenge: how to smuggle Jews away from the Nazis and into Switzerland. Freely using every conceivable method at hand — from well-placed bribes to ringing humanitarian arguments — Recha Sternbuch created an entire network of border smugglers, a broad Swiss spectrum ranging from taxi drivers to villagers. (Some villagers helped Jews across; others simply notified her when refugees were caught.) Her name was passed among the desperate, fearful people; her telephone number was scrawled in way stations along the border.

SHE VOICED A THOROUGH CONCERN for the Swiss laws of refoulement, i.e., the key victims of Jewish refugees — a direct

The Sternbuchs Helped any Jew refutation of such historians like Yehuda Bauer, who incorrectly read the Sternbuch's response as solely concerned with fellow Orthodox Jews. On the contrary, the Sternbuchs helped *any* Jew, regardless of observance or party.* Others like Saly Mayer may have voiced humanitarian concerns for the *Klal,* for everyone — but did relatively little to help. Moreover, in the case of Mayer there is substantial evidence that he himself set in motion the events leading up to her arrest and the deposing of Paul Grueninger.[2]

Once the escapees were inside Switzerland, Recha Sternbuch was often able to use her good connections with sympathetic Swiss officials to help them stay. One notable example was Paul Grueninger, the St. Gallen police chief, who was virtually indefatigable in his efforts to help. Sadly, Grueninger had to pay dearly for his humanitarian dignity, for in 1939 he was summarily dismissed from his post; thereafter, his livelihood came largely from the grateful Sternbuchs. (In an even more tragic footnote, it was nearly thirty years later, and only after due publicity by Yad Vashem for his role as one of the "Righteous of the World," that the Swiss government restored Grueninger's pension.)

Further, Recha Sternbuch helped hundreds of refugees into Switzerland, and with the help of Dr. Kuhl's Polish papers, insured that at the very least they would be kept in Swiss internment camps and not sent back to the Germans. And as she herself pointed out to the court during the proceedings against her, she helped roughly several thousand Jews pass through Switzerland to safety in Italy, Palestine and elsewhere. To that end, she obtained all sorts of visas, notably Latin American — often for substantial sums of money. In one instance, she herself traveled to Italy to obtain 400 Chinese end-visas, which were used to get Jews out of Europe and, illegally, into Palestine.[4]

At one of the usual crossing points, near Lac Leman on the French border, Swiss guards had apprehended two illegal refugees, the Blum brothers, and were preparing to send them back —

---

* Even non-Jews were included among those she rescued. Nor did this in any way negate her special affinity to and concern for Torah scholars. Though personally an Agudist, in her trips to postwar Poland, etc. to help rescue many hundreds of Jewish orphans, she acted only in this "neutral" capacity as representative of Vaad Hatzalah. In contrast, when Chief Rabbi Yitzchok Halevy Herzog came to Poland at about the same time, to help with the rescue of children, he was always accompanied by Dr. Zev Gold, president of American Mizrachi, to assure the Mizrachi political perspective in all matters.[3]

certainly to concentration camps. Quickly, an informant reported the situation to the Sternbuchs, adding that only immediate action could prevent deportation. After weighing any number of options, Recha Sternbuch finally went to see Saly Mayer, at that time clearly the most influential Jew in Switzerland. (Aside from being the Joint's representative, he was the former head of the Swiss community organization SIG — for *Schweizerischer Israelitischer Gemeindebund* * — and a personal friend of Dr. Rothmund.)[5] Recha Sternbuch stated her case simply, asking Mayer to help save these two unfortunate Jews.

"Frau Sternbuch," Mayer answered, "I know you quite well. You are surely a good patriotic Swiss citizen and you are quite familiar with the Swiss laws. You don't really want to violate these laws. There is no alternative but to send these escapees back across the border."

"Herr Saly Mayer," Recha Sternbuch replied angrily, "you obviously *don't* know me. I am a Jewish mother. I don't know what the Swiss law says. I only know that according to the Torah, we have to save these boys. And if you refuse to be of any help then I will have nothing further to do with you!" When Mayer continued to refuse despite all her humanitarian arguments to the contrary, she told him flatly that he would never see her again and left.[6]

Despite his being a Sabbath observer, Mayer was the paradigm of the assimilationist Jew whose adherence to normal social rules was based on authorities other than Torah. Sadly, he — and others — were completely inappropriate in their response to the German war against the Jews. Mayer, like others, was a decent and honest man who, tragically, in such abnormal times could not see beyond his own narrow ideology, who was out-of-place when flexibility was a prerequisite to real action.

MAYER KNEW AND UNDERSTOOD the real pressures placed by the Swiss on the Jewish community generally, and individual Jews specifically, *not* to speak too loudly about clearly Jewish causes. This generally negative if not hostile atmosphere of most Swiss, is typified by the advice one

Swiss Facade of Humanitarianism

newspaperman gave to the Jews, and goes far to help explain the attitudes of a Saly Mayer and other assimilationist Jews like him in Switzerland and elsewhere. The editor wrote:

---

* Association of Swiss-Jewish Communal Organizations

> We should like to ... counsel the Jews in Switzerland as a Jewish mother advises her children: Precisely because you are Jews, you should not push yourselves too far up, otherwise you will be disliked, and arrogance brings on contempt and persecution ...[7]

Chief Rothmund in effect described Mayer, whom he considered a friend:

> The good Jew, the assimilated Jew ... was the frightened, quiet, inconspicuous Jew who made himself as unobtrusive as he could and, if possible, denied his Jewishness and his origins. Then he would be left in peace, accepted, tolerated ...[8]

Therefore, Rothmund could write of Mayer and this type of Swiss Jew:

> "The Swiss Jews are cooperating with us, and they clearly see their own stake in the matter."[9]

However, the Swiss had to be careful in not being too obviously antisemitic or the (alleged) Jewish world-wide influence, especially in the West, would ruin the Swiss facade of humanitarianism, as he noted:

> If they [the Jews] begin to protest internationally, instead of exerting their influence in their international circles on behalf of the measures that we have adopted, *as they are doing today* [i.e., in accepting the harsh laws of refoulement], we take the risk of setting the whole civilized world against us ...[10]

THE STERNBUCHS ALSO KNEW and understood such pressures very well — and simply chose to ignore them. Where others felt fear

Some Truly Humanitarian Non-Jews

and trepidation, the Sternbuchs knew only strength and commitment — at least their actions indicate as much. What's more, they were fortunate that they could rely heavily on the enlightened support of a number of non-Jews, among them Paul Grueninger, Alexander Lados, the Polish Ambassador at Bern, and Fillippe Bernardini, the papal nuncio.

Lados allowed them to use the Polish cable; it alone proved to be virtually the sole reliable method of quick and confidential trans-Atlantic communication. The role of Papal Nuncio Bernardini was somewhat different. Known as the so-called dean of ambassadors, he was pre-eminent in both prestige and influence in Swiss diplomatic circles — and he rendered all his powers to the service of the Sternbuchs. His men, for example, were used as couriers to Rabbi Weissmandl in Slovakia, a region impenetrable by either Polish or Allied diplomats. Moreover, because of his very office, he carried great weight in Switzerland itself.

FROM ALL ACCOUNTS, THE STERNBUCH HOUSEHOLD — first in St. Gallen, later in Montreux — was hardly what one might think of as a typical Swiss household. Punctuality —

Extraordinary Circumstances, Extraordinary Responses

or even normal hours — were unheard of; income-producing and domestic activities were often held in abeyance indefinitely; the cast of characters was infinitely changeable and impossible to keep straight. Like many Orthodox-Jewish women, Recha Sternbuch's initial goal was to be a wife and mother and creator of a household — hardly minor tasks at any time; she was the last woman who would have chosen a career for its own sake.

Yet, extraordinary circumstances necessitate extraordinary responses, and Recha Sternbuch quickly recognized the gravity of the situation and she plunged into the fray. Fortunately, a number of people surrounding the Sternbuchs took over their various daily routines, thereby freeing them for their more difficult and taxing services to *Klal Yisroel*. So much, in fact, did the twin spirits of *hatzalah* and hospitality permeate the Sternbuch home that new and unwary visitors often thought it a small refugee hostel.

Ironically, Recha Sternbuch's greatest triumph — i.e., the release of 1,200 inmates of the Theresienstadt camp through the Musy-Himmler negotiations, which she inspired and kept going — she considered her greatest failure. This was so because, as we have seen, the great promise of the release of 300,000 surviving Jews in the camps was not to be fulfilled. It was thwarted by a combination of human factors that included intrigue by SS factions, the Swiss socialist press, the Socialist-Zionist opposition and assimilationist Jewish fears under Swiss pressure, abetted by the negative role of the American representative of the War Refugee Board in Switzerland.

Still, her influence was able to save many, often with the help of men such as Papal Nuncio Bernardini. They once changed Swiss policy through the simple force of their convictions — and Bernardini's office. The official policy had been to let refugee couples with small children remain in Switzerland, while turning back all others. In quick measure, hundreds of people used orphans to create "artificial" families, thereby gaining berths in civilian internment camps and avoiding deportation. Once in the camps, however, they parted — and when the Swiss officials discovered the mass charade they wanted to send all the offenders back to occupied France. With all other avenues seemingly blocked, Recha Sternbuch turned to Bernardini for help. The papal nuncio acceded, publicly announcing that it was perfectly acceptable for the refugees to alter the facts when their lives were in danger. Suitably shamed, the Swiss changed their policy, rescinded the deportation orders, and the Jews remained in safety.[11]

TYPICAL OF THE WAY RECHA STERNBUCH operated is an incident related to this author by the individual involved.[12] It occurred some

The Two Suitcases time during the Musy negotiations in the winter of '44-'45, when desperate attempts were being made to keep the rescue plan alive in the face of opposition by the Mayer-Kastner-Schwalb group.

Recha called a young lady from the Orthodox community who had just become engaged and was going to live in a town near the German border. "Come to my house at once; I have a matter of vital importance to discuss with you," the messenger told her. Interrupting the preparations for her wedding the bride-to-be rushed to the Sternbuch home, where Recha pointed to the two suitcases and said to her, "Take these two suitcases to [an address in a certain town] near the border. A Gestapo agent will meet you there. Give him the two suitcases and then turn around and go home. I will see you afterward."

The woman, who told the author that she was not normally the kind to follow someone else's bidding, said she was mesmerized by Recha Sternbuch and didn't even inquire about the contents of the suitcases. She could have been arrested had the Swiss police caught her in an illegal act; yet, she obediently took the suitcases and went on her mission.

That night at about midnight, she met her Gestapo contact, who was in civilian guise, and delivered the suitcases. Then she went home.

About 3 a.m. she heard a knock on the door. Her first thought was that the Swiss police had come to arrest her. As she peeked out the door, in came Recha. Skipping all formalities, she asked, "Did you accomplish your mission?" When told yes, she slumped down on the couch and fell asleep. An hour later Recha jumped up and disappeared into the night as mysteriously as she had come.

The young messenger eventually learned that one of the suitcases was filled with cartons of cigarettes, but she never learned the contents of the second. Most likely it was cash for bribing the

Nazis during the Musy negotiations. We do know that no one but Mr. and Mrs. Sternbuch and Mr. Herman Landau were originally involved in delivering the 500,000SF that Musy took on his mission as bribes for Nazi officials.

D. DR. JULIUS KUHL[1]

At the end of summer 1942, Dr. Georg Brunswig, one of the leaders of the Swiss-Jewish community, received a long memorandum which began:

> Before setting down the following lines, I must beg of you to keep the source of this information secret. I am fully aware that I am violating the obligation placed upon me by the embassy to keep all classified information strictly confidential. As a Jew, however, I cannot remain silent.
>
> Recently, a prominent person came to us directly from Poland and reported about a pogrom that took place in Lemberg, as a result of incitement of the Polish masses against the Jews. I felt obligated to immediately report this to Saly Mayer, the President of the Swiss Jewish community board.
>
> Yesterday again, a trustworthy messenger came from Poland and reported the following:
>
> (a) The Warsaw ghetto is in a process of liquidation. Many Jews, regardless of age or sex, are being dragged away in groups, shot, and their bodies are being used for the manufacture of soap and fertilizers. The mass executions are not taking place in Warsaw but rather in special camps. One of those camps is in

Belzec. Most recently fifty thousand Jews were murdered on the spot ...[2]

Three closely-written pages followed, an extraordinary document compiling data on the myriad executions taking place in Eastern Europe. Although the memorandum was intended to be secret and therefore not signed, Dr. Brunswig was well acquainted with its author, Dr. Julius Kuhl, an Orthodox Jewish official at the Polish Consulate in Bern. Indeed, this was hardly the first such communication from Dr. Kuhl to the Jewish leadership in Switzerland, for beginning in 1940, when he became a consulate staff member, he was a constant source of vital information on events in occupied Europe. Yet beyond his immeasurable contribution to official Jewish circles, Dr. Kuhl was also a vital part of virtually all the rescue and relief projects initiated or continued by the Sternbuch family. Indeed, it is hardly surprising that in an October 14, 1944 letter to Yaakov Rosenheim, then the president of the Agudath Israel World Organization, Recha Sternbuch wrote that "without the help of the Polish ambassador [Alexander Lados] we could not have saved anyone at all."[3] The link between Lados and the Sternbuchs was Dr. Kuhl, whom the ambassador had appointed as his personal representative to the Swiss-Jewish community.

❀ ❀ ❀

AS A YOUNG MAN JULIUS KUHL WENT TO SWITZERLAND to study at a yeshivah and at a university; he received a doctorate and became an official at the Polish Consulate — a

Position Afforded a Rare Opportunity
rare achievement, since at that time there were virtually no Jews in the Polish Diplomatic Service. Dr. Kuhl quickly realized that his new position afforded him the rare opportunity to serve Europe's endangered Jews; after meeting Recha Sternbuch, who had traveled to his office to seek help for some Polish refugees, he knew that he could do much.

During and after the war years, Dr. Kuhl's services were invaluable. First, he was able to supply the Sternbuchs with thousands of Polish passports for many Jews whom they had smuggled into Switzerland — literally a lifesaving act for those Jews, often from Belgium or France, who had come across the border illegally, and who faced immediate deportation if caught. Further, those with passports then had the chance of obtaining a visa for the

United States, Palestine, South America, or other havens; without a passport, such visas — and therefore such travel — was impossible. In one dramatic 1943 case, Dr. Kuhl used the diplomatic mail to rush a passport to Rabbi Aaron Rokeach — the Belzer Rebbe — in Budapest. Having been previously smuggled-from Poland into Hungary, the Rebbe was literally stuck without good papers, despite a British entry-permit to Palestine. The passport which the Rebbe received from Dr. Kuhl enabled him to travel, first to Turkey, then to *Eretz Yisrael*.

Dr. Kuhl's work did not go unnoticed by Ambassador Lados, and he was rewarded with a promotion to head of the refugee department. In his new office, Dr. Kuhl was in a position to do even more, initially by obtaining a monthly allocation of 15 Swiss francs, later increased to 30, for Polish-Jewish refugees, many of whom were held in internment camps. Although the amount may seem small, perhaps, when judged on a per-family per-month basis, in reality it meant an expenditure of millions of dollars for needy Jews.[4] Later, Dr. Kuhl increased his involvement, often risking his own position by helping Recha Sternbuch bringing Jews illegally from Germany, Austria, and Nazi-occupied France. More than once, for example, he placed calls to the Swiss border police, requesting them — on behalf of the Polish Embassy, he said — to permit the entry of particular Jews, even though he had no such authority to do so. Indeed, Dr. Kuhl fought so frequently with Swiss authorities over these and other rescue activities that they asked Ambassador Lados to dismiss him. Lados, a great humanitarian in his own right, refused.

THE POLISH AMBASSADOR ALSO PRESENTED his assistant to Papal Nuncio Bernardini, and Dr. Kuhl in turn introduced the

The Polish Cable Service

prelate to the Sternbuchs. Bernardini became a great ally of theirs. Kuhl was responsible for making the connections with a Mr. Huigly, the Paraguayan consul in Zurich, who provided, for a steep price of 500-3,000SF, Paraguayan passports, the first of the Latin American papers that became so popular later. There were other successes, none greater than Dr. Kuhl's persuading Ambassador Lados to place the Polish Embassy's secret code department at the Sternbuch's disposal. Needless to say, this action took on enormous significance after December 1941, when America entered the War and virtually all correspondence between Europe and the United States ceased. Whatever communication did get through other channels often took months because of delays caused by war censorship. Yet, despite the high cost, by using the Embassy's cable, and especially the services of Stanislaw Nachlik, the sympathetic Polish code-operator, the Sternbuchs were in steady contact with the Vaad Hatzalah and Agudath Israel in New York. Among the more notable transmissions was the earlier-mentioned September 1942 message about mass deportations to death camps. Similarly, the Embassy helped channel desperately needed support funds to the 500 rabbis and Torah scholars stranded — and penniless — under Japanese rule in Shanghai.

E. GEORGE MANDEL-MANTELLO [1]

THE STERNBUCHS, ALONG WITH YISROEL CHAIM EIS, pioneered the use of Latin American passports for Jewish refugees. However,

The Price Was too Steep the cost of such life saving papers — from 500 to 3,000 Swiss francs per document — was prohibitive, so that, for the most part, only the wealthiest were able to use that escape route. This obstacle seemed insurmountable until it was removed by a Rumanian textile manufacturer named George Mandel-Mantello.

Scion of a well-known rabbinic family,* and himself an

---

* His grandfather, Rabbi Yitzchok Yaakov Mandel, was the *rav* and *halachic* authority in Lechnitz and the surrounding province of Hungary (near Bistrice). He was a colleague of the Admor of Siget (R' Yekuthiel Judah), father of R' Joel Teitelbaum. Mantello's father, Yosef Yehudah Boruch, had studied in his yeshivah, though he earned his livelihood as the owner of a large flour mill.

Orthodox Jew, Mandel-Mantello was a Revisionist-Zionist who early in 1942 set aside his business activities and settled in Geneva as the Secretary General of the El Salvadoran Mission. During his frequent business trips throughout Europe he had, of course, become completely aware of what was happening to the Jews in Nazi-occupied lands; indeed, Mandel-Mantello was one of the first to know the full details of both *Kristallnacht* in Austria on November 9-10, 1938, and the invasions of Prague and Yugoslavia in 1939 and 1941 respectively. During those first war years Mandel-Mantello traveled frequently as Secretary-General of El Salvador to Czechoslovakia, Hungary, and Yugoslavia. He was thus able to experience how the Jews were being treated in those countries as well as in others which had already been occupied by the Nazis. He then decided to intervene in their favor and help as many of them as possible to emigrate to Hungary and Rumania, from where they could then migrate to Palestine, England and the U.S.A.* As a Latin American diplomat in neutral Switzerland then, he hoped to be able to unite representatives of both local and international Jewish organizations — as well as other activists — in a joint effort to provide relief. Sadly — almost predictably — his hopes were frustrated again and again. Project after project failed to receive necessary support due to personality and ideological clashes among various Jewish representatives, Swiss legal pettifogging, and a general resignation in the face of ongoing events.

UNDAUNTED, HOWEVER, MANDEL-MANTELLO turned to the Orthodox activists, his most consistent — and most consistently

Maitre Muller supportive — allies. Indeed, one of his key contacts was a Paris lawyer, Maitre Matthieu Muller, the long-time president of the French Agudah. Maitre Muller was relatively new to Switzerland himself, having just escaped from Vichy France — a journey made possible because *le Maitre* was accompanied by his wife, five daughters, and varied Jewish girls whom he personally rescued. This was possible by the "humane" Swiss laws which permitted entry to those refugee families with children under sixteen, while sending all other adults between sixteen and sixty back across the border. Almost immediately, Maitre Muller was placed by Mandel-Mantello in charge of a newly

---

* In this he was greatly helped by his former Rumanian business partners General Draganescu (a WWI hero who had defeated the famous German Gen. Mackensen at Marasesti); Col. Ralya, the Minister of Interior's brother, and Capt. Vasilescu, brother-in-law of the Chief of the Rumanian Secret Service.

created division of the Salvadoran Mission — an operation housed in its own separate building which with the help of Jewish and Catholic Hungarian students, who knew how to spell the difficult Hungarian names, mass-produced Salvadoran citizenship papers for refugee Jews. The first to request Salvador citizenship papers was Dr. Max Kimche, a lawyer, who was to be helpful to Mantello in later rescue projects. This rescue effort was, of course, enormous, and involved gathering Jewish names from German-occupied Hungary, Poland, Czechoslovakia, Holland, Belgium, and France, and stamping out seemingly authentic Salvadoran citizenship papers and then sending them to Jews all over Europe in the sometimes vain hope that they would be in time. Yet even then, the papers could be used — by relatives, neighbors, or others facing deportation to the camps; or sometimes by certain Nazis who had created the rather lucrative business of selling them.

INDEED, THE FINEST TRIBUTE TO MANDEL-MANTELLO'S work with the Salvadoran papers came in a cable sent to the U.S. State

U.S. Ambassador Winant's Tribute Department in the middle of 1943 by John Winant, the U.S. Ambassador to Great Britain. In it he described the sale of such Latin American documents.

> ... The average price of a passport was approximately 700 Swiss francs. Only the Secretary-General of El Salvador has acted from purely humanitarian motives. There is little doubt that the German authorities are aware of what has been going on but for reasons of their own they have hitherto not adopted a set policy of withdrawing passports. Some estimates are as high as 10,000.[2]

Mandel-Mantello produced thousands of Salvadoran documents free of charge, of course, causing an ironic depression in the for-pay market.* What's more, many Jews, notably in Budapest, forged further copies of the false papers, flooding the market even further. Still, there were some who continued to act as middlemen and make a profit on the sale of human lives. As we have seen, by the end of 1943, there arose a real danger to the holders of these "bogus" papers, as a consequence of a demand by the Germans for verification from the supposed host Latin American countries that they had indeed issued the papers in question and were willing to accept the corresponding parties. Many countries, of course, refused

---

* There were people who were still willing to pay for the other Latin American passports under the illusion that these were superior to the Salvador citizenship papers. As they discovered later, the opposite was true.[3]

to do this — thereby sending thousands of Jews to their deaths. El Salvador, led by its president General Castenendu Castro, under the influence of Ambassadors Col. I. H. Castellanos and Jose G. Guerrero, later President of the High Court of The Hague, cooperated from the outset.

WHILE MANTELLO'S DISTRIBUTION of free Salvador papers was extraordinary enough, his second rescue feat was even more so. **The Auschwitz Protocols** With it he was able to accomplish what no one else was, though many tried. This was the instigation of a press campaign which actually stopped the deportations to Auschwitz from Budapest by early July 1944. It was probably the single most incredible and successful rescue attempt during the Holocaust. This occurred in the following manner.

By mid-1944, after Eichmann's brutally efficient deportation of Hungarian Jews to Auschwitz, there were roughly 100-200,000 Jews remaining in and around Budapest. Mantello, of course, realized that those Jews were in serious jeopardy, and took steps to help as many as he could. His work, as it turned out, however, depended in no small degree on two young Slovak-born Jewish inmates of Auschwitz, Alfred Wetzler (also known as Josef Lanik) and Walter Rosenberg (Rudolph Vrba) who had escaped with the help of the underground in Auschwitz, and desperately sought to inform the world about the incredible atrocities that were being committed in the Polish death camp. The two men had not only seen the worst of Auschwitz, they had also witnessed the elaborate preparations — in the gas chambers and elsewhere — for the extermination of the one million Jews who were still living in Hungary under the Fascist Regent Admiral Horthy. The Hungarian Jews had, of course, been relatively safe until March 1944, when the Germans had occupied Hungary to keep her from surrendering to the Soviet Union.

Wetzler and Rosenberg had worked at the Auschwitz registry, and had memorized an enormous amount of data. Once safely with the Jewish underground in Slovakia, they provided material for a 30-or-so-page report, usually referred to as the Auschwitz Protocols. The Jewish underground forwarded copies to Budapest, Geneva and Jerusalem. Rabbi Weissmandl, after his personal interrogation of the two escapees, wrote his own brief Hebrew version of the report, attaching a plea to bomb the gas chambers and especially the railroad tracks leading to the camp.

Many copies of the Protocols reached Switzerland, whose

Jewish organizations brought them to the U.S. Consulate in Geneva and to the representative of the U.S. Refugee Board, McClelland. However, the Allies quietly tucked these heart-rending reports in their "official" wastebaskets and did nothing about them, as 12,000 Jews a day were efficiently murdered by the Nazi death factory at Auschwitz. None of the Jewish representatives gave or even showed a single copy of the Protocols to the El Salvador Secretary General. He found out about it when his special envoy, whom he had sent to Transylvania to rescue his family, brought two copies of it back, tragically, three months late.

Already in March 1944, as soon as the German army occupied Budapest, Mantello organized what was known as the Swiss Committee for Assistance for Jews in Hungary, headed by a Hungarian-Swiss Jew, Michael Banyai, and a rabbinical body chaired by Rabbi Dr. Zvi Taubes, and including Maitre Muller, Rabbi A. Kornfein and Rabbi Tuvia Lewenstein and his sons, to try to publicize the plight of Hungarian Jewry and to try to help them.

HUNGARY WAS THEN CUT OFF FROM THE REST of the world and even the usual couriers were not successful in obtaining any **1,000** concrete information from that now unfortunate **Salvadoran** country. In order to secure some reliable information about the situation, and **Papers** simultaneously rescue his aged parents living in Bistrice, Transylvania (then part of Hungary), Mantello decided to send his friend, Dr. E. Florian Manoliu, Counselor of the Rumanian Legation in Bern, as a reliable courier. At the same time, Mantello sought to provide 1,000 of his Salvador citizenship papers already signed and ready for anyone to place their data and photos on them. These would at least provide that many families with some protection.

Although the German Embassy was very obstructive because of Manoliu's reputation as an anti-Nazi, he was finally able to obtain a transit visa to travel through Hungary on his way to Bucharest. So by the end of May 1944, Manoliu left on his fateful trip on which the suspicious Nazis detained him for a week, and he finally reached Bistritz, only to find that he was too late. Mantello's parents, together with all the Jews of Bistritz had already been shipped to Auschwitz. He then went to Budapest with the Salvador papers to a Moshe (Miklos) Krausz, head of the *Palaestina Amt*. Mantello had obtained a visiting card for Manoliu from Chaim Posner, Krausz' counterpart in Switzerland with remarks in Hebrew stating that Manoliu could be trusted, since Mantello did not personally know Krausz. Manoliu gave the 1,000 certificates to Krausz and in turn Krausz provided him with two reports. The first was an abbreviated version of the Protocols which covered the gassing of almost 1,765,000 Jews through April 1944. By mid-June, however, further Hungarian deportations had raised the total another 335,000, and that further information was included in the second report, this one prepared by Philip Freudiger of the Budapest *Judenrat* and head of the Orthodox community of Budapest. Mandel-Mantello, in turn, read the reports, and had them translated into English.

Along with the two reports Moshe Krausz sent a desperate letter addressed to Chaim Posner requesting that he do something to help, since all the remaining Jews in Budapest were also in danger of being sent to Auschwitz. He especially requested that Posner send him and his family a British passport.

TO MAKE THE LETTER MORE EFFECTIVE, since neither the British nor Swiss knew of either Moshe Krausz, or even Chaim Posner of

Publicizing the Protocols

Switzerland, Mantello changed the addressee from Posner to himself. He also inserted his own name into the middle of the letter, adding a plea to help all the Jews and especially to "publish this letter and the enclosed reports ... so that the world may learn of the cruelties committed in the 20th century in so-called civilized countries." At the bottom he also added the plea, "Helfet, Helfet, Helfet!"

Accompanying Krausz's letter and the two reports was another letter signed by four of Switzerland's most highly respected Protestant theologians and philosophers, namely, Professor Karl Barth, Emil Brunner, W.A. Visser t'Hooft and Rev. Paul Vogt, which noted that:

> They come from an *absolutely reliable source* and were brought into Switzerland through diplomatic channels. These reports have shaken us profoundly. Our sense of responsibility compels us to bring these two reports also to your knowledge ...[4]

This letter was unequivocal in its assertion of the horrible facts and the belief that it came from unimpeachable sources via a neutral diplomat. This is in marked contrast to the Riegner cable of August 28, 1942, which left room for doubt. Amazingly enough, due to the emergency, Mantello affixed the names of the four theologians without asking any of them first; yet when these clerics were questioned by the Swiss police, they all voiced their unqualified approval of what Mantello had done. In fact, thousands of copies of the Protocols were made and circulated by the clergy to politicians, MP's and other prominent people, telling them to spread the news and within a month, one of them, Rev. Paul Vogt, published a small, but powerful book entitled *Soll ich meines Bruders Hueter sein* (Am I My Brother's Keeper?) based on the reports publicized by Mantello. In it he condemned the passivity of the free world as onlookers to the world's greatest crime, and helped to turn the atmosphere in Switzerland into a much more sympathetic one vis-a-vis the Jewish plight. Mantello handed two copies of the Protocols to the British military attache, General F. M. West. He was stunned by the content. He immediately called his American counterpart, Allen Dulles, of the Office of Strategic Services (OSS). They were both surprised as none of them had seen the Protocols before. They decided to call their respective governments to inform them of these documents.

Along with Dr. Max Kimche, Mantello then went to Zurich to see Walter Garrett, director of the British Exchange Telegraph — Independent News Agency and a British intelligence agent. With the two reports and the covering letters, Mantello persuaded Garrett, who meanwhile on the same day had received approval from his own embassy, to send cable-form summaries of the Protocols to all the major news agencies and Western embassies in Switzerland, including the United States, Britain, Sweden, the Vatican — and even Hungary.

The text itself, though abbreviated, is still stirring:

I.

NEUTRAL DIPLOMAT AND CATHOLICCHURCH HUNGARY VOUCH ABSOLUTE TRUTH FOLLOWING DETAILED REPORT REVEALING FATE HUNG-JEWS''CONCENTRATION HUNGJEWS BEGAN APRIL 16 FORTYSIX COMMUNITIES AROUND NYIREGYHAZA THEN RAPIDLY SPREADING ALL PROVINCES STOP NYIREGYHAZA GHETTO COVERED 9665 SQMETERS WHERE 10759 PERSONS SQUEEZED TOGETHER SLEPT BARE EARTH INCLUDING PREGNANTS BABIES SICK ALDERLIES STOP ADDITIONAL CONCAMP OPENEED BARON MOLNARS FARM STOP DAILY RATION ONLY HUNDREDGRAMS BREAD BEANS TWO GLASSES WATER STOP BY MAY 10 TENTHOUSANDS MORE JEWS ARRIVED EXALL PARTS HUNGARY CONCENTRATED TOBACCO BARNS SIMAPUZZTA, VARJULAPOS AND

NYIRJES STOP HUNDREDS DIE DAILY EXHUNGER UNATTENDED ILLNESS STOP ON MAY 15 DEPORTATION BEGAN UNKNOWN DESTINATION BUT LATER REVEALED AUSCHWITZ IN WAGONLOADS 70 STOP JUNE 6 POLICE OFFICIALLY STATED ALL JEWS PROVINCE NYIREGYHAZA LEAD BY CHIEFRABBI DOCTOR BELA BERNSTEIN TRANSPORTED AUSCHWITZ STOP MEANTIME BETWEEN APRIL 30 END MAY ALL JEWS PROVINCE MUNKACS — COMITAT BEREG ALSO DEPORTED TOGETHER THOSE ARYANS WHO HELPED THEM OR PROTESTED HUNGGOVERNMENT AGAINST INCREDIBLE BRUTALITY STOP FORMER PREMIER IMREDY OFFICE PROUDLY ANNOUNCED JUNE 10 TO HOMEOFFICE BUDAPEST "FOLLOWING PARTS HUNGARY COMPLETELY FREE JEWS: SUBKARPATHIA DEPORTATION FIGURE K57 THOUSAND 500 STOP TRANSYLVANIA 94000 UPPERHUNGARY 35000 UPPER TISZA DISTRICT 75000 SOUTHERN HUNGARY 25000 STOP ALTOGETHER THIRTYSIX TOWNS ABOVE PROVINCES CLEARED EXJEWS STOP TOTAL 335000 HUNGJEWS DEPORTED CHIEFLY UPPER SELESIA"

II.

CATHOLIC CHURCH HUNGARY TWO QUOTE CONCENTRATION JEW BUDAPEST BEGAN JUNE 16 END JUNE 21 IN HOUSES CHESSBOARD SYSTEM AS GOVERNMENT BELIEVED REST BUDAPEST WOULD EXPOSED HEAVY BOMBARDMENTS IF JEWS LIVED ABSOLUTELY SEPARATELY ONE SPECIAL PART TOWN STOP FORMERLY SOME EXCEPTION MADE BUT TODAY NONE STOP PROTECTIVE POWERS REPRESENTATIVE CATHCHURCH INVAIN SOUGHT HELP STOP JUNE 22 JEWS OFFICIALLY INFORMED DEPORTATION BEGINNABLE END NEXT WEEK WHICH UNDOUBTLY MEANS JOURNEY TO DEATH STOP AS ALL APPEALS WARNINGS BRITAMER GOVERNMENTS FAILED DIPLOMAT SANSALVADOR WITH SPECIAL AUTHORIZATION PRESIDENT SANSALVADOR UNDERTOOK ONLY WAYOUT SAVE LARGE NUMBER FAMILIES ANNIHILATION BY GRANTING THEM NATIONALITY CERTIFICATES SANSALVADOR WHEREBY JEWS ENJOY INTERVENTION POSSIBILITY ALLIIE [sic] PROTECTIVE POWER HUNGARY WHICH HOWEVER UNABLE INTERVENE WITHOUT WASHINGTON CONSENT STOP MAYBE EMPHASIZED

SANSALVADORS ENDEAVORS MERELY DICTATED
UTMOST NECESSITY RENDER IMMEDIATE HELP AND
WITHOUT SLIGHTEST REMUNERATION STOP
NEUTRAL DIPLOMATS REPRESENTATIVE
CATHCHURCH EMPHITICALLESTLY UNDERLINE
SALVADOR ATTITUDE ONLY MEANS SAVE FURTHER
VICTIMS FROM TERREBLE [sic] DISASTER END

III.

FOLLOWING DRAMATIC ACCOUNT ONE
DARKEST CHAPTERS MODERN HISTORY REVEALING
HOW ONEMILLION 715 THOUSAND JEWS PUT DEATH
ANNIHILATION CAMP AUSCHWITZ BIRKENAU AND
HARMANSEE BRACKET UPPER SILESIA UNBRACKET
WHERE ALSO AWFUL DESTINY HUNGJEWS TODAY
FULFILLING ITSELF STOP REPORTS COME EXTWO JEWS
WHO ESCAPED BIRKENAU CORRECTNESS WHEREOF
CONFIRMED RESPONSIBILITY THEREFORE ACCEPTED
EXONE NEUTRAL DIPLOMAT TWO HIGH
FUNCTIONARIES CATHCHURCH STOP QUTOE BE-
TWEEN APRIL THIRTEENTH 1942 TO BEGINNING JUNE
1944 FOLLOWING NUMBERS JEWS GASSED DEATH
AUSCHWITZ: BRACKET IN THOUSANDS UNBRACKET
EXPOLAND NINEHUNDRED EXHOLLAND ONE HUN-
DRED EXGREECE FORTYFIVE EXFRANCE ONEHUN-
DREDFIFTY EXBELGIUM FIFTY EXGERMANY SIXTY
EXYUGOSLAVIA ITALY NORWAY FIFTY EXBOHEMIA
MORAVIA AUSTRIA THIRTY EXSLOVAKIA THIRTY
STOP GASSING OF FURTHER THREE HUNDRED
THOUSANDS FOREIGN JEWS WHO ARRIVED EXDIF-
FERENT POLISH CAMPS TOOK PLACE SAME PERIOD
BUT NATIONALITY UNKNOWN STOP ON ARRIVAL
AUSCHWITZ CAMP WE IMMEDIATELY TATOOED
NUMBER LEFTSIDE CHEST WHICH IN FEBRUARY 1943
BEGAN WITH 28600 STOP WHEN WE ESCAPED
BEGINNING JUNE 1944 TATOOED NUMBERS REACHED
180000 WHICH THEN BEING TATOOED LEFT FOOT
STOP BORDERING AUSCHWITZ CAMP ARE NEW
FACTORIES CALLED DEUTSCHE AUFRUSTUNGSWERKE
MUTUALLY KRUPP SIEMENS AND BUNA WORKS
UNDER CONSTRUCTION WHERE MANY PRISWAR
EMPLOYED STOP AUSCHWITZ CAMP GUARDED
ELECTRICCURRENT FENCE S. MASCHINEGUN-
STOWERS [sic] SEARCHLIGHTS STOP CAPTURED
ESCAPEES HANGED PRESENCE WHOLE CAMP BODY
LEFT ENTRANCE CAMP BEARING POSTER QUOTE HERE

I AM UNQUOTE STOP OUR WORKING GROUP
EMPLOYED CONSTRUCTION DAWERKE AND OWING
BAD INSUFFICIENT FOOD CONSTANT BEATING EXOVE
[sic] RSEERS OF 650 ONLY 150 JEWS ALIVE AFTER
FORTNIGHT STOP CORPSES BROUGHT BY US TO
AUSCHWITZ CREMATORIUM MORE.

IV

CONTINUATION ONE QUOTE MARCH 1943
SOCALLED SELECTION BEGAN STOP TWICE WEEKLY
DOCTOR DECIDED WHICH INTERNEES BE GASSED
WHEREAFTER BURNT STOP TWO THOUSAND DIED
WEEKLY SICKHOUSE 800 WHEREOF WERE GASSED
STOP ONE DAY TRANSPORT 1600 FRENCH JEWS
ARRIVED 600 WHEREOF TATOED [sic] RUNNING
NUMBER FROM 38000 ONWARDS WHILE REMAINING
THOUSAND MOSTLY ELDERLY MEN WOMEN AND
CHILDREN IMMEDIATELY GASSED AND BODIES
CREMATED STOP FROM BEGINNING JUNE 1943
NINETYPERCENT INCOMING JEWS GASSED DEATH
STOP EXECUTIONERS SOCALLED SONDERCOMMAND
UNDER SUPREME COMMAND SS STURMFUHRER
SCHWARZHUBER EXTYROL SUPERVISED THREE
GASCHAMBERS FOUR CREMATORIUMS BIRKENAU-
AUSCHWITZ STOP EACH CREMATORIUM CONSIST
THREE BUILDINGS A FURNACES B BATHINGHALL C
GASCHAMBER STOP CAPACITY FURNACES TWO
THOUSAND CORPSES DAILY STOP EACH OVEN
CAPABLE THREE CORPSES AT TIME STOP SOCALLED
BATHINGHALL WITH IMITATION SHOWERS ROOM
FOR 2000 PEOPLE IS WHERE VICTIMS BROUGHT TOLD
THEY GETTING BATH EVEN GIVEN TOWEL AND SOAP
WHEN UNDRESSED BRACKET MEN WOMEN
TOGETHER UNBRACKET WINDOWS ROOF CLOSED
HERMETICALLY AND GAS DISTRIBUTED EXSHOWERS
STOP GAS PRODUCED EXTINNED POWDER LABELLED
QUOTE SCHAEDLINGSBEKAEMPFUNG UNQUOTE
MANUFACTURED HAMBURG BELIEVED CYANIDE
STOP DEAD [sic] TAKES THREEMINUTES THEN
CREMATION FOLLOWS STOP SOMETIME PROMI-
NENTS EXBERLIN WATCH PROCEDURE THROUGH
PEEPHOLES STOP FIRST TRANSPORTS EX-
THERESIENSTADT ARRIVED SEPTEMBER 1943 CHIEFLY
CZECHS LATER MOSTLY GERMANS INCLUDING
UNIVERSITY PROFESSORS GREAT PERCENTAGE
INTELLECTUALS STOP VICTIMS FORCED REQUEST

FRIENDS ABROAD FOODPARCELS ONE WEEK BEFORE DEATH WHICH PARCELS WERE THEN TAKEN EXCAMP ADMINISTRATORS STOP WHEN WE LEFT GASSING AND CREMATIONS 24-HOUR SHIFT REACHED 600 END.
    GARRETT ADDS ABSOLUTE EXACTNESS ABOVE REPORT UNQUESTIONABLE AND DIPLOMAT CATHOLIC FUNCTIONARIES WELLKNOWN VATIKAN DESIRE WIDEST DIFFUSION WORLDWIDE END EX-CHANGE.[5]

Ironically, one of the most difficult outlets for Holocaust news was the Swiss press, governed by strict neutralist censorship. Indeed, before Mantello's press campaign, Swiss newspapers carried virtually no news of the conflagration that was taking place just across their borders. They were supersensitive about the publication of any unfavorable report concerning the Nazis, particularly atrocity stories, unless they had been previously published in another neutral country. Therefore, Mantello and Garrett obviated this obstacle by using an Ankara (Turkey) dateline for the cables. Yet, in this case, and despite vehement protests made by the Hungarian and German embassies in Switzerland, virtually the entire Swiss press — more than 400 newspapers — carried the story of 12,000 Jews being killed every day, often with front-page coverage. Such searing headlines included: "A Cry of Pain Fills the World," "The Guilt of Silence," "The Protest of the Swiss People," "For such a Crime There Can Be No Neutrality." The names of Professors Barth and Brunner added further weight to those stories.[6]

THE RESPONSE WAS AS SUDDEN AS IT WAS UNIVERSAL. Within days after the cables had been dispatched on June 24-26, even

"Europe is much Sicker ..."

quarters that had previously kept a discreet silence began to respond loudly and angrily. President Roosevelt sent a particularly fierce warning to Hungary through Cordell Hull, the Secretary of State, to stop the deportations, as did Pope Pius XII and King Gustav V of Sweden. The latter went so far as to dispatch Raoul Wallenberg to Budapest as his special envoy (with the authority of the War Refugee Board as well), with great yet tragic results. Britain's Anthony Eden also publicly condemned the atrocities and warned the Germans that at the end of the war they would be tried as war criminals — while the BBC broadcast the Protocols' essence to the world. Even the International Red Cross, which until then had refused to address the severe problem of the specifically Jewish victims, began to act, as did the Swiss, who tightened their protection of Jews in Budapest carrying Salvadoran papers.

The long-range impact of these reports on the Swiss themselves can be gauged from the response of a highly distinguished Swiss editor. The opening of his provocative essay begins with:

> The attached reports were received by us from a quarter which leaves no doubt as to their veracity ... Something in us, however, still refuses, regardless of undisputed proofs, to believe them. More than in the extirpation of European Jewry, we are stung by the destruction and renunciation of humanity ... this method of putting a conflict out of the way by the most ghastly, inhuman and disgusting means. These are the things we somehow cannot accept as true, inasmuch as the consequences for the future of civilization will be immeasurable and eternal ... Europe is much sicker than we would like to admit ...

Every two days Mantello would send copies of the latest Swiss headlines blasting the Nazi barbarism and cruelty to the German Embassy in Bern. To each package, Mantello would add the warning that the Germans will have to reckon with the world's wrath someday and be prepared to pay the price. The enraged Germans unsuccessfully tried to put a halt to this heated press campaign. The Swiss warned them, however, that any attempt to censor these revelations about Auschwitz would only exacerbate the debate and enrage the Swiss even more.

Finally, even the Nazis themselves, in fact, had to respond, for even they did not wish to be identified with the systematic murder of nearly two million human beings.[7] The Deputy Chief of the German Propaganda Ministry Suendermann declared a few days later in a press conference that the International Red Cross had visited the model camp at Theresienstadt where they were shown how well Jewish families lived together.

Suendermann concluded his defensive article with the remarks:

> The Jews incite newspapers and other organizations with the intention of defamatory canards concerning alleged mistreatment. There is sufficient evidence to prove that the Jewish question is not only a problem for us but also for our enemies as well. The world will have peace only when a world-wide quarantine is instituted for this disruptive element ...[8]

This was therefore supposed to sustain the German argument that all that was written against them in Switzerland was false. Ironically, Rudolph Kastner, who was busy at the time getting out his train from Budapest, warned Mantello not to publicize the

Protocols, from fear that his agreement with Eichmann and Becher could fail. In fact, Kastner had been made to believe by Eichmann that the Zionist convoy would be bound for Spain and eventually to Palestine. The press campaign actually helped to stop the train while on its way to Auschwitz and its insistence had the effect of detouring it to Bergen-Belsen, a less cruel camp, from where, a few months later it was brought into Switzerland (without Swiss permission).

It all worked — to a greater or lesser degree — for Admiral Horthy felt the impact of world opinion and ceased all Auschwitz-bound deportations on July 7, 1944. That same day Capt. Rothmund of the Swiss Alien Police was compelled to modify, at least on paper, the severe regulations concerning *refoulement*. For the first time the category of those permitted entry cited ... those who out of political and other reasons find themselves in physical danger ... *for example*, *Jews*. [Emphasis added] Directly then, the publicity generated by the Secretary General of the El Salvadoran Consulate saved Budapest's last remaining 100,000 Jews — and another approximately one hundred thousand more hiding in different parts of the country. While life in Budapest was not easy for the Jews by any means — especially since the Hungarian Nazi Arrow-Cross would frequently shoot Jews on sight, regardless of papers or the protective houses set up by the Swiss, the Spanish and Swedish (the latter under Raoul Wallenberg), and one small transport of Jews did leave Budapest, still the vast majority survived the last few harrowing months due to Mantello's brilliant and courageous act.

F. FRANZI GOLDSCHMIDT: AN INTREPID WOMAN[1]

Saving the Rosmans

AS EVEN THE MOST CASUAL OBSERVER of the Second World War era undoubtedly knows, the September 29, 1938 Munich Agreement between Great Britain and Germany — dubbed the so-called "peace in our time" pact by Prime Minister Neville Chamberlain — directly resulted in the German annexation of the Sudetenland section of Czechoslovakia. And if that action did not serve effective notice on Europe generally, and Jews specifically, as to what was assuredly coming, the terror and violence of *Kristallnacht* but a month later, on November 9-10, 1938, clearly indicated to most Jews the path the Third Reich would take. By then, most Jews living in Greater Germany (including annexed Austria) wanted to leave — but there was no place open to them in sufficient numbers. As individuals cast about for various methods to get out, one family was fortunate enough to find a haven in Switzerland, with the help of a remarkable woman named Franzi Goldschmidt.

Franzi Goldschmidt, the daughter of Zurich's Rabbi Tuvia Lewenstein, had always been active in Jewish community affairs, having founded and led N'shei Agudath Israel — the world organization's women division. She was the key speaker at the N'shei section of the 1937 World Agudath Convention in Marienbad, Czechoslovakia, where she befriended a Mrs. Feyge Rosman of Chust.[2]

The Rosmans, fully cognizant of the troubled times ahead, had left their home in Chust, Czechoslovakia, hoping to relocate in Switzerland. Like many other Jews, however, they could not cross the closely guarded border, and therefore found themselves homeless — and waiting — in Milan, Italy. Facing an understandably uncertain future, the Rosmans contacted Mrs. Goldschmidt, who thereupon dispatched her husband, a businessman, to help with the Rosmans' passage across the border. In Milan, Mr. Goldschmidt, who knew the difficulties involved, advised Mr. Rosman to leave all his luggage behind in his hotel room and bring only one suitcase with him — making it appear as if he were merely leaving the hotel on a short business trip. Then they met in the Swiss-Italian border town of Pascciavo, where they duped the border guards at the customs house by chatting nonchalantly about their plans for Switzerland as a pair of wealthy businessmen on a trip. To lend credence to their appearance, Goldschmidt went so far as to smoke a *Stupen* cigar, something of a status symbol.

Even so, it was no small problem to get Hershel Rosman across the border. Even though he held a Czech passport, which was recognized, there was only a small chance that he would be permitted to enter Switzerland — because the Swiss government felt that Jews were more interested in permanent residence rather than temporary stays. And as we have seen already, many more Jews were turned away than permitted to enter. Yet, because of Rosman's and Goldschmidt's ruse, the guards wound up stamping the Czech's passport — despite the fact that he had no official Swiss visa.

Rosman, then, duly crossed over into Switzerland — on a Friday afternoon. The following Sunday he was required by Swiss law to go to the Alien Police and register for a four-week visa — another possible stumbling block. Yet once more Goldschmidt's formidable voice — and anger over the bureaucratic wrangling — helped Rosman, and he was given his permit. It did not hurt Rosman's cause, too, that there were a few among the police who clearly realized that their racially-motivated policy toward Jews was not in the classic Swiss tradition of refuge.

The four weeks were up in December 1938, and Rosman, along with his family, had to register for a six-month visa extension — the most that the Swiss allowed. This time, however, Franzi Goldschmidt herself took charge of the Rosmans' case, and bypassing the local authorities, went directly to the immigration officials in charge. Perhaps it was her own strong character combined with the Rosmans' plight — Mrs. Rosman was then pregnant — that gained them this one small victory. Challenging the stolid Swiss bureaucrats, she demanded to know how in good conscience they could deny such people permanent entry. Where, she asked, were their values, consciences, and love for their fellow men? Despite ample precedent against her, she indeed convinced the immigration authorities that the Rosmans' claim was valid.

FRANZI GOLDSCHMIDT SAVED MANY OTHERS in addition to the Rosman family. Throughout the war, she was particularly involved **Organizing** in the spiritual rescue of children, by having **Children's** children's transports shipped from Germany to Holland to Switzerland, and by taking children **Transport** from Swiss sanitariums and non-Jewish missionaries and institutions. (With the help of Joseph Heidingsfeld, a Swiss school teacher, she prevented many institutionalized children from being converted to other faiths.) In fact, she herself went to Germany in 1938 and 1939 — and even as late as 1941 — to bring people out.

No task was too small for her. In one instance, for example, her husband took receipt of a letter written from an institutionalized ten-year-old Jewish girl to a friend on the outside. "You are angry with me that I have not written to you," she wrote in part, "but anyway I will leave Judaism and become Protestant soon." The Goldschmidts immediately dispatched their ally, Joseph Heidingsfeld, who told this institution's authorities that although he was a bachelor, the girl was his illegitimate daughter and should therefore be in his custody. The Church opposed the girl's release, but with Heidingsfeld applying pressure in front, and Franzi Goldschmidt talking to the authorities, they soon had the girl in their care; the girl grew up an observant Jew and eventually became the mother of three *kollel* children.

Franzi Goldschmidt was one of many Orthodox activists who worked industriously for Jewish rescue and relief during and after the war. Yet perhaps she is somewhat unique in her extraordinary thoughtfulness even in minor matters. During the war all sorts of food were rationed in Switzerland — which meant that the fare in the Jewish internment camp was something less than wholesome. In order, though, to insure that the children in the camps had at least a taste of childhood's delight, she convinced the Orthodox Swiss children to give up their allotted weekly chocolate bar and instead share it with their less fortunate fellow Jews.

CHAPTER TWELVE
Sweden

A. INTRODUCTION

THOUGH IT WAS NOT AS IMPORTANT in a number of ways as Switzerland — notably as a communications center — nevertheless, neutral Sweden offered a number of unparalleled

Chief Rabbi Against Sweedish Haven

opportunities for Europe's Jews, especially the Orthodox. Of course, there were the famous rescue operations — 900 from Norway and 8,000 from Denmark, both taken literally from the grasp of German troops.

During the late 1930's, Sweden's Jewish community was roughly 7,000 — out of a total population of six million. Perhaps because of the continued high unemployment rate in the country, there was a substantial amount of antisemitism as well as anti-foreign sentiment. To make matters worse, as the Nazis tightened their grip on Europe, Chief Rabbi Marcus Ehrenpreis, a Reform Jew, stood against the use of Sweden as a haven for Jews. Rabbi Ehrenpreis generally refused to use his considerable personal influence in Swedish society to aid Jewish rescue and relief efforts. Instead — like many Jews in America, England and Switzerland — he preferred to avoid raising the so-called Jewish issue, in part because of a feared antisemitic backlash.

The work performed by a very small group of Orthodox activists, however, had in all likelihood some effect on the efforts of Hillel Storch of the Swedish section of the World Jewish Congress,

Mr. and Mrs. Hans Lehmann

who tried to use the Swedes to rescue survivors.[1] Indeed, there was ample precedent, even for one of an assimilationist bent, for nearly half of all the Swedish-Orthodox Jewish families were actively involved in rescue efforts. Clearly, as impotent as the American Jewish community was in the 1940's — despite far greater numbers — the relative handful of Swedish counterparts was infinitely weaker. In such circumstances, then, it is all the more remarkable that these few Jews carried out some minor local matters, as well as some not-so-minor relief and rescue programs as well.

ONE IMPORTANT REASON FOR THE ORGANIZATIONAL success of Sweden's Orthodox Jews was their cohesiveness — and the **Hans Lehmann** literally essential support of a long-time resident and highly visible champion — Hans (Chaim) Lehmann. Lehmann was a successful Stockholm merchant who continued to commute to Sweden after he moved his family back to his native Hamburg, Germany in the late twenties, to insure that his children received a thorough Orthodox education and upbringing. After the rise of the Nazis, however, he came back to Stockholm permanently, and insured the continuance of his children's Jewish education by hiring Rabbi Shlomo Wolbe, a young German graduate of the Mirrer Yeshivah, and sending his two older sons to that great Torah institute.[2] Lehmann's standing among Sweden's Orthodox Jews was further solidified after *Kristallnacht* when a back-alley *klaus* (a small, private synagogue) in Hamburg miraculously escaped the destruction unscathed. Rabbi Dr. Josef Carlebach, who was later murdered by the Germans, appealed to Lehmann to salvage the *Klaus* in toto — a request that the wealthy merchant heeded, transferring every movable piece to Stockholm, where the reconstructed *klaus* became a new focal point — and symbol of hope — for the Orthodox community.[3] It was no accident, then, for example, that the last boatload of Torah scholars leaving Poland in 1940 — including Rabbi Joseph I. Schneerson, the former Lubavitcher Rebbe — rested briefly in the Lehmann home.[4]

Shortly thereafter, the Wolbe-Lehmann link proved to be of enormous importance in the Vaad Hatzalah's network, especially when Rabbi Wolbe was designated by Rabbi Kalmanowitz as his personal contact in Sweden. Among the early Vaad successes, for example, was convincing the Dutch Ambassador in Stockholm to secure additional "Curacaoan visas" so that more yeshivah students in Soviet-occupied Lithuania could travel to Japan — a necessity after both Dutch Ambassador Dekker and Consul Zwartendik fled Lithuania after the June 1940 occupation by the Soviet Union. Similarly, Wolbe and Lehmann served as a vital link in the later efforts to save the Mirrer yeshivah — plans which originated with Rabbi Abraham Kalmanowitz. To be sure, much of the communication came through Switzerland, yet throughout the period much had to be channeled through Sweden — through Rabbi Wolbe and Hans Lehmann. Indeed, when Manfred and Bert, two of the Lehmann sons, were sent to the United States, the former to study at the Ner Israel Yeshivah, they helped Rabbi Kalmanowitz maintain contact via letter and at times long-distance telephone calls.[5]

Events dictated courses of action, and each of Sweden's Orthodox rescue activists developed a different sphere of interests, although they all cooperated when necessary. At the suggestion of Rabbi Kalmanowitz, for example, Rabbi Wolbe joined with Rabbi Binyamin Zev ("Wolly") Jacobson in 1944 to try to convince the Swedish government to provide visas for 500 Torah scholars to come to Sweden from Shanghai. The Jacobsons, too, like Rabbi Yaakov Yisroel Zuber and his son Mendel, worked to save the spiritual as well as the physical lives of the postwar Jewish refugees — notably, the girls in Rabbi Jacobson's own school in the Stockholm suburb of Lidingo.

B. THE POTENTIAL SWEDISH MAGIC CARPET: RABBI SHLOMO WOLBE AND THE MIRRER YESHIVAH IN SHANGHAI[1]

SHANGHAI IS NEARLY 10,000 MILES FROM GERMANY, yet, as the Jews living in that Japanese-occupied city discovered, the Gestapo's influence was so great that it extended even there.

Japan Had Its Own Reasons

Roughly 500 students of the Mirrer Yeshivah — and others, including dozens from Kletzk, Lubavitch, and Lublin — who in 1940 had been stranded in Lithuania, were granted passage through the Soviet Union, and Siberia, to the port city of Vladivostok and finally to Kobe, Japan. Yet after they had been in Japan for a few months, the Japanese government, which was a partner with Germany in the Axis, felt that an escalation of the Second World War was imminent and shipped these refugees to Shanghai. There the group of about 1,000 Polish refugees, which included the 500 or so yeshivah students and rabbis, joined 16,000 other Jewish refugees — largely German and Austrian — who had also found a haven in what was once East Asia's great international city. Although the International Settlement in Shanghai had been largely under Japanese control since 1937, the Jewish community had enjoyed a relatively stable life — and since the Torah scholars were coming from Japan itself, they needed no visas or official documents of any kind to enter. All that was required was Japan's approval to settle in their sector of the International Settlement of Shanghai. Unknown to the Jews, or anyone else for that matter, was the fact that for its own reasons, amplified by this author elsewhere, this Asian ally of Hitler adopted a pro-Jewish policy which was responsible for the rescue of over 17,000 Jewish refugees.[2]

The new, largely Polish-born refugees received help both from Russian and Sephardic Jews led by Rabbi Meir Ashkenazi as well as Vaad Hatzalah and Joint. Shortly after their arrival, then, the yeshivah refugees were able to continue their studies in a beautiful Sephardic synagogue — a first, to be sure, for East Asia.[3]

IN JULY 1942, OR SOON AFTER America's entry into the war and the commencement of actual fighting in the Pacific, rumors began to **Soviet** circulate that the Germans had convinced their Axis **Veto** partners to follow their policy of exterminating Jews. One particularly gruesome plan — created by several **Power** Japanese junior officers who were personal admirers of Hitler — called for all the Jewish refugees to be placed aboard ships and then sent, unmanned, into the sea. Fortunately, this and other death plans never materialized, yet the Japanese did eventually yield to German pressure and in mid-1943 created a ghetto in Shanghai. While on the one hand conditions in the Shanghai ghetto were hardly as barbarous as those in Europe — the residents were free, for example, to travel to their *bais hamidrash* outside the ghetto proper — life inside was often strained at best. Indeed, when the ghetto was created, no one, either in Shanghai or in Europe or America, knew how closely it might resemble the Nazi models.[4]

Rabbi Kalmanowitz and the Vaad Hatzalah moved quickly to circumvent wherever possible any harmful effect on the hundreds of yeshivah students. They contacted a variety of possible support agencies, from the State Department in Washington to the Vatican to representatives of the Mexican government. Finally, they called Rabbi Wolbe in Stockholm: would the Swedes take the yeshivah, and could they help in an evacuation, by land, sea, or air? The entire operation depended on whether the Swedish government would provide a collective visa for the 500, and Rabbi Wolbe, along with "Wolly" Jacobson, brought the case to Crown Prince Gustaf Adolph. The Prince said he would consider the matter, and did: the next day a Swedish State Department messenger brought the necessary papers to the Vaad Hatzalah office.

There was, however, one problem: transit. The only feasible means of transportation was by ship, and then rail through the Soviet Union. The Japanese authorities had already assented to the plan — but would the Soviet Union? They didn't, and the yeshivah remained in Shanghai, where it survived through the continued support of Rabbi Kalmanowitz and the Vaad.[5]

C. RABBI YAAKOV YISROEL ZUBER[1]

Rabbi Yaakov Yisroel Zuber

Mendel Zuber

ONE DAY IN LATE 1940, after the German invasion of Holland, an elderly Jew with a long beard, and his clean-shaven son, approached the German Embassy in Stockholm. It seemed that a group of Dutch Jews — desperate, nearly frantic — had come to this man, the rabbi of a small Lubavitcher *shtibel*,* and asked for help in rescuing a group of endangered girls in Holland. So while the rabbi waited nervously outside, his son, who looked and sounded like any other Swede, went in and asked the Nazis for help in providing papers so that he could marry one of the girls in question. Without the slightest difficulty — even helpfully — the German Consul, who was fully aware of the man's true intentions in the matter, gave the rabbi's son all the necessary papers. It did not take long for the young man's Dutch "bride" — whom he had never before seen — to arrive safely in Sweden. Nor did it take much time for young Mendel Zuber, son of Rabbi Yaakov Yisroel Zuber, to repeat his action, again and again, always with the full cooperation of the "Nazi" official, until he had married — and rescued — half-a-dozen Dutch "brides."

My Dutch "Bride"

---

* A small, informal (Chassidic) synagogue, usually housed in a private house or other distinct non-synagogue structure.

The marriage operation was hardly the first or the last Zuber relief and rescue effort carried out during the War. As early as 1939, Rabbi Zuber began to receive letters — often including photographs and personal data — asking for help out of occupied Europe. Somehow, numerous people had discovered that there was an Orthodox rabbi in Stockholm, and had turned to him for help. He, in turn, could not refuse, and tried many consulates hoping to secure visas for these people, unfortunately without initial success. Soon after, however, his son became acquainted with three Honorary Consuls (so called because, unlike career diplomats, these were businessmen, who served officially only on a part-time basis) who eventually helped rescue dozens of families. When Mendel Zuber told his three non-Jewish associates of the plight of the people who had written to his father, they responded positively and decisively. Representing such diverse nations as Honduras, Haiti and Afghanistan, each man made out visas for every family who had written to Zuber. These visas were never intended to be used for immigration; instead they were intended as protection, for the holders of such visas were often shipped to Vittel, a detention camp for the so-called privileged (including political prisoners, those with visas, and those slated for exchange) or to a similar special section in Bergen-Belsen. None of the Honorary Consuls took any remuneration for his work. What's more, the three tried to make matters easier for the Jews holding visas for their countries by sending fact sheets about their supposed new homes — a hedge against untimely and intrusive questions about lands they had never seen and barely heard of. Sadly — tragically — despite these and many other efforts, on a number of fronts, as we have noted, the Vittel inmates eventually ended up in Auschwitz. Ultimately, though, 25 families or so were able to use the Zuber-generated papers for survival and escape.[2]

LIKE NUMEROUS OTHER ORTHODOX RESCUE ACTIVISTS, Rabbi Zuber was highly active in the Swedish Committee of the Vaad

Rabbi Ehrenpreis Blocked Entry Hatzalah.[3] Understandably, within this group, though, he had a special interest in the Lubavitcher Yeshivah and the remnants of that yeshivah that survived in Shanghai; similarly, Rabbi Wolbe paid special attention to those members of his former school, the Mirrer Yeshivah, then also in that East Asian metropolis. The main obstacle to any of the rabbis' rescue plans was Rabbi Ehrenpreis, particularly if the plan involved bringing any refugees into Sweden. His role was so minimal that even non-Jewish government officials did more for rescue — and wondered aloud about his superpatriotic stance.[4] (Indeed, Ehrenpreis' stand cut so deeply against the more humane policies of the Swedish government that officials eventually began to disregard him and allowed thousands of Jewish survivors into the country.) As late as 1940, for example, there was the opportunity to save a small Latvian yeshivah — indeed, an American Jew had even guaranteed the Swedish government a half-million dollars for its upkeep. Yet, Rabbi Ehrenpreis singlehandedly blocked entry, citing the idea that Jews should in no way draw attention to themselves. "This will lead to antisemitism," he was wont to say. Similarly, on a lesser scale, he even prevented the notable Vilna publisher of the Talmud (the widow and Rom Brothers), and other classic Jewish works, from obtaining asylum in Sweden on the same grounds that his appearance would only have negative repercussions.[5]

STILL, RABBI ZUBER CLAIMED ONE TRIUMPH which even Rabbi Ehrenpreis could not take from him: enabling hundreds of *agunos*

Rabbi Zuber's Triumph to marry. An *agunah* is a woman whose husband is presumed but not proven dead and who therefore cannot remarry, and there were literally thousands of such women after the War. Working endlessly, Rabbi Zuber systematically researched death lists in Sweden, then corroborated the names with Displaced Persons authorities in Germany. His thoroughness is the kind of highly accurate information which was recognized by Rabbi Yecheskel Abramsky of the London Bet Din and Rabbi Shlomo Dovid Kahane of the Warsaw and later the Jerusalem Bet Din. This saved many from remaining in the perpetual limbo of a technically deserted wife.[6]

D. LIDINGO, SWEDEN: SPIRITUAL AND PHYSICAL REJUVENATION

IN THE WEEKS PRECEDING THE HOLIDAY of *Shevuos* (May) 1945, hundreds of concentration camp survivors, largely from

With Official Sanction Ravensbrueck concentration camp (released shortly before the end of the war through the Sternbuch-Musy negotiations), flooded southern Sweden. The group, by and large Hungarian women and children,

Rabbi Binyamin Zev Jacobson

were exhausted, starved, drained; yet, along with the food and rest and shelter they needed, many of them also asked for *siddurim, Shabbos* candles — ways to fulfill *mitzvos*. Rabbi Eliezer Berlinger of Malmoe, unable to perform such an extensive service by himself, called upon Rabbi Shlomo Wolbe and the Vaad Hatzalah for help. Rabbi Wolbe, along with the Vaad secretary, Rabbi "Wolly" Jacobson, immediately suggested that the Vaad support a number of the refugees, emphasizing especially the need for continued Jewish education. Following this policy, Rabbi Avrohom Yisroel Jacobson (formerly of Norway — not to be confused with his colleague, Rabbi "Wolly" Jacobson) successfully negotiated with the Swedish government for permission to establish an Orthodox school for an initial sixty women, and later more.[1]

Swedish policy was so favorable to Jews, that the government permitted the school to operate without interference and actually funded it for two years. In due course, Rabbi "Wolly" Jacobson became the dean of the Lidingo school, and his *rebbitzin* the headmistress. Utilizing the talents of teachers gathered from all over Europe, the Jacobsons were able to offer these women a good home, refreshed spirit, and complete Torah atmosphere — all of which would not only be beneficial per se, but would act as effective counters against the assimilationism prevailing in Sweden.[2]

TO BE SURE, MANY OF THE WOMEN were in Lidingo — and Sweden — temporarily, yet Rabbi Jacobson worked to provide a

A New Home — No Hurt Feelings

stable, warm home for them, one virtually indistinguishable from his own home. Indeed, he asked that his own children call him Rabbi Jacobson, and their mother "Frau Rabbiner" so that those without parents would not have their feelings hurt. Similarly, he shared all financial matters with the girls at Lidingo so that not only would they develop a sense of responsibility, but also that they would never feel like outsiders.

The Polish girls began to come on *Shabbos Chazon*, the Sabbath immediately preceding Tishah B'Av, the fast day commemorating the destruction of the Temple in Jerusalem. One dazed young girl, free for the first time in six years, was so overwhelmed by the sight of so many trees without barbed-wire fences in between that she began to cry and recited *shehecheyanu*, the blessing of thanks for renewal. Others, too, tearful and lonely, were moved by the fact that for a while, at least, they were going to live in an authentic Orthodox community, much as they had with their parents. Rabbi Jacobson blessed the girls as a father would his own daughters, and told them how their parents' souls rejoiced in their children's Sabbath observance.

In time, the girls developed deep friendships with the Jacobsons and others, notably Rabbi Wolbe and Rabbi Avrohom Yisroel Jacobson. The latter, in fact, was so concerned about the girls' possible intermarriage that he himself traveled to Washington in an attempt to secure visas for his charges. Sadly, his failure weighed enormously on him, and he died soon after his return to Stockholm. Later, perhaps spurred both by Rabbi Avrohom Jacobson's desire as well as his failure, Rabbi "Wolly" Jacobson retraced the other man's steps and was in fact successful.

In his own memoirs, Rabbi "Wolly" Jacobson writes eloquently of the young women's character and *mitzvos*, nourished, perhaps, by the Lidingo teachers, but obviously rooted in their destroyed homes.

The girls' collective love for Torah is nowhere better illustrated than by their collective efforts to live in *Eretz Yisrael*. At one time, due to the efforts of Rabbi Solomon P. Wohlgelernter, Mizrachi leader and the American representative of the Vaad Hatzalah, the girls were given a collective visa to emigrate to the United States. In due course a vote was taken, and the offer was turned down. Instead, the girls decided to wait for permission to emigrate to Palestine — and went so far as to adopt Hebrew as the Lidingo language of instruction. Interestingly, for most the wait was worth it, for many did indeed resettle in Palestine. Many married well; some reached the top ranks of Israeli education. And many continue to think of themselves as daughters of the Lidingo family and proudly say that they owe their present well-being to the Jacobsons.

CHAPTER THIRTEEN
Turkey, Eretz Yisrael, Tangier

A. INTRODUCTION

TURKEY, WHICH LIKE SWEDEN and Switzerland, remained neutral during the Second World War, played — by virtue of its proximity to the Balkans — a unique role as a listening post **Turkey:** and center for rescue activities. Although Turkey **Listening** had been used in a number of important ways **Post** before, it took on increased importance from 1943 on, but especially in 1944, when the problem of rescue in Rumania, Bulgaria and particularly Hungary became paramount.

Following the 1944 German occupation of Hungary, rescue opportunities, paradoxically, began to increase in the Balkans, notably via Rumania. Moreover, much — if not most — of the information on conditions in these countries, as well as original rescue ideas, came from Rabbi Weissmandl in the Slovak-Jewish underground.

Istanbul hosted a delegation of the Vaad Hahatzalah, the rescue committee of the Jewish Agency created in 1942.[1] (This group is not to be confused with the Orthodox New York-based Vaad Hatzalah of the *roshei yeshivah* and Orthodox laymen.)[2] While both the Agudah and the Revisionist-Zionists did not belong to the Jewish Agency, both joined the united rescue efforts; and while all parties were granted representation on the committee, they were decidedly not equal, due in no small degree to the domination of the socialist Jewish Agency.[3]

Whereas, in fact, the official body of the Jewish Agency was in Jerusalem, where David Ben-Gurion held a more dominating position than Yitzchok Grynbaum, the Agency's nominal chairman, its most active section was in Istanbul, due especially to the diligence of the Orthodox and Revisionist-Zionist activists.

The Istanbul group, generally known as the *Moetza*, was headed by Chaim Barlas, who had served in the *Aliyah* department since 1940. Barlas was also the lone officially recognized spokesman for the group, and as one historian has put it in a great understatement, "the other members of the delegation subsequently complained about this situation."[4]

Despite — or perhaps because of — Barlas' outward dominance of the organization, Dr. Yaakov Griffel of the Agudah, and Dr. Joseph Klarman of the Revisionists, both *de facto* outside the Zionist mainstream, worked well together. Griffel became enormously important to the rescue movement — a fact which Barlas, in his memoirs, simply glosses over.[5]

DURING THE FINAL YEAR OF THE WAR, a vital link in the Vaad Hatzalah chain was added in Tangier, the Spanish-controlled

Tangier: International Zone of Morocco. Tangier became
Food increasingly important for food shipments, given
Parcels relative scarcity of foodstuffs in Europe. Mrs. Renee Reichmann helped Vaad Hatzalah send countless food packages from Tangier to starving Jewish inmates in Nazi concentration camps in Europe.

In mid-1944, Mrs. Reichmann, owing to her good connections with the Spanish authorities and the American charge d'affaires, was instrumental in rescuing 1,200 Jewish children from Nazi-occupied Budapest.

B. OUR MAN IN ISTANBUL: DR. YAAKOV GRIFFEL[1]

IN THE LATTER WAR YEARS, neutral Turkey became a key link — second only to Switzerland — in the Jewish intelligence and rescue network. Already toward the end of 1942, the Jewish Agency in Jerusalem, responding to the frightened pleas of European Jewry, created its own Vaad Hahatzalah and opened offices in both Istanbul and Ankara, the Turkish capital. This decision of the Agency was to a great extent a result of pressure from a few Orthodox activists, such as Dr. Yaakov Griffel, Chief Rabbi Yitzchok Isaac Halevy Herzog, Shimon Kornitzer, Binyomin Mintz, and Dr. Isaac Breuer. The task was judged to be so important, in fact, that the Palestinian delegation in Istanbul, led by Chaim Barlas who had headed the Agency's Istanbul Aliyah office, included representatives from virtually every political faction, from Hashomer Hatzair on the extreme left to the Agudah on the right.

Orthodox Pressure the Agency

As always, the Agudah worked closely with anyone who was interested in the common goal of rescuing Jews. Thus, in the spring of 1943 they sent Dr. Yaakov Griffel to Istanbul to represent the Agudath Israel, although he was not an official member. Some time later he was joined by the Slovakian Agudist, Ludwig (Lajos) Kastner (not to be confused with Dr. Rudolph Kastner, who negotiated with Eichmann).

Because Barlas established himself as the only Vaad spokesman recognized by the Turkish government, the Allied governments, and the International Red Cross, the alliance was rocky, with virtually all the other members, including Griffel, protesting his domination. Barlas, clearly representative of the Jewish Agency's left wing, was less than receptive to an Orthodox ideology or agenda.[2] Griffel himself was a strong activist, and he refused to be restricted by the narrow rescue concepts espoused by the Zionists who usually equated rescue with *aliyah*.[3]

DR. GRIFFEL, OR REB YAAKOV AS HE WAS KNOWN to those close to him, was a most extraordinary man. Born of a Polish chassidic

Dr. Joseph Klarman
family, he was a rare Orthodox Jew in that period to earn a doctorate in law. Although he was familiar with secular Polish life between the wars, Griffel nevertheless remained not only a devout Jew, but also retained his chassidic fervor when it came to fulfilling *mitzvos* and, as it turned out, saving Jewish lives. Like virtually all of the Orthodox activists, he too literally embraced all Jews, regardless of religiosity or party registry — a fact mirrored by the high regard the Istanbul-based Marxist atheists had for him. Indeed, Dr. Joseph Klarman, himself not Orthodox, described Griffel as

> ... a most fascinating person and unique ... He fled Poland [in 1939] to Eretz Yisrael, having lost his wife and children, who were trapped in Warsaw, and immediately set out to work on rescue matters. A strictly Orthodox Jew, he was blessed with the character and tolerance of the sage Hillel — yet with an aristocratic posture. Personally most stringent in the observance of Torah, he never yielded an iota, yet he never hesitated to take any step possible to save a Jew — any Jew. He was a man of tall bearing and broad horizons, though reserved and even bashful by nature. He had the charisma and talent to establish good relations with the highest circles in Turkey, Jewish and non-Jewish — wherever necessary to help in the rescue process.[4]

While Griffel actually never belonged to any party — throughout his life he studiously maintained his independence — he served as a representative of both the Agudah and the Poalei Agudah in Istanbul from spring 1943 to the end of the war. When the American War Refugee Board was created in January 1944, Yaakov Rosenheim and Julius Steinfeld arranged to have Griffel represent the American Vaad Hatzalah as well — thereby giving him a unique status outside the Jewish Agency, and more importantly, insuring Griffel's personal access to American Ambassador

Steinhardt and War Refugee Board representatives Ira Hirschmann and Herbert Katzki.[5]

The invaluable American connection enabled Griffel to use the far superior and cheaper cable facilities at the American Embassy in Ankara, as well as to receive money from the U.S. Nevertheless, as the Sternbuchs did in Switzerland, Griffel also made full use of the Polish Government-in-Exile's secret diplomatic cable whenever he had to transmit a message that did not agree with War Refugee Board policy. And in Turkey he developed a very close relationship with Dr. Joseph Klarman of the Revisionist-Zionists, which he represented in the *Moetza*. So much so, that when Griffel became the Vaad's representative vis-a-vis the WRB in early 1944, Klarman joined him as co-representative.[6]

Vaad Contacts GRIFFEL KEPT UP VARIOUS VAAD CONTACTS even before his official designation by New York. He maintained a dialogue with Yisroel Chaim Eis in Switzerland, until Eis' death in late 1943.[7] Griffel also communicated regularly with the Sternbuchs, who frequently relayed his messages to New York, forwarded Vaad funds to him, and generally worked together on several major rescue efforts; and since his own stay in Rumania in 1940, after escaping from Poland, Griffel maintained close relations with Rabbi Eliezer Hager, the Rebbe of Vishnitz, and Rabbi Zusha Portugal, the Admor of Skulen, who passed on vital information on the condition of Rumania's Jews, notably the original 180,000 sent to Transnistria.[8]

Most important of all, however, was the fact that Griffel kept in close touch with Rabbi Weissmandl, who knew that he could trust Griffel more than anyone else on the Jewish Agency's Istanbul delegation. Indeed, Rabbi Weissmandl sent his astounding plea — for the Allies to bomb the rail lines leading to Auschwitz — directly to Griffel, mailing it to the office Griffel maintained separately from the one shared with the delegation. Ironically, Rabbi Weissmandl entrusted his message to the regular mail, coding and signing it "Dr. Michel-Beer," then mailing it from the post office in Bratislava.[9]

Yaakov Griffel's dedication to rescue, despite often remote chances of success, understandably caused frequent long-standing conflicts with other members of the *Moetza* who generally dismissed him as "unrealistic" — a strong Marxist pejorative.[10] Griffel characteristically responded by saying that he cared little about such epithets; further, he added that although in legal or business matters one does indeed weigh avenues of practicality, in matters of rescue one seizes *any* opportunity, regardless of how dim the outcome might seem.[11]

THE ONGOING DISAGREEMENT BETWEEN Griffel and the other factions took on many aspects — from the heights of ideology to the

Chastised by Secularists

depths of penny-pinching. To give but a single example of the difficulties Griffel had to contend with, he was even chastised for spending too much money on Istanbul-Jerusalem cables. When people in German-occupied countries wrote and asked for certificates to Palestine, Griffel invariably forwarded every request via the fastest means possible — by cable to Jerusalem, whether it came from an Orthodox Jew or an atheistic rabidly anti-Orthodox member of Hashomer Hatzair. Naturally, cables cost more than the slower surface mail, and Griffel was taken to task for raising a so-called panic in Jerusalem because he was allegedly wasting valuable funds. His response was characteristic of his lifelong attitude toward rescue work:

> As long as there exists a post office accepting my cables I cannot refrain from forwarding to Jerusalem in the speediest manner the request of a person appealing to me for a certificate. To what extent such an appeal will bring favorable results is none of my concern. My duty is to forward the information immediately to Jerusalem and there is no power in the world that could stop me from doing so, neither political nor financial arguments (such as the cable expenses).[12]

MORE AND MORE PREDICTABLY, Griffel was unable to work within the narrow confines of the Jewish Agency's bureaucracy,

Independent of the Bureaucracy

especially the one run by Chaim Barlas, a man who controlled all aspects of the operation. Griffel, then, with his friend Klarman, sought out independent rescue means — and once Barlas had turned down the profferred help, Griffel felt free to work independently. After the German occupation of Hungary in March 1944, for example, the *Moetza* was ready to give up using Palestine certificates as a means of rescue. Yet Griffel wasn't, reasoning that since Yisroel Chaim Eis and the Sternbuchs had used Latin American papers in occupied territory to keep Jews alive, using Palestinian documents in Hungary was worth a try. Although Barlas threw the familiar charge of "unrealistic" at Griffel, he nevertheless agreed to pursue such a plan — provided that it was implemented by Dr. Joseph Goldin of the Palestine office in Istanbul. As matters turned out, though, the bureaucratic Goldin simply couldn't — or wouldn't — produce a high number of certificates, and was content to let the matter rest by listing all the names and data necessary for subsequent British approval.

Yet Griffel and Klarman were hardly going to let such a rescue opportunity die because of what amounted to bureaucratic technicalities. Instead, they quickly mobilized a large volunteer staff of Orthodox girls from the Istanbul Jewish community, rented additional offices, and supplied them with all the requisite equipment. For their part, the girls worked until midnight — and in some cases afterward — to process the certificates (with all the data that had to be filled in) which were then sent by diplomatic courier to Hungary. As it turned out, these papers sent out by Griffel and his staff saved thousands of Hungarian Jews who were later able to secure the protection of the Swiss and Swedish Red Cross.[13]

IN ANOTHER EVENT, GRIFFEL LEARNED through the Vishnitzer Rebbe that the surviving 70,000 Transnistrian Jews (Rumania) were

Danger in Transnistria

in imminent danger of annihilation. In turn, he told Saul Meyerov, a more sympathetic and influential member of the Istanbul branch of the Histadrut, and less bureaucratic than Barlas, that a major campaign must be mounted to save as many of these Jews as possible. Because of the difficulties encountered in this case, Griffel decided to involve a large number of influential individuals, including *Yishuv* and American-Jewish leaders, and high-ranking functionaries in Turkey, Rumania, and the Vatican. Perhaps most difficult of all was the fact that all the preparations had to be kept secret — or at least away from Barlas, who would never have permitted such independent action. For his part, Meyerov agreed, and went to Jerusalem to try to convince various leaders to support the Griffel plan. First, he succeeded with Rabbi Herzog and his son Yaakov, who had not only been involved in rescue work since the late 1930's, but had also taken a personal hand in helping the Mirrer Yeshivah receive Soviet approval to traverse Siberia to Japan. Griffel himself brought in Dr. Mordechai Eliash, a prominent Orthodox attorney who later became Israel's first ambassador to Great Britain, and tried — unsuccessfully — to get Ben Gurion to come to Istanbul to further discuss rescue matters.[14]

DESPITE ALL ODDS AND THE COMPLEXITY of Ankara politics, Griffel and his allies could claim considerable success. This is in no

"You Could Have Saved More Lives!" small measure due to the high level of support they received from two top American officials in Turkey. Ira A. Hirschmann, representing the U.S. War Refugee Board since early 1944, proved very helpful. So did Ambassador Laurence Steinhardt, who had become more sympathetic toward the cause through the influence of Yaakov Rosenheim and a persuasive talk by Rabbi Herzog on refugees and American interests. So primed, Steinhardt set the stage for what would become a highly productive meeting in Ankara between Hirschmann and the Rumanian Ambassador Alexander Cretzianu. Remarkably, when Hirschmann told Cretzianu of his great concern for surviving Transnistrian Jews, whose number had by now dwindled to 48,000, the Rumanian said quite honestly, "If this means so much to you in the United States, why didn't you come sooner? You could have saved more lives."[15]

In addition, Griffel along with Rabbi Herzog had several interviews with the Patriarch of Istanbul's Orthodox Church, who helped them with his Rumanian contacts, especially Queen Mother Helena. Dr. Griffel and Rabbi Herzog also met with Cardinal Roncalli (the future Pope John XXIII) who was also sympathetic and helpful.[16]

As a result of the rescue efforts by Jewish activists in Turkey, approximately 5,000 Rumanian Jews, including 1,000 orphans from Transnistria, were transported to Palestine in 1944. The Rumanian government, after the devastating Swiss press campaign concerning the Auschwitz atrocities, instigated by Mantello, and witnessing the defeat of the German armies in the east, and fearing postwar retribution for its part in the destruction of Rumanian Jewry, agreed to bring the remainder of the Jews from Transnistria to Bucharest. There the rescue advocates intensified their efforts to get as many survivors as possible to Palestine, either directly by chartered boats to Haifa or via Turkey. The latter included the cumbersome and rather dangerous overland route through Syria. However, the greatest impediment to this emigration was the British refusal to issue Palestine certificates or at least to continue the meager allotments provided for in the 1939 White Paper. The British government claimed that the situation for the Jews in the Balkans had "stabilized" and that there were no valid reasons for their emigration. With this line of reasoning, they persuaded Ankara to seal off the Turkish route to Palestine.

In mid-1944, however, the situation was far from stabilized. Hungarian Jews were being transported to Auschwitz en masse. Some of them escaped the Nazi dragnet and reached Rumania.

For Griffel and other Orthodox activists, the failure to save the Hungarian Jews was a devastating experience. They tried then to help the Hungarian refugees in Rumania by getting for them some of the Palestine certificates still available.

GRIFFEL HAD LEARNED THAT MORE THAN HALF of these refugees were Orthodox and that the *Moetza* was assigning to them **Barlas'** only six percent of the available certificates, based **Inhuman** on an outdated formula that allotted this share to the Agudah since the 1920's. Griffel was naturally **Practices** furious, claiming that the Jewish Agency was *still* confusing emergency rescue with voluntary *aliyah.*[17] (See Appendix.) When the news of this clearly discriminatory policy spread, the Vishnitzer Rebbe called Yitzchok Sternbuch from Bucharest to complain bitterly, suggest that proper protests be made, and that the policy be changed immediately. The Rebbe "demanded that a separate ship be chartered to solve this problem" and take all the "rejected" Orthodox refugees to Turkey.[18]

In a thoroughly justified response, Vaad Hatzalah and Agudath Israel applied pressure on the War Refugee Board and the World Jewish Congress. On September 13, 1944, they cabled their reply to Sternbuch:

> Your cables of August 11th and 12th have been answered on August 18th through the Embassy. We should like to add, only, that concerning the permanent discrimination against Agudist, religious and non-Zionist Jews in general by the Jewish Agency, we have undertaken energetical [sic] steps through the American Embassy in Ankara. The Ambassador is fully informed and has repeatedly admonished Mr. Barlas, the representative of the Jewish Agency in Ankara, to stop these inhuman practices and not to destroy the Jewish name in this hour of general danger by party-policy. Barlas has promised to do everything in his power to comply with the request. Nevertheless, interventions have also been made in London and Jerusalem at the Agency leaders.[19]

It seems as if Barlas had given his assurance that such policies had ceased; yet the same — or similar — negotiations had been ongoing and evidently Barlas was not to be taken at his word. An earlier cable, from June 8, 1944 sent to Barlas by Dr. Nahum

Goldmann, indicates the difficulties the Vaad had in working with the *Moetza:*

> Yours 2420 implied Griffel Klarman agreed their action [to rent a separate ship] unnecessary stop cable seventeenth from Griffel [Ludwig] Kastner Klarmann to Vaad Hatzalah strongly differs stop War Refugee Board anxious have all rescue work coordinated stop we here endeavoring reach agreement Vaad Hatzalah please cable suggestions settlement
>
> Nahum Goldmann
> Signed
> Dr. Leon Kubowitzki
> Head, Rescue Department[20]

Sadly, because of Barlas' obstruction, including his threats against the shipping company itself, the rescue boat simply never made it — and those Jews were not saved.[21]

Yet Griffel never held Barlas' restrictionist rescue policies against the other members of the *Moetza,* and he went to great length to help some of them. It was fairly common knowledge, for example, that Griffel was duly licensed by the War Refugee Board to spend the American dollars sent by the Vaad in New York. One time, then, several *Moetza* members, including Ehud Avriel, requested a loan, citing a specific need for American dollars. Griffel discussed the matter with his Vaad Hatzalah committee — Ludwig Kastner and Dr. Joseph Klarman — and gave them the money. Soon after, the same *Moetza* figures came back to him and requested a second, much larger loan — and Avriel then dictated a cable in Griffel's name to the Vaad in New York, detailing his need. Again, Griffel and his co-workers approved.

Barlas, in the meantime, had returned from a trip to discover that Griffel had this special War Refugee Board license, and promptly said that no one could work for both the *Moetza* and the New York Vaad. Then he particularly criticized Griffel's requests for money — requests which had actually been made by his own colleagues. Later, in fact, at a *Moetza* general meeting, Barlas demanded to know where the money was going, and Griffel steadfastly refused to say, for he was not willing to embarrass the people who had asked for his help. Instead, Griffel said that he saw no disadvantage in obtaining a double mandate and merely requested that the complaint be aired before a smaller committee. He left it to the *Moetza* to decide if he should remain. Griffel never heard about the issue again, and Saul Meyerov, for one, later expressed his appreciation to Griffel in private for the work he had done. The loans themselves, however — a figure amounting to thousands of dollars — were never returned to Vaad Hatzalah. Griffel had, of course, discussed it with Rabbi Chizkiyahu Yosef Mishkovsky in Palestine and both men agreed to drop the matter. Because the funds had indeed been used for rescue, they thought it best not to create any trouble for the *Moetza.*[22]

Postscript

WHEN THE WAR ENDED, Griffel shifted the focus of his rescue to helping Jews from Eastern Europe make it to the free world, primarily France. Most of his efforts were concentrated in Prague, since for several years after the war, Czechoslovakia was the only country adjoining Eastern Europe which permitted Jews to use it as a transit center. All that was required was an end-visa to another country.

Griffel was aided by Rabbi Avigdor (Victor) Vorhand of Prague, whose indefatigable efforts and high governmental connections were utilized in helping many Jews reach Prague and to provide them with all the amenities. At the same time, George Mantello provided him with hundreds of Salvadoran papers which enabled them to leave Poland for the West.

In Italy, another postwar center for Jewish refugees, Griffel spent much of his time in helping Jews — Orthodox and non-Orthodox alike — obtain both physical and spiritual relief.

More than any other rescue activist, however, Griffel struggled in seeking to locate and rescue Jewish children hidden during the war by non-Jewish families or religious orders such as convents in Western Europe and in Poland — long after this problem of the Displaced Persons was solved. He pursued this goal, against all odds, indifference and neglect, even in the Orthodox circles, until his dying days in 1962. Those hundreds and perhaps thousands of Jewish children and later on even youths and adults, who were saved for the Jewish people through Griffel's efforts, are a personal testament to his persistent drive to fulfill the dictum of *pikuach nefesh* to the utmost.

C. RABBI DR. YITZCHOK ISAAC HALEVY HERZOG: THE CHIEF RABBI AND RESCUE DURING THE HOLOCAUST[1]

Rabbi Yitzchok Isaac Halevy Herzog, Palestine's Ashkenazi Chief Rabbi and leader of Mizrachi, received many desperate pleas for help during the Hitler era. Despite his warmheartedness, his love for *Klal Yisroel*, and his particular affection for Torah scholars, circumstances often prevented him from responding to these entreaties. The Allies' indifference to the plight of European Jewry and Britain's pro-Arab Mideast policy were major obstacles to rescue throughout the War. Prior to the outbreak of the War, even though Britain's White Paper of 1939 limited the total number of Jews eligible for immigration to Palestine, over 75,000 Jewish refugees reached the shores of *Eretz Yisrael*.

In theory, the British Mandatory Government in Palestine had control over most of the criteria governing the distribution of the life-saving permits to enter *Eretz Yisrael*. In practice, however, the Jewish Agency led by Ben Gurion and his supporters such as Yitzchok Grynbaum and Eliezer Kaplan, was in a position of authority to "recommend" which would-be emigres should receive permits. As we have seen, the Agency's immigration policy, based on a narrow Palestinocentric *Weltanschauung*, was biased to encourage the entrance of young, secularist, ideologically committed *chalutz* types or veteran Zionist leaders. Rabbinical scholars and Torah students did not fit the Agency's standards: the Zionist leaders considered these "old-fashioned" bearers of the Torah tradition the worst representatives of the *galut* image, who had to be eliminated from the new society of the future *Eretz Israel.*

The Agency exercised complete financial control over the office of the Chief Rabbinate. Despite Rabbi Herzog's heartfelt petitions on behalf of his fellow Jews throughout the world, the Agency continued to promote its particularist Zionist policy, focused on bringing refugees only to *Eretz Israel,* to the exclusion of all other possible countries of admission. Regardless of the White Paper restrictions that threatened the feasibility and viability of a Jewish homeland in Palestine, the Jewish Agency sought immigrants who would be most "useful" in establishing a Jewish state.

Besieged with desperate calls from all parts of Europe and as far away as Vladivostok, Kobe, Singapore, and Bombay, Rabbi Herzog faced many difficulties and frustrations. His gentle, conciliatory manner contrasted sharply with that of his good friend Rabbi Aaron Kotler, the "uncompromising fighter." But despite all obstacles, the courageous and persistent Rabbi Herzog devoted inordinate amounts of time and effort to rescue. During more than twelve years of rescue activity, he was instrumental in the escape of thousands of Jews.

LIKE OTHER *GEDOLIM* OR LAY JEWS involved in rescue work, Rabbi Herzog believed in the Torah dictum of *pikuach nefesh.* He **Concern** implemented this belief in his concern for all of *Klal* **for All** *Yisroel,* Orthodox or not, who sought a safe haven anywhere — not necessarily Palestine — from the **Jews** dangers of the war. At his installation as Chief Rabbi of Palestine in 1937, he clearly stated what he considered his responsibility for the safety and welfare of all Jews, whether in the *golus* or in *Eretz Israel.* Though he was dedicated to the upbuilding of *Eretz Israel,* the chief rabbi in his inaugural address stressed his commitment to the Jewish community the world over.

The first of Rabbi Herzog's rescue efforts involved the legalization of "illegal" immigrants. Between 1936 and 1939, thousands of Jews made their way from Europe to Palestine without British permits under the sponsorship of the Revisionist Zionists and one faction of the Socialist Zionists. The Jewish Agency took a negative attitude toward this illegal immigration because it did not wish, at that time, to antagonize the British Government, as well as the fact that many Revisionists and Orthodox Jews were among the escapees.

The immigrants who entered *Eretz Yisrael* without permission suffered great privation. They could not leave on personal or business matters, and they were in constant danger of expulsion if they were caught by the British police. The British Mandate Government proposed a legalization solution for illegals in Palestine with families still in Europe and the Jewish Agency refused to agree to it. Since the British solution which would have deducted the illegal immigrants from the approved number of certificates obviously meant less potential *chalutzim*, therefore the Jewish Agency constantly fought for exclusive control over immigration; the Zionists sought to retain their sole symbol of sovereignty and increase the potential *chalutzic* immigration to *Eretz Yisrael*. With the encouragement of the Chief Rabbinate, the immigrants themselves exerted sufficient public pressure to force the Jewish Agency to accept the British solution. The Jewish Agency still resisted British control by allotting only a small percentage of the certificates to the illegal immigrants.

Throughout this pre-war period the Chief Rabbinate served as the rallying station for these hapless souls, whether Orthodox or atheist. In contrast to the indifferent Jewish Agency, Rabbi Herzog constantly defended the illegal immigrants and insisted that no political considerations take precedence over the Torah dictum of *pikuach nefesh*. In turn, the illegals looked to Rabbi Herzog for moral sanction and encouragement in their successful protest against the Jewish Agency's immigration policy.

RABBI HERZOG INTIMATELY CONCERNED HIMSELF with the rescue issues involving fictitious marriages. Frequently a Palestinian **Fictitious** Jew would marry someone in Europe by proxy, thus enabling the new spouse to enter Palestine. An **Marriages** entire family could obtain a safe haven through the protection of a single certificate (or an end-visa). Someone possessing such a certificate would usually "create" an entire temporary family thus allowing more refugees to flee to safety. When such "families" arrived in Palestine they sought quick divorces to end their marriages of convenience. To the immigrants' dismay, the British authorities frowned on such means of rescue and ended them in 1939. The Jewish Agency not only disapproved of illegal methods but also declined to petition the Mandate Government on behalf of such "illegal" immigrants.

The Chief Rabbinate openly fought the Jewish Agency's stand. The arrangement and dissolution of fictitious marriages involved both the rescue of a large number of Jews and the weighty halachic concerns of marriage, divorce, and potential *mamzerim.** In addition, Rabbi Herzog sought to prevent additional *agunos*** — wives whose husbands' fates were unknown and who were thus unable to remarry. Despite their political overtones, these questions lay directly in the legitimate domain of the Chief Rabbinate. The Jewish Agency's concept of the future *Eretz Yisrael* and its new men and women reflected little concern for the denigration of the sanctity of the Jewish marriage, the family, and family purity. The Zionist leadership only feared using the certificates to save individuals they considered "ill-suited" to the task of building a postwar state. Rabbi Herzog weighed both sides of the issue in light of the Torah's higher dictum of *pikuach nefesh* since these "phony" marriages provided a meager hope of rescue for those trapped in Europe. To restore the integrity of the Jewish family, the chief rabbi readily granted the divorces — their statistics increased tremendously — that had enabled the rescue of untold numbers of Jewish lives.

IN AN EARLY RESCUE ATTEMPT, RABBI HERZOG utilized the good relations he had established with Prime Minister Eamon De Valera of the Irish Free State, during his tenure as chief rabbi of Ireland. He first sought a refuge for German-Jewish physicians who lost their licenses during the early days following Hitler's rise to power. This small channel for such physicians' rescue operated throughout the war.

German Physicians and Lithuanian Scholars

While the rabbi was intensely concerned about all Jews, the yeshivah world which had been deliberately abandoned by the Jewish Agency, remained closest to Rabbi Herzog's heart. In January 1941 he received a touching appeal from the yeshivah of Jassy, Rumania: "Your brother's blood is crying out to you for rescue ... for we are covered by shame and disgrace to see that there is a mass *aliyah* of adults, youth, children, individuals ... *aliyah* of veteran Zionists *(vatikim)*, etc., but no *aliyah* of Orthodox Jews and members of yeshivos."

The Jewish Agency showed the same indifference to the Polish Torah scholars stranded in Lithuania and even acted to prevent their rescue. The Zionists preferred to use the certificates Herzog sought for the immigration of more "productive" elements. Rabbi Herzog

---

* Product of an illegal union.
** This would occur if the "husband" of such a marriage disappeared or refused to give a *get* or religious divorce.

played an important role in the complicated rescue of hundreds of these Polish yeshivah students and scholars in Lithuania and their passage to East Asia.

Rabbi Herzog wished to travel to London to negotiate with the British authorities on issuing certificates for the stranded Polish Torah scholars. The Jewish Agency attempted to interfere with his trip but, undaunted, Rabbi Herzog went to London. Once there, he managed to obtain only a small number of certificates that brought a few chosen *roshei yeshivah* and their families to Palestine. But he achieved one important gain: he managed to persuade Ivan Maisky, the Soviet ambassador to London, to obtain from his government Soviet exit permits for yeshivah groups with the so-called Curacao end-visas. The Soviet government's approval of this necessary step enabled the yeshivos to reach Japan by the first half of 1941, while the USSR was still a reluctant ally of Nazi Germany.

However, Rabbi Herzog was aware that the situation of the refugee yeshivos in East Asia was precarious. In August 1941, he therefore approached the Jewish Agency in a further effort to obtain certificates for the teachers and students and their families. After much debate, the Jewish Agency approved fifty certificates* for the five hundred or so individuals in the Polish yeshivah group. Jewish Agency executive members Yitzchok Grynbaum, the head of the Jewish Agency's own rescue committee, the Vaad Hahatzalah, and Eliezer Kaplan, the Jewish Agency's treasurer, among others, vehemently opposed the entry of the Talmudic scholars. They demanded assurance that when these individuals arrived in *Eretz Yisrael* they would stop studying Torah and engage in "constructive" work instead. Rabbi Jehuda Leib Fishman (later Maimon) of the Mizrachi and Moshe Shapiro of the Hapoel Hamizrachi — neither of them great admirers of the Yiddish-speaking European yeshivos — strongly objected to Grynbaum's and Kaplan's compromise "provisos," saying that, in effect, admission to *Eretz Yisrael* is barred to members of *yeshivos* ... Their opposition was strictly ideological. In this instance, the fifty certificates — even if all had been utilized — would not have discriminated against any Polish Zionists in Japan, for all the Zionist refugees from Poland who had made their way to East Asia had already arrived in Palestine.

---

* Very few of the possessors of the fifty certificates ended up going to *Eretz Yisrael*, just as only about forty of the American Emergency Visitor's Visas obtained by Vaad Hatzalah were ever utilized out of an original list of 500. See *Fifth Agudah Report*, p. 1 [Ed].

1946 Rescue
Conference.
l. to r. R' Z. Gold,
M. Shapiro, R' S.P.
Wohlgerlernter,
R' C. Mishkowski,
Chief Rabbi Herzog,
B. Mintz, H. Landau.

LATE IN 1943, RABBI HERZOG FURTHER displayed his opposition
to the exclusivist Palestinocentric perspective on rescue in his

**Further
Rescue
Work**
activist support of like-minded intellectuals such as
Martin Buber, Professor Hugo Bergman, the Orthodox
writer known as "Reb Binyamin," and members of the
Revisionists concerned about the fate of European
Jews. This small group cogently argued that the Zionist
Establishment's emphasis on *aliyah* to Palestine incurred the wrath
of the British and precluded any effort to open world doors to the
Jewish refugees. As we have seen, in February 1944, Rabbi Herzog,
his son Yaakov and Dr. Mordechai Eliash journeyed to Turkey on a
successful rescue mission originating with Dr. Griffel, while Ben
Gurion refused his request to join. (See chap. 14B).

Rabbi Herzog also participated, in varying degrees, in many
other successful and unsuccessful rescue endeavors during the war,
including the rescues of such Chassidic leaders as the Admorim of
Gur, Belz and Bobov as well as Rabbis Shmuel David Ungar,
Michoel Ber Weissmandl and S. Schreiber in Bratislava.[11]

After the cessation of hostilities, Rabbi Herzog made a postwar
trip to Europe with Dr. Zev Gold of Mizrachi. In Poland, Rabbi
Herzog's considerable influence and prestige enabled him to
convince the Polish Communist regime to permit the exit of
hundreds of Jewish children. Recha Sternbuch, who had secured
exit visas for many hundreds of children, willingly permitted her
youngsters to travel to *Eretz Yisrael* under the auspices of Rabbi
Herzog. En route to Palestine, Rabbi Herzog stopped in Montreux to
confer with Recha Sternbuch and other leaders on Vaad Hatzalah on
rescue matters.[2]

D. THE MOTHER-DAUGHTER RESCUE TEAM: MRS. RENEE AND MISS EVA REICHMANN AND THE TANGIER CONNECTION[1]

Introduction

AFTER FAILING TO OBTAIN PALESTINE Certificates, the Reichmann family fled from Vienna to Paris by *Shevuos* 1940, then **Spain Returns the Favor** to Orleans, staying one step ahead of the Nazis. The French police advised them to get to Spain, to avoid capture by the Nazis, which they did in July 1940, crossing the border with a ten-day transit visa.

Mr. Reichmann, who went on before the rest, had no problems at the Spanish border. It was not even necessary to have a passport. And once in Spain you simply registered with the government. There were times when single men might encounter problems if suspicious as potential communists or spies, but to his knowledge, families never encountered any difficulty. At the border, Mr. Reichmann asked the guards if he could come in and they agreed. Then he asked if he could bring his family in as well. The guard said, "As long as they come in before six (p.m.) when we close."

The Reichmanns brought in with them a Hungarian girl who had been stranded in France, and when a Spanish policeman noticed six children, not seven, listed on the passports, he went out of his way to straighten out the problem with the help of the Hungarian Embassy, instead of just blowing the whistle. His benevolent attitude, which was shared by most of the Spanish authorities, was attributed to the fact that France had accepted all Spanish refugees during Spain's recent civil war and Spain was just returning the favor.

The family then went to Tangier in Morocco, which was under Spanish rule and had an old Sephardic community as well as a Jewish refugee group that eventually numbered several hundred. There were also available *kashrus* and a *minyan*. One of the brightest stars in Vaad Hatzalah's firmament was Renee Reichmann, who served as the Vaad's representative in Tangier.

❀ ❀ ❀

Here Eva Gutwirth (nee Reichmann) picks up the story:

My mother's involvement in helping refugees arose from our acquaintance, from Vienna days, with the Klein family who went on to establish Barton's Candy company in the United States. In 1941, one of the women of the Klein family wrote to my mother in Tangier from the United States and asked whether we could mail food packages to her in-laws in Poland. My mother did so and, when some of the packages were returned because the addressees had been deported, she decided to send parcels directly to the concentration camps. She cabled her brother, Hesky Gestetner, in Bratislava, asking for the names and addresses of deported Jews. He sent 1,800 names, mostly of young women deported from Bratislava and Prague to Auschwitz-Birkenau.*

To finance this operation, my mother collected money from all the refugees (Ashkenazim and Sephardim) who had come to Tangier and had prospered in business there. She was not a woman ever to take no for an answer. We knew that the Auschwitz inmates were receiving the packages because of the postcards we received. The Nazis made them write postcards so the world would think they were well-treated, but they were afraid to write to their relatives in Slovakia, for fear of giving away identities. Therefore, they were glad to be able to write to Tangier, far from their homes, and did so.

Our operation continually broadened, staffed by our own family and some girls from the Jewish community of Tangier. After school hours, for example, my brothers helped fill the packages and load them onto the trucks. We began to get names and addresses from Vaad Hatzalah, especially through Recha Sternbuch and HIJEFS in Switzerland. Parcels were sent to all these addresses. By 1943 4,000 parcels were being sent out every two weeks. As the number of packages increased, money was sent by Vaad Hatzalah in New York in the then large sums of $5,000 and $10,000. The packages went to Auschwitz-Birkenau and Theresienstadt and to other camps. The Vaad remained the

---

* In fact, these were the first group of deportees sent to Auschwitz in the spring of 1942. [Ed.]

most important source of names, although we accepted names from anyone who submitted them. The packages weighed five kilos (or about ten pounds) each; and they contained primarily sardines, chocolate, almonds, and raisins — nutritious foods in compact form.

There were two major factors in our success. First, we had the fullest cooperation from the Spanish authorities, not only in Tangier but also from Madrid. Second, we were able to obtain many thousands of dollars to pay for these parcels from the Vaad Hatzalah. When my mother asked the Spanish authorities for permission to send out food parcels to German-occupied territory, she not only obtained it without restrictions, but El Conde de La Granja, president of the Spanish Red Cross in Madrid, which was under government control, gave us permission to send the parcels under its label, even allowing us to print the labels ourselves. (See Appendix.) Since the Red Cross could send such packages without postage, this saved us quite a sum, and also spared us from having to write out all those addresses. We just had to write the person's name above the printed address. We used to go to the office with the packages — tell them that we had — say 1500 of them — and they would usually give us the official stamp and papers allowing us to complete the transaction. They rarely ever counted the packages; they took our word for it. And the Spanish Red Cross labels classified the Jewish inmates as "prisoners of war," which made it more likely the packages would reach their destinations than if they'd simply been sent to Jews per se.*

Because Spain was an ally of Germany, the Spanish Red Cross and the Spanish government were able to carry out relief operations four years before the Swiss International Red Cross. And even then, when the packages were sent by the International Red Cross via Geneva, they weren't addressed to an individual, and this caused problems. Verification was impossible since no receipts were sent and there were even times when the IRC would destroy the packages, claiming that Spanish chocolate or other food were not up to Swiss standard.

With the help of the Vaad, we continued to send money and food via the IRC, knowing that only a small percentage would get through.

As noted before, the financing of the packages came mostly

---

* It is important to remember that until late 1944, some time after the mass exposure to the horrors of Auschwitz by the Swiss press campaign, the International Red Cross (IRC) had refused to designate Jewish inmates of concentration camps as "prisoners of war," the only category the IRC was willing to send packages to. Yet, from the beginning of 1942, the Spanish Red Cross readily utilized this simple designation for Jews in order to assure delivery to Jews. [Ed.]

from Vaad Hatzalah via Recha Sternbuch and later also from the Joint whose representative in Tangier was Isaac Lorado, a Sephardic Jew and an uncle of a good friend of mine. That's when we obtained the use of a large warehouse from Aaron Cohn, another prosperous Sephardic merchant. From that time on, our work each day began shortly after 5 p.m. and frequently extended far into the night.

In 1944, Mother was able to send matzos for Pesach to Birkenau, although she had to pressure on the Tangier Jewish community to get the matzos prepared in time. Before long we were sending over 4,000 packages a week at that time. Then she began sending clothing. I remember that one time I went with a friend to the largest city in Spanish Morocco to collect decent clothing from the Jewish community there. It took a little convincing to make the president of that community understand the tragedy that had overtaken European Jewry. These Jews really had no idea of the tragedy in Europe. The next day he apologized for his initial reluctance to help.

My mother's most dramatic achievement was the rescue of at least 1,200 Jewish children in Budapest sometime in mid-1944. This was after the Nazi occupation of Hungary, when the deportations of Jews from Hungary had already begun. When we found out that foreign papers, even mere entry-visas to another country, provided Jewish bearers with a measure of protection, my mother obtained the names of 500 children — that were already in detention camps and headed for Auschwitz — from Philip Freudiger and Chaim Roth of the Orthodox community of Budapest, and from the Sternbuchs in Switzerland. She then went to J. Rives Childs, charge d'affaires of the American Legation in Tangier, who was known to have good relations with General Luis Orgaz, the Spanish High Commissioner for Tangier, to see what he could do about obtaining entry visas to Tangier for the children. As Mr. Childs noted in his memoirs, General Orgaz "gave his accord without hesitation."[2]

The entry-visas, which no one expected anyone to use, did the trick and the 500 children were transferred to safe houses in Budapest, under the protection of the Spanish Red Cross, and so they were saved from the gas chambers. In the meantime, we received the names of 700 additional children and again my mother went to Mr. Childs. Again, he and General Orgaz proved their humanitarianism by immediate action, and another 700 children joined the first 500 in the safe houses under Spanish protection.

What was interesting about the second group of children is

that when we got their names, I told my brother to ask the Spanish governor for permission to provide papers for another hundred. My mother, always one to think big, suggested otherwise. 'Let's ask for 700 and let him cut it down to 500.' Well, she did ask for 700 and got the approval for all 700.

"In her letter of thanks to Mr. Childs, my mother wrote:

The International Red Cross in Budapest was able, thanks to the entry visas for Tangier, to obtain the release of 1,200 Jews from a Nazi concentration camp, put them in safety in a house rented for the purpose, which, through the authorization given for visas, was protected by the Spanish Consulate in Budapest. Thus, 1,200 innocent souls owe their having been saved to Your Excellency.

Signed
Mme. Renee Reichmann[3]

Mr. Childs very humbly acknowledged the real role of General Orgaz as well as my mother's.[4]

SOME FACETS OF MRS. REICHMANN'S rescue efforts with food packages via the Vaad and the Sternbuchs can be gleaned from the following brief exchange of cables in 1944.

An Exchange of Cables
A terse exchange of cables and memos highlights but one rescue effort that Renee Reichmann was deeply involved in with Vaad Hatzalah. In a brief memo dated August 12, 1944, Mrs. Reichmann reported the following:

Send out the sum of $3,000 ... necessary for sending [packages] to Theresienstadt and Birkenau [Auschwitz] ... the International Red Cross should get permission to help Jews in concentration camps. A great deal of money is essential to secure the necessary packages for Hungarian Jews ... Except for those in Budapest, they are all in concentration camps.[5]

From the Tangier connection, then, particularly close contact was established between the Vaad and Theresienstadt. As such, Mrs. Reichmann periodically sent out packages to designated names and addresses there, receiving notices of confirmation on a regular basis.

On December 5, 1944, Yitzchok Sternbuch cabled a request to Renee Reichmann asking for political assistance and support:

In response to your phone conversations with Madrid [Spain], the Jewish community of Budapest and the Red Cross were notified — reported an urgent cable by the Spanish Consulate in Budapest, to make a contact with the Jewish community ... Request your leaders to conduct urgent personal intervention by the authorities in Madrid concerning the following ... citizens of Paraguay [i.e., who were sent such passports from Switzerland] including a number of personalities, some from Antwerp, some from Poland, who were transported on April 18, [1944] and May 16, [1944] from the concentration camp in Vittel [France] to Drancy near Paris, and from there they were transported on April 30 and May 30 to an unknown destination in upper Silesia [really to Auschwitz] — The Spanish Embassy in Berlin was informed but will not divulge the information ... The Vaad Hatzalah notified us that the Paraguayan government requested that the Spanish government take the most dramatic steps to save the people, with the proposition of exchanging them for German nationals in Paraguay ... We cabled Madrid on this matter on November 30, but received no reply ... Urgent request to intervene in Madrid, to send a special delegate to Berlin in an attempt to save and return them [the camp inmates] to an official internment camp.[6]

Mrs. Reichmann responded that she

... received your cable of December 5 [1944] yesterday from Madrid ... arranged with the help of the American Embassy in Madrid ... I cabled to Madrid from here via the Consulate ... attempts to intervene in the same manner. I requested a Spanish visa and hope to receive one in a few days ... Inform if trip is necessary.[7]

On December 23, 1944, she again cabled Vaad Hatzalah:

Received 5,000 dollars through Cohn ... sent 2,056 packages in October, now 3,000 ... Funds all spent ... Please cable money for packages for January's shipment ... One can send more packages if funds are increased ... send money order and cable respond.[8]

Then, on January 15, 1945, Mrs. Reichmann again sent a detailed report in which she said she

... received your cables of December 30 [1944] and January 2 [1945] through the American Embassy in Tangier. I can already reply to your first [inquiry]. I am pleased that it was completed so quickly, because I have already received 6,000 dollars. I will arrange for the sending of packages in the shortest possible time, and in the best way. I work with all my strength and heart so that the money which I have received through your good will should be utilized in the best manner. The packages were sent out from here on the 12th and 14th of December [1944], left Barcelona [Spain] on the 25th and 27th to the [International] Red Cross in Geneva, and the representative of

Vaad Hatzalah in Montreux [i.e., Sternbuchs] will receive the [packages] from them and mail them out first of all to the addresses in Theresienstadt and Birkenau while the rest [will be sent] to the most needy [elsewhere].

In response to your second inquiry, it is possible to send packages amounting to about 10 to 15,000 kilo [about 20,000 to 30,000 lbs.]. I hope to obtain permission for this amount, since it is clear that without permission it is impossible to send such large amounts. The price of chocolate rises daily, therefore I am seeking permission to mail other products.

In response to a request by the Vaad Hatzalah representative in Switzerland, I began a campaign to collect clothes. Considering the small [Jewish] population of our city [Tangier] it must be considered a success. On the 12th of December I sent out 74 sacks of warm clothing, underwear, socks and shoes through the Spanish Red Cross to the address of the International Red Cross at the disposal of the Vaad Hatzalah in Switzerland. My daughter, and my friend, Mrs. Rosenfeld, gathered so much in Tetuan [capital of former Spanish Morocco] that I was able to send out 98 sacks [of clothing] by January 4 [1945]. My sister, in Madrid, likewise made a similar collection of this size. She is presently in Barcelona for another [clothing] campaign. We will visit every city in [Spanish] Morocco where it is at all possible to collect.

I conclude my letter with a request to the Al-mighty to bless your work and thank you for all that you do on behalf of our suffering brethren.[9]

AFTER THE WAR, THOUSANDS OF FOOD packages were sent to the large groups of survivors who kept streaming into France from **Postwar** Siberia via Poland, Czechoslovakia, etc. So efficient an operation had her package project become, that the Joint Distribution Committee used them from the time of the liberation in mid-1944 until they were set up in Europe by early 1946. Such packages were sent with the labels of the Joint [see appendix] via the IRC in Geneva. As private citizens they got the best exchange for the dollar, enabling them to ship more for the money. Moreover, the free postage provided by the Spanish Red Cross, and the assurance that the packages would arrive in Paris via the IRC in Geneva, made the Tangier connection the best all-around solution during the early, hectic year and a half after the liberation of France.

In addition to the packages sent to the JDC in postwar Paris, she also sent packages directly to Agudath Israel in Paris.[10]

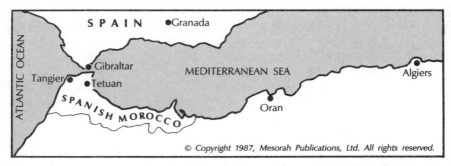

Although both the letter by the American Charge d'Affairs and Mrs. Reichmann mention only the number 1200 rescued, this was not the total.

In a confidential cable of September 29, 1944, by the American Secretary of State, Cordell Hull, to the American Legation in Tangier, he informs the latter that [in addition to the 500] ... another fifteen hundred Spanish visas have been authorized for Jews in Hungary.* To ensure their safety, Intercross in Hungary is requested likewise to assume supervision of the beneficiaries of these additional visas as soon as feasible.[11]

---

* If the 1500 replace the additional 700 then the number adds up to at least 2,000 in addition to adults (70 for the first 500) that were to be assigned to the children. If these were beyond the 700, then the total would add up to at least 2,700. Actually, this figure tallies closely with the report given by Mr. Albert Reichmann that in the Spanish protected houses there were about 3,000 Jews, since the Spanish Ambassador who returned from Budapest to Spain had left word for his charge d'affairs, Angel Sanz-Briz, in Budapest to approve papers for any additional Jews that request them. If those with forged copies of such papers [and we know that many such existed] it is quite within reason to assume the approximate accuracy of the figure of 3,000 Jews rescued this way. [Ed.]

CHAPTER FOURTEEN
Occupied Europe

A. INTRODUCTION

BEFORE THE GERMAN ARMY marched unopposed into Austria on March 13, 1938, Vienna had a Jewish population of roughly 185,000. Throughout the latter part of the nineteenth

Germany and Vienna century, and into the early years of the twentieth, Jews had been fortunate enough to live in relative peace in the capital of the former Austro-Hungarian Empire. There they served as a catalyst for most of Vienna's vibrant cultural and scientific scene. This peaceful existence was abruptly destroyed after the *Anschluss*, and conditions for Jews quickly became even worse in Austria than they were in neighboring Germany at the time: it was in Vienna that Adolf Eichmann promoted "forced emigration" as a first-stage solution for rendering Europe *Judenrein*.

At the Evian Conference on refugees, held in the middle of 1938, the Jews of Greater Germany were offered to any and all takers but, of course, to no avail. While the Evian Conference was called by President Roosevelt with perhaps all the best intentions, it did not accomplish much. For though it served to publicize the plight of the Jews, the Western world's indifference not only made many nations shy away from accepting Jews, but also strengthened the Nazi resolve to expel them in one way or another. Subsequent events show that if the Western democracies had opened their doors instead of tightening restrictions much would have been different.

Certainly, the Germans might have moderated their policies and many Jews would have been spared. As it was, however, the world turned its back and the *Kristallnacht* pogrom took place in November, 1938.

Jews were caught in an ever-tightening noose of chaos, and feared the impending pogroms. Alternatively, terror and transit were the bailiwicks of the Gestapo, the worst Nazi police apparatus of all, and of its Vienna chief, Adolf Eichmann. Eichmann operated the so-called Central Office for Jewish Emigration, and furthered the Reich's oft-stated goal of rendering Germany *Judenrein* by shipping out as many Jews as possible, either by legal emigration or by illegal flight.

THOUGH HUNGARY, UNDER ITS REGENT, Admiral Miklos Horthy, was officially a German satellite during the Second World **Hungary** War, she managed to retain a considerable degree of independence until it was actually occupied by German forces in March 1944. Hungary was certainly antisemitic at this time, and indeed had its own anti-Jewish laws and sent forced Jewish labor battalions to the Eastern front, but it had neither a Hitler nor an Eichmann. As a result, the majority of the Jewish population felt relatively safe. After March 1944, however, Eichmann himself took charge, and instituted a savage and efficient system for deporting the Jews en masse for extermination in Auschwitz.[1]

Indeed, the tragedy was greater than what it may seem at first, for the Germans had initially swelled the borders of Hungary to include large sections of Czechoslovakia, Rumania and Yugoslavia, thereby enlarging the country's Jewish population to between 750,000 and one million Jews.[2] There were, besides, more than 12,000 Polish Jews who had managed to escape from Poland by crossing illegally into Hungary, and who were cared for by Hungary's Jews. Those caught coming over the border were either sent back or placed into detention centers in Budapest, where they also received help from the Jewish community, including forged papers. So many, in fact, were given forged papers that there grew up in Budapest a sizeable Slovak and Polish underground counterfeiting industry offering Jews at least some measure of safety. There was such a demand for the false papers that one underground activist, Samuel Frey, kept a steady stream of appointments — while Rabbi Chaim Roth, head of the Budapest

Chevra Kadisha and Frey's institutional contact, issued the papers to the refugees.[3]

Many secondary figures helped in the distribution of such false papers to Jews who crossed the Hungarian border, among them Rabbi Yaakov Bein. He was the chaplain at one major Budapest detention center and a contact for Frey's organization. In this capacity he was responsible for providing false papers to hundreds of refugees, including Rabbi Yekusiel Y. Halberstam, the Admor of Klausenberg (Cluj).[4] Rabbi Bein used to get the illegal papers into the center by hiding them in the false bottoms of large metal kosher-food canisters.[5]

When the deportations began from the puppet state of Slovakia in 1942, thousands of Jews crossed the border into neighboring Hungary to escape. But a scant two years later the pattern was reversed when the deportations began in Hungary as well and Hungarian and Polish Jews found a temporary haven in Slovakia.[6] After the so-called Kastner Train left Budapest in July 1944, carrying among its 1,700 Jews much of the Zionist, secular, and Orthodox leadership, Frey and Roth again surfaced to fill a desperately needed role. Frey was fortunate enough to meet with Raoul Wallenberg, who helped him accomplish what seemed even then to be improbable — the maintenance of the lone yeshivah in Nazi Europe. Frey's yeshivah was such a success that after the war, with the help of Rabbi Schonfeld its several hundred boys were sent to England, the United States, and Israel — a testimony, in part, of his ability to keep them alive.[7]

Frey and Roth were not alone. There were others in Budapest, notably Chaim Stern (see below, section D), who like Yaakov Griffel in Turkey officially belonged to no organization but worked extensively throughout the war to help Jews, notably Torah scholars and yeshivah students who had fled to Hungary with no means of support.

IN THE OCCUPIED NETHERLANDS, a man named Herbert Kruskal was an integral part of the relief effort. Kruskal (see below, section

The Netherlands C) was at one time a close associate of Germany's Yaakov Rosenheim in the World Agudath Israel. He put his background to good use by opening what he called the Agudah's Migration Division; headquartered in his own home, Kruskal had flour and other food sent through Belgium to the Polish ghettos — at times even utilizing the Nazi-controlled German Red Cross for the purpose.

B. SHTADLAN OF VIENNA:
YAAKOV SHLOMO (JULIUS) STEINFELD[1]

JULIUS STEINFELD, THE ORTHODOX RESCUE ACTIVIST, was a product of the Viennese (Hungarian) Orthodox Jewish community **Judenrein** which reached its high point at the time of the First World War. (At this time the community was augmented by literally tens of thousands of Galician refugees, including numerous Chassidic Admorim and other Torah scholars, who fled southwest away from the advancing Russian armies.) As a young man, Steinfeld was already active in communal and relief work, a twin course of action which he merely intensified after the *Anschluss.* *

Some time after the *Anschluss* in March 1938, the Nazis officially dissolved most Jewish organizations and institutions in Austria, thus immediately depriving Austria's Jews of almost every officially recognized representation. The void was as frightening as it was instantaneous, yet it was filled up, in part at least, by the quick reactions of Yaakov Steinfeld, an extraordinary *shtadlan* and organizer in the occupied Austrian capital. He created a Jewish relief committee — which, in turn, not only set up a kosher kitchen, but also cared for many of the city's new Jewish refugees. In one notable instance, Steinfeld and his committee took the responsibility of resettling hundreds of Jews from Burgenland — the *"Sheva*

---

* Steinfeld was to continue his important work even after he came to the United States, helping to reestablish a kind of Viennese Jewish community among refugees in Williamsburg.

Kehillos," or the so-called Seven Communities where Jews had resided for hundreds of years, and which the Nazis had decided to render *Judenrein* a few days before Passover. Without warning, Jews were loaded onto trucks and literally dumped in Vienna — where Steinfeld managed to resettle them all into private homes or the Hotel Barshak.

ALTHOUGH THEY WERE SAVED FOR THE MOMENT, the Jews of Burgenland still faced further dangers from the Gestapo. In what

Into the Jaws of the Gestapo

seemed a sudden change in Gestapo policy, the heads of the Jewish families from Burgenland were taken to Gestapo headquarters, where they were forced by beatings and threats to sign papers promising that they would leave the country — even if they had no prospects of doing so. Steinfeld resolved to intervene with the Gestapo on their behalf. Many of Steinfeld's friends warned him against taking such action, for not only was he advocating an extremely dangerous position, the mere act of appearing at Gestapo headquarters meant literally taking his life into his hands; other Jews had gone there with minor personal requests and never returned.

Yet, Steinfeld, though decidedly not a foolhardy man, refused to listen to these warnings. He had dealt with the Viennese police and other officials before; he had learned how to talk to them and whom to bribe. In virtually no time he was able to reach Eichmann himself — who actually pointed a pistol at Steinfeld's head. Steinfeld, however, was not frightened; he managed to convince Eichmann that they were allies of a sort, because he, Steinfeld, could help the Nazis make Austria *Judenrein*. Steinfeld made Eichmann believe that he, Steinfeld, had many important contacts who would help him secure visas for Jews, especially deportees from Burgenland. Given this promise, along with a well-timed bribe, Eichmann stopped what amounted to his steady persecution of Burgenland Jews.

Steinfeld's talks with Eichmann made two things clear: First that Eichmann and, obviously, his superior Heinrich Himmler were willing, and even interested that as many Jews as possible should leave Austria. Second, that he, Eichmann, was willing to take bribes and, in return, to ease harsh antisemitic decrees. Steinfeld's reputation as a rescue activist and helper of unfortunate Jews became so widespread that Eichmann began to doubt that Steinfeld was working on emigration at all. Upon encountering Steinfeld at another official's door in Gestapo headquarters, Eichmann would shake his finger at him and say, "Steinfeld, you're just a real Jewish swindler."

STEINFELD WORKED IN MANY DIFFERENT AREAS to help Jews. In some cases, he arranged for the release of Jews who had been **Many** placed under arrest. He provided shelter for others and **Areas** kosher food for prisoners. In short, Steinfeld became the focus for all Jewish problems in Vienna — a role he fulfilled with great skill and concern. Perhaps his finest service, though, was providing visas. He himself made numerous trips to Switzerland, London, France, Belgium and Holland, where he procured as many visas as he could (along with matzos and kosher meat). In Holland, for example, his audience with Queen Wilhelmina resulted in some visas. In London, too, he helped the redoubtable Dr. Solomon Schonfeld wrangle from the British Home Office a large number of visas which were especially earmarked for Jewish youth.[2] In fact, Steinfeld was the immediate inspiration for Rabbi Solomon Schonfeld to become involved in the rescue of Jews from Austria. Similarly, in Switzerland, he obtained numerous visas and made all necessary arrangements for refugee transports. What's more, after each of these journeys, Steinfeld reported to Eichmann the number of visas he had received. True to form, Eichmann invariably screamed, "Not enough!" and threatened Steinfeld. For his part, Steinfeld was less concerned with Eichmann than with his chosen task of sending hundreds of Jews safely abroad.

In one remarkable episode Steinfeld helped in the larger — and illegal — effort to bring hundreds of Jews into Palestine.[3] Organized by both Agudath Israel and the Austrian Revisionist-Zionists (the latter headed by Yitshaq "Mike" Ben-Ami and Dr. William R. Perl), the Viennese *aliyah* was aided in no small measure by Steinfeld's knowledge of official channels and his contacts, both technical and financial, in Zurich, London, and Paris. Although Eichmann preferred that the largest number of Jews possible leave Austria, official policy required an exist visa marked for a specific destination. Since the visas could not be marked "Palestine," as such, the entire Palestinian operation was in jeopardy until Steinfeld, and the others, managed to obtain 1,000 forged Liberian visas from the Liberian Consul. Still, at that time, Eichmann was inordinately concerned with the *appearance* of legality, and therefore he made all the Jewish emigrants purchase travel tickets for Liberia, despite the fact that as far as he was concerned, they were going only a few kilometers down the Danube. Why Eichmann had the Jews play this charade still remains unclear, although one cogent theory has it that since the Nazis were currying favor with the Mufti of Jerusalem, they did not wish to appear to be organizing the emigration of Jews to Palestine. With full Nazi cooperation, the largest transports of illegal immigrants to Palestine left from Vienna on November 4, 1938.

BECAUSE OF HIS FREQUENT TRIPS THROUGH EUROPE, Steinfeld had many visas and identification cards of his own, but did not ever **To Cuba** consider emigrating himself as long as he felt it was still possible for him to work for his fellow Jews in Austria. Only when conditions had deteriorated so badly that the Nazis no longer considered him a negotiating partner and he himself was in immediate danger of arrest, did Steinfeld prepare to leave Austria. When he applied for a visa to the United States, he found to his surprise that he was not permitted to enter on the dubious grounds that the State Department had been informed that he was a Gestapo agent. Steinfeld and his family took the road chosen by many others who wanted to settle in the United States but were refused an American visa: they went to Cuba.

Steinfeld maintained his high level of activity even in Cuba. He continued activities in communal work — both for his fellow-refugees in Cuba and in rescue endeavors for those still in Vienna. Meanwhile the World Agudath Israel, which now had its headquarters in the United States under the leadership of Yaakov Rosenheim, tried to convince the State Department that its information about Steinfeld was incorrect. Unfortunately, it was not until Dr. Perl's arrival — and his own enlistment in the American army — his testimony under oath, and a letter he presented from a noted British official attesting to the quality of work they performed in Vienna, that Steinfeld received his American visa. Once in the United States, of course, Steinfeld continued his activities, joining forces with Vaad Hatzalah to raise funds and provide homes for hundreds of refugees.

C. A ONE-MAN RELIEF AGENCY:
HERBERT KRUSKAL SENDS FOOD TO THE GHETTOS[1]

HERBERT KRUSKAL, A LONG-TIME FRIEND and assistant of Yaakov Rosenheim in the World Agudath Israel headquarters in

Ingenious Distribution of Flour Germany, was fortunate enough to arrive in Holland just prior to the Second World War. Yet on May 15, 1940, when the Dutch surrendered to the German army, Kruskal and 30,000 other German Jews again found themselves under the rule of the Third Reich. Despite some oppression, things in Holland remained relatively calm, at least for two years, until May 1942 when Jewish businesses and assets were confiscated. Two months later the deportation of Jews from the Netherlands began.

Still, prior to 1942, Holland's indigenous and refugee Jews did not suffer in the same manner as did Poland's Jews, who were reported, with alarming frequency, to be starving. Upon receipt of this data, Kruskal began a one-man operation to send food from Holland to the Ghettos, combining remarkable ingenuity and audacity to accomplish his goal. First, Kruskal realized he would need an official-sounding entity to serve as a basis of operations: he therefore set up what he called the Dutch Migration Department of the Agudas [sic] Israel World Organization at his own home in The Hague. Next, he utilized his ingenuity to gather the funds necessary for buying thousands of pounds of flour and shipping the flour to the Jewish community in Poland. This flour, which was intended for Passover, was routed from Belgium so ingeniously that the Nazi-controlled German Red Cross actually aided in its distribution. Kruskal, who had remained in close contact with Rosenheim (who in turn had fled earlier to England), managed to keep the shipments up for three years until he himself was taken to the Westerbork concentration camp. Mercifully, he survived.

D. CHAIM STERN: A LIFE OF RESCUE[1]

CHAIM STERN, A PROMINENT CHASSID IN BUDAPEST, was the manager of Philip Freudiger's textile mills. Even prior to the Second

Indefatigable Community Activists World War, Stern had been an energetic community worker. As Nazism spread to Austria and Czechoslovakia, Stern turned all his efforts toward rescue activities. Thus he organized the crucial 1938-39 food transports to Austria, and the supply of food, shelter, and forged papers to Polish and Slovak Jews who had escaped into Hungary. He transformed his own home into a shelter for refugee Torah scholars, and set up many refugees in business so that they could earn their own living with dignity. Like many other Orthodox rescue activists, Stern was less concerned with his own safety than he was with that of his fellow Jews. He accomplished many spectacular missions, including the liberation (with the help of other Orthodox rescue activists) of Rabbi Aaron Rokeach, the Admor of Belz, and of the latter's brother, Rabbi Mordechai Rokeach, the Rabbi of Bilgoraj, both of whom Stern helped to bring to Palestine.

By the spring of 1944, Hungary herself was occupied by the German army, and Stern redoubled his rescue work, preparing forged visas, exposing himself and his family to severe danger if he was caught. Unfortunately, Stern and his own family could not escape the concentration camps; in June 1944 he and his family were sent to Bergen-Belsen as part of the so-called Kastner group. While incarcerated, though, he continued his relief activities, using his position as Block Elder to help as many people as he could, notably Torah scholars. Indeed, such was Stern's dedication that once, while he was procuring a lamp for fellow-detainee Rabbi Joel Teitelbaum, the famous Admor of Satmar, Stern talked down a knife-wielding man who would have prevented him. "I need this," Stern said unafraid, "for the Rebbe who is studying Torah day and night." Cowed before such fearlessness, the young man let him pass.

Stern was, of course, one of the fortunate Jews, for he spent only five months in Bergen-Belsen before being taken to Switzerland on December 6, 1944. Yet, instead of spending time to recover from what at best was an ordeal, Stern again continued to work, resettling survivors, feeding them, helping them to rebuild their lives. Later he emigrated to the United States, and until his death in 1977 worked to rebuild Vishnitz, Belz, Satmar, and other chassidic communities to their earlier strength.

CHAPTER FIFTEEN

Working with Rabbi Weissmandl:
A. Two Vignettes[1]

Introduction

T IS ONLY FITTING that this volume, which tries to convey the response of Orthodox Jewry to the Holocaust, should conclude with several personal vignettes of Rabbi Michoel Ber Weissmandl, the genius of rescue, and the very embodiment of Jewish diplomacy in action. An extraordinary personality, he was the peerless rescue activist who personified to the ultimate the Torah perspectives of rescue. While a most devout Jew, a true *tzaddik*, his name was mentioned with awe by all those he came in touch with, Orthodox and freethinker alike. Even the Marxist-Zionists — whether in the Slovak underground, the *Moetza* in Istanbul or Jerusalem — with their deep seated hatred for Orthodox Judaism, held him in the highest esteem. They recognized not merely his creative genius, but his total dedication to rescue of *Klal Yisroel*. As Yaakov Griffel put it, "His name was always mentioned with awe — even by the leftists — both in internal meetings and public assemblies in Palestine."[2]

Peerless, Creative, Ingenius and Frustrated

He was the first to apply the age-old Jewish practice of *pidyon shevuyim*, the ransoming of Jewish captives, on a grand scale, and his efforts, despite the failures, remained the basis for any of the other ransom plans attempted.

While he had difficulty in convincing the secularists, especially the Marxist-Zionists, in the underground of the feasibility

Rabbi Michael Ber Weissmandl

("realism") of the ransom plans, his charismatic personality won them over.

He also developed a smuggling operation near the Slovak-Polish border, which enabled thousands of Jews — though at a high monetary price — to reach then-relatively safe Slovakia or Hungary. Following the German invasion of Hungary, he shifted the escape routes into Slovakia until the tragic failure of the Slovak uprising in the fall of 1944.

His Holocaust memoir *Min Hametzar*, published posthumously, is the most profound and heart-stirring work to emerge from the ashes of the Holocaust. Though the book is unfinished and poorly edited, its accuracy has yet to be disproved despite many attempts by ideologically-motivated historians to do so.[3]

Throughout this volume, the genius of this great man is clearly seen in the various plans for the rescue and help he sought for his fellow Jews throughout the Holocaust. For the most part he was behind the warning signals sent out to the free world as well as to the next potential victims of Hitler's genocidal plans. This great Torah scholar was able to conceive, within the narrow confines of occupied Slovakia, plans that amazed the outside world with their different approach.

YET HE SPENT MOST OF THE WAR YEARS in frustration, operating on many fronts at the same time, trying desperately to **Accurate** inform the Allies and the Jews of the free world **Information** of the atrocities being committed against the **to the West** Jewish people: to drive the Jews into sending the necessary money required by his many rescue efforts; convince them of the efficacy of his ransom and other rescue plans; and to spread the message and plea to the Allies to bomb Auschwitz and the rail lines leading to the crematoria.

He is the one, for example, who tried to extend the Europa Plan to ransom European Jewry to Hungary when they became the Nazi victims; he encouraged the tragically unsuccessful Joel Brand mission to Turkey. And, when that failed, it was his frantic genius and great heart that sought and found means of reestablishing negotiations with the Gestapo after they had almost collapsed. The messages he sent to inform the Nazis of the availability of 300 trucks in Switzerland, as a means of continuing the negotiations, were typed on a Swiss typewriter and on stationery from one of the finest hotels in Switzerland, under the name of "Ferdinand Roth," Weissmandl's fictitious representative of American Jewry in Switzerland. Ferdinand Roth served as Weissmandl's mouthpiece in his negotiations with the Nazis.[4]

It was his series of urgent cables at the end of 1943 that eventually mobilized the Orthodox in the United States to achieve an independent channel for rescue. This road had been neglected earlier because the Orthodox felt financially and politically powerless and they had hoped to realize their elusive dream of unity among American Jews for rescue. It was this newly forged determination by the Orthodox to go it alone that, despite all the failures, enabled them to achieve far more success in 1944-45 than they dreamed of.

As we have seen, from 1942 on, a great deal of accurate information on conditions in occupied Europe emanated from Bratislava.

HIS FELLOW JEWS, BOTH WITHIN THE UNDERGROUND Working Group as well as those in the free world were profoundly startled by **Epitome of** his unique ideas. They — the socialist-realists — **Real Jewish** came to an amazing conclusion. Those classic **Diplomacy** weapons of Jewish diplomacy, which they had long discarded as a product of the *golus* mentality, should now be resurrected as the most practical means of dealing with the most unprecedented tragedy befalling the Jewish people. As the epitome of the real Jewish diplomacy, he thus had to contend not merely with the outside world, but frequently enough with those in his own underground circles, most of whom had been brought up on secular ideologies very foreign to these classic Torah ideas, such as ransom and dealing with fascists and murderers. Yet, part of his genius was his great Jewish heart, his sense of humility and total disregard for material things and an even greater disinterest in matters of personal vanity or honor. All these were necessary ingredients for this "ultra-Orthodox" rabbi, not only to be accepted within the essentially secular group, but to go much further. They honored, respected and revered him, as one of the following stories will convey.

In fact, his charismatic and bewitching personality, despite his disheveled appearance and the retention of his beard, shone through to influence normally very strong-minded individuals who, otherwise, would not have given a rabbi a second glance. This was brought home to this author by Andre Steiner, the engineer, who was an important member of the Working Group. This man, a city-planner in a major U.S. city for 35 years, was born into an assimilated family — very far from Judaism. He had been working for the underground, creating labor camps for the Jews in order to make them appear "constructive" in the eyes of the Slovak authorities. In this way he hoped to prevent their deportation by the Nazis.

He had first met Rabbi Weissmandl when the latter came one day to inquire about the possibilities of providing kosher food for the observant Jews in the camps. For Mr. Steiner, who said that though this was the farthest thing from his mind, an incredible thing happened. "Rabbi Weissmandl looked at me with his piercing, yet kind, eyes and said to me softly, 'You will provide kosher food, won't you?' " Steiner, even in retrospect over forty years later, couldn't explain why he, the non-believer, suddenly got the urge to fulfill this "strange" request, but he did so unhesitatingly.[5]

Moreover, at a certain stage in the negotiations with the Nazis, Steiner had taken the key role in serving as the intermediary with Dieter Wisliceny, Eichmann's assistant for Jewish Affairs, in negotiating for Weissmandl's ransom plans. "At every stage," Steiner recalled, "Weissmandl would feed all the arguments to me, and even present all the counter-arguments that Wisliceny would bring forth. It is incredible," Steiner remarked, "how cogent and brilliant were his arguments and how well he understood the mind of Wisliceny as well as those of his chief, Eichmann, and the SS

Chief and arch-murderer Heinrich Himmler."[6]

It is this personality in action that we hope the next few episodes will convey, including a close look at the first ransom deal, that of Slovak Jewry, essentially as portrayed in his *Min Hametzar*.

THROUGHOUT HIS OWN VITAL WORK, Rabbi Weissmandl depended on a man named Shloime Benjamin Stern, whose **Shloime** supporting role is made clear in Rabbi Weissmandl's **Stern** own book.[7] Stern's own work in the Slovakian underground put him in close touch with a range of people, from smugglers to diplomats — *anyone* who was capable, and willing, to serve as couriers to Switzerland, Turkey, and of course Budapest.

The first two vignettes are based on interviews with Reb Shloime Benjamin Stern and his son "Brudi"; the latter helped Rabbi Weissmandl sketch the map of Auschwitz on Weissmandl's Hebrew version of the Auschwitz Protocols.

I. BENJAMIN SHLOIME STERN STOPS THE TRAIN[8]

IT SEEMED THAT THE TRAIN FROM BUDAPEST, its supposed destination Spain, wasn't like the others — or so the Slovakian **"Kosher"** partisans thought. They were well-paid allies of **Ham** Rabbi Weissmandl, and closely watched all the trains to gather information about shipments of Jews. In this specific case, the partisans told Benjamin Shloime Stern, a close associate of Rabbi Weissmandl, clearly it was no regular Auschwitz carrier, for it had open wagons, made frequent stops, and indeed had a relative liberty about the way the passengers embarked and disembarked.

Thus alerted, Stern bribed the Slovakian railroad workers to use a pretense of fallen power lines and stop the train near Bratislava — and then gave them extra money to take the train's German guards for drinks at a nearby bar. It all happened without a hitch, and Stern boarded the unguarded train himself to see who its passengers were and where they were headed. Stern was shocked by what he saw: the people on board had not eaten for the seven days they had been in transit. The seemingly special train, allegedly en route to Spain, appeared to be another Nazi ruse.

Stern, undaunted, did what he could. Desperately racing against the German guards' imminent return, he called Bratislava and asked that someone buy food for the passengers. The war had brought scarcities and little could be found. Meanwhile, the German officers were growing impatient to leave. Finally, Stern, admittedly fearful of not being able to help the trapped Jews, bought up the entire railway canteen, including all the non-kosher foodstuffs, and distributed it to the passengers. Indeed, Stern went so far as to convince a number of extremely Orthodox Jews that the railway ham was really *kosher* meat, basing his quick-thinking actions on the Torah law that suspends dietary restrictions when life is endangered. What's more, despite the fact that his perusal of the passengers was understandably brief, he nevertheless recognized Rabbi Joel Teitelbaum, the Admor of Satmar, to whom he gave a bottle of whiskey and a pack of cigarettes. Some time after the War, in London, Rabbi Teitelbaum recognized Stern, embraced him, and told him that his gift had kept him alive; he had traded it for bread and potatoes.

The train, of course, finally left, but not before Stern was able to provide one further service by taking several young people off the train and hiding them in his wagon. One of them was the son of a Budapest woman who had placed him on the train thinking that it was a so-called "safe" train bound for Spain. Stern managed to get him — and others — off, hide them, and eventually secure their passage to Switzerland.[9]

II. THE MESIRAS NEFESH OF A YESHIVAH STUDENT

THROUGHOUT THE WAR, RABBI WEISSMANDL devised numerous plans to halt — at least temporarily — the roughly 12,000 daily deaths at Auschwitz. Perhaps his most cogent

Bombing the Rails

— and feasible — one was the plan calling for the destruction of the rail lines, especially those running from Hungary through Slovakia. Rabbi Weissmandl's initial intent was to spare the thousands being transported daily — yet he quickly realized the real beauty of his plan was not in its awesome simplicity. Instead it lay in the fact that the same rail lines were major military supply lines, and that a concerted air strike — for whatever reason — would mean a major German military setback. What's more, since so much of the German war effort in 1944-45 — including large numbers of wagons, men, and machinery — had been thrown into the destruction of Europe's Jews, any massive air raid on the rail lines would of necessity eliminate large quantities of war material and thousands of soldiers. This was pointed out by

Rabbi Weissmandl who noted in one of his letters that the railroads to Auschwitz carried thousands of Axis soldiers and much war material.[10] There is little doubt that the Nazis, who were fully aware of Weissmandl's letters, realized that because "only Jewish lives" were at stake these railroads would not be bombed.

It was an excellent plan, farsighted and workable, and Rabbi Weissmandl wrote letters, which the Jewish messengers in different countries brought to the attention of every Allied government, outlining a course of action, including maps with exact routes detailing Auschwitz and its exact geographical environs. As an added impetus, too, he urged major Jewish organizations to exert all possible pressure on their governments to act. Yet all the efforts — on the part of other Jews as well as Rabbi Weissmandl — were ignored. According to Meir Springer, for example, Czech President Benes, who unstintingly cooperated with Jewish rescue efforts personally, spoke to British Prime Minister Winston Churchill about Rabbi Weissmandl's plan — to no avail. "There is a war on," Churchill replied, "and I cannot endanger even one single English soldier for the Jews." The truth was, sadly, as Professor David Wyman has unequivocally demonstrated, that there was no significant military obstacle to a successful raid on the rail lines or Auschwitz itself.[11] (And if there were to be casualties, the Allies could simply have asked for Jewish volunteers. Assuredly, there would not have been a dearth of qualified Jewish and non-Jewish airmen ready to assume the risks of such a mission.)

While the Allied governments were unwilling to act, nevertheless individual Jews were. In one notable example, Yankel Lowy, a Nitra Yeshivah student, volunteered to sabotage a major tunnel on the line from Hungary to Auschwitz. At first, he had thought that he would load himself with dynamite, enter the engine of the train when it was moving through the tunnel, and blow it up along with himself. The partisans, however, devised a means by which the tunnel could be blown up without losing the boy's life. They planned to release two engines in the tunnel, with dynamite in between them: the damage would take weeks to repair and thousands of Jews would be spared.[12]

Unfortunately, this plan was never carried out because Rabbi Weissmandl and his Vaad in the Jewish underground decided, after much understandable debate, that the Nazis would simply retaliate, in this case by killing the remaining 25,000 Slovakian Jews, and that the underground did not have the right to put so many Jewish lives in danger.

B. RANSOMING SLOVAK JEWRY

I. Introduction

LIKE HUNGARY, SLOVAKIA WAS SEMI-INDEPENDENT and a satellite of Germany; unlike its neighbor, however, it was virulently

Himmler Could Be Bribed antisemitic. Headed by President Josef Tiso, a Catholic priest and leader of the Nazi-inspired Hlinka People's Party, Slovakia was far more willing to accede to Eichmann's request to rid the country of

its Jews. Hence, deportations began in spring 1942; yet after roughly 60,000 had been sent to Auschwitz, Rabbi Michoel Ber Weissmandl was able to ransom the remaining 25,000 through Dieter Wisliceny, Eichmann's assistant, with the approval of SS Chief Heinrich Himmler himself. At the same time, Rabbi Weissmandl helped his father-in-law, Rabbi Shmuel Dovid Ungar, the rabbi of Nitra, operate the last active adult yeshivah in occupied Europe. The Nitra Yeshivah, known as the Little Vatican because of its semi-protected status achieved by bribery, was remarkable in another way; it had specially constructed moving walls and hideaways. Through all of this Rabbi Weissmandl continued to direct the Working Group — the Jewish underground — in Bratislava (Pressburg), 60 kilometers away.[13]

Following the decimation of Slovak Jewry between Passover and Yom Kippur, 1942, Rabbi Weissmandl undertook an attempt to spare the lives of the remaining 25,000 bewildered and impoverished Jews. In his investigations, he discovered that a lone Jew had been able to purchase a deportation exemption from Dieter Wisliceny. Rabbi Weissmandl wasted no time, but set about to learn if Wisliceny was willing to put a price on the lives of Slovakia's remaining Jews. He was, and stated his willingness to halt the twice-weekly death trains for $50,000 in American dollars, paid in two equal installments. The first would be due in 10 days, the second in seven weeks. As his own demonstration of good faith, Wisliceny offered to halt three death trains immediately. Rabbi Weissmandl quickly realized that Wisliceny himself would not set such a course on his own initiative, but was in fact working as an agent for Heinrich Himmler.[14]

Wisliceny offered Rabbi Weissmandl hope, but there were two problems. First, how to raise or borrow $25,000 American dollars with an already weakened and impoverished Jewish community? And second, once raised, where could one find trustworthy couriers to bring it in from Switzerland, the only reliable source? Yet Rabbi Weissmandl solved both problems virtually overnight; for a close friend, Binyamin Shloime Stern, gave the first half of the ransom — all in dollars, literally unearthed and cleaned. The rabbi called upon gold smugglers with whom he had previously worked — Gestapo officers and foreign diplomats eager to receive a fee for bringing money over the border. It all worked: the payment was on time, and Wisliceny stopped the deportations.

THE SEVEN WEEKS' RESPITE LIFTED AN ENORMOUS BURDEN from Rabbi Weissmandl — but he soon realized that the first half of
The Other $25,000
the ransom was a great deal easier to raise than the second. Rabbi Weissmandl had initially been optimistic about obtaining the funds from Saly Mayer, the Joint's Swiss representative, for one dollar per person was not an unreasonable sum for ransom. Yet he quickly discovered that his hopes had been premature. In fact, his father-in-law, Rabbi Shmuel Dovid Ungar, had been more skeptical and had cautioned Rabbi Weissmandl to contact Orthodox as well as secular groups, and to choose as his representative someone respected by both. He chose Gisi Fleischmann, a distant relative, dedicated community worker, and Slovakian Jewry's representative for the Joint, the World Jewish Congress, and the Jewish Agency. As a person with established credentials, she could minimize the Jewish Establishment's expected skepticism about the accuracy of the Slovakian reports and suggestions. Rabbi Weissmandl knew that Orthodox rabbis were not well respected by secular Jewish organizations, particularly by those on the left.[15]

The Weissmandl party worked diligently. Letters sent via courier were dispatched to the major Jewish organizations in Switzerland and Hungary, and Gisi Fleischmann herself had made several trips to Budapest. They expected results in Hungary, for despite antisemitic legislation and forced labor battalions, the large Hungarian-Jewish community continued to live in relative peace. Yet the responses were negative because the Jewish organizations refused to accept ransom as a viable course of rescue. Nor were they ready to provide the necessary illegal U.S. dollars. (The small Budapest-Orthodox community was an exception.) Saly Mayer, for one, suggested that the money not be paid, but be placed instead in a Swiss bank account and paid out after the war. Representatives of the World Jewish Congress and the Jewish Agency refused to send funds illegally to Slovakia, standing fast to a policy which called for

Jews to borrow money locally on Joint guarantees of postwar repayment in American dollars.[16]

Rabbi Weissmandl was dismayed by the attitude of Saly Mayer and others who were unable to realize that the Nazis would not bargain without getting something — in this case money — in return. "Did they really think," he asked, "that the Nazis were such fools as to give up their [human] merchandise upon a promise to collect the money after the war?" Later he added, "We were the merchandise, the deadline for payment was near, and the buyer was bickering with impossible demands." Yet a Hungarian leader, Samuel Stern, told Rabbi Weissmandl why they could not raise the money. First, it would be unlikely that Hungarian Jewry would again come to the aid of the Slovakians, and second, the use of the black market "will not be done in any circumstances [because they would not] commit such a crime against the government — especially during these times, when we are in need of their grace."[17]

Finally the Joint relented. Word arrived from Switzerland that monies budgeted for Slovakia and previously deposited in Switzerland could be used for Wisliceny's ransom — but only after a complicated series of currency exchanges. Rabbi Weissmandl had already arranged for two trusted allies — Philip Freudiger, head of the Orthodox community in Budapest, and Zvi Heilbrun, of Nitra — to expedite matters, but it was all too late. Wisliceny, angered by the delay, had sent 3,000 more Jews to Auschwitz. The clear implication was that more would follow shortly, and Rabbi Weissmandl sent a special messenger to the Budapest-Orthodox community demanding the money. When no answer was forthcoming, he sent cables from Bratislava to the three prominent Hungarian Orthodox leaders summoning each to the High Court. The message was clear: the High Court was the heavenly tribunal to which they would be responsible for responding too slowly to save the lives of their fellow Jews.[18]

THE FOLLOWING DAY A MESSENGER FROM BUDAPEST arrived with the $25,000 — despite the fact that the Hungarian police,

Deportations Stopped for Two Years suspecting espionage in the cryptic cable, closely monitored the Jews' activities. (The messengers skirted the danger by informing the police that the matters were religious in nature.) Rabbi Weissmandl immediately took the ransom to Wisliceny, hoping to halt the trains. Yet he was not in luck, for a furious Wisliceny said, "You miserable Jews, until I pressed you to the wall there was no money. You found all kinds of excuses — hoping all the time that the war would end and you'd save both lives and money, while my friends and I would be killed. Now you have the money, but the transport won't return. From now on, you keep your word and we will keep ours."[19] And he did, for despite his anger, Wisliceny stopped the deportations — other than one further train — for the next two years, and relative calm prevailed once again for Slovakian Jewry.

As soon as Rabbi Weissmandl stepped into Orthodox headquarters, though, he was seized by the Slovakian police, who questioned him about receipts and other papers he had relating to aid for Jews deported to Poland, and then took him to prison. In his cell he decided that should he be released, he would attempt to ransom all Jews still held prisoner by the Nazis. Although his 1943 two-million dollars Europa Plan eventually failed, as did his other ransom plans, ransom per se was made acceptable as a means of rescue when dealing with a superior enemy — and eventually saved the lives of thousands more Jews. After ten days in prison, Rabbi Weissmandl was released and continued his work to save Jewish lives.

Rabbi Weissmandl had acted forcefully in 1942 to save *all* Slovakian Jews regardless of religious or political affiliation, a course he continued to follow throughout the war. By his acts, he not only gave direction to the greater Orthodox efforts around the world, he also enlarged the scope of his activities as the war continued. For while the Nazis increased the killings, at the same time they showed a greater willingness to bargain.

II. Genius of Rescue:
Personal Vignettes from Oscar [Yirmiyahu] Neumann's *In the Shadow of Death*[20]*

The Place: Nitra, a small town in Slovakia
The Time: June, 1942

THE ANCIENT PROVINCIAL TOWN OF NITRA, situated pictures-quely on the spur of a mountain chain of the same name, was a
Nitra citadel of faith for two religions. On the top of a characteristic hill, a thousand-year-old church dominated an entire city of Catholic clergy with its Episcopalian Theological Seminary, libraries, and dormitories for the young seminarians. But this city was at the same time home for an eminent yeshivah of

---

* Selected and translated by Asher Forst

Torah learning and a great Orthodox community.

The old and venerable head of this yeshivah, the authoritative Chief Rabbi [Shmuel Dovid] Ungar, was at the same time the real head of Orthodox Jewry in Slovakia. The impressive appearance of this great leader — his lean, ascetic frame crowned by scholarly features and a white-bearded face — bespoke his great inner spiritual strength. The citadel of Orthodoxy was the yeshivah, Rabbi Ungar's particular domain, and was humorously called the Vatican. This expansive complex of buildings set into one another became increasingly important as a place for Jews who hid to escape deportation. Great numbers of Jews hid there, for it was possible to cross the border from there into nearby Hungary.

But the most interesting and — in terms of rescuing Jews — most important personality in the strictly Orthodox milieu of "the Vatican" was the Talmudic scholar Rabbi Michoel Ber Weissmandl, the son-in-law of Chief Rabbi Ungar.

AT THIS TIME, the orthodox Central Office (*Landeskanzlei*) in the capital, Bratislava, had lost its leader, with no outstanding personality left. That was when this apparently strange man Weissmandl began to appear and take matters into his own hands.

Appearances Are Deceiving

Whoever met him for the first time could not possibly imagine the amazing personality hidden beneath his unassuming exterior. His face was not handsome, his black beard was not groomed and his clothes were not neat and tidy. If he had done nothing else but move around the streets of the capital filled with Germans and members of the notorious Hlinka Guard, he would have been a heroic figure. His [obviously Jewish] appearance alone acted like a magnet on momentarily dormant instincts of brutality.

Rabbi Weissmandl was physically attacked and insulted many times, yet could never be persuaded to change his appearance or to withdraw from open danger. Nothing in his appearance indicated his genuine humility and bashfulness, his ardent soul, his sharp intellect, the wisdom and practical philosophy of his sparkling mind, and basic serene and cheerful temperament. Who could have guessed that behind that maturity of heart and mind, and behind the appearance of a fifty-year-old, was a very young man.

This man, whose appearance was so misleadingly unimpressive, immersed himself totally into a society completely foreign to his own background. The odds against his achieving any kind of success were overwhelming, but his careful, thought-out-manner, his humility and his humaneness, won the hearts of all. Because of the boldness of his plans, they called him the Partisan Rebbe. Though he could not, on account of his appearance, visit government offices and authorities, he was an inexhaustible motor of energy and ideas, a perpetual motion machine, untiringly swinging between the Orthodox Central Office in which the group was constantly meeting and all the various other places of his activity. He was the uncontested authority of the strictest Orthodoxy, and a close collaboration with him meant at the same time the closest contact with the people who placed themselves at his disposal at the slightest hint. They were people whose assistance was actually indispensable in that increasingly desperate situation.

IT WAS STILL SPRING, 1942. Deportation trains were rolling, train by train, with incessant regularity. The trains carried away parents,

Shocking Reports brothers and sisters, relatives and friends, removing a flourishing upright Jewish community to a cruel fate whose real nature was still unknown.

In the meantime, messages and shocking reports began to arrive by clandestine routes. It had been announced officially by the German propaganda that transported families would stay together, but immediately after getting off the train, after the fatigue of a journey which lasted eight to fourteen days, the family members were separated. It became painfully clear that the earlier reports had been lies, calculated to lull Jews into the false hope that things were not bad. No clothes, linen, watches or jewelry were left which could be bartered for bread and potatoes. What had escaped the eyes of the train guards was robbed by the camp guards. We read these reports with deep shock and chagrin. The reports were not about people unknown to us; just a short while ago we had lived together with them and we knew each and every one of them. Something had to be done immediately. At that time the two rabbis, Weissmandl and [Armin] Frieder,* started to work. A vast supply of watches and jewelry was bought and stored, and a very active secret service began its work between Slovakia and our brothers in Poland. Reliable non-Jewish messengers were found who were familiar with the routes and with the Polish language. These men made clandestine contacts, smuggled valuables and letters, and brought back receipts. Most of the valuables reached their destination and the receipts were signed by the recipient's own hands.

---

* Rabbi Dr. Armin Frieder, rabbi of reform (Neologue) congregation, was an important member of the Slovak-Jewish underground. [Ed.]

In the midst of all this exhausting work, one day news came like a thunderclap. Pale and shaking with agitation, Rabbi Weissmandl appeared in the office, his eyes pouring tears, his voice shaking with sobs. From the terrified group around the table came fluttering questions. Weissmandl took from his pocket a piece of crumpled paper that looked as if it had been torn from a prayerbook, and we saw that on it were scrawled with a shaky hand a few words in pencil, "For Heaven's sake, brothers, help us, we are all about to be murdered."

"One of the messengers had just arrived from Poland," panted Rabbi Weissmandl. And with nervous hands he produced more scraps of similar paper from his pockets. What was there to do? These horrifying documents must immediately be brought to the knowledge of the Chief of State, of the Slovakian people who were cooperating in the deportations with the Germans. The clergy must see them. A report must be sent without delay to the Pope in Rome.

❧ ❧ ❧

Rabbi Weissmandl's own account of those fateful days was recorded in his work, *Min Hametzar — Out of the Depths.*[22]

THE IDEA OF INTERVENING DIRECTLY WITH THE POPE was based on the following assumption. The president of the Slovak

Two Letters to the Pope

Republic, Monsignor Tiso, was still the parson of his parish of Banovce and as such he was under the jurisdiction of his Church superior. Therefore, the threat of excommunication would at least have made him think twice. (Tiso had requested the Germans to take over the Jews and deport them for payment of 5,000 Slovak Crowns per person, to be paid for by the Slovak treasury.)

Two letters were sent to Pope Pius XII in Rome. One was written in the German language in the name of the Central Office of the Orthodox as well as in the name of the liberal Jewish representations. The second letter was a personal petition of the rabbis, and it fell to me to compose it. How many hours did I sit over this piece of paper! The tears and the groans which filled our days and nights formed themselves into letters and words. The letter was signed by many rabbis — those who had somehow managed to remain alive. Karol Sidor, the Slovakian Ambassador to the Vatican, undertook to deliver it — for good money. (I think it was 30,000 Crowns.) The Minister of Education, Josef Sivak, promised — for 1,000 Crowns — to let us know immediately if and when there might be any reaction to our letters. We did not have to wait too long.

Ambassador Sidor personally delivered the reply from the Papal Secretariat of State, signed by Cardinal Maglioni on March 14, 1942. Its essence was the following paragraph:

> These people, approximately 80,000, according to some 135,000, are allegedly transported to Poland, to the district of Lublin, and men, women and children are separated during these transportations. The Secretariat of State hopes that these reports do not correspond to the truth, for such measures, painful for so many families, could not be executed by a State which claims to be guided by the principles of the Catholic Church.

On May 8, the Ministry of Foreign Affairs in Bratislava ordered Ambassador Sidor to inform the Holy See that the Slovakian Jews would remain together. Jews of the Catholic faith would, according to the assurances of the Reich, be settled elsewhere.

In May 1944, when the Slovakian government was busy deporting the last remnant of the Slovak Jews, and the entire world already knew all the details of the extermination process, the following note was sent by the Vatican to the Slovak government:

> The Holy See is convinced that the Slovak government will take no steps to deport forcibly people of the so-called "Jewish race." The more painful to the Holy See is the report that such deportations are actually taking place. This pain is increased by the reports which arrived from several sides that the Slovak government intends to carry these deportations through completely, regardless of women and children, and even not to exempt those who belong to the Catholic Church. The Church cannot react with indifference to decrees which will cause physical suffering and spiritual distress to so many of the faithful as a result of isolation from their Church.

IN THE TOWN OF NITRA LIVED the Catholic Archbishop Karol Kmetko for whom President Tiso worked several years as private

Archbishop Kmetko secretary when he was still a simple cleric. My father-in-law, Rabbi Ungar, was somehow acquainted with the archbishop. I assumed that the old prelate had no knowledge of all these events, and that a personal petition by the rabbi might perhaps produce some positive results. I persuaded my father-in-law to visit the archbishop. It was between Purim and Passover, 1942. At that time the public did not yet know of any systematic extermination of the Jews, and the protestations and ardent entreaties of my father-in-law concerned themselves with the deportations only, since at the time there was as yet no mention of death camps.

"This is not just a deportation of the Jews," said the archbishop. "There you will not die of hunger and pestilence. There you will be killed, young and old, women and children. And that will be your punishment for your killing of our Saviour."

In autumn 1944 came the final blow against the last remnant of Jews who tried to escape into the surrounding woods.

AT THAT TIME I DECIDED to make an attempt to escape from the Sered concentration camp where we all were imprisoned. That

The Papal Nuncio in Bratislava particular moment seemed to be favorable to try to see the papal nuncio in Bratislava. The Allied armies had already advanced far on the one side, and the Russians on the other. The war was already in its last stages. Simultaneously, warnings had been issued to the Hungarian Government by President Roosevelt and the King of Sweden to stop the deportation of the Jews.* Cardinal Justinian Seredi of Hungary also made efforts in the same direction. All this gave me the impression that the Vatican might also have some positive interest in such efforts.

An attempt to intervene with the nuncio therefore seemed to hold some prospect for the small remnant of Jews for whose lives I wanted to plead. I succeeded in penetrating the ranks straight to the Nuncio's office, where I told him of my escape from the camp, and that I had come to him to plead for his help to save the lives of 20,000 Jews who were about to be transported to the slaughterhouse. I also mentioned as an example the intervention of the Hungarian Cardinal Seredi with the Hungarian Regent Horthy, whom he threatened with excommunication if the deportations were not put to an end. Why should that not be possible with Tiso?

"First of all, today is Sunday and on Sunday we do not deal with profane matters," said the nuncio.

I could not believe my ears. In my delusion and the folly of my heart, I still tried not to believe. Could it be possible that he doesn't know about Auschwitz? "Your Eminence," I said, "we are all going to be slaughtered; is the blood of thousands of innocent children a 'profane matter'? I beg of you, Your Eminence, go immediately, the Al-mighty will bless you for it." I cried before him. I cried very

---

* He was unaware of Mantello's Swiss press campaign which was responsible for this world-wide outcry. [Ed.]

much. My wife and my children, my entire family, and so many, many people were in that camp and they all knew just as I did what was awaiting them.

And that man, the personal representative of the Pope, stood there with his face distorted from rage and his eyes sparkling with hate, and he said,

> There is no such thing as blood of innocent Jewish children — all Jewish blood is guilty. What about the fact that Seredi had threatened the Regent Horthy with excommunication? Seredi himself should be excommunicated. Who gave him the right to intervene on your behalf? As to you, I shall call the Gestapo immediately to arrest you.[22]

In his book Oscar Neumann concludes this episode:[23]

> After a long discussion with our friends in Camp Sered, Rabbi Weissmandl decided to make a renewed attempt with Brunner to stop the deportations and take up the plan of merchandise for lives. Brunner received the rabbi as was his habit with satanic-cynical friendliness, and the rabbi spent almost two hours in the office of that beastly man. He must have pleaded there in his usual courageous and convincing manner, because he himself told us later that in the course of the discussion he pounded several times on the table in excitement.

> But the discussion ended, as was expected, without any results. The fourth transport was arranged, and with it went, to our unspeakable grief, Rabbi Weissmandl with his young wife and his many small children. His friends insistently suggested to him to make an attempt to jump from the train — he could not help his family by staying on because they were lost anyway. This deeply religious man fought then the greatest struggle of his life. Should he, who knew exactly the meaning of Auschwitz, let his family roll towards death and save himself? Should he, before the eyes of his wife and children, jump out of the train and leave them to their bitter fate?

> Can anyone imagine the thoughts of this man who devoted his life entirely to the rescue of his people? Can anyone imagine the tragedy of his inner conflict? He knew precisely, on the other hand, that immediately after arrival he would be separated from his family and they would all have to go separately to death. His friends did not give up their attempts to persuade the rabbi to save himself. His mission was not yet at an end; he might be successful in reaching Bratislava and so in some way alarm the outside world. After a horrible inner struggle, Rabbi Weissmandl decided to jump from the train.

> And the miracle happened. His escape succeeded, and he reached Bratislava where he hid in a bunker. We in the camp

soon heard the news about his escape, and this news also told us that the man almost went insane with grief, and that he cried and lamented day and night. But we knew that he had done the right thing, because sacrificing himself would have been senseless. Many months later, shortly before the Russians entered the Slovak capital, he arrived with a few others in Switzerland.

III. Rabbi Weissmandl: A Personal Retrospect
by Asher Siegmund Forst, artist, thinker, and close friend of Rabbi Weissmandl[24]
Introduction:

This great and tragic *tzaddik*, whose brilliant mind created the most spectacular rescue schemes of the Holocaust period, and whose heart was fully consumed in his quest to save Jewish lives, emerged from his bunker a broken man. Until his dying day twelve years later, Rabbi Weissmandl mourned this greatest of Jewish tragedies. This is evidenced not merely from testimony of numerous friends and acquaintances, but also from the anguish permeating every line in *Min Hametzar*, his great, unfinished work — the most profound book to appear on the Holocaust. Through months of despair hovering on the abyss, Rabbi Weissmandl slowly was nursed back to relatively tolerable physical existence, through the compassion and help of a few close friends in Williamsburg and in the Nitra Yeshivah which he recreated in Mt. Kisco, New York.

... After the War, shortly after his arrival in the United States, Michoel Ber Weissmandl issued a flaming *J'accuse* in which he put ten "Yes-or-No" questions to the leaders of the Jewish Agency.

One must understand the motive and the nature of Rabbi Weissmandl's statements and vehement accusations. Though he addressed himself to a political group, dealing with practical issues, though of enormous dimensions, his motivation was not "political" — it was basically religious, because Rabbi Weissmandl was a religious man par excellence. He conceived Jewish nationalism as the great sin of assimilation in a national disguise, as a substitution for a universal religion which, like all religions, has the purpose to give sense to one's life and solve the personal and collective dilemma of man in this world. One has to understand what went on in the mind of this man who stood in the midst of the fire, waiting day after day, month after month with terrible anxiety for that answer to his hundreds of frantic letters, telegrams and messages. He could not comprehend what had happened only until after all was over. It was only after the war, when the crushing realization dawned upon him that a group of people, having lost their roots, in possession of power and influence, commanding publicity, journalists, politicians and professional pulpiteers, with almost irrational delusion had substituted an ideal after their own image, for the most basic, the most elementary and vital Jewish command at that hour — to save Jewish lives.

With incessant compulsion, Rabbi Weissmandl hunted for documents and rummaged in libraries and archives among the huge body of material which has been collected after the war. He traced his own letters and communications, some of which found their way to the highest authorities, like his proposal to bomb the rails leading to Auschwitz. Allied bombers did successfully strafe the oilfields of Ploesti, Rumania, but they let the trains to Auschwitz roll undisturbed until the last minute, a fact which the Nazis amusedly interpreted in their own way.

Rabbi Weissmandl was a restless and brooding man. He became ever more restless and brooding with the passing of time as the process of oblivion had set in. People wanted to forget what had happened, and they succeeded astonishingly.

And so we see Rabbi Weissmandl as he came back after the war into a world which he could not accept anymore as it appeared. He had seen reality breaking into pieces and displaying in horrible inconceivability its content of an unfathomable mystery. Reality could not serve anymore as a pretext for a life of "normality" — he saw it as the fragile and brittle layer it is and was from now on possessed by the potential danger of a terrible eruption of its content. Of course, Rabbi Weissmandl did what his Jewish instinct almost automatically compelled him to do — he grasped at Torah, which appeared now, more than ever, to be the only constant in the vanishing illusion of reality. He built a yeshivah which was the elementary and natural thing to do, and the few remaining years of his life were filled with agony and torment. He went around begging for his yeshivah, though he knew that his heart was failing. Perhaps, that also was the elementary and natural thing for him to do — and then the flickering light went out ...

Rabbi Michoel Ber Weissmandl was possessed by the restlessness of the seeker and he was always on the spiritual move. Once — he was at that time a very young man, he bought himself a railway ticket which enabled him to travel over the length and width of Poland, the largest and most colorful Jewish community. He came to know all Jewish leaders of importance. He spoke with R' Chaim

Ozer Grodzenski and with the Chofetz Chaim; he saw how people lived in Warsaw and in Lodz. In *Eretz Yisrael* he spoke to Sephardim and in Oxford to English Jews and non-Jews. He liked to listen to other people, regardless of whether they were *rabbonim* or porters, taxi drivers or doctors. Generally, he was fascinated by people. He was especially attracted by the "outsiders" of society because he was tired of the self-righteous philistine ...

In a way, the yeshivah [that he built] in Mt. Kisco is a remarkable symbol for the man Rabbi Weissmandl and his life. One remembers the time when he brought over some sixty-odd young boys, all orphans. For a short time they settled in a place in New Jersey; from there they came to Mt. Kisco, New York. That place belonged to an industrialist who wanted to sell it. Rabbi Dr. Leo Jung of New York succeeded to interest a well-meaning philanthropist, Israel Rogosin, to buy the estate and donate it to the yeshivah. All seemed well and then trouble started. First it was zoning trouble, initiated by real estate interests who feared a devaluation of their properties in that residential area in which the yeshivah and its inhabitants were an unusual and strange-looking sight. The Westchester County Jews did not feel too happy either about the sudden emergence of that group which proved to be stubbornly resistant to all friendly attempts to be educated in the "American Way of Life," of which the Westchester County Jews felt themselves to be the chosen experts. When the zoning debate became a public issue with some antisemitic undercurrents, and some non-Jews became interested, the big Jewish organizations — but especially one prominent non-Jewish society woman — came to the support of the yeshivah, which finally assured its right to stay.

During the following years the yeshivah went from one crisis to another. There was no money to pay the food bills, no money for oil, telephone and electricity. Rabbi Weissmandl was at that time already a very sick man. He had no days of peace and no nights of rest. The man who one time had disposed of hundreds of thousands of dollars, money and jewelry, collected by the underground resistance in Slovakia and Hungary, was spending sleepless nights agonizing about paying the butcher's bill of the yeshivah. He completely — perhaps deliberately — forgot about himself. He possessed nothing but the shabby clothes he was wearing and the wooden cane with which he supported his tired body. One remembers that cane. One remembers also Rabbi Weissmandl dragging himself through the hot streets in summer and the cold slush in winter, borrowing money here to pay a debt there. There was first that slight, impatient annoyance and then that shrug with the shoulder, that slightening movement of the head pointing knowingly towards him: oh yes, that's Weissmandl! After the first heart attack, the pains in the chest became more frequent and the body more frail and exhausted — but there was still no rest.

One remembers the kindness of his eyes which rested lovingly on simple piety wherever he found it. He admired simplicity, straightforwardness of character, even naivete which, he felt, is somehow related to saintliness. He had an instinctive dislike of the artful, the oversophisticated and especially of the showy, even if all these came under the mantle of Torah. He admired and he was impressed by the scholar, but it was the saintly who would move him lastingly and genuinely. There were probably very few in this postwar generation who were so deeply concerned about the Torah — not Torah learning in its usual quantitative sense, but rather the entire complex of Torah in a qualitative way.

There was once a great light which emerged on the sky like a meteor consuming itself in its vehement rapidity. On its way it warmed and unforgettably inspired many Jewish hearts.

Epilogue
"Some Old-fashioned Rabbis and Inepts"

A LOT MORE PEOPLE TODAY, certainly, think that rescue should have been the first priority during the Holocaust than thought so at the time — ahead of statehood, bans on trading with **"Will Some Old-Fashioned Rabbi Succeed?"** the enemy, loyalty to a U.S. president in wartime, or the ideology of those one is willing to work with. But choosing the right priority when worthy priorities conflict is a challenge of the human condition and always will be. Perhaps it can be said that the Orthodox, for whom Torah values are a way of life, had less trouble with that choice during World War II than any other group in American Jewry. Both the Torah perspective and the general skepticism of the efficacy of the efforts by the Orthodox leaders, which is still common today even among ideologically motivated historians, are reflected in the following episode involving Rabbi Eliezer Silver, founder of the Vaad Hatzalah. More than twenty years after the Holocaust he wrote the following account of a conversation he had back then with a philanthropist who was being asked to give a considerable sum:

> He asked me ... "With all due respect ... it is difficult for me to understand why in ... saving Jews in Europe there is no one who can do anything; not one of our famous help organizations ... and none of our political leaders — only a

handful of Orthodox rabbis. Forgive my frankness, but *will some old-fashioned rabbis and inepts succeed in such an undertaking?"*

I answered ... "When it is a matter of rescuing Jewish lives we, the rabbis, are forbidden to be inept ... By command of our Holy Torah we are prepared to violate many laws ... to save lives. We are ready to pay ransom for Jews and deliver them from concentration camps with ... forged passports. For this purpose we do not hesitate to deal with counterfeiters and passport thieves. We are ready to smuggle Jewish children over the borders, and to engage expert smugglers for this purpose ... We are ready to smuggle money illegally into enemy territory ... to bribe ... the killers of the Jewish people, those dregs of humanity! We are even ready to send special emissaries to plead with the chief murderers ... and try to appease them at any cost!"

"Now I understand ...," said the man and handed me a fine gift.

Yes, we the rabbis and the Orthodox community ... attempted to do many a thing in all these fields. Not all we did was crowned with success, but the success that we had showed us that we were on the right path. And it is precisely because of these limited successes that our hearts ache to this day.[10] [emphasis added]

Footnotes

Foreword

1. The first scholarly paper devoted to the role of the Orthodox is my chapter (Appendix 4-3) entitled, "Orthodox Ends, Unorthodox Means," in the so-called Goldberg Commission Report [*Goldberg Report*] *American Jewry During the Holocaust*, edited by Prof. Seymour M. Finger. (New York: American Jewish Commission on the Holocaust, 1983.) The first mention of the work of Rabbi Abraham Kalmanowitz and his efforts on behalf of the yeshivah groups in Shanghai during World War II is found in this author's *Japanese, Nazis and Jews: The Jewish Refugee Community of Shanghai 1938-1945* [*Kranzler, Shanghai*] (New York: Yeshiva University Press, 1976). Two other popular works on the role of Orthodox rescue activists by this author are (with Gertrude Hirschler) *Solomon Schonfeld: His Page in History* [*Kranzler, Schonfeld*] (New York: Judaica Press, 1982), and *Heroine of Rescue* (with Joseph Friedenson) (New York: Mesorah Publications, 1984).

Introduction

1. *Rescue attempts During the Holocaust: Proceedings of the Second Yad Vashem International Historical Conference.* [*Rescue Attempts*] April 1974 (Jerusalem: Yad Vashem, 1977). See also Bernard Wasserstein, *Britain and the Jews of Europe 1939-1945* [Wasserstein] (London: Oxford U. Press, 1980), pp. 311-313. Wasserstein mentions Chaim Weizmann's plea to bomb Auschwitz apparently unaware of Rabbi Weissmandl as the originator of the plan, although in his bibliography Wasserstein cites David Wyman's article, "Why Auschwitz Was Never Bombed" [Wyman, "Auschwitz"], *Commentary* (May 1978), pp. 37-45. Wyman had no hesitation in giving Rabbi Weissmandl full credit.

2. Yehudah Bauer, *The Holocaust in Historical Perspective* [Bauer, *Holocaust*] (Seattle, Washington: U. of Wash. Press, 1978), p. 139. In his later works, Bauer does give more credit to Rabbi Weissmandl. See his *American Jews and the Holocaust: The American Jewish Joint Distribution Committee, 1939-1945* [Bauer, *JDC*] (Detroit: Wayne State U. Press, 1981), p. 357. See, however, pp. 492-3, note 23.

3. Wasserstein, *op cit.*

4. Yaakov Griffel *Memoirs*, p. 1. The author is grateful to Mr. Charles Silber for providing him with a copy of this manuscript.

5. See Bauer, *JDC*, in the index.

6. Taped interview with Mr. Landau. Mr. Landau was the executive secretary to the Sternbuchs' relief organization called HIJEFS.

7. *Disaster and Salvation* [VH], p. 33.

8. *San.* 37a.

9. *VH*, p. 38.

Preface: Four Episodes

1. Based on an interview with Mr. Irving Bunim.

2. This unit is a brief adaptation of a chapter in this author's forthcoming work *Stand Not Idly By*. See below, Chaps. 3, 7E for more on Vittel and Latin American papers. See also *Heroine of Rescue*, Chap. 9.

3. *Morgenthau Diaries* [MD] 4/6/44, p. 86.

4. *Ibid.*, p. 87.

5. *Ibid.*, p. 108.

6. *Ibid.*, p. 87.

7. *Ibid.*

8. *Ibid.*

9. *Ibid.*, 4/7/44, p. 221.

10. *Ibid.*

11. *Ibid.*

12. *Ibid.*

13. *Ibid.*

14. *Ibid.*, p. 222.

15. *Ibid.*

16. *Ibid.*

17. *Ibid.*, 4/10/44, p. 169.

18. *Ibid.*, pp. 180, 182; p. 181.

19. *Ibid.*, p. 184.

20. *Ibid.*, p. 182

21. Based on an interview with Rabbi Moshe Schwab, son of Rabbi Shimon Schwab and a participant in the event.

22. Reprinted from Kranzler, *Schonfeld*, pp. 57-61.

Chapter I: Pikuach Nefesh: The Jewish Foreign Policy

1. Bauer, *JDC*, p. 378.

2. *Ibid.*

3. *San.* 37a.

4. *Sifra* 19:18.

5. *Lev.* 19:16.

6. *Minchas Chinuch*, Com. 37.

7. *San.* 37a; *Yoma* 85b.

8. *Lev.* 18:5

9. *Yad Matnas Aniyim* 8:10.

10. *Hor.* 3:7, 13a.

11. *Yad Matnas Aniyim* 8:10. Cited by Salo Baron, *The Jewish Community* [Baron, Community] Vol. II (Phila.: S, 1942), p. 333.

12. Colon, *Responsa*, Root 5. Cited *op cit. ad loc.*

13. *Shevuos* 39a; *San.* 27b; *Sotah* 37a; *Rosh Hashanah* 29a. Rashi s.v. *Af Al Pi.*

14. Irving Agus, *The Heroic Age of Franco-German Jewry* (New York: Yeshiva U. Press, 1969), p. 33. See also Chap. 1. Cf. Elkan N. Adler, *Jewish Travellers* (New York: Sepher-Hermon Press, 1966).

15. Baron, *Community* II, pp. 333-337.

16. Selma Stern's *The Court Jew* (Phila.: JPS, 1950), especially Chap. VII and *Josel of Rosheim* (Phila.: JPS, 1965), especially Chap. 9.

17. *Court Jew.*

18. Celia Heller, *On the Edge of Destruction* [Heller, *Edge*] (New York: Columbia U. Press, 1977), see especially pp. 168-181.

19. *Ibid.*, p. 176.

20. *Ibid.*, pp. 176-180.

21. *Ibid.*

22. *Ibid.*, pp. 274-275.

23. *Ibid.*, p. 181.

24. Cf. Ezra Mendelsohn, "The Dilemma of Jewish Politics in Poland: Four Responses," in *Jews and Non-Jews in Eastern Europe 1918-1945* edited by Bela Vago and George L. Mosse (New York: John Wiley and Sons, 1974), pp. 209-213.

25. Heller, *Edge*, pp. 274-275.

26. *Ibid.*, esp. p. 176.

Chapter II: Pikuach Nefesh in Action

1. See Reuben Ainsztein, *Jewish Resistance in Nazi Occupied Eastern Europe* [Ainsztein, *Resistance*] (London: Paul Elek, 1974), p. 853, n. 7.

2. Heller, *Edge*, p. 181.

3. *Ibid.*, pp. 57-60.

4. Cf. Bauer, *Holocaust*, p. 23, where he fails to understand the ideological implications of the Bund's statement. Compounding the

error, he ascribes this "muddle and disorientation" to "all sections of Jewry in the 'Free World.' "

5. Kranzler, *Shanghai*, p. 470, n. 21. For an extremely sympathetic view of Joseph Schwartz's role during the War see Bauer, *JDC*, index. Similarly, Laura Margolies Jarblum, *JDC's* representative in Shanghai and Europe during WWII, gave the same sympathetic portrayal of Dr. Schwartz. Taped interview.

6. Rabbi Michoel Ber Weissmandl, *Min Hametzar (From the Depths)* [Min Hametzar] (New York: n.p., n.d., p. 54.

7. *Ibid.*, pp. 160-1..

8. *Ibid.*, p. 133

9. See below, Chap. 7H.

10. See, for example, Livia Rothkirchen, *The Destruction of Slovak Jewry* [Rothkirchen, Slovak] (Jerusalem: Yad Vashem, 1961), pp. XLVI-XLVII. When this author questioned Andre Steiner about his statements in a previous interview at the Hebrew U. Institute for Contemporary Jewry, that Rabbi Weissmandl had approved and even promoted the purchase of arms by the Jews in the labor camps in Slovakia, Mr. Steiner agreed that he had erred. Taped interview with Andre Steiner.

11. Taped interview with Shloime Stern.

12. Taped interview with Joseph Klarman. Dr. Klarman was a close collaborator of Griffel during the period of 1943-1945.

13. Taped interview with Rebbetzin Sarah Kotler-Schwartzman, daughter of Rabbi Kotler. Rebbetzin Schwartzman served as personal secretary to her illustrious father during this era, and was a doctoral student at Columbia University in political science. By the end of the summer of 1941, several months after the arrival of Rabbi Kotler, who constantly pushed for Orthodox unity vis-a-vis rescue, we find Mizrachi part of Vaad Hatzalah, despite earlier reservations. See Efraim Zuroff, "Rescue Priority and Fund Raising as Issue During the Holocaust: A Case Study of the Relations between the Vaad Ha-hatzalah [sic] and the Joint, 1939-1941," [Zuroff, "Vaad"] *American Jewish History*, Vol. LXVIII, No. 3 (March 1979), p. 310. Zuroff does not understand the specific role of Rabbi Aaron Kotler.

14. Taped interview with Rabbi Alex Weisfogel.

15. Taped interview with Mr. Irving Bunim. Some units from this volume on Mr. Bunim's rescue effort have been deleted upon the

request of his son Amos Bunim. The latter is publishing a biography of his father, for which I did the research and wrote the first draft. Mr. Bunim therefore desires that this book appear first.

16. See the accountant's figures for 1944. *Disaster and Salvation* [VH] (New York: "Vaad Hatzalah" Book Committee, 1957), p. 517.

17. Taped interview with Dr. Gershon G. Kranzler. Dr. Gershon Kranzler was very active with Zeirei Agudath Israel's refugee and immigration work during 1938-1942. See below, chap. 9G.

18. *Ibid.* Also taped interviews with Mr. Frank Newman, Mr. Louis Septimus. See below, *ibid.*

19. Bunim interview.

20. Taped interview with Mr. Herman Landau.

21. See *Heroine of Rescue*, Chap. 3.

22. See above, p. 15. Also taped interview with Dr. Manfred Lehmann, son of Hans Lehmann.

23. Interviews with the children of twelve rescue activists.

24. Rothkirchen, *Slovakia*, p. 241.

25. Taped interview with Rabbi Joseph Brody, a student and close observer of Rabbi Weissmandl during the Holocaust.

26. Herman Landau interview. Cf. also the protocols of her trial. Sternbuch Papers (SP).

27. Weisfogel interview. Cf. also taped interview with Mr. Joshua Ashkenazi, who was pressured by Rabbi Kalmanowitz into performing such illegal money transfers during World War II. See Kranzler, *Shanghai*, p. 472, n. 40.

Chapter III: Influence of the Rabbis

1. Zuroff, "Vaad," p. 312.

2. Steiner interview.

3. Taped interviews with Dr. Judith Grunfeld. See also photos of Rabbi Schonfeld in this author's book. Dr. Grunfeld worked closely with Rabbi Schonfeld for over 40 years.

4. For a different view of the "rabbinate" as a training ground for rescue activists, see Walter Laquer, *The Terrible Secret* [Laqueur, *Secret*] (Boston: Little, Brown, 1980), pp. 158-160. For the remarks by the Joint representative, see Kranzler, *Shanghai*, p. 342, n. 47.

5. Emanuel Celler, *You Never Leave Brooklyn* [Celler, *Brooklyn*] (New York: Day, 1953), pp. 89-93.

6. Weisfogel interview.

7. Contrary to the assertion of several historians of the Holocaust, it was not the major factor. The rabbis' march on Washington and the follow-up congressional hearings on rescue were of greater significance in creating the pressure on Roosevelt during this "election year." See below, pp. 7D. Cf. for example, Henry Feingold, *The Politics of Rescue* [Feingold, *Rescue*] (New Brunswick, NJ: Rutgers U. Press, 1970), pp. 239-241, and Bauer, *Holocaust*, pp. 82-83.

8. *Ibid.*

9. Memo re visit of JCH[yman] and MAL[eavitt] to Washington DC, July 22, 1942. JDC archives.

10. Taped interview with Dr. Joseph Schwartz.

11. Interview with Naphtaly Levy. Professor Levy was present at the dinner. Mr. Pehle confirmed this story to this author in a taped interview.

12. *MD* 2/28/44, p. 2.

13. *Ibid.*, p. 2-3.

14. *Ibid.*, p. 3.

15. *Ibid.*, p. 4.

16. McClelland-State 12/9/44. WRB.

17. *MD* 2/28/45, p. 5.

18. *Ibid.*

19. *Ibid.*

20. Zuroff, "Vaad," p. 315.

21. See below, chap. 15B.

22. Stern interview.

23. This author participated in the three-day campaign. The citation is from *Tal. Shab.* 119b.

24. Gershon Kranzler interview. Cf. also *Agudah Reports*, No. 5, pp. 15-16.

25. Gershon Kranzler interview.

Chapter IV: Orthodox Jews, Unorthodox Approach: Ideology at Work

1. Petuchowski, *Zion Reconsidered*, pp. 126-127.

2. Ronald Steele, *Walter Lippmann and the American Century* [Steele, *Lippmann*] (Boston: Little, Brown, 1980), p. 187. See also Naomi W. Cohen, *American Jews and the Zionist Idea* [Cohen, *American Jews*] (New York: Ktav, 1975), p. 6.

One must not confuse the assimilationist

perspective as necessarily negating a concern for fellow Jews. For example, Ambassador Morgenthau himself was extremely helpful to the Jews in Palestine during W.W.I and to the Jews of Post W.W.I Poland. Prof. Jacob Katz noted the heart and the head were not always synchronized.

3. Stanley F. Clujet, *Lives and Voices of American Memoirs* (Phila.: JPS 1967), p. 124.

4. For Wise's view of Zionism and Brandeis' influence see George L. Berlin, "The Brandeis-Weizmann Dispute" *American Jewish History* Vol. LX No. 1 (Sept. 1970), pp. 38-40; Melvyn Urofsky, *A Voice That Spoke for Justice: The Life and Times of Stephen S. Wise* [Urofsky, *Wise*] (Albany, NY: SUNY Press, 1982), esp. 118 ff. and his *Louis D. Brandeis and the Progressive Tradition* (Boston: Little, Brown, 1983), esp. Chap. 5. For an in-depth analysis of Wise and his role during the Holocaust see this author's forthcoming *American Leadership* and the article entitled, "Stephen S. Wise and the Holocaust."

5. For the keen contemporary observation of the Jews' worship of Roosevelt as well as the "Jewish" role in the New Deal, see Judd L. Teller, *Strangers and Natives: The Evolution of the American Jew from 1921 to the Present* [Teller, *Strangers*] (New York: Delacorte Press, 1968), Chap. 5.

6. Steele, *Lippmann*, Chap. 15, esp. pp. 373-374.

7. *Hapardes*, (October 1940), p. 23.

8. *Ibid.*

9. *Ibid.*

10. *Ibid.*

11. *Ibid.*

12. *Liberal Judaism*, Vol. No. 4. Spring, 1944, p. 3.

13. Herbert Druks, *Failure to Rescue* [Druks, *Failure*] (New York: Speller and Sons, 1977), p. 69. I elaborated on the theme in my draft of Amos Bunim's book re his father.

14. Moses Leavitt to Samuel Goldsmith (Chicago), June 27, 1941. JDC Archives.

15. *The Jewish Floridian*, August 15, 1941. See also Moshe R. Gottlieb, *American anti-Nazi Resistance 1933-1941* [Gottlieb, *Boycott*] (New York: Ktav, 1982].

16. For Tenenbaum's remark see "*Peklach Kayn Poilen: A Blutiger Frage*," *Der Tog*, July 22, 1941. For "sacrifice by blood" remarks, see Rael Jean Isaac, *Party and Politics in Israel* [Isaac, *Party*] (New York:

Longman, 1981), p. 53, n. 47 and p. 55, no. 63.

17. Rabbi Schonfeld to *The Jewish Observer*, reiterated to this author on a taped interview of Rabbi Schonfeld.

18. *Min Hametzar*, pp. 92-93.

19. *Ibid.*

20. *Ibid.*, p. 94.

21. See above, chap. 7A.

22. Bauer, *JDC*, p. 35.

23. *Ibid.*

24. Kranzler, *Shanghai*, pp. 461-462.

25. See for example the exchange of letters by Bernard Wasserstein and this author in *Midstream* (March 1981), pp. 59-64. See also Chaim Pazner's response to Haim Avni's paper, entitled, "The Zionist Underground in Holland and France and the Escape to Spain," in *Rescue Attempts*, pp. 595-596. Cf. Bauer, JDC, pp. 256-257.

26. See Kranzler, *Shanghai*, pp. 355, 462. See also Wyman, *Abandonment*, p. 248; *MD* 2/27/45, p. 13; 2/28/45, p. 2.

27. Kranzler, *Shanghai*, p. 573, no. 57.

28. Bunim interview.

29. O'Dwyer Speech at Vaad Hatzalah Dinner, Dec. 12, 1945.

30. Interview with Ernest Seewald. Mr. Seewald worked with one of these "Lehmann relatives."

31. See Kranzler, *Heroine of Rescue*, pp. 34-35.

32. *Ibid.*, chap. 4.

33. *Min Hametzar*, pp. 70-72, 90-91. Cf. Kranzler, *Shanghai*, pp. 459-460, 560-561. See also below, chap. 8.

34. *Ibid.*, p. 59; Rothkirchen, *Slovakia*, p. XXVII.

35. Based on taped interviews with Dr. Manfred Lehmann, Yaakov Zuber and Rabbi Shlomo Wolbe, all of whom worked for hatzalah via Sweden, at the time.

36. Laqueur, *Secret*, p. 179.

37. See below, Chap. 7B.

38. Yehuda Bauer, *My Brother's Keeper: A History of the American Jewish Joint Distribution Committee 1929-1939* [Bauer, *Brother's*] (Phila.: JPS, 1974), p. 279.

39. *Ibid.*, p. 287. See also pp. 278-292.

40. Taped interview with Herbert Kruskal, who provided substantiating documentation to this author. See appendix.

41. Taped interview with Mr. George Mandel-Mantello.

42. See below, chaps. 10D, 13D.

43. Kranzler, *Heroine of Rescue*, Chap. 8. Cf. also Wyman, *Abandonment*, p. 46, MD 2/28/44, pp. 2, 7, 8.

44. Corres. Joseph C. Hyman [Executive Vice President of JDC] to the Hon. Jan Ciechanowski [Polish ambassador] April 14, 1942. See cable by International Red Cross representative Marc Peter to Joint Distribution Committee June 27, 1942; Cable, Polish Minister Kwapiszewski to [Arthur] Leavitt of the Joint, June 5, 1942; another cable by same correspondees for July 10, 1942; Joint Distribution Committee. China Archives [JDCCA].

45. Kranzler, *Heroine of Rescue*, chaps. 3-4. See also MD 4/28/45, p. 2.

46. Taped interviews with Mr. Herman Landau and Mr. Hugo Donnenbaum.

47. Gershon Kranzler interview.

48. Nathan Eck, "The Rescue of Jews with the Aid of Passports and Citizenship Papers of Latin American States," [Eck, "Latin American Papers"] *Yad Vashem Studies I*, p. 135.

49. *Ibid.*, p. 136. The Sternbuch "Brothers" should rightfully read Recha and Yitzchok, since Mrs. Sternbuch was the primary rescue activist. This confusion reigns in most histories that mention the Sternbuchs. See, for example, the recently published *The Politics of Genocide: The Holocaust in Hungary* [Braham, *Politics*] (2 vols.) by Randolph A. Braham (New York: Columbia U. Press, 1981). See Index. Although Yitzchok wrote and signed almost all the documents, this author's *Heroine of Rescue* set the record straight.

50. Taped interviews with Mr. Maitre Muller and his wife as well as Mr. Mantello. See below, Chap. 11E.

51. Eck, "Latin American Papers," pp. 138-141. See also Abraham Shulman, *The Case of Hotel Polski* [Shulman, *Hotel*] (New York: Holocaust Library, 1982).

52. See above, Introduction and chap. 3.

53. Mantello interview.

54. He was Abraham Silberschein of the World Jewish Congress, who "created" a relief organization called RELICO which sent food, Latin American papers and other aid to his fellow Jews in Poland. See Silberschein Papers at Yad Vashem. See also Eck, "Latin American Papers," pp. 128-129; Penkower, *Expendable*, pp. 124-125.

55. Landau interview.

56. See for example *Sixth Agudah Report*, pp. 15-16.

57. See Samuel Halperin, *The Political World of American Zionism* [Halperin, *Zionism*] (Detroit: Wayne State U. Press, 1961), Chap. 8, esp. pp. 204-5.

58. Cited by Yitshaq Ben-Ami, *Years of Wrath, Days of Glory* (New York: Speller and Sons, 1982) [Ben-Ami, *Years*], p. 320. For the attitude re Yeshivah students see below, pp. 247-248.

59. See Ben-Ami, *Years*. For the conflict of the JA and the Joint, see Bauer, *JDC*, p. 184.

60. See below, chap. 13B.

61. Taped interview.

62. Lewis Strauss, *Men and Decisions* (London: Macmillan, 1963), p. 107.

63. Yoab Gelber, "Zionist Policy and European Jewry," [Gelber, "Zionist"] *Yad Vashem Studies* 13 (Jerusalem: Yad Vashem 1979), pp. 199-200.

64. *Ibid.*, p. 199.

65. *Ibid.*

66. Aaron Berman, "American Zionism and the Rescue of European Jewry: An Ideological Perspective" [Berman, "American Zionism"] *American Jewish History* (March 1981), p. 319. See also Halperin, *Political Zionism*, pp. 220-222.

67. For his lifetime of liberal and Progressive causes see Urofsky, *Wise*, esp. Chaps. 3, 5, 7, 17.

68. See his opening speech at the American Jewish Conference. Wise reiterated this "affirmation" in 1941 as head of the American Emergency Committee for Zionists. See Doreen Bierbrier, "The American Zionist Emergency Council: An Analysis of a Pressure Group," *American Jewish Historical Quarterly* Vol. LX No. 1 (Sept. 1970), p. 83.

69. See the chapter on Wise in my forthcoming *American Leadership*.

70. Carl H. Voss, *Stephen S. Wise: Servant of the People* (Phila.: JPS, 1969), p. 242.

71. Zuroff, "Vaad," p. 313.

72. See David S. Wyman, *Paper Walls: America and the Refugee Crisis 1938-1941* [Wyman, *Walls*] (Amherst: U. of Mass. Press, 1968), Chap. 7, esp. pp. 137-138. Cf. also Kranzler, *Goldberg Report*, chap. 4-2; Bauer, "Rescue," p. 222.

73. Zuroff, "Vaad," p. 312.

74. Bauer, *JDC*, p. 123.

75. Bauer, "Rescue," p. 222.

76. Bauer, *JDC*, p. 123.

77. See above, "Shabbos Ride," p. 6.

78. See for example, Naomi W. Cohen, *Encounter With Emancipation: The German Jews in the United States 1830-1914* [Cohen, *Encounter*] (Phila.: JPS, 1984), pp. 110-114.

79. Bauer, "Rescue," p. 222.

80. The entire project of Emergency Visitor's Visas approved by President Roosevelt was an elitist one by definition, since its purpose (as originated by the Jewish Labor Committee) was to rescue the politically endangered elite, the labor leaders, intellectuals, etc. If the JLC could submit lists of over 7,200 names and the Zionists 100, plus those submitted by a dozen other Jewish and non-Jewish organizations, why were the Orthodox not entitled to select as many of their "elite" in a program of unlimited numbers? Why is it that Bauer sees no elitism in the 100% selection process practiced by the Zionists, or any other group, although the Zionists spoke in the name of the world's Jewry when it suited their purpose? Why, for example, doesn't Bauer cite the "universal," "all Jews being equal" formula, when he knows fully well that Nathan Schwalb's rescue program from Switzerland was geared solely to members of his ideological group?

Chapter V: Cooperation and Ideology

1. Weisfogel interview.

2. Taped interviews with Dr. Joseph Klarman and Andre Steiner.

3. For a brief analysis of the role of the Bergson Group see Eliyho Matzozki, "An Analysis of a Pressure Group: The Activities of the Bergson Group in the Year 1943," *Gesher* (Vol. 8, 5741-1981), pp. 185-188. Cf. also Monty N. Penkower, "The Bergson Boys," *American Jewish History* (March 1981), p. 308. The full-scale scholarly work on this group has yet to be written.

4. See the WRB which contain letters of congratulations by almost every Jewish organization.

5. McClelland to Sternbuch, Oct. 26, 1944, WRB; Sternbuch to VH, Nov. 10, 1944; Nov. 21, 1944 (SP).

6. See below, p. 108.

7. Confidential cable by Sternbuch to the Vaad, Aug. 3, 1944 (SP). Everybody at the time assumed all the 1200 passengers (really 1,684) were Orthodox rabbis. See for example, McClelland to Sternbuch August 18, 1944. Yet by July 5, 1944, Landau, in a phone conversation with Mayer, tried to disabuse him of this mistaken notion that only Orthodox were involved. As he noted to Mayer this plan originated with Weissmandl, who even Mayer understood by then worked for *all* Jews, not merely the Orthodox, yet Mayer remained unconvinced. See memo of Phone Conversation by Landau with Mayer July 5, 1944 (SP). All historians of the Holocaust still seem perplexed by the discrepancy in the documentation between the 1,200 "Orthodox" rabbis and the 1,684 cited for the train from Budapest. Actually a thorough analysis of the relevant documents resolves the discrepancy readily. See, for example, Braham, *Politics*, p. 247; Penkower, *Expendable*, p. 201.

8. See, for example, Vaad to Sternbuch (via McClelland) Aug. 18, '44 (WRB).

9. Herman Landau, memo of phone conversation with Saly Mayer, July 5, 1944 (SP).

10. Saly Mayer had originated the myth of his sole concern for all Jews *(Klal)* in contrast to the Orthodox particularist interest solely in their own. This was perpetuated by Dr. Joseph Schwartz in an interview with Prof. Bauer. In that interview Bauer himself cites the Zionists' narrow, particularist concerns. The latter has continued to propagate this canard throughout all his writings. See, for example, Bauer, JDC, p. 441.

11. Sternbuch to the Vaad, July 5, 1944 (SP).

12. Sternbuch to Vaad, July 13, 1944 (SP).

13. Sternbuch to McClelland, July 12, 1944 (WRB).

14. Interview with Mr. Hugo Donnenbaum. Cf. also McClelland to Sternbuch, July 14, 1944 (WRB).

15. See notes 99-100 to my "Orthodox Jews Unorthodox Means," pp. 45-46.

16. *New York Times*, Dec. 119, 1938. Cf. also Gottlieb, *Boycott*, Chap. 30.

17. Elizabeth E. Eppler, "The Rescue Work of the World Jewish Congress During the Nazi Period" *Rescue*, p. 50; *American Israelite*, April 9, 1936, p. 11.

18. See below, pp. 248-255.

19. *Ibid.*, p. 601.

20. *Ibid.*, pp. 595, 600.

21. Leon Kubowitzki (WJ Cong.) to John Pehle, 3/9/44 WRB.

22. *Rescue*, p. 613.

23. *Ibid.* Cf. also Daniel Carpi, "The Rescue of Jews in the Italian Zone of Occupied Croatia" in *Rescue*, pp. 465-526.

24. See Hans Habe, *The Mission* (New York: Coward-McCann, Inc. 1966) et passim, re Trujillo's offer, and Kranzler, *Shanghai*, esp. Chaps. 1, 7, 8, esp. pp. 227-229.

25. *Ibid.*, Chap. 11.

26. See Chap. 7 for an overall picture of Japan's unique, favorable policy toward the Jewish refugees. For the Zikman incident see pp. 227-9.

27. *Ibid.*, p. 228.

28. *Ibid.*, pp. 228-229.

Chapter VI: Not Giving Up

1. Raul Hilberg, *The Destruction of the European Jews* (Chicago: Quadrangle, 1967), p. 719.

2. *Ibid.*

3. Bauer, *Holocaust*, pp. 18, 25. This theme of Jewish powerlessness became *the* theme of another of Bauer's books, entitled, *The Jewish Emergence from Powerlessness* (Toronto: U. of Toronto Press, 1979). It is part of his widespread and widely accepted, but quite distorted thesis. For a thorough analysis of this thesis see this author's forthcoming *American Leadership*, Chap. 12.

4. Bauer, *Holocaust*, pp. 18-24.

5. *Ibid.*, p. 159, n. 25.

6. Naomi Cohen, *Not Free to Desist: The American Jewish Committee 1906-1966* [Cohen, *American Jewish Committee*] (Phila.: JPS, 1972), pp. 227-228. Especially after the debacle of the Bermuda Conference in April 1943, American Jews tended to accept the government's view that the best way to save Europe's Jews was to help America and its Allies win the war as quickly as possible. None dared even to demonstrate before the American Government except its "benign neglect" of European Jewry, except for the Orthodox, the Bergson group, and the Jewish Labor Committee.

7. *Ibid.*

8. Bauer, *Holocaust*, p. 26.

9. Dalia Ofer, "The Activities of the Jewish Agency Delegation in Istanbul in 1943," [Ofer, "Istanbul] in *Rescue*, pp. 443-445. Cf. also Bauer, *Holocaust*, pp. 24-25.

10. *Ibid.*, p. 91.

11. *Lev.* 19:16.

12. Vaad to Sternbuch.

13. See below, pp. 112-113.

14. Joan Fredericks'interview with Irving Bunim. This author is grateful to the late Mrs. Fredericks for permission to make copies of her collection of documents (Fredericks Papers).

15. See the *Final Summary Report of the War Refugee Board [WRB Report]*, pp. 43-44 for the refusal to permit the use of the money for ransom. For the Joint's condition that the money borrowed from them go via the WRB, and thereby assure the restrictions of its use, see Vaad Hatzalah, p. 359. Bauer, in "The Negotiations Between Saly Mayer and the Representatives of the S.S. in 1944-1945," [Bauer, "Negotiations"] in *Rescue Attempts*, pp. 38-39, is unaware of the fact that the Vaad Hatzalah wanted to have the money sent only care of Sternbuch to give him leeway. But the Joint refused to lend the money unless it was used strictly according to American law and the directives of the War Refugee Board. Even so, the Joint had to send the money to Sternbuch without Mayer's knowledge or consent, because he no doubt would have tried to squelch any deals with the Nazis.

16. See, for example, McClelland-State, 5/16/45 (WRB).

17. Isaac Lewin, *Churban Europa* [Lewin, *Churban*] (New York: Research Institute for Post-War Problems of Religious Jewry, 1948), pp. 78-83, esp. p. 83.

18. *Ibid.*, pp. 43-78.

19. *Ibid.*, p. 44.

20. *Yiddishe Shtimme*, Feb. 1943, p. 1.

21. Lewin, *Churban*, pp. 45-46.

22. *Ibid.*, p. 54.

23. *Ibid.*, pp. 55-56.

24. *Ibid.*, pp. 63-67.

25. *Ibid.*, pp. 67-70.

26. *Ibid.*, pp. 74-77.

27. *Ibid.*, p. 77.

28. *Ibid.*, p. 78.

29. *Ibid.*, pp. 83-86.

30. *Ibid.*, p. 87.

Chapter VII: Survey of the Orthodox Rescue Activities During the Holocaust

1. "Shall Jewish Organizations Send Food Parcels," [Food Parcels"] *The* (Paterson, NJ) *Jewish Post*, Aug. 28, 1941. This and other clippings on the boycott were found in the Orthodox Jewish Archives at Agudath Israel (AA).

2. Taped interview with Rabbi Asher (Osher) Rand, the Secretary of Agudath Israel. He was directly involved with the food package project.

3. *Ibid.*

4. *Ibid.*

5. For Nahum Goldmann's recollections, see Shabtai Bet-Zvi, *Post-Ugandian Zionism in the Crucible of the Holocaust* [Bet-Zvi, *Post-Uganda*] (Tel Aviv: Bronfman, 1977), p. 252. After the war, Dr. Tenenbaum became a Holocaust historian. See his *Race and Reich* (New York: 1956). He also wrote an article on this subject called, "The Anti-Nazi Boycott Movement in the United States," in *Yad Vashem Studies Vol. III* (Jerusalem: Yad Vashem, 1959), pp. 141-159.

6. B.Z. Hendeles, "Nochmol Vegen Peklach Kain Poilen," a response by an Agudah representative to Dr. Tenenbaum's charges *(Der Tog,* July 27, 1941) (AA).

7. *Ibid.*

8. Editorial (Washington D.C.) *National Jewish Ledger,* Aug. 29, 1941 (AA).

9. See Hendeles, "Nochmol." For the precedent of World War I see Naomi Cohen, *American Jews and the Zionist Idea* [Cohen, *Zionist*] (New York: Ktav, 1975), p. 18.

10. "Food Parcels."

11. Dr. Joseph Tenenbaum, "A Lezt Vort Vegen Peklach Kain Poilen" *Der Tog,* Aug. 10, 1941 (AA).

12. "Food Parcels."

13. "Peklach Kain Poilen: A Blutige Frage" *Der Tog,* July 22, 1941 (AA).

14. Editorial *The Jewish Floridian,* Aug. 15, 1941.

15. *Ibid.*

16. "Food Parcels."

17. Dr. Israel Goldstein to Rabbi Eliezer Silver, May 6, 1941. Papers of Rabbi Eliezer Silver (ESP). Courtesy of his son, Rabbi David Silver.

18. *Ibid.*

18a. *Nachla L'Yehoshua* Responsa Nos. 39, 40, (Constantinople, 1731).

19. This unit was first published as Appendix 4-3 of the *Goldberg Report.* Even the two more sympathetic works, by Wyman and Penkower, don't grant the Sternbuch cable and the Orthodox response any significance in terms of alerting the American Jewish public. See Wyman, *Abandonment,* Chap. 3, esp. pp. 45-46; Penkower, *Expendable,* p. 68. Penkower misunderstands Lewin. Nowhere does he note that Wise showed or even mentioned the Riegner cable to the Orthodox. See below, note 31.

20. See Yehuda Bauer, "When Did They Know," in *Midstream,* April 1968, p. 51-58.

21. See Morse, *While Six Million Died* [Morse, *Six Million*] (New York: Random House, 1968), Chap. I; Henry Feingold, *The Politics of Rescue* [Feingold, *Politics*] (New Brunswick: Rutgers U. Press, 1970), pp. 169-170. He mistakenly identifies Jacob (Yaakov) Rosenheim, president of World Agudath Israel, as "a representative of the World Jewish Congress"; Laqueur, *Secret,* pp. 77-80.

22. This was in keeping with his penchant for avoiding any pressure on President Roosevelt.

23. Isaac Lewin, a key representative for both Agudath Israel and Vaad Hatzalah, first "discovered" the existence of the Riegner cable in January 1948. See Lewin, *Churban,* pp. 287-289. Lewin also recounts how it was the Orthodox that pressured Wise into calling a meeting in the first place.

24. See "Agudat Israel," *Encyclopaedia Judaica,* Vol. 2, p. 422. No scholarly history of this organization exists.

25. See Isaac Lewin, "Attempts at Rescuing European Jews with the Help of Polish Diplomatic Missions during World War II." Part I [Lewin I] *Polish Review,* Vol. XXII, No. 4 (1977) pp. 5-7.

26. Lewin I, pp. 5-7; Lewin, "American Jews," p. 26.

27. Ibid. Re the phone call to Kalmanowitz, see Weisfogel interview. See this author's correspondence with the Bell Company's historical division which verified the phone connections and the average number of calls from Switzerland at the time of 1-½ per month. The phone episode had been related orally to this author by Rabbi Weisfogel already during the 1950's. Only in 1978-79 did he put this and many other memories of those years on tape during several interviews with this author.

28. Wyman, *Abandonment,* p. 28.

29. Laqueur, *Secret,* p. 44. Professor Laqueur seems to be unaware of the source of Mann's broadcast.

30. Morse, *Six Million,* p. 8. Laqueur, *Secret,* p. 79-83.

31. For example, Dr. Lewin, who participated in almost every meeting involving the Orthodox rescue efforts, only found out about the Riegner cable in 1948. See *Churban,* pp. 228-229, 287-289. Cf. also Laqueur, *Secret,* p. 82, where he contends that the Sternbuch cable made things worse.

32. Lewin I, pp. 5-7. Cf. also *Churban*, p. 129. Cf. also Aryeh Leon Kubovy [Kubowitzki] "Criminal State vs. Moral Society: Bettelheim to Arendt's Rescue," *Yad Vashem Bulletin*, No. 13 (October 1963), p. 6. Kubowitzki recalled: We suggested protest meetings, *a march on Washington*, etc. The rabbis fiercely opposed our programme and expressed this in the harshest terms imaginable: "You are the grave diggers of our people. *You have chosen to antagonize Hitler. You proclaimed a boycott against* Germany, you published strongly worded resolutions. Hitler is not the first Haman in our history. The experiences of centuries have taught us how to deal with Haman. Stop your provocations! Let us rescue our people through our tested methods." [Emphasis added]

Kubowitzki's claim of having demanded public demonstrations and a march on Washington sounds rather hollow in view of the oath of silence imposed — and not protested by him — by Stephen S. Wise, over the protests of the Orthodox. Moreover, his dates are a bit mixed-up. Nor did Wise call upon the rabbis after he had received the alarming news from Europe. Not a word of the Riegner cable went out to other Jewish organizations, let alone the Orthodox rabbis who, at that time, were not even considered sufficiently important to consult on rescue matters. It was only a slow development of the rise in power by the small Orthodox group which made itself felt in the Jewish Establishment. Only as a result of the very strong personal pressure and magnetism of Rabbi Kalmanowitz, following his receipt of the Sternbuch cable, did Rabbi Wise, the acknowledged leader of American Jewry and "friend" of President Roosevelt, consent to come with two aides to see the rabbis.

33. See below, n. 34 re the lack of proper response to the earlier Bund Report.

34. See the invitation by cable to Rabbi Kalmanowitz. Copies of the Kalmanowitz Papers in this author's possession, courtesy Mrs. Abraham Kalmanowitz and Rabbi S. Moshe Kalmanowitz. This meeting, of all Jewish organizations, was the first on such a scale concerning the tragedy of European Jewry. This did not occur after the arrival of the Bund Report of June 1942. See Yehudah Bauer, "When Did They Know?" *Midstream* (April, 1968), pp. 51-58. Cf. also A. Leon Kubowitzki, *Survey of the Rescue Activities of the World Jewish Congress 1940-1944* [WJ Cong. Survey] (Unpublished manuscript WJ Cong. Archives. Courtesy

Eliyohu Matzozki), p. 18. Kubowitzki notes that the meeting was "called" on the 6th. It actually took place on that day.

For the *"Greuelmarchen,"* see Meir Shenkolewski interview. Mr. Shenkolewski attended the meeting on behalf of World Agudath Israel.

35. *Yiddishe Shtimme*, Nov. 1942, p. 1.

36. For the news see the *New York Times*, November 25, 1942, p. 10. See also WJ Cong. *Survey*, p. 18-20. For the meeting with FDR see Eliyohu Matzozki, "An Episode: Roosevelt and the Mass Killing" [Matz: "FDR"] *Midstream* (Aug.-Sept. 1980), pp. 17-19; Bernard Wasserstein, *Britain and the Jews 1939-1945* [Wasserstein, *Britain*] (London: Institute of Jewish Affairs, 1979), pp. 172-174. For the U.N. condemnation and follow-up see John Fox, "The Jewish Factor in British War Crime Policy in 1942," *English Historical Review* (Jan. 1977), pp. 91-92.

37. See Kranzler, *Heroine*, Chap. 8. See also letter by this author to *Commentary* (January, 1984), pp. 6-7.

38. Morse, *Six Million*, pp. 15-16.

39. Interviews with Dr. Julius Kuhl. Dr. Kuhl personally sent these reports to the above-mentioned individuals. See also the Kuhl Papers; Kranzler, *Heroine*, pp. 67-68.

40. See the Minutes of Joint Emergency Committee on European Jewish Affairs [JEC], especially March 6, 1943. The four Zionist organizations were the American Jewish Congress, B'nai Brith, American Zionist Emergency Council (AZEC), Synagogue Council of America. The four non-Zionist organizations were Agudath Israel, American Jewish Committee, the Jewish Labor Committee and the Union of Orthodox Rabbis of America. While Wise attempted to include Hadassah immediately, this was rejected. It was pointed out to him that Hadassah was already represented on two of the eight organizations, the American Jewish Committee and American Jewish Congress. Wise's ability by November 5, 1943 to eventually maneuver the acceptance of Hadassah, as a fifth overriding vote, enabled him to dissolve JEC. Cf. also *Fourth Agudah Report*, p. 5; Emanuel Pat, *In the Struggle: Jacob Pat and His Generation* [Pat, *Struggle*] (New York: Jacob Pat Family Fund, 1971), pp. 352-353.

For the role of Ambassador Lados, as well as Dr. Kuhl, see *Heroine*, chaps. 6, 9 et passim.

See interview by this author with Dr.

Reuven Hecht. Dr. Hecht, a Revisionist-Zionist, was the only non-Orthodox member of the Sternbuch's rescue team. It was Sam Woods who suggested that Hecht work with the Sternbuchs on rescue matters. See the Sam Woods' files in the Hecht Papers. Copies of most of these files were made for the author, courtesy Dr. Hecht. See also Laqueur, *Secret*, pp. 96-97, re Sam Woods. Dr. Hecht was particularly active in Sternbuch's Musy negotiations with Himmler. For detailed scholarly analysis see this author's *Stand Not Idly By*, chaps. 12-13.

Cf. also Min. JEC, Sept. 28, 1943, American Jewish Archives. For the dissolution of the ad hoc committee see also M[ax] Gottschalk to [Morris] Waldman, Nov. 27, 1942, American Jewish Committee archives.

For a first, though incomplete, review of the dissolution of the JEC, see Edward Pinsky, "American Jewish Unity During the Holocaust — The Joint Emergency Committee 1943," [Pinsky, "JEC"] *American Jewish History* [AJH], Vol. LXXII No. 4 (June, 1983), pp. 477-494.

41. See especially Samuel Halperin, *The Political World of American Zionism* [Halperin, *Zionism*] (Detroit: Wayne State U. Press, 1961), chap. 9, esp. pp. 220-224. Cf. also Monty N. Penkower, "Ben-Gurion, Silver and the 1941 UPA National Conference for Palestine" [Penkower, "Ben Gurion"] *American Jewish History* (Sept. 1979), pp. 74-76; Aaron Berman, "American Zionism and the Rescue of European Jewry: An Ideological Perspective" [Berman, "Silver"] *American Jewish History* (March, 1981), pp. 314-316; Memorandum of the talk by Adolph Held and others with Ben Gurion and the Jewish Labor Committee, April 15, 1942. Jewish Labor Committee Archives.

42. Halperin, *Zionism*, chap. 9. For an ideological analysis see this author's forthcoming *American Leadership*, chap. 9.

43. Halperin, *Zionism*, pp. 272 and 382, n. 16. Cf. also Melvyn I. Urofsky, *We Are One* [Urofsky, *One*] (New York: Anchor Press, 1978), p. 21. Alexander S. Kohansky, ed. *The American Jewish Conference: Its Organization and Proceedings of the First Session, August 29 to September 2, 1943* [Kohansky, *Conference*] (New York: 1944), p. 46. Cf. also *Yiddishe Shtimme*, November 1943, p. 5; the invitation to the Pittsburgh Conference which, as Hilberg already pointed out over 25 years ago, never mentioned rescue. Raul Hilberg, *The Destruction of European Jewry* (Chicago: Quadrangle Books, 1967), p. 719; Haskel Lookstein, *American Jewry's Public*

Response to the Holocaust 1938-1945 [Lookstein, *Press*] (Unpublished doctoral dissertation, Yeshiva U., 1979), pp. 270-274.

44. *Yiddishe Shtimme*, Nov. 1943, p. 5. The text is from a stenographic copy of the minutes.

45. Urofsky, *One*, p. 25.

46. Ibid. Cf. also Halperin, *Zionism*, p. 224; *Fourth Agudah Report*, p. 7. Also *Fifth Agudah Report*, pp. 9-10.

47. *Fourth Agudah Report*, p. 7.

48. *Ibid.*

49. Halperin, *Zionism*, pp. 224, 233-36; Urofsky, *One*, pp. 22-30. The verse from the Daily Prayer is derived from Psalm 133. The original term "assembly" with possible implications of a rump parliament or Jewish government drew the fears by the assimilated American Jews of "dual loyalty" and an "International Jewry." See Kranzler, *Stand Not Idly By*, chap. 2, for further analysis. The "Conference" as an umbrella organization lasted until 1945.

50. The entire speech is found in Arthur Hertzberg, *The Zionist Idea* [Hertzberg, *Zionist*] (New York: Atheneum, 1970), pp. 592-600. The text of Monsky's speech as well as that of Judge Proskauer is found in the Conference Files of the American Jewish Committee Archives.

51. *Ibid.*

52. One observer from the American Jewish Committee noted this derision of refugee "humanitarian philanthropic" perspective at least spells out the political phase of Zionism rather than the humanitarian one, which had been popularized earlier. See "My Impressions of the American Jewish Conference" by Dr. Louis Wolsey, pp. 9-10, American Jewish Committee Archives [Wolsey, "Impressions"]. Cf. also Halperin, *Zionism*, p. 222.

53. Proskauer felt particularly grieved about this disavowal of unity by Silver because he had been in touch with Silver for a long time, and as late as May '43 requested that both look over their respective platforms in order to avoid friction. After an unequivocal oral agreement, Silver later reversed himself. See Memo by Judge Proskauer on "Who Really Destroyed Jewish Unity," Dec. 28, 1943, p. 3, American Jewish Committee's Archives. For the description of the impact of Silver's speech, see Wolsey, "Impressions," p. 9.

54. Halperin, *Zionist*, p. 239.

55. Berman, "American Zionism," p. 327.

56. *Orthodox Tribune*, July-August 1943, p. 1.

57. Rosenheim to Proskauer, October 28, 1943. American Jewish Committee Archives cited by Pinsky, "JEC," p. 492.

58. See *Minutes of American Jewish Conference Rescue Committee Aug. 31 — Sept. 1-2, 1943* (Unpublished manuscript at the American Jewish Historical Society Archives), pp. 159-160.

59. Minutes of JEC, Nov. 5, 1943, the final meeting of JEC.

60. Wise to Goldmann, April 23, 1943. Stephen S. Wise Manuscripts Box 1001 (AJHSA).

61. Minutes of JEC, Nov. 5, 1943, pp. 1-2.

62. See, for example, *Hapardes*, Jan. 1944, pp. 8-9.

63. For example, Rabbi Weissmandl's cables concerning the possibilities of rescue of Jews from Poland to then-relatively-peaceful Slovakia, see *Hapardes*, Jan. 1944, pp. 8-9. That Rabbi Weissmandl, usually labeled an "ultra-Orthodox rabbi," was the peerless rescue leader was admitted at the time even among the most vehement secularist marxist anti-Orthodox members of the rescue committee of the Jewish Agency in Jerusalem, in Istanbul, Turkey, as well as in his own underground in Slovakia, which contained mostly secularist Jews. For the latter, see this author's interviews with Andre Steiner, a member of Weissmandl's "Working Group," who did most of Rabbi Weissmandl's negotiations with Dieter Wisliceny, Eichmann's assistant, to ransom Slovakian Jewry in the fall of 1942. Steiner noted how, upon first meeting with Weissmandl, inexplicably he immediately fell under his "spell." It was Weissmandl who provided literally almost all the arguments, and even potential counter-arguments, that Steiner used in negotiating with Wisliceny. For the views of the Jewish Agency's *Moetza* in Istanbul, see the unpublished memoirs of Dr. Yaakov Griffel, p. 12. (The memoirs were written in the late 1950's at the instigation of Rabbi Weissmandl. Cf. also Rudolph Vrba and Alan Bestic, *I Cannot Forgive* [Vrba, *Auschwitz*] (London: Sidwick & Jackson, 1963), pp. 258-259.

64. The close cooperation between the Orthodox and the Bergson group is manifest in the fact that Rabbi Eliezer Silver was on their board. See letterhead of the "Emergency Committee to Save the Jewish People of Europe." See also *Churban*, p. 82.

65. See *The Answer*, October 15, 1943 (the publication of the Bergson group) for much of the details of this rabbis' march.

66. The quote is from the *Yiddishe Shtimme*, October 1943, p. 1. For a detailed description of the rabbis' march, see *Stand Not Idly By*, chap. 3. For a deeper analysis, see my *American Leadership*, chap. 7.

67. Wise's role is evident from the very sarcastic editorial on the rabbis' march in the Hebrew journal *Bitzaron* (edited by Prof. Chaim Tchernowitz, known as *Rav Za'ir*) (Tishri 5704), pp. 67-68. For Rosenman's remarks see William D. Hassett, *Off the Record with FDR 1942-1945* (New Brunswick, N.J.: Rutgers U. Press, 1958), p. 209.

68. See Memo of Interview with Judge Samuel Rosenman, Oct. 6, 1943 (Zionist Archives. Courtesy Eliyohu Matzozki).

69. For some of the steps following the march, which led to the creation of the War Refugee Board, see *Vaad Hatzalah*, pp. 290-293.

70. See the *Yiddishe Shtimme*, October 1943, p. 1. It lists all the points. For the origin of the separate agency by Schonfeld, see JTA, Jan. 27, 1943, p. 2. While it attributed the idea to Chief Rabbi Hertz of Britain, it was really that of Rabbi Dr. Schonfeld. He created the Chief Rabbi's Religious Emergency Council as a one-man rescue committee utilizing (with permission) the name of the Chief Rabbi, his father-in-law. See this author's *Solomon Schonfeld: His Page in History* (New York: Judaica Press, 1981), pp. 24-26. Rabbi Schonfeld passed away on his 72nd birthday, Feb. 6, 1984.

71. Hearings. House Resolutions 350 and 352. 78th Congress. 1st Session [*Hearings*]. Reprinted in *Problems of World War II and Its Aftermath*, Vol. II (Washington D.C.: 1976), pp. 187, 245.

72. *Ibid.*, p. 241.

73. *Ibid.*, p. 243-244.

74. Cited by Sarah Peck in "The Campaign for an American R1sponse to the Holocaust 1943-1945." *Journal of Contemporary History* (London), v. 15 (1980), p. 391.

75. Halperin, Zionism, p. 239, 272-280. Cf. also Daniel J. Silver, *In the Time of Harvest* (New York: Macmillan, 1963), pp. 13-17.

75a. Feingold, *Politics*, pp. 230-238, esp. p. 238.

76. Though many historians fail to see the relation between the heated political climate

of opinion in an election year and the creation of the War Refugee Board, this author has little doubts about it. Davidowicz's note that the exact text for the government agency was Arthur Cox's version is quite irrelevant. See *Commentary* (Sept. 1983), p. 26. It matters little whose version was used. The pressure on FDR during an election year is the real factor, and that was caused primarily by the Bergson-Vaad Hatzalah cooperative actions. See also Cox's copy of the rescue *Hearings*, attached to his letter to Morgenthau on Dec. 20, 1943, concerning "a draft of" a proposed Executive Order on the "subject" [of a War Refugee Board]. Cox continued, "... getting the Executive Order signed would *forestall* some of the *action* on the Hill in connection with the *Rogers-Gillette Resolution.*" [emph. added] (CPF 3292. Stephen S. Wise FDRL).

77. Yehuda Bauer, *The Holocaust in Historical Perspective* [Bauer, *Historical*] (Seattle: U. of Washington Press, 1978), p. 83.

78. At a symposium on "Jewish Leadership During the Holocaust," CUNY Graduate Center.

79. For the sums see War Refugee Board. Amounts contributed to the work of the War Refugee Board. WRB History. Relief Programs. Box 53. See also Morse, *Six Million*, p. 382. See also Jewish Labor Committee Archives. Budget. And Vaad Hatzalah Budget, see *Vaad Hatzalah*, p. 516. Vaad actually spent over $1,135,000, half of which was transferred by Silver, see *Yiddishe Shtimme*, Feb. 1945, p. 1. Cf. also Doreen Bierbrier, "The American Zionist Emergency Council," *AJHQ* (Sept. 1970), p. 87.

80. For this episode in brief see *Heroine*, chap. 9. Fuller treatment in *Stand Not Idly By*, chap. 8.

81. *Ibid.* A large segment of the Sternbuch Papers revolve about the Vittel affair.

82. Nathan Eck, "The rescue of Jews With the Aid of Passports and Citizenship Papers of Latin American States," [Eck, "Passports"] *Yad Vashem Studies I*, pp. 125-152, esp. pp. 128, 135-136, 140. Cf. also Isaac Lewin, *Churban*, pp. 162-164, 172-176. Dr. Kuhl interview. See esp. Sternbuch Papers.

83. Winant to State, June 17, 1943. WRB.

84. Herman Landau interview.

85. Interview with Mrs. Miriam Weingort. She and her husband (Dr. Saul Weingort, a nephew of the Sternbuchs) were the main contact for the entire Vittel affair. The question was really why the Nazis suddenly decided to question the papers. For the details of this sordid affair and the documentation on a possible "informer," see *Stand Not Idly By*. For Dr. Hillel Seidman's view see interview with author.

86. See unpublished text of speech on a record by Henry Morgenthau at the dinner given by Rabbi Abraham Kalmanowitz in honor of the War Refugee Board heads, including John Pehle, William O'Dwyer, as well as Morgenthau. Bunim Papers in author's possession, courtesy of Mr. Irving Bunim. For the "two rabbis," traveling on Passover, see Dr. John Slawson to Simon Segal, April 20, 1944. American Jewish Committee Archives.

87. *Ibid.* For the Hungarian episode see Randolph A. Braham, *The Politics of Genocide: The Holocaust in Hungary* [Braham, *Hungary*] (New York: Columbia University Press, 1981), pp. 780, and chapter 26. Also see taped interviews by this author of Mr. Samuel Frey and Chaim [Charles] Roth, the first, an Orthodox Slovak refugee in Hungary who specialized in forging foreign passports with the help of Raul Wallenberg, the heroic representative of the Swedish Red Cross in Budapest. Roth was head of the Budapest Orthodox *Chevra Kadisha* (Burial Society) that specialized at the time in caring for the thousands of Polish refugees in Hungary during 1940-1944. Mr. Roth provided the lists to the author of thousands of names of such individuals who received "bogus" papers in possession of this author. See Pehle to Vaad Hatzalah, October 9, 1944, re Roth and Levy. WRB re the recognition of the Latin American Papers.

88. *Heroine*, chap. 6.

89. [Recha] Sternbuch to Roswell McClelland, June 22, 1944, p. 1; July 13, 1944, p. 1-2 SP.

90. See Rudolph Vrba, *I Cannot Forgive* (New York: Grove Press, 1964), pp. 250-2. See also Erich Kulka, "Five Escapees from Auschwitz" in Yuri Suhl, *They Fought Back* (New York: Crown, 1965), pp. 206-207. See various versions of the "Protocols" in the papers of the War Refugee Board, also in Yad Vashem and Zionist Archives in Jerusalem.

91. See *Min Hametzar*, pp. 110-111. His emphasis was on bombing the rail lines not the camp. See also *op. cit.*, pp. 229-252; Livia Rothkirchen, *The Destruction of Slovak Jewry* [Rothkirchen, *Destruction*] (Jerusalem: Yad Vashem, 1961), pp. 236-242,

especially pp. 239, 242. Vrba, *I Cannot Forgive*, pp. 248-250; Braham, *Politics* pp. 708-716. Braham accepts Krasznyansky's view that he was the one to attach 'the plea to bomb Auschwitz,' to the *Protocols*, rather than Weissmandl. Andre Steiner, whose wife, Krasznyansky, typed the Protocols, told this author that it was absolutely Weissmandl's idea, not Krasznyansky's. Steiner interview.

92. See, for example, copies to War Refugee Board via Sternbuch, June 2, 1944. See especially Sternbuch to McClelland, June 22, 1944. Copy of Sternbuch's original received courtesy of Professor David Wyman, as well as the message of June 12 transmitted via Sternbuch to Rabbi Solomon Schonfeld in London (SP). He personally pleaded with members of the British Government on behalf of Rabbi Weissmandl's plea — unsuccessful like all the others. Rabbi Weissmandl had been Schonfeld's teacher during the early 1930's. See this author's book *Solomon Schonfeld*.

Among the first is the message in mid-May 1944 by Sternbuch to Vaad Hatzalah SP. Though the coded message read the "Neutra Rabbi," meaning Rabbi Dovid S. Ungar the well-known rabbinic personality, it really refers to his son-in-law, Rabbi Weissmandl, who used the more famous name for the same reason Rabbi Schonfeld called his rescue organization the Chief Rabbi's Religious Emergency Council. Chief Rabbi Joseph Hertz became his father-in-law soon after.

See the excellent article on the plea to bomb Auschwitz by Professor David Wyman, "Why Auschwitz Was Never Bombed," *Commentary* (May 1978), pp. 37-40. See the cables of May 16 and May 23 in the files of McClelland. WRB. Cf. also Martin Gilbert, *Auschwitz and the Allies* (New York: Holt, Rinehart and Winston, 1981), esp. pp. 216-7, 236-7, 246-8, 303-6. For Griffel's efforts re Weissmandl's plea, see [Griffel, *Memoirs*] pp. 27-8.

For the distribution to the others, see Braham, *Politics*, pp. 710-711.

93. Herman Landau interview with author. Mr. Landau was the executive secretary of HIJEFS from 1942 to 1948. Verified by Dr. Kuhl. Kuhl interview.

94. See Sternbuch to McClelland, June 12, 22, 1944. SP; Wyman, "Auschwitz," p. 40; McClelland to *Washington Post*, April 27, 1983.

95. Vrba, *I Cannot Forgive*, pp. 248-249. Cf.

also Kulka, "Five Escapees," pp. 205-207; Braham, *Politics*, pp. 710-711, 729 n. 81. Kastner asked George Mantello not to publicize the Protocols, but Mantello refused to listen. Interviews with George Mantello. Mr. Mantello's papers are in the possession of this author, courtesy of Mr. Mantello. See also Jeno Levai, *Zsidosors Europaban* (Budapest: 1948), pp. 68-72. For some odd reason, Gilbert mentions Walter Garrett and the press campaign but ignores Mantello, the man behind it. *(Auschwitz*, pp. 248-249) See also copy of the *Auschwitz Protocols* and the letter to Mantello by Moshe Krausz, WRB. The figure of 1,715,000 is due to an error on Mantello's version of the "Protocols," in contrast to the figure of 1,765,000 in the other versions. It is Mantello's figures that show up in the entire Swiss press and in the thousands of copies he had distributed throughout Switzerland and the world.

See for example, Braham, *Politics*, pp. 712-713 and chap. 31. Cf. also Gilbert, *Auschwitz*, pp. 248-249. The names of the four Swiss theologians that signed a covering letter to the report sent to the newspapers, were Karl Barth, Emil Brunner, W.A. Visser t'Hooft, and Paul Vogt. All were courageous men who fought against the silence of the Holocaust in Switzerland. Copies of many of the Swiss newspapers which publicized the Protocols in the author's possession, courtesy Mr. Mantello.

96. Mantello interview. His motivation, most likely, was the same as that which led him already in April '44 to withhold the *Protocols* from Hungarian Jewry.

97. See above note especially Braham, *Politics*, chap. 31. See also *op. cit.*, pp. 762-771. A longer analysis will appear in this author's *Stand Not Idly By*.

98. See, for example, Braham, *Politics*, chap. 31, and pp. 762-771.

99. For the change from 600 Zionists to 750, see "Report on Hungary: March 19 — August 9, 1944," by Philip Freudiger, et al., ["Freudiger Report"] in Randolph Braham, ed. *Hungarian-Jewish Studies*, vol. 3, p. 118. Cf. also Lewin II, p. 56. The certificates were given only to "bonafide" Zionists. Moshe Krausz interview.

100. See above note. For the 80 Orthodox provided for by Freudiger, see Braham, *Politics*, p. 955.

101. See especially letter by Rudolph Kastner to Nathan Schwalb, July 24, 1944 (WRB). In his *Bericht*, Kastner no longer acknowledges the Freudiger-Link connection

with the tractors, see pp. 155-6 and Harrison to WRB, August 11, 1944 (WRB). *Min Hametzar*, pp. 134-136. Weissmandl gives the figure of 250 while Kastner mentions 300.

102. Harrison to WRB, August 11, 1944.

103. Sternbuch to Vaad Hatzalah, July 21, 1944, Sept. 7, 1944 (SP); *Freudiger Report*, p. 122; Lewin II, p. 58. Among the many cables by Weissmandl warning of the danger to the "train," unless payment were made for the tractors, see the one sent by Sternbuch to McClelland, July 20, 1944, warning, in code, that "the entire train would be sent to Auschwitz unless a letter of credit were established within 24 hours" (WRB).

The Vaad Hatzalah had pressured both the Joint and the WRB to urge Mayer and McClelland to do something about this train. In a cable of July 18, to McClelland, Secretary of State Cordell Hull noted that the "Joint Distribution assumes that Mayer is doing his utmost to prevent the reported deportation." (Hull to McClelland, 7/18/44. WRB). A copy of this was naturally sent to Mayer. See note by McClelland on this document.

104. Interview with Hugo Donnenbaum. Mr. Donnenbaum was brought to the American Legation where present were McClelland, members of the Swiss police and a representative of Interkommerz, which was to have furnished the tractors. Cf. also McClelland's negative reply to Sternbuch re the tractors upon appeal by Weissmandl in cables of July 14, 17, 1944. On the 17th, McClelland told Recha Sternbuch, that, "I could not give my approval to this plan." McClelland memo on the "Tractor Affair," July 21, 1944 (WRB).

105. In a confidential cable to Vaad, Landau of Sternbuch's Committee, complains, "Lately the police investigated Sternbuch. They were well informed about details which should have been known only to the Committee." Further, Landau told the Vaad, "... because of indiscretions we can no longer rescue people on the French and Italian border in the previous manner." Lewin II, p. 59. For Recha's arrest trial, and the role of the Jewish "informer," see Kranzler, *Heroine*, chap. 4.

106. See Lewin II, p. 56. Saly Mayer first became involved in the negotiations on August 21, the day the first transport arrived in Switzerland. Moreover, it was the additional payments for the tractors by Mayer during the next few months as a result of Vaad pressure on both the WRB and the Joint that remained a crucial factor in the Kastner-Mayer-Becher negotiations.

107. See Harrison to WRB, August 11, 1944, p. 3.

108. For Mayer's fear of flooding Switzerland from the 1930's on, see *Heroine*, chap. 3. See also *American Leadership*, for a further analysis of Mayer and his policies.

109. *Morgenthau Diaries*, v. 760, August 1, 1944, p. 3 (FDRL). Cf. also McClelland to Sternbuch, 8/18/44 (SP).

110. For the payments that Mayer made to the Sternbuchs, see Sternbuch to Vaad, Sept. 25, Oct. 6, 1944 (SP). See also Bauer, "Mayer Negotiations," p. 34. For the cable by Kastner see *ibid.* p. 32. While the negotiations by Kastner-Mayer-Becher were undoubtedly a major factor in the release of the 'second' train from Bergen Belsen, Bauer ignores the role of the 'real' payment for 'Sternbuch's tractors' that spelled a very practical return for Becher in contrast to the stalling tactics for the 5 million dollars. See esp. Confidential cable Sternbuch to Vaad, Oct. 6, 1944; Dec. 5, 1944 (SP).

111. *Ibid.* See also Sternbuch to Vaad, Nov. 10, 1944; ST-VH 10/6/44 (SP).

112. Harrison to WRB, August 11, 1944 (WRB).

113. Kastner to Schwalb, July 28, 1944 (WRB); ST-VH, Oct. 6, 1944 (SP).

114. See *Report to the Union of Orthodox Rabbis of the United States and Canada Concerning Action Undertaken Toward the Freeing of Jews Detained in German Concentration Camps*, by Dr. Jean-Marie Musy [mid-1945] [Musy, *Report*] pp. 1-2. Unpublished 32-page report in French on his rescue efforts. For a scholarly analysis of this complicated affair, see *Stand Not Idly By*, chaps. 12-13.

115. Musy, *Report*, pp. 2-3. (The pagination refer to the English translation.) For the 60,000 SF and the half million in checks, see Agreement [between Sternbuch and Musy, Oct. 18, '44] (SP). For the 200 litres of rationed gasoline, see Buchler to Sternbuch, Jan. 17, 1946 (SP).

116. Sternbuch to Vaad, Nov. 21, 1944 (SP). This ransom negotiation, like those of Weissmandl's, involved stages during which releases would precede any payment. At no time, in any of these negotiations — so disparaged by some historians as unfeasible, or better, a hoax — were the Jewish negotiators double-crossed on such matters.

The real tragedy lies in the inability of the West in general and Western Jewry to accept the feasibility of such methods of dealing with an enemy. See *Stand Not Idly By*, chap. 2, for an analysis of this problem.

118. See Vaad to Sternbuch, Oct. 26, 1944. This note, also sent to McClelland, was handed to Mayer by Sternbuch on Oct. 29, 1944. For the rejection by JDC see Sternbuch's 13-page written testimony re the so-called Kastner Trial on Feb. 8, 1954 [*Sternbuch Testimony*], p. 5-8, 10-11. The Sternbuchs tried to coordinate efforts with Kastner since August '44, first upon Gisi Fleischmann's suggestion. See also Sternbuch's "Open Letter to Judge [Chaim] Cohen and Halevy," July 9, 1954 (SP) [Open Letter]. Another ten-page testimony re the so-called Kastner Trial, p. 8.

118. See Vaad to Sternbuch, Oct. 26, 1944. This note, also sent to McClelland, was handed to Mayer by Sternbuch on Oct. 29, 1944. For the rejection by JDC see Sternbuch's 13-page written testimony re the so-called Kastner Trial on Feb. 8, 1954 [*Sternbuch Testimony*], p. 5-8, 10-11. The Sternbuchs tried to coordinate efforts with Kastner since August '44, first upon Gisi Fleischmann's suggestion. See also Sternbuch's "Open Letter to Judge [Chaim] Cohen and Halevy." July 9, 1954 (SP) [Open Letter]. Another ten-page testimony re the so-called Kastner Trial, p. 8.

119. *Ibid.* Only in the later stage of negotiations did Mayer even try to get the Nazis to accept the Red Cross supervision of the camps. See Bauer, *Joint*, p. 423.

By Jan. 7, 1945, Mayer had obtained a license for 5 million dollars from the War Refugee Board which restricted its use solely as a bargaining chip and which had to be countersigned by McClelland. After that, Mayer had no more bargaining chips and his stalling could no longer work. That is why, by January 15, when Musy met Himmler a second time, Himmler decided to work with Musy, who seemed to offer something more concrete. See *Musy Report*, pp. 6-7; McClelland-Sternbuch, Jan. 17, 1945 (SP). Cf. also Sternbuch to Vaad Hatzalah (Polish cable), Jan. 17, 1945.

After Musy 'discovered' the Mayer team's obstructions in Berlin during his first trip to Berlin in Oct.-Nov. '44, he refused to go back. Only after Musy received reassurances re the Vaad's influence and Sternbuch's designation as the official representative did he return to Germany in mid-January, 1945.

See *Sternbuch Testimony*, p. 3. Also Vaad to Sternbuch, Feb. 19, 1945 (SP).

120. *Musy Report*, pp. 10-11. See cable by Sternbuch to Vaad Hatzalah. Sternbuch-Vaad Hatzalah (Polish cable), Feb. 5, 1945 (SP). Bauer, "Mayer," p. 40. Although Gestapo agent Krell was asked to halt negotiations with Mayer on February 5, it was right after the January 15 meeting with Musy that shifted the negotiations from Mayer to Musy. Sternbuch-Vaad Hatzalah (Polish cable), February 16, 1945 (SP).

121. *Ibid.*, p. 2. Among others, see McClelland to WRB, Feb. 8, 1945, pp. 1-3. *MD*, Bk. 818.

122. See the articles in the Sternbuch Papers. Other papers included the *St. Louis Star, Detroit News, Chicago News*, etc. See, for example, cable to Vaad, Feb. 18, 1945 re Swiss press and radio, which were full of this event. Dr. Hecht was the official representative of the Vaad for the press campaign. See for example, Vaad to Musy, Feb. 24, 1945 (SP). Dr. Hecht even hired a clipping service for the numerous Swiss reports.

123. See Testimony by Kurt Becher at Nuremberg, June 6, 1948, in *Holocaust Docs.*, v. 16, p. 2.

124. Among others, see Sternbuch to Mrs. Musy, Feb. 23, 1945; Dr. Reuven Hecht to Benoit Musy, Feb. 28, 1945, for some of the leftist press. Also interviews with Dr. Hecht. See also *Musy Report*, pp. 11; Testimony by Walter Schellenberg, June 18, 1948, p. 6. See also Sternbuch's response to some of the negative leftist press, Sternbuch to the editor of one unnamed newspaper, whose article, "Merci Monsieur Musy," was particularly vicious. No date (ca. mid-March, 1945) (SP). Also Sternbuch to Mr. Marx, Feb. 8, 1945 (SP).

125. See the (London) *Jewish Weekly*, March 30, 1945, p. 1, for an editorial on the nasty PALCOR article sent to London from Geneva. Cf. also *op. cit.*, April 13, 20, 1945. See also nasty cables about the Sternbuch rescue effort sent around the world by "someone who hates us." These cables include information that stems from the early agreements with Musy (which mentioned payment to Musy and the original ransom price of 20 million SF) (SP). Undoubtedly this reference is to Schwalb, whose PALCOR office sent out such negative reports. See *Griffel Memoirs*, pp. 51-53, for the effect of PALCOR in Jerusalem; *Jewish Weekly*, March 30, 1945, p. 1.

126. All accounts agree on the role of Kaltenbrunner and his role with the negative press. See, for example, *Schellenberg Testimony*, p. 6; *Becher Testimony*, p. 3.

127. See copy of this message in the SP. Cf. also *Musy Report*, p. 12. Even in Sweden, Benoit Musy was made aware of Mayer's obstructionism. *Ibid.*, p. 23. See also Sternbuch to Vaad, March 3, 1945 (SP).

128. Interview with Irving Bunim. He was the one who arranged for this loan. Bunim finally convinced a very reluctant Joint by threatening to publicize its refusal to help rescue Jews.

129. For the battle to convince a reluctant WRB to grant the license for transferring the million dollars, see *Stand Not Idly By*, chap. 7. For McClelland's negative role re Musy even after the arrival of the 1210 inmates, see McClelland to WRB, March 23, 1945, "of the Nazis and all their doings ... and a very dangerous individual," WRB. For his remarks re the money for relief, see McClelland to Sternbuch, May 5, 1945, (WRB).

130. See *Heroine*, chap. 13. Dr. Kuhl notified Saly Mayer of this threat to liquidate all the camps (see letter, p. 140). We are unaware of his response, if any. The Vaad, however, acted immediately, p. 141.

131. See Musy Report, pp. 17-23, which contains sections of the report by Benoit incorporated into that of Musy Sr. Benoit spent eleven weeks on his own traveling to and from Berlin as well as to all the camps in order to assure them safe transfer. He also went to Sweden where he again spoke with Schellenberg and paved the way for the Kersten, Masur and Storch last-minute negotiations. For the agreements re the protection of the guards, see, for example, Sternbuch to the Vaad, April 24, 1945; *Musy Report*, pp. 15-16.

132. *Ibid.*

133. *Musy Report*, pp. 12, 20-21. Cf. also *Work of the IRC for Civilian Detainees in German Concentration Camps from 1939-1945* (Geneva: IRC, 1975), Part III. Schellenberg Testimony, p. 3.

134. *Musy Report*, p. 13. While Becher claims credit for this, as well as for the transfer of the camps to the Allies, there is little to support his claim, despite the fact that he might have visited them. At that point, past mid-January, Becher had nothing tangible to offer Himmler, neither the good press, nor later the agreement for the transfer of the guards. This makes dubious Becher's

claim that Himmler guaranteed him the release of the 69 (61 in *Musy Report)* Slovak Jews hiding in the bunkers, including Rabbi Weissmandl. It was Musy's Schellenberg connection that worked both in Germany and in Sweden for last-minute-attempt releases to provide a good press, or later at least provide a better appearance for Germany, in the West. This was part of his long-time drive to negotiate a better deal with the West for Himmler — and himself — ever since 1942. See, for example, Heinz Hohne, *The Order of the Death's Head* (London: Secker & Warburg, 1969), pp. 521-524. See *Stand Not Idly By*, chap. 14, for an analysis of the two Nazi-Gestapo factions and Himmler's peace and ransom negotiations.

Chapter 8: 'If ...'

1. McClelland to WRB, Oct. 12, 1944 (WRB).

2. Sternbuch-VH, Nov. 28, 1944 (SP).

3. WRB to McClelland, Nov. 28, 1944 (WRB).

4. All from the WRB Papers. The remark re McClelland and bribery sent by Sternbuch-VH via the confidential Polish pouch, July 12, 1944.

5. Sternbuch-McClelland, Sept. 26, 1944. WRB.

6. *Ibid.*

7. *Ibid.*

8. Sternbuch-McClelland, June 22, 1944 (SP).

9. *Ibid.*

10. *Ibid.*

Part II: Personality Portraits

Chapter 9: The United States

A. Introduction

1. Teller, *Strangers*, p. 196.

2. Gay Talese, *The Kingdom and the Power* [Talese, *Kingdom*] (N.Y.: Andros Books, 1978), pp. 98-101. With one exception, in Nov. 1944, none of the news of the holocaust made the front page.

3. McClelland Papers Financial Records.

4. See *Vaad Hatzalah*, pp. 153-165. Also interviews with Rabbi Asher Rand and Dr. Gershon Kranzler.

5. Interviews with Dr. Gershon G. Kranzler and Dr. Isaac Lewin. See also the Minutes of the JEC.

6. Interview with Rabbi Asher Reichel, rabbi of the West Side Institutional Synagogue,

son-in-law and successor to Rabbi Goldstein.

7. Interview with Rabbi Alex Weisfogel.

8. Gershon Kranzler interview.

9. *Ibid.*

10. See the papers of Michael G. Tress for the volume of the postwar affidavits. Also Gershon Kranzler interview.

11. See *Vaad Hatzalah*, pp. 153-165, esp. pp. 162-3.

12. Irving Bunim interview. More details about Mr. Bunim in his forthcoming biography.

13. Interview with Rabbi Joseph D. Epstein, former secretary of the Mirrer Yeshiva during its long trek from Kovno in Lithuania throughout its stay in wartime Shanghai. See also Dov Levin, "The Attitude of the Soviet Union to the Rescue of Jews," in *Rescue Attempts*, pp. 228-236, 238-239.

14. Kranzler, *Shanghai*, chap. 11.

B. Siberia, Tashkent, Samarkand

1. Adapted from *Vaad Hatzalah*, pp. 212-227.

2. See above, chap. 4.

3. P. 216.

4. *Ibid.*

5. P. 221. See below, chap. 13C.

6. Pp. 222-223. See also David Kranzler, "The Role in Relief and Rescue During the Holocaust by the Jewish Labor Committee," [Kranzler, "JLC"] in the *Goldberg Report*, Appendix 4-2, pp. 19-20.

7. *Vaad Hatzalah*, p. 222.

C. Rabbi Abraham Kalmanowitz

1. Based primarily upon interviews with Rabbi Alex Weisfogel, who served as his secretary and aide during 1940-1942.

2. L.S. Lesser to [John] Pehle, April 18, 1944 (WRB).

3. David S. Wyman, "Why Auschwitz Was Never Bombed," *Commentary*, May 1978, p. 41.

4. Pehle VH Speech.

D. Rabbi Eliezer Silver

1. The introduction is based partially on Weisfogel interview.

2. Interview with Mr. Yitshaq Ben-Ami. See also Ben-Ami, *Years of Wrath*, document opposite p. 265.

3. Interview with Peter Bergson.

4. See, for example, the *Yiddishe Shtimme*, Sept. 1943, p. 1.

5. This is adapted and translated from an article by Dr. Isaac Lewin from *Personalities and Events: Essays and Speeches* [Lewin, *Personalities*] (New York: Orthodox Library, 1978), pp. 55-60.

E. Rabbi Aaron Kotler

1. Based primarily on two taped interviews with Irving Bunim and on five taped interviews with Rebbetzin Sarah Kotler-Schwartzman. The balance, especially the quotes, are from Aaron Surasky, "Rabbi Aaron Kotler," [Surasky, "R' Kotler"] in *Marbitze Tora Umasar*, Vol. 3 (New York: N.P., 1977). Details concerning Irving Bunim and his close association with Rabbi Kotler and rescue are in the forthcoming biography of Mr. Bunim, *Soul on Fire.*

2. Surasky, Rabbi Kotler, p. 43.

3. *Ibid.*, p. 19.

4. Kotler-Schwartzman interview.

5. See *Soul on Fire.*

6. Kotler-Schwartzman interview. Confirmed in Bunim interview.

7. *Ibid.*

8. Rabbi Asher Rand interview.

9. Bunim interview.

10. *Ibid.*

F. Irving Bunim

1. Bunim interview.

2. Kranzler, *Shanghai*, chap. 11.

3. Pehle. VH Speech.

G. "Mike" Tress

1. This article is based largely upon the article by Gershon Kranzler entitled "Setting the Record Straight," *Jewish Observer* (Nov. 1971) vol. 7 No. 10, pp.9-14.

2. Dr. Kranzler has served as a pioneering educator on the Orthodox scene during the quarter century after leaving as head of Agudath Israel's Refugee and Immigration Service in 1942. He helped establish the secular high-school departments in the Beth Jacob schools and several yeshivos. At the same time, he taught sociology at NYU, Townsend State College and John Hopkins U. He is the author of many works including *Williamsburg: A Community in Transition.*

3. G. Kranzler interview. Also interview with Rabbi Leo Jung. Rabbi Dr. Jung was probably the leading English-speaking Orthodox rabbi during the 1920's and 1930's. A foremost supporter of the early Beth Jacob movement in Poland, he was also a leader of the Rabbinical Council of America

and the Union of Orthodox Jewish Congregation of America. Later, he served as professor at Yeshiva University. He was still on the Advisory Committee of Agudath Israel World Organization in 1941, although he later severed relations due to his pro-Zionist leanings. See *Agudah Reports*, July-Dec. 1941. See also Leo Jung interview.

4. *Ibid.* Also interview with Meir Shenkolewski. Dr. G. Kranzler also pointed out that it was Dr. Nelson Lasson of Baltimore who initiated the contacts for Vaad Hatzalah and Agudath with members of the State Department. Dr. Lasson, an Orthodox Jew, had worked for years as secretary to George Lovick Radcliffe, the junior senator from Maryland. Corres. G. Kranzler to this author, December 7, 1979. Confirmed also by two other long-time Baltimore residents, Rabbi Shimon Schwab and Ms. Gertrude Hirschler, the well-known author and translator.

5. Bunim and G. Kranzler interview.

6. *Ibid.* Also interview with Mr. David Turkel.

H. Yaakov Rosenheim

1. Interview with Rabbi Joseph Elias. Rabbi Elias worked closely with Rabbi Schonfeld in London as well as with Mr. Rosenheim. He was also one of those German-Jewish refugees interned at first in the Isle of Man and later sent to Canada. See also the issues of *The Jewish Weekly*.

2. See *Comfort Comfort My People*: A collection of Essays and Speeches by Moreinu Jacob Rosenheim [Rosenheim, *Comfort*] edited by Isaac Lewin (New York: Research Institute of Religious Jewry, 1984), pp. 251-253.

According to Rabbi Jung he was responsible for obtaining over 1,000 affidavits through the members of his influential Jewish Center.

3. *Fourth Agudah Report.* Jan.-June 1943, p. 6-7.

4. *Ibid.*, pp. 8-9.

5. Rosenheim, *Comfort*, pp. 256-259; *Fifth Agudah Report*, pp. 9-10; *First Agudah Report*, p. 7. By the beginning of 1944, over $120,000 had been sent to Slovakia and a little over one-third that sum was sent to Shanghai, to the 500 members of the yeshivah group. This was to become a point of contention, since the general approach by Vaad Hatzalah included the Weissmandl cables which he rightfully claimed helped stir up the large response during 1944.

6. *Ibid.*, pp. 1, 15, 16.

7. *Ibid.*, pp. 15-16; *Sixth Agudah Report*, p. 17.

8. See below, chap. 13B.

9. See above, chap. 7F.

10. Lewin, *Nochem*, pp. 201-202.

I. Oswego

1. Based primarily on an interview with Mr. Louis Septimus and his article, entitled, "The Refugee Shelter at Fort Ontario," in the *Orthodox Tribune*, Oct. 1944, p. 3 and news article, p. 1. Mr. Septimus, a successful professional and businessman, was one of the "volunteers" working for rescue under the inspiration of "Mike" Tress. He remains a major supporter of yeshivos and Torah institutions.

Actually Agudah was not the originator of the plan for a "Free Port." See, for example, Wyman, *Abandonment*, pp. 260-276.

2. Septimus interview.

Chapter 10: Great Britain

A. Introduction

1. Interview with Dr. Judith Grunfeld. Dr. Grunfeld worked closely with Dr. Schonfeld, especially involving the Jewish education of the refugee children in the secondary schools as headmistress of one (Hasmonean School) and as head of the approximately 500 students evacuated from London to nearby villages during the ill-famed London "Blitz." See her charming book, entitled *Shefford: The Story of a Jewish School Community in Evacuation 1939-1945* (London: Soncino Press, 1976).

2. See Wasserstein, *Britain*.

3. Interview with Mr. George Mandel-Mantello.

4. See Wyman, *Abandonment*, pp. 280-284.

B. Harry Goodman

1. Based upon documents in the Harry Goodman Papers in this author's possession, courtesy of Simon and Naphtaly Goodman and Mrs. Arens, children of Harry Goodman.

C. Rabbi Solomon Schonfeld

1. This is adapted from a selection from this author's work, *Solomon Schonfeld*, pp. 35-53.

2. *Solomon Schonfeld*, pp. 25, 42-43; *Min Hametzar*, p. 31. Mr. Retter became an assistant to Rabbi Schonfeld and in this capacity spoke a number of times with Rabbi Weissmandl during his stay in London. Also

interviews with Mr. Charles Richter, son-in-law of Mr. Julius Steinfeld, and himself active in rescue affairs in the U.S., especially the food package project.

3. *Solomon Schonfeld*, p. 36.

4. This is based on a count of the lists of individuals found in the Schonfeld Papers, copies of which are in this author's possession. These papers had been lying in an attic of one of the day schools.

5. See "Appreciation," by Rabbi Dr. Sir Immanuel Jacobovits, *Solomon Schonfeld*, pp. 14-15.

6. Interview with Rabbi Joseph Elias who served as translator for Rabbi Schonfeld.

D. Meir R. Springer

1. Based primarily on interview with Mr. Springer and the Springer Papers, copies of which are in this author's possession, courtesy Mr. Springer. While one historian credits Harry Goodman with instigating the food-package project, it was actually Mr. Springer, his assistant, who initiated it, in his role as "Official Spokesman to the Czechoslovak Ministry of Interior for the Orthodox Jewish Community in Czechoslovakia" during the period of 1941-1945.

Mr. Springer showed this author the volume of names of Theresienstadt inmates collected by the Czech underground from the nighttime broadcasts by the Nazi camp administration.

Chapter 11: Switzerland
A. Introduction

1. See Bauer, *Holocaust*, p. 90. Yet, most of his statistics are highly suspect. For a popular, yet more accurate picture of the Swiss refugee policy, see Alfred A. Hasler, *The Lifeboat is Full: Switzerland and the Refugees 1933-1945* [Hasler, *Lifeboat*] (New York: Funk & Wagnalls, 1969). For a scholarly study, upon which much of Hasler's book is based, see the official Swiss government report entitled, *Die Fluchtlingspolitik der Schweiz seit 1933 bis zur Gegenwart* [*Ludwig Report*] (Bern: Verlag Herbert Lang, 1957).

2. Hasler, *Lifeboat*, chap. 3 "Marked Men."

3. See Bauer, *Holocaust*, p. 90, also his *JDC*, p. 230. The "over" 5,000 figure exists nowhere, and Bauer's "calculations" fly obviously in the face of the official statistics. The lowest figure of 9,751 refoulees refers to the officially reported number for the period of August 1942 through 1945. This ignores

the period from 1938 on until mid-1942. Including emigrants, plus civilian refugees, the Jews accounted for approximately 28,000 out of a grand total of close to 300,000 or less than 10%, though only 21,858 remained in Switzerland for any length of time.

The *Ludwig Report* notes that though precise statistics cannot be given for the complete number of refoulees returned into Nazi hands, it is surely in the many thousands. This, as the key point made, excludes the even larger number that never attempted the near impossible task of entry into Switzerland (pp. 318-319). It also excludes, as Sternbuch pointed out, those refoulees who were sent back as frequently as five, six or more times (ST-McClelland 1944, SP).

While Recha Sternbuch estimated the number of refoulees at over 150,000, Mr. Landau, her secretary who worked closely with her since 1942, told this author of his estimate of at least 200,000. At any rate, Bauer's figures were clearly reduced in order to mitigate the negative Swiss role, especially vis-a-vis the Spanish.

4. Interviews with six survivors of the Swiss camps. While some were more lenient than others (the harsher ones were really labor camps), all were guarded by armed Swiss soldiers who saw little distinction between refugees from Hitler's persecution and deserters from the army. In contrast, the Swedish not only refrained from placing all entering survivors (including the 8,000 rescued Danish Jews) in any camps, they permitted them to work and provided for both physical and spiritual sustenance of the refugees. (See below, chap. 12D re Lidingo.)

5. See Kranzler, *Heroine*, pp. 30, 36-37. See also *Rescue Attempts*, pp. 645-646, where Sternbuch's role is totally ignored.

6. Kranzler, *Shanghai*, chap. 6.

7. Laqueur, *Secret*, chap. 6.

8. See below, chap. 16.

9. Interview with Dr. Reuven Hecht. Dr. Hecht not only gave several taped interviews; he also provided the author with copies of his papers as well. More information on Dr. Hecht's activities will be found in this author's above-mentioned, two forthcoming volumes on rescue.

10. See Kranzler, *Heroine*.

11. *Ibid.*, chaps. 5, 7. Cf. also Sternbuch-Harrison [mid-July 1944] (SP). Also Lewin, *Nochem Churban*, pp. 87-94, and Lewin, "Rescue II," pp. 58-59.

12. The pleas to bomb Auschwitz is but one of many examples. See also Lewin, "Rescue II," pp. 52-54.

13. *Ibid.*, p. 59. Also see interviews with Dr. Kuhl, Herman Landau.

14. Interview with Mr. Lebowitz. Also documents his rescue work via R' Weissmandl. Copies in the possession of this author courtesy Mr. Lebowitz.

B. Chaim Yisroel Eis

1. Adapted from an article by Dr. Isaac Lewin, entitled, "R' Chaim Yisroel Eis" in *Nochem Churban*, pp. 163-166.

C. Recha and Yitzchok Sternbuch

1. See Kranzler, *Heroine*. Also based on the Sternbuch Papers, the Kuhl Papers and dozens of taped interviews, including those with Herman Landau, the Sternbuch children: Rabbi Avrohom Sternbuch, Rabbi Chaim Siegel and Mrs. Nettie Siegel and Mrs. Esther Gutterman.

2. See letter by Grueninger to Sternbuch, Nov. 29, 1945 [HIJEFS — History], also History of HIJEFS, a 7-page manuscript (SP).

3. See Aaron Rakeffet-Rothkopf, *The Silver Era* [Rakeffet, *Silver*] (Jerusalem: Feldheim, 1981), p. 230.

4. HIJEFS-History, p. 2.

5. Bauer, *JDC*, p. 233.

6. Rabbi Chaim Siegel interview. He claims that his mother-in-law, Mrs. Recha Sternbuch, told him this among many other incidents. It fits in neatly with all the other evidence about Saly Mayer and Recha Sternbuch.

7. Hasler, *Lifeboat*, p. 18.

8. *Ibid.*

9. *Ibid.*, p. 43.

10. *Ibid.*

11. Interview with Mr. Eli Sternbuch, a brother of Yitzchok who also helped in rescue matters.

12. Telephone interview with Mrs. D. Gromb.

D. Dr. Julius Kuhl

1. Based both on a series of interviews with Dr. Kuhl as well as the Kuhl (KP) and Sternbuch Papers SP. These were the primary sources for Kranzler (and Friedenson), *Heroine*.

2. (KP) This document was received by the Sternbuchs from someone in Warsaw who sought Latin American papers such as sent to many Jews in Poland. This letter and several other confirming letters and postcards re the summer '42 deportations from Warsaw were given by the Sternbuchs to Dr. Gerhard Riegner of the World Jewish Congress. One of these was cited by Morse, *Six Million*, pp. 15-16. For some strange reason, Dr. Riegner never acknowledged the Sternbuchs as the source for this information.

3. SP

4. See the expenditure sheets from Dr. Kuhl's office.

E. George Mandel-Mantello

1. Based upon a series of taped interviews with Mr. Mantello, Matthieu Miller and Moshe Krausz, as well as on their respective papers. The Mantello Papers include, for example, a sworn testimony of June 27, 1946 about his rescue activities by the Commission of the Swiss Jewish Command Association, signed by Dr. Georg Brunschwig, Prof. P. Guggenheim, Obberrichter Dr. M. Gurny in Bern. See also Jeno Levai, *Zsidosors Europaban* [Levai, *Zsidosors*], (Budapest: Magyar Teka, 1948).

2. WRB.

3. Herman Landau interview.

4. WRB.

5. Levai, *Zsidosors*, pp. 68-72.

6. Copies of scores of such newspapers in this author's possession, courtesy Mr. Mantello.

7. See *Pester Lloyd*, 1944 (MP).

8. *Ibid.*

F. Franzi Goldschmidt

1. Based on interviews with Mr. Herschel Rosman, Mrs. Franzi Goldschmidt and her son, Dr. Alex Goldschmidt, in addition to the Goldschmidt Papers in this author's possession, courtesy of Mrs. Goldschmidt.

2. Incidentally, Mrs. Goldschmidt had the unusual opportunity of a "repeat performance" with a keynote speech at the Convention of World Agudath Israel in Jerusalem, 1980.

Chapter 12: Sweden

A. Introduction

1. See *Rescue*, p. 68.

2. Interviews with Eric and Dr. Manfred Lehmann.

In early October 1938 Poland's antisemitic government started a vicious cycle by rescinding the passports of all Polish Jews residing in foreign countries unless they had been validated within five years, thereby making most of them stateless. Germany, with its over 30,000 Polish Jews, took the cue and decided to expel all these now "stateless" Polish Jews although most resided in Germany for tens of years. On October 28, 1938, there took place the "Polish aktion," whereby thousands of these Polish Jews were rounded up and sent back to the Polish border town of Zbonzyn, where many languished in "no-man's-land" until they were accepted into Poland. Poland in turn expelled all its German-Jewish residents including many students in the yeshivos of Mir and other higher institutions. Rabbi Wolbe was then brought to Sweden by Mr. Hans Lehmann.

It was the "Polish aktion" that directly provided the Nazis with the excuse to foment the mass pogrom of Kristallnacht of November 9-10, 1938. Herschel Grynspan, a 17-year-old lad in Paris, distraught over the fate of his parents deported to Zbonzyn, fatally shot Ernst von Rath, a minor German official whom he took to be the German Ambassador to France. The Nazis used this event to instigate Kristallnacht following the death of von Rath.

3. Manfred Lehmann interview. See Appendix for part of one letter by Hans Lehmann to his sons with a paragraph of messages to Rabbi Kalmanowitz. See also the certificate by the rabbinical part of Vaad Hatzalah, Rabbis Wolbe, Zuber and W. Jacobson, in Stockholm honoring Mr. Lehmann with the title of *Moreinu*, a German-Jewish custom granted to privileged Jews for singular dedication to the needs of the broader Jewish community, such as the title bestowed upon *Moreinu* Yaakov Rosenheim.

4. Weisfogel interview. Rabbi Weisfogel was also a passenger on this boat.

5. Manfred Lehmann interview. See also the correspondence between Manfred and his father in Sweden, copies in this author's possession, courtesy of the Lehmann family.

B. Rabbi Shlomo Wolbe

1. Based on interview with Rabbi Wolbe who also supplied supporting documents.

2. See Kranzler, *Shanghai*, especially chap. 7.

3. *Ibid.*, esp. pp. 431-435.

4. Interview with Rabbi Joseph D. Epstein, secretary to the Mirrer Yeshiva in Shanghai.

5. Kranzler, *Shanghai*, pp. 556-447. See also document in the appendix, pp. 625-626.

C. Rabbi Yaakov Yisroel Zuber

1. Based on an interview with his son, Mendel Zuber, who was closely involved with his father's rescue work.

2. *Ibid.*

3. In addition to the chairman, Mr. Hans Lehmann, other members included Rabbi Shlomo Wolbe and Rabbi "Wolly" Jacobson, the local Vaad Hatzalah included Israel C. Hasdan, Dr. Tanchum, M. Finyas and Samuel Samson. See Rabbi Wolf Jacobson's *Zichronos* (Jerusalem: Center for Orthodox Literature in Israel, 1953), pp. 159-160.

4. Interviews with Zuber and Eric Lehmann and Rabbi Wolbe. Cf. also Jacobson, *Zichronos*, p. 418.

5. Zuber, and Lehmann interview. The publisher was called *The Brothers and Widow Rom*, who put out the classic Vilna edition of the Talmud.

6. Zuber interview.

D. Rabbi (Zev) Wolf Jacobson

1. Rabbi Binyomin Zev ("Wolly") Jacobson originally hailed from Germany. There he served as head of the *Keren Hatorah Fund* which raised money for yeshivos and Beth Jacob schools in Poland. He also officiated as rabbi in Copenhagen, Denmark, from 1934 until the eve of Rosh Hashanah in 1943 when he was rescued along with the rest of the 8,000 Danish Jews and brought to Sweden by fishing boats.

2. In Sweden, he joined the handful of Orthodox rabbis and laymen in the marvelous relief and rescue work described here. This episode is translated and adapted from Rabbi Jacobson's second, enlarged volume of memoirs, entitled, *Esa D'ee L'merchak* (Bnei Brak: Netzach, 1967), chaps. 27-29.

Chapter 13: Turkey, Eretz Yisrael, Tangier

A. Introduction

1. See Dalia Ofer, "The Activities of the Jewish Agency Delegation in Istanbul in 1943" [Ofer, "Istanbul"] in *Rescue*, pp. 435-450. The role of the Orthodox in the creation of the Jewish Agency's Vaad Hahatzalah is described in this author's *Stand Not Idly By*, chap. 10.

2. The New York Orthodox Vaad Hatzalah was represented in Eretz Yisrael by Rabbi Chiskiyahu Yosef Mishkowski, formerly rabbi of Krinki, Poland, and Rabbi Levy in Teheran, both described in the above-mentioned work.

3. Ofer, "Istanbul," p. 439.

4. *Ibid.*

5. See index in Chaim Barlas, *Hatzalah Bimei Hashoah* [Barlas, *Shoah*] (Beit Lochamei Hagetaot: Kibbutz Hameuchad, 1975).

B. Dr. Yaakov Griffel

1. Based primarily on the Sternbuch Papers and the Griffel *Memoirs* as well as four taped interviews with Dr. Joseph Klarman, who worked closely with Dr. Griffel in Istanbul and later in Europe, and Mr. Shimon Kornitzer, a member of the Jerusalem-based Vaad Hahatzalah.

2. Ofer, "Istanbul," p. 439.

3. See below, pp. 222-223.

4. Joseph Klarman, "A Friday Evening in Istanbul with the Previous Belzer Rebbe," *Algemeiner Journal*, July 16, 1982.

5. Griffel, *Memoirs*, pp. 29-32.

6. *Ibid.*, p. 31.

7. *Ibid.*, p. 12.

8. See SP. See also Griffel, *Memoirs*, et passim.

9. *Ibid.*, p. 27.

10. See this author's forthcoming *American Leadership* for a detailed analysis of this theme.

11. Griffel, *Memoirs*, pp. 7-8.

12. *Ibid.*, p. 8.

13. *Ibid.*, p. 33.

14. *Ibid.*, p. 13-15.

15. *Ibid.* See also Ira Hirschmann, *Caution to the Winds* [Hirschmann, *Caution*] (New York: McKay, 1962), pp. 158-159.

16. Griffel, *Memoirs*, pp. 15-16.

17. See Appendix.

18. Sternbuch to VH, August 7, 1944 SP.

19. VH to Sternbuch, Sept. 13, 1944 SP.

20. WRB.

21. Griffel, *Memoirs*, pp. 48-49. See also John Mendelsohn, *The Holocaust, Vol. 14, Relief and Rescue of Jews from Nazi Oppression 1943-1945* [Mendelsohn, *Rescue*] (New York: Garland, 1982), pp. 47-51.

22. Griffel, *Memoirs*, pp. 31-32.

C. Chief Rabbi Dr. Yitzchok Isaac Halevy Herzog

1. Based largely on the article by Shulamit Eliash, "The Rescue Policy of the Chief Rabbinate of Palestine Before and During

World War II," *Modern Judaism*, Vol. 3, No. 3 (October 1983), pp. 291-308.

2. See Kranzler, *Heroine*, p. 178.

D. Mrs. Renee and Miss Eva Reichmann

1. This is based on the interview with Miss Eva Reichmann [Gutwirth] who was directly involved with her mother's rescue work throughout World War II. The documents derive primarily from the Sternbuch Papers and the papers of the Vaad Hatzalah at Yeshiva University Archives (YUA). A number of documents were also obtained from the Reichmann family. Interviews were also conducted with Mrs. Renee Reichmann and two sons, Hashie and Albert.

2. Rives Childs, *Foreign Service Farewell* [Childs, *Memoirs*], pp. 116-117. See also letter to Mrs. Renee Reichmann by Rives Childs dated June 13, 1945. Copy Reichmann papers.

3. Childs, *Memoirs*.

4. *Ibid.*

5. R. Reichmann to Sternbuch, Aug. 12, 1944 SP.

6. SP.

7. *Ibid.*

8. *Ibid.*

9. *Ibid.*

10. Eva Gutwirth interview.

11. WRB.

Chapter 14: Occupied Europe

A. Introduction

1. See Braham, *Genocide*, chaps. 14-25.

2. *Ibid.*, chap. 4.

3. Interviews with Samuel Frey and Chaim Roth. See also WRB re their leadership of the Jewish community following the departure of the large number of leaders in the so-called "Kastner Train" from Budapest to Bergen-Belsen.

4. Interview with Rabbi Yaakov Bein.

5. Frey interview.

6. See Braham, *Politics*, pp. 267-270, 915-917.

7. Frey interview.

B. Julius Steinfeld

1. Adapted from the article by S.Y. Sonnenfeld entitled, "Der Shtadlan Fun Vien," in *Dos Yiddishe Vort* (Adar-Nissan 5735 — March 1975), pp. 26-28.

2. See below, chap. 10B.

3. See William Perl, *The Four-Front War* (New York: Crown, 1978); Ben-Ami, *Years of Wrath*, Parts III-IV.

C. Herbert Kruskal

1. Based on an interview with Mr. Kruskal and the supporting documents provided by him. See appendix.

D. Chaim Stern

1. Adapted from Shlomo Rosman, *Zichron Kedoshim*, Vol. II (New York: N.P., 1979), pp. 89-103.

Chapter 15:

Rabbi Michoel Ber Weissmandl

1. Based on interviews with Benjamin Shloime Stern and his son "Brudi." Benjamin Shloime Stern, a close associate of Rabbi Weissmandl, participated in all his activities and travails in the underground in Slovakia. He personally dealt with smugglers, diplomats and members of the underground, who sent and brought the hundreds of messages to Switzerland, Turkey, England, and the U.S. It was he who, with his "illegal" dealings in currency, was able to keep the wheels of their incredible intelligence network rolling. See *Min Hametzar* for Rabbi Weissmandl's notes of gratitude. See also Bauer, *JDC*, p. 366.

Whenever Rabbi Weissmandl stayed in Bratislava, which was most of the time, he lived at the Sterns. Brudi Stern, though a youth at the time, helped prepare the maps of Auschwitz and the railroad lines, which Rabbi Weissmandl sent out.

2. Interviews with Andre Steiner. For the quote see Griffel, *Memoirs*, pp. 12, 27.

3. For example, see Livia Rothkirchen, "The 'Europa Plan': A Reassessment," in the *Goldberg Report*, Appendix 4-7. For a detailed response to Rothkirchen's and other criticism of the Weissmandl rescue plans, see this author's forthcoming *Stand Not Idly By*, chap. 9.

4. Mr. Steiner admitted to this author that he was unaware of the fictitious aspects of Weissmandl's "Ferdinand Roth" creation.

5. Steiner interview.

6. *Ibid.*

7. *Min Hametzar*, P. 53. Also Bauer, *JDC*, p. 366.

8. Shloime Stern interview.

9. *Ibid.*

10. Letter in Rothkirchen, *Slovak*, p. 239.

11. Wyman, *Abandonment*, chap. 15.

12. *Min Hametzar*, pp. 118ff. Also S. Stern interview.

13. Interviews with Rabbi Joseph Brody, a student at the yeshivah during this period.

14. *Min Hametzar*, pp. 43-53.

15. *Ibid.*, pp. 56-59, 133, 160-161.

16. *Ibid.*, pp. 88-91.

17. *Ibid.*, pp. 56-60.

18. *Ibid.*, pp. 61-62. While Weissmandl doesn't identify the names of the three Jewish leaders, the identity of two, Rabbi Strasser of Debrecin and Mr. Samuel Kahan-Frankl, head of Orthodox Jewry of Hungary, was obtained from Mr. Kahan-Frankl, the son of the latter. He added that in his desperation Rabbi Weissmandl didn't realize that these cables could easily have jeopardized Budapest Jewry — as the entry of the Hungarian Secret Service indicates. In fact, Mr. Kahan-Frankl noted, that after the war, Rabbi Weissmandl apologized for being responsible for this inadvertent danger. Interview with Mr. Kahan-Frankl.

19. *Min Hametzar*, p. 62.

20. *B'Tzel Hamoves* (Tel Aviv: Sefarim, 1958).

21. Adapted from pp. 18-26.

22. Pp. 25-26.

23. *Shadow*, pp. 79-82.

24. Mr. Forst was friendly with Rabbi Weissmandl yet from his youth in Vienna, when Rabbi Weissmandl would stay at his home. After the war, when Rabbi Weissmandl came to the U.S. broken in body and in soul, he spent many weeks at the Forst home. There he poured out his anguish and frustrations to this close friend, who in turn became inspired by this extraordinary human being.

Cartoon by Andre Steiner of Rabbi Weissmandl, representing General Montecucolli, the 17th century Austrian officer, whose motto was, "There are three ways of winning a war, with money, money, and more money."

DEN HAAG, (Holland)   3. April 1940
MECHELSCHESTRAAT, 8.

American Joint Distribution
        Comittee

      W a r s c h a u

      Jasna 11

        Unter Bezugnahme auf unser Schreiben v. 26.März
        teilen wir Ihnen hofl.mit,dass wir nunmehr doch
        glauben,dass wir Ende der Woche noch die Geneh-
        migung für die Verladung von ca. 1500 Pakete
        Mazzoth erhalten werden. Die Sendung würde als-
        denn an den Beauftragten des Deutschen Roten
        Kreuzes nach Krakau für den American Joint
        Distribution gehen. Es werden Pakete von 2 & 3
        Kilo verladen. Ein Teil der Pakete soll an be-
        stimmte einzelne Personen in Krakau oder auch
        ausserhalb Krakau's, wie Lublin, Warschau usw.
        gehen. Wir bitten Sie, uns bei Erhalt dieses
        Briefes an unsere Telegrammadresse:

        Elundeka Haag

        zu telegrafieren, ob dieses möglich ist. Eine
        grössere Anzahl der Pakete wird der Krakauer
        Gemeinde zur Verteilung überlassen.

                        Hochachtungsvoll
                        Dutch Migration Department
                             of the
                        Agudas Israel World Organisation

*Herbert Kruskal's one-man relief campaign
from occupied-Holland to Poland (especially Krakow).*

דער וויי-געשריי

פון די גערעטעװעטע ישיבות אין שאנכאי.

פון גרויסען פייער און חורבן װאו אונזערע ברידער אין שוועסטער געפינען זיך אין יודאם איז געלונגען ברחמי השם ארויסראטעװוען הונדערטער תלמידי חכמים, ראשי ישיבות און ישיבה בחורים פון ליטע און פוילען דורך סיביר קיין יאפאן. צווישען זיי די גרעסטע צאל אן ערך 300 פון דער אלטער באנאוטטער מירער ישיבה, און אויך פון אנדערע ישיבות. זיי האבען זיך גערא טעוועט נען עטליכע מאנאטען אין יאפאן און יעצט זיינען זיי צוליב די לעצטע מלחמה געמווסקלונגען טראנזיש אהויסגעטריבן געװארן אין שאנכאי, כינע, װאו זיי װאלגערן זיך אין א שוהל אין א שטיינערנער פלאר אן קיינע מיטלען צום לעבן און צענדליקער ליגן קראנק אונטער עפידע מישע אוסברוכן.

אין דער דרינגענדער שעה האט דער וועד הרבנים און וועד הישיבות פון דעמעריקע גענומען אויף זיך דעם הייליגן חוב צו העלפן ראטעװוען פון בלוטיגן טרערן-טאל די טראגיש אומגליקליכע בני תורה און עס איז ספעציעל איינגעלאדן געװארן

דער באװאוסטער גאון ר'
אברהם קאלמאנאװיץ
פרעזידענט פון מירער ישיבה
און הרב אשר קאצמאן

איינער פון די אריבערנעקומענע תלמידים װעלכער ברײנגט א לעבעדיגן גרוס פון די ישיבות אין יאפאן, אנצופירן די ארבעט פאר אן עלפארגרייכן קאמפיין.

ברידער און שוועסטער! יעצט צום יום הדין האט דעם

זכות און רופט זיך אפ װוארעם אויף די אפילם װעלכע וועלן געמאכט

אין אלע שוהלן פאר דעם צוועק ראש השנה און יום כפור.

מאנטאג, דעם ערשטען טאג ראש השנה, 5 א זייגער וועט געגעבן װערען

א קבלת פנים לכבוד דעם גרויסן גאסט הגאון ר' אברהם
קאלמאנאװיץ אין בית תפלה עמנואל שוהל
טיילאר און װאודהראו װילדמאן

פראמינענטע רבנים װעלן באגרוסן און נטע רעדנער װעלן אדרעסירן

קומט אין מאסן הערן דעם גרוים נאסט און װאונדערבארן רעדנער!

תנו כבוד לתורה!

Appeal in Detroit by Rabbi Abraham Kalmanowitz
for yeshivos stranded in Shanghai [1941].

W.T. 16/180/41.

BRITISH EMBASSY,
WASHINGTON, D.C.,
August 13th, 1941.

Dear Dr.Rosenheim:

When you called on me on August 6th the question of the sending of food parcels into the German occupied areas of Europe was mentioned between us, and I promised briefly to indicate to you the view of His Majesty's Government.

This is an extremely difficult question for any of us who have friends and relations living in those tragic districts, but you will realize that His Majesty's Government have been obliged to look at it having in mind the chief charge that lies upon them today — to defeat the Nazi power and force the withdrawal of the armies of occupation as soon as possible.

From the point of view of the exigencies of that duty, we is bound to recognize that the sending of extra foodstuffs into occupied countries increases the strength of the enemy in several ways. It adds to the total supply of food of which the enemy can dispose and makes it possible for him to organize his occupation more effectively. His Majesty's Government have, moreover, conclusive evidence that parcels sent from Portugal to Poland either are not received by the addressees, or that the latter, if they receive them, suffer a corresponding reduction in their rationed food allowances. Further, Portugal itself is not self-supporting in food supplies, and can thus only make good the quantities that may be sent out in food parcels by importing them through the blockade and this, as you will appreciate, cannot have the approval of His Majesty's Government.

The financing of the despatch of food parcels to the occupied areas has always been regarded by His Majesty's Government with serious concern. People sending food parcels regularly have paid several times the value of the food actually delivered. Moreover, they paid forwarding and insurance charges in American Dollars and these accrue to the account of German interests in this country. Nazi propaganda and Fifth Column activities in North and South America, German purchases in the United States to fill South American orders, and Germany's purchases to supply her own war machine, have been financed in part by funds built up this way.

I think I need hardly develop these points further. This brief summary of them will, I hope, make it clear to you that, while they do not fail to understand the generous motives that prompt such action, His Majesty's Government cannot regard the despatch of food parcels to the occupied territories otherwise than with disapproval.

Yours sincerely,
sgd. HALIFAX.

Dr.Jacob Rosenheim,
Agudas Israel,
New York City.

Ambassador Lord Halifax giving Britian's position re Agudah's breach of the naval blockade of Axis territory [Aug. 13, 1941].

Postcard to H. Kruskal on conditions in Poland. It includes: "Aunt Fear (Pachad) visits us daily and Uncle Bread (Lechem) only once a week [Feb. 20, 1942].

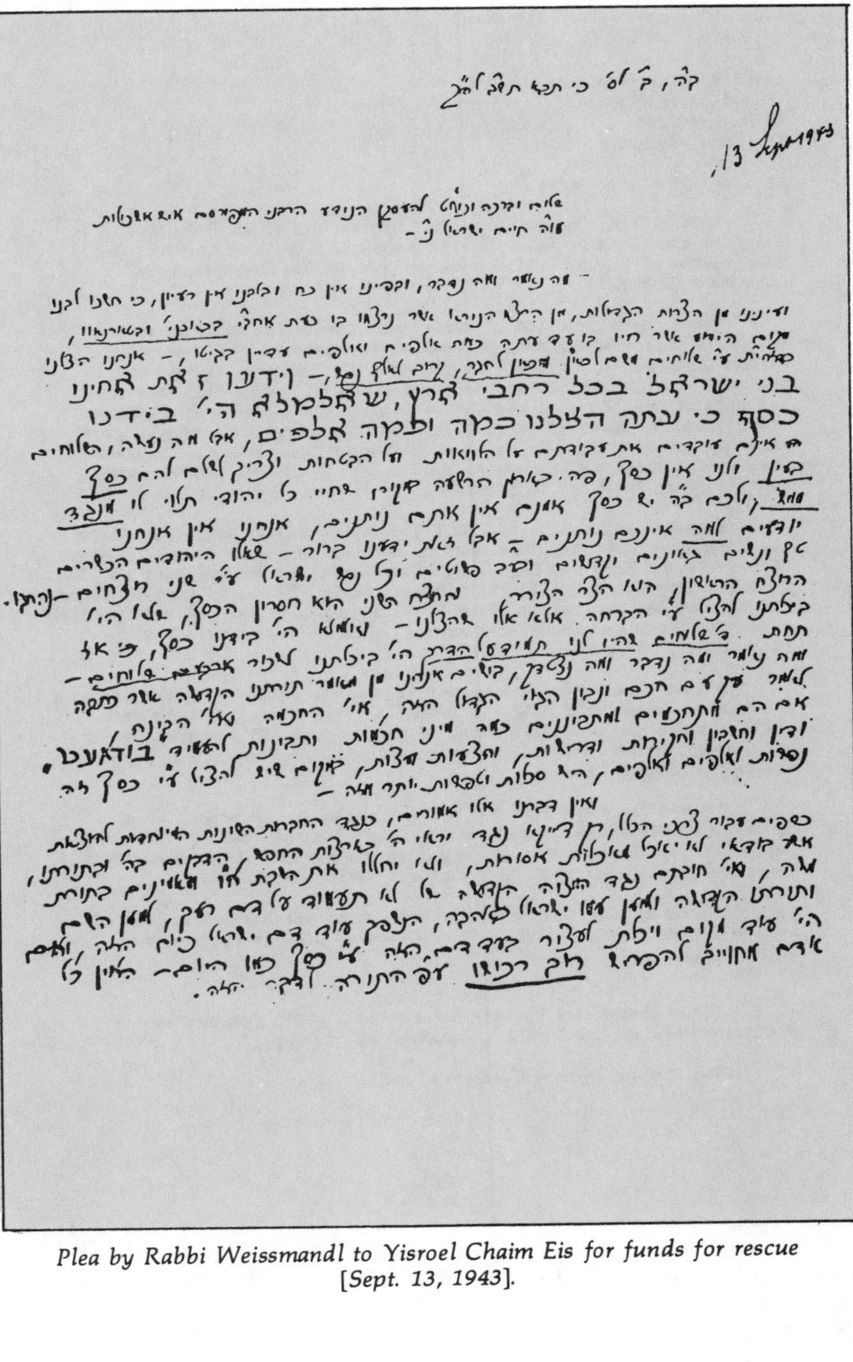

Plea by Rabbi Weissmandl to Yisroel Chaim Eis for funds for rescue [Sept. 13, 1943].

January 5, 1944

Rabbi Michael Bernstein
Inwood Jewish Centre
66 Nagle Avenue
New York 33, N.Y.

My dear Rabbi Bernstein:

I am writing to you in answer to your letter of January 3rd and I am glad to know that you are contemplating raising funds for the purpose of saving Polish Jews who are in the Hungarian and Slovakian border.

There is no question of doubt that the monies raised can be forwarded to a reputable agency in Switzerland and then forwarded to the necessary individuals in Slovakia and Hungary. Of course, you must realise that this entire procedure is a very delicate one and must be handled with the utmost discretion. Funds are forwarded via diplomatic channels of an Allied Government in this country, and in turn, are given to our representatives in Switzerland. This entire method does not conform to the "legal" statutes, but we cannot at this time, think of this matter.

In addition, let me add that the entire matter cannot be given too much open publicity, but must be handled in a very careful manner. We have in the last ten days been instrumental in raising over $50,000 for this purpose, of which the student body of the Mesifta Torah Vodaath and its faculty has raised $20,000. I can also inform you that regular receipts, which are income-tax exempt, will be issued by our organization for this purpose.

I know that I need not stress to you the vital necessity of doing all that is humanly possible in behalf of this very important work. I feel, without qualification, that we must expend all the energies at our command to rescue while it is yet possible. Every delay may mean the loss of human lives.

I therefore hope that you will organise the necessary forces to raise a substantial sum of money. May I further add that not one penny will be divulged for any expenses whatsoever. Everything that is raised will go in total for the designated purpose.

I am also enclosing a copy of the cable which gives us the entire matter in a nut-shell. It seems that $380 is necessary to save a human being.

If you desire any further information, would you be kind enough to call me and I will be glad to be of help.

With kindest personal regards, and

With Torah greetings,

Michael G. Tress,
Chairman

"Mike" Tress trying to raise funds for Rabbi Weissmandl's efforts to smuggle Jews from Poland into the relatively "safe" Slovakia and Hungary. Note the closing of the Mesivta Torah Vodaath to enable the students to participate in the fund-raising [Jan. 5, 1944].

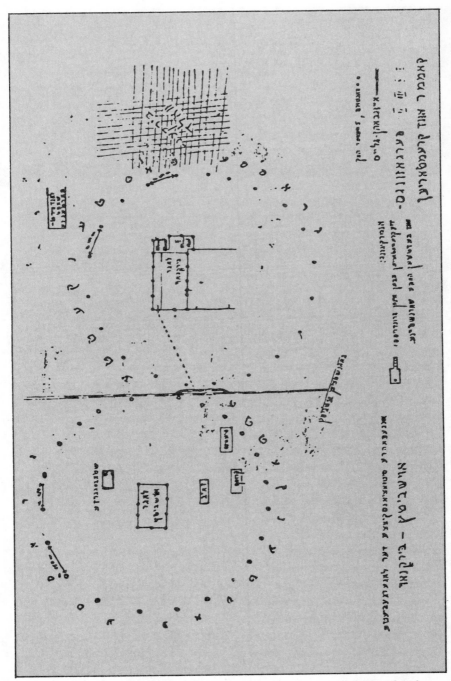

*Copy of plan of Auschwitz-Birkenau highlighting Camps and Gas chambers.
From Rabbi Weissmandl's version of the Auschwitz Protocols.*

CONGRES JUIF MONDIAL ∴ CONGRESO JUDIO MUNDIAL

330 WEST 42nd STREET
NEW YORK 18, N. Y.

LONDON
55 New Cavendish St., W 1

GENEVA
37 Quai Wilson

BUENOS AIRES
Corrientes 2024-9c

JERUSALEM
Vaad Leumi, P. O. B. 471

MONTREAL
1121 St. Catherine St. W

MEXICO CITY
Sonora 174-4

CABLES: CONGRESS, NEW YORK
TELEPHONE: LOngacre 5-2600

March 9, 1944

Hon. J. W. Penle, Acting Executive Director
War Refugee Board
Executive Office of the President
Washington 25, D. C.

Dear Mr. Penle:

I beg to bring to your attention the following information
which has been conveyed to one of our representatives in
Lisbon by one of our Geneva representatives.

Since the report was of November 26, 1943, it may well be
that it is outdated. It is, however, of such serious
character that I felt you would want to check on it. The
information reads textually:

"You certainly heard that only young people below sixteen
are permitted to enter Switzerland; in addition families
with children. Others are being sent back. You can picture our state of mind. The authorities stick to these
rules. A month ago people arrived here from Belgium. We
registered them in the Interior in the town of Z. The result was that those who took care of them were arrested
and held in prison for a week. This is not as important as
the fact that people are being sent back. Our proteges
finally remained, but I am worried about the others still
to come.

"The situation of our brethren and our youth who have
suffered everywhere and who are now compelled to take
refuge here should be explained to the Swiss authorities."

This information has been quite a shock to us even as it
would be to public opinion were it to learn that Switzerland is rejecting refugees. I repeat, however, that this
information may be obsolete.

May I suggest that the War Refugee Board approach the
Swiss Government and request it to open its doors to all
the Jews who manage to escape. If Switzerland would up-
hold a policy such as described in this report it would
mean a terrible blow to the possibilities of rescue from
France and Italy.

I would greatly appreciate hearing from you soon.

Sincerely yours

Dr. A. Leon Kubowitzki, Head
Department European Jewish Affairs

ALK:ter

*World Jewish Congress reporting on serious problems
re entry of Jewish refugees into Switzerland.*

The Jews of Poland and of other occupied countries who have succeeded in obtaining
foreign passports, particulary South American passports, have been put by the Germans
into several special camps for foreigners. One of the largest of these camps, containing 2000 to 3000 Jews, was established in Vittel, Alsace. The conditions in
the Vittel camp were relatively good. Of course the Germans knew very well that
the people who held the foreign passports were not citizens of those countries,
but they were keeping them as hostages for the exchange of Germans held by the
United Nations.

Several weeks ago I had suggested, and our Polish Advisory Committee had discussed,
that the American Jewish Committee should approach the War Refugee Board and
particularly the State Department. We asked that the State Department should
notify, through Switzerland, the German government that at least some token exchange would be considered in the near future. Such a declaration would have
saved not only the Jews who are already in the camps but would have permitted also
for the sending of further passports to other Jews and the Germans would have had
interest to continue to recognize the validity of these passports. Unfortunately
nothing was done in the matter.

In the meantime the Agudath Israel, the Orthodox organization, has received from
their people in Switzerland a telegram that there is immediate danger that the camps
for foreigners, especially the camp in Vittel, will be liquidated. They went to
see the people of the War Refugee Board in Washington and also talked to Breckenridge Long and others of the State Department. The State Department was non-commit-
tal and the War Refugee Board expressly asked that the Jewish organizations should
exert strong pressure upon the State Department to make a declaration that an exchange would be considered. Dr. Lewin of the Aguda immediately contacted us and
asked us to intervene with the State Department. Mr. Landau happened to be in
Washington that day and we asked him to verify with the War Refugee Board Dr.
Lewin's information. The information proved entirely correct and the War Refugee
Board re-emphasized the need for pressure upon the State Department. While we were
hesitating the War Refugee Board informed us that they had succeeded themselves in
convincing the State Department that such a declaration was necessary for the saving
of the Jews in the camps and that the State Department had instructed the American
minister in Switzerland to notify the Germans through the Swiss government that the
people in the camp would be considered in the future exchanges.

A few days later the Aguda received further telegrams that the camp in Vittel had
already been liquidated. Two Orthodox rabbis, in spite of Passover, immediately
went to Washington and through the intervention of Senator Wagner and some Congress-
men got to see the Secretary of State Cordell Hull. They asked him to intervene
with the Spanish government, whose ambassador seems to be very influential in
Berlin, to stop the liquidation of the camps. They also asked that the Jews who
had already been deported from Vittel should be returned or sent to another camp
for foreigners. They have succeeded in convincing Mr. Hull that this was an extremely urgent and important matter and the State Department instructed the

The rabbis travel on Pesach to Washington to press for rescue on the Vittel Affair.

✚ CRUZ ROJA ESPAÑOLA

T A N G E R

ENVIO PARA PRISIONEROS DE GUERRA

EXPEDIDOR — EXPEDITEUR   FRANCO DE PORTE
                                          FRANC DE PORT

NOMBRE Y DIRECCION: DIRECCION DEL PRISIONERO:
NOM ET ADRESSE: ADRESSE DU PRISONNIER:

Renée   CROIX ROUGE
REICHMANN   INTERNATIONAL

TANGER   G E N E V E
                             SUISSE

*Label for food packages sent to Auschwitz. Notice the Jews are labeled
"Prisoners of War" by the Spanish Red Cross.*

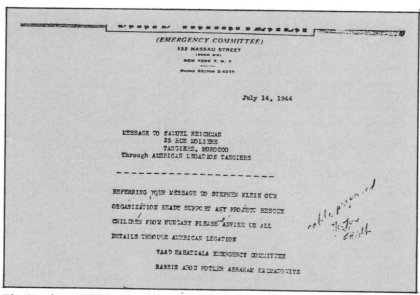

The Vaad Hatzalah ready to support any rescue plans for Jews of Hungary.

Truck-load.
of food packages
sent by the Reichmann's
from Tangier to the camps.

September 20, 1944

Cable to ChiefRabbi Marcus Ehrenpries
Stockholm (Sweden)
Through American Embassy in Stockholm

Greatly disturbed growing danger to group of 500 Rabbis and Rabbinical
scholars (with almost complete Mirer Rabbinical College) in Shanghai.
Have directed several pleas to Vatican to intervene with Japanese Government
for unilateral release of entire group. Negotiations in progress stop
Respectfully urge you contact Swedish Government that presentations be
made by Swedish Government and King to Japanese Government for release of
group. Necessary also consult Swedish Government and request make available
ship for transport of group and permit temporary entry into Sweden. Almost
entire group possess final entry visas to Palestine, Canada, United States
and other lands. We guarantee cost of transport and maintenance while in Sweden
stop This group represent the remnant of the great Rabbinical Colleges of Poland
and Lithuania. Their rescue and rehabilitation would be an historic undertaking.
We appeal to you to consult Rabbi Wolbe and lend your influential support to our
Committee in Switzerland

VAAD HAHATZALA EMERGENCY COMMITTE

RABBIS ISRAEL ROSENBERG
ARON KOTLER
ABRAHAM KALMANOWITZ

Unsuccessful appeal by Vaad Hatzalah to Chief Rabbi Ehrenpreis to enlist the help
of the Swedish Government to ship the yeshiva groups from Shanghai to Sweden.

WESTERN UNION

S1CC 1G INTL

CD STOCKHOLM VIA RCA 81 31

NLT RABBY ABRAHAM KALMANOWITZ

540 BEDFORDAVENUE BROOKLYNNY (EMD)

PROFESSOR EHRENPREIS CANNOT DO ANYTHING OUR COMMITTEE DEPENDENT UPON
OURSELVES REGARDING HELP FOR RABBINICALCOLLEGE PLEASE DONT EXPECT
SUPPORT FROM OTHER QUARTERS HERE AND DONT RECOMMEND US COLLABORATION
WITH OTHER PERSONS APART STORCH OF JEWISHCONGRESS POSSIBILITY OBTAIN
IMMIGRATION FINLAND FOR COLLEGE PROVIDED PROVISIONS AND LIVINGCOSTS
GUARANTEED I WILL BE THERE SHORTLY ACCOUNT MY RECEIVING RABBISHOP
COULD NEGOTIATE FURTHER THERE IF RECEIVING YOUR AUTHORIZATION PLEASE
REPLY THROUGH DIRECT CABLE PLEASE INFORM ABOUT PURPOSE STEAMERSPACE.

WILHELM WOLBE

1250A NOV 7 1944

APOSTOLIC DELEGATION

UNITED STATES OF AMERICA

3339 MASSACHUSETTS AVENUE
WASHINGTON 8, D. C.

Nº 581/42

July 24, 1944

THIS NO. SHOULD BE PREFIXED TO THE ANSWER

Rabbi Abraham Kalmanowitz
Union of Orthodox Rabbis of the U.S. and Canada
132 Nassau Street
New York City

Dear Rabbi Kalmanowitz:

I wish to acknowledge your letter of July 20th, and I am pleased to inform you that I have received another communication concerning the Jewish people of Hungary from His Eminence, the Cardinal Secretary of State.

His Eminence states that according to a communication of July 15, 1944, from the Apostolic Nunciature in Budapest, the personal appeal of the Holy Father to Regent Horthy has lead the latter to assume a more determined attitude of opposition to the racial laws. Likewise the members of the Catholic Hierarchy were encouraged to carry on a more intense activity in favor of the victims of persecution.

In seems that the Government of Hungary has now given assurance to His Eminence, Cardinal Seredi, Primate of Hungary, that deportations of Jewish people will cease. The Apostolic Nunciature adds that in fact the whole racial situation is somewhat improved.

I regret that there has been no further word from the Holy See concerning the Rabbinical College of Mir, but as I stated in my previous communications the Holy See, while anticipating great difficulty in this problem, will let nothing undone to obtain the desired result.

With sentiments of esteem, and every good wish, I remain

Yours very sincerely,

A. G. Cicognani
Archbishop of Laodicea
Apostolic Delegate

Local Britconsulate informs local Jewishagency representancy

inspiteof greatnumber accorded certificates immigration from

Bulgaria Rumania together fixed 5000 persons from October till

March stop local and Bucarest Jewishagency tries reviviscency

Agudacontingent six percent intervention urgently needed firstly

because thereare many impartial religiousjews secondly because

uptonow religiousjews neglected weobserve that before afew months

Jewishagency agreed toelevate contingent eight percent besides

Bucarest Jewishagency representancy will give sixpercent oncondition

renounce separateships severest prkotest necessary against reprisals

weremark according information Jerusalem exists tendence general

collaboration Jewishagency with orthodoxie especially in America

very necessary tocondition really loyal agreements and practical

loyal realistic settling by all representancies informs Rosenheim wire

[Ludwig] Kastner Griffel

Gonderen: Jakob Griffel
Kontinentaloteli

17/11/44

["impartial" religious jews = non-party Orthodox Jews]

CONGRES JUIF MONDIAL .·. CONGRESO JUDIO MUNDIAL

330 WEST 42nd STREET
NEW YORK 18, N. Y.

LONDON
55 New Cavendish St., W 1

GENEVA
37 Quai Wilson

BUENOS AIRES
Corrientes 2024-9e

JERUSALEM
Vaad Leumi, P. O. B. 471

MONTREAL
1121 St. Catherine St. W

MEXICO CITY
Sonora 174-4

CABLES: CONGRESS, NEW YORK
TELEPHONE: LOngacre 5-2600

June 8, 1944

In reply refer
to No. 85

Mr. Lawrence S. Lesser
War Refugee Board
Treasury Building
Washington, D. C.

Dear Mr. Lesser:

I beg to let you have below the text of a cable sent by
Dr. Goldmann to Mr. Barlas as a result of a conference
which took place between representatives of the World
Jewish Congress and the Vaad Hahatzalah.

"YOURS 2420 IMPLIED GRIFFEL KLARMAN AGREED THEIR
ACTION UNNECESSARY STOP CABLE SEVENTEENTH FROM
GRIFFEL KASTNER KLARMAN TO VAADHATZALA STRONGLY
DIFFERS STOP WAR REFUGEE BOARD ANXIOUS HAVE ALL
RESCUEWORK COORDINATED STOP WE HERE ENDEAVORING
REACH AGREEMENT VAADHATZALA PLEASE CABLE SUGGESTIONS
SETTLEMENT

NAHUM GOLDMANN"

Very sincerely yours,

Dr. A. Leon Kubowitzki
Head, Rescue Department

ALK:bn

*World Jewish Congress appeals to Chaim Barlas of the Moetza in Turkey
to halt the discrimination vs. the Orthodox refugees
seeking refuge in Eretz Yisrael via Rumania-Turkey.*

Dear Sirs:

The War Refugee Board has recently received the following very confidential information which will be of interest to you.

Our representative in Switzerland is attempting to secure information concerning the camp at Krotingen and other camps in East Prussia in which Baltic Jews are concentrated. However, he has pointed out that the International Red Cross is not able to exercise supervision considered capable of preserving the inmates of such camps from death, and ability to render effective intervention in their behalf is made doubly difficult by the fact that East Prussia is presently a very active theater of military operations./ Our representative in Sweden recently reported that Lithuanian refugees reaching Sweden have stated that on July 1 of this year there were only about 500 Jews in Krotingen and it was believed that no more than that number are presently in Krotingen unless there has been a heavy demand for conscript labor in this area. Special efforts are also being made to obtain information concerning camps in Austria by our representative in Switzerland.

Mrs. Sternbuch advised our representative that she has informed your organization of a plan upon which she is working personally for bringing 5,000 Jewish children from Hungary to Switzerland. In this connection, she advised him that a diplomat who recently came to Switzerland from Hungary told her that he had received information from "competent German quarters", indicating that if either the United States or Great Britain gave concrete assurances that these children would be admitted to the United States and to the British Isles, the Germans would permit them to leave Hungary by way of Switzerland. She explained that the question of the Swiss Government regarding as insufficient the guarantees given that such children would be evacuated from Swiss territory did not therefore arise, and that she fully understood that the Swiss Government has in fact received appropriate guarantees to that effect.

While the names and addresses of Mr. Sternbuch's principal confidential agents in Slovakia were said to be already known to the Union of Orthodox Rabbis in the United States, he gave our representative the names of Rabbi Samuel David Ungar, Berthold Donnebaum, and M. B. Weissman in Bratislava. His main contacts in Hungary were Julius Link and Philip Freudiger, both of whom fled to Bucharest some weeks ago; Charles Roth, Sch. B. Frey, and Dr. Reiner are his present men in Budapest. Mr. Sternbuch is out of contact with the Rabbi of Neutra at the present time and has received no news concerning any special rescue plan recently evolved by the latter.

The last report from Neutra, which was received early in September, refers to the Rabbi's need of funds primarily for financing the rescue and flight of refugees from Hungary and Poland at an estimated cost of 6,000 Slovakian crowns per person in the case of Hungary and 10,000 Slovakian crowns per person in the case of Poland. Approximately 100 refugees per day were said to be arriving from Hungary. False papers incident to these operations are secured at a cost of 3,000 Slovakian crowns per person and an estimated 4,000 Slovakian crowns per month are required for hiding refugees. Other activities include general maintenance for all such refugees newly arrived as well as Jews "normally" in Slovakia and special relief to Orthodox Jews in camps. It was reported that Slovakian crowns are obtainable at the rate of 20 to 25 per Swiss franc, and that during the period from July 15 to September 15 the sum of 305,000 Swiss francs were sent by Mr. Sternbuch to Slovakia for Jewish relief and rescue operations. In an effort to secure late news from the Rabbi of Neutra, and information concerning the general situation with respect to Jews in Slovakia, Mr. Sternbuch has sent a wire to Bratislava.

Very truly yours,

(Signed) J. W. Pehle

J. W. Pehle
Executive Director

Some rescue efforts by Vaad Hatzalah in Slovakia and Hungary in late 1944.

Wed. April 25th.

Frau Sternbuch and Musy telephoned from
St. Margarethen at about 3:30 today
and stated that they were in contact with
the chief of the Gestapo for southern
Germany who was bearing a message from
Schellenberg and Himmler. Latter claimed
that in the capture of Bergen-Belsen
"the Allies had not kept their word about
treating the SS guards et al as pows &
soldiers." I informed Musy that no such
word had been given officially or formally
but that I had merely stated as a personal
opinion that it was not the practice of
our Army to shoot such persons who surrendered without resisting. Musy said
Germans claimed that SS men taken in BB
had "been photographed in humiliating
positions, etc." I said I didn't know
anything about this, which anyhow didn't
seem very serious. Frau Sternbuch stated
that an answer had to be given for Schellenberg by 5 o'clock about our "guarantee" not
to mistreat SS guards in o camps, etc.
I replied that no such answer could be given
but that I could only repeat my personal
opinion.
     Musy stated that Frau S. was trying to
get a "visa" or permission to go to Theresienstadt where there were many of her relatives. Musy added that Th. was not yet
captured, implication being that if we
could give the Germans no such assurance
about treatment of guards then things might
go badly for the internees.
     A nice business, all this!

                                   RDMcC.

News by Roswell McClelland re last-minute rescue action instigated by the
Sternbuchs. Notice code of letter, negative view of the rescue effort by McClelland.

Vaad Hatzalah notifying Sternbuch (and Musy) of the favorable news report in the New York Times re the release of 1200 inmates of the Theresienstadt camp on Feb. 7, 1945 (The news appeared the following day Feb. 8).

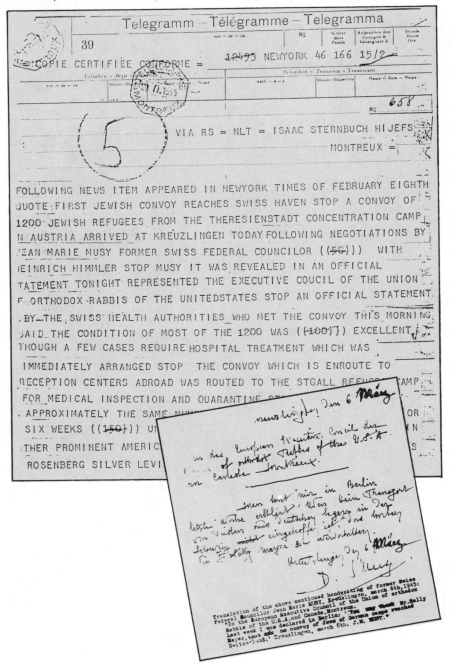

Telegramm — Télégramme — Telegramma

39

COPIE CERTIFIÉE CONFORME =

12493 NEWYORK 46 166 15/2

N° 658

VIA RS = NLT = ISAAC STERNBUCH HIJEFS
MONTREUX =

FOLLOWING NEWS ITEM APPEARED IN NEWYORK TIMES OF FEBRUARY EIGHTH
QUOTE:FIRST JEWISH CONVOY REACHES SWISS HAVEN STOP A CONVOY OF
1200 JEWISH REFUGEES FROM THE THERESIENSTADT CONCENTRATION CAMP
IN AUSTRIA ARRIVED AT KREUZLINGEN TODAY FOLLOWING NEGOTIATIONS BY
JEAN MARIE MUSY FORMER SWISS FEDERAL COUNCILOR ((50)) WITH
HEINRICH HIMMLER STOP MUSY IT WAS REVEALED IN AN OFFICIAL
STATEMENT TONIGHT REPRESENTED THE EXECUTIVE COUCIL OF THE UNION
OF ORTHODOX RABBIS OF THE UNITEDSTATES STOP AN OFFICIAL STATEMENT
BY THE SWISS HEALTH AUTHORITIES WHO MET THE CONVOY THIS MORNING
SAID THE CONDITION OF MOST OF THE 1200 WAS ((100)) EXCELLENT
THOUGH A FEW CASES REQUIRE HOSPITAL TREATMENT WHICH WAS
IMMEDIATELY ARRANGED STOP THE CONVOY WHICH IS ENROUTE TO
RECEPTION CENTERS ABROAD WAS ROUTED TO THE STGALL REFUGE CAMP
FOR MEDICAL INSPECTION AND QUARANTINE
APPROXIMATELY THE SAME NUM   OR
SIX WEEKS ((150)) U   WN
OTHER PROMINENT AMERIC   S
ROSENBERG SILVER LEVI

Translation of the above mentioned handwriting of former Swiss
Federal Councilor Jean Marie MUSY, Kreuzlingen, march 6th 1945:
To the European Executive Council of the Union of orthodox
Rabbis of the U.S.A.and Canada,Montreux. 'You may thank Mr.Sally
Mayer, last week I was declared in Berlin no convoy of German camps reached
Switzerland. Kreuzlingen, march 6th. J.M. MUST.'

Index

Abramsky, Rabbi Yecheskel, 226
Acheson, Dean (Secretary of State), 150
Adas Yisroel, Congregation (London), 179
Adler, Cyrus, 77, 150-151
Affidavits (guarantee of refugee support), 32, 126, 128f, 134, 148, 156f
Collective affidavits, 128, 187
Afghanistan, 225
Agudas Harabonim, See Union of Orthodox Rabbis in the US and Canada, 154
Agudath Israel, England, 160, 161; France, 59, 205, 253; Poland, 23-24; Switzerland, 59; US, 31, 32, 36, 51, 59, 60, 67, 82, 84-88, 111, 124ff, 134, 139, 143, 145-146, 152, 154f, 162; Vienna, 180, 260
Agudath Israel World Organization, See also England, 172; in Germany, 261-262; Hague, 262; Istanbul, 30, 104, 164, 231, 232, 233, 234, 239; N'shei (Women's division), 216; Rosenheim, Yaakov, 7, 23, 24, 25, 58, 60, 71, 82, 90-91, 94, 124f, 201, 203, 238, 257, 261, 262; World convention, 216
Agudath Israel Youth (Zeirei Agudath Israel), See also Tress, Mike, 125f, 154ff
Agunah (pl. agunos), 226, 244
Akiva, Rabbi (Tannaitic scholar), 19
Akzin, Benjamin (WRB), 138
Aliyah, See also Jewish Agency; Moetza, US-rescue 30, 61-64, 233, 234, 238, 239, 240, 244, 245, 246, 260, 261
Alliance Israelite (France), 22
Allied governments, See also Allies; Trading With the Enemy Act, 18, 93, 105, 107, 242, 256
Alter, Rabbi Avrohom Mordechai (Admor of Gur) 246
American Civil Liberties Union, 65
American Jewish Committee (Jewish defense organization), 3, 22, 54, 61, 70, 77, 79, 94-99, 162
American Jewish Conference, 82, 95-99, 100, 101, 162
American Jewish Congress (American Zionist Organization), See also Wise, Stephen S., 3, 22, 67, 69, 71, 77, 80, 85, 125, 162; World Jewish Congress
American Jewish Establishment, See also Political power, 123-124; Secular Jewish ideologies, 58, 67-69, 71, 79, 82, 136
American Jewish Joint Distribution Committee, See Joint Distribution Committee
American Jewry (in general), See also Individual organizations, 18, 37, 78, 90-91,

163, 192; Secular Jewish ideologies
Amshenov, Admor of (Rabbi Shimon Kalish), 59, 130
Ancona, 89
Angola, Portuguese, 172
Ankara (Turkey), 164, 213, 232, 237, 238
Antisemitism, 56, 58; Hungary, 256; Japanese, 76; Polish, 23; Sweden, 219; Switzerland , 186-188, 197ff; US, fear of, 48, 68-69, 123-124
Antwerp, 194
Arrow-Cross (fascist antisemitic party), 215
Ashkenazi, Rabbi Meir, 223
Assimilation, See Assimilationists
Assimilationists, 1, 26, 43-50, 54ff, 60, 61, 74, 168, 220ff, 267, 281; Conflict with the Orthodox, 65, 74, 135, 171, 220; Fear of antisemitism, 68-69, 108, 124, 188, 197ff, 198, 219
Associated Jewish Charities (of Baltimore), 12
Auschwitz—Birkenau, See also Bomb railroad to, 29, 138, 164, 172, 266, 270f; Weissmandl, M.B., 29, 103-106, 114, 116, 206, 207, 208, 211ff, 212ff, 225, 238, 248, 249, 250, 251, 253, 268, 269, 280
Auschwitz Protocols, See also Auschwitz; Cable text, 209-213, 230, 249; Weissmandl, M.B., 104ff, 116, 206ff
Australia, 161
Austria, See also Vienna, 13-16, 62, 64, 107, 113, 123, 176-180, 194, 202, 204, 216, 255, 256, 258ff, 262
Avni, Haim, 75
Avriel, Ehud, 239

Balfour Declaration (1917), 64
Baltimore, Jewish leadership of, 12
Banyai, Michael, 207f
Barcelona, 253
Barlas, Chaim, See also Vaad Hahatzalah of the Jewish Agency, 231, 232, 235
Barth, Prof. Karl, 106, 208, 213
Baruch, Bernard (Presidential advisor), 47, 123
Bauer, Yehuda, 2, 19, 54, 57, 68, 78, 79f, 90
BBC (British Broadcasting Corporation), 91, 171, 213
Becher, Kurt, 111-112, 215
Bein, Rabbi Yaakov, 257
Belgrade, 84
Belz, Admor of, See Rokeach, Rabbi Aaron
Belzec (concentration camp), 201

58, 72, 100f, 108, 140, 144f, 155f, 266; Insignificance, 49-50, 111, 124-5; Propelled to forefront, 50, 71, 98, 99, 102, 126-128, 130, 141f, 152, 153, 162ff, 267f; Rabbis (Orthodox); View of, 27, 47ff, 67-9, 87, 95-98, 154;

Orthodox rescue activists, See Orthodox rabbis

Orthodox rescue leadership, See Orthodox rabbis

Orthodox Tribune, 97

OSS (Office of Strategic Services), 209

Oswego (detention Center Oswego, N.Y.), 166ff

Our Crowd (by Stephen Birmingham), 46, 50

Palaestina Amt (Jewish Agency office handling Palestine Certificates), See also *Aliyah;* Certificates, Palestine; Jewish Agency, 63, 207; in Istanbul, 236

PALCOR News Agency, 112

Palestine, See also *Eretz Yisrael*, 30, 45, 51, 61, 62, 64, 74, 77, 79, 86-87, 94, 100-101, 124, 132, 145, 164, 170, 181, 183, 189, 195, 202, 204, 206, 215, 263; illegal immigration into, 195, 261, 262

Palestine Certificates, See Certificates, Palestine

Palestine Resolution (1944), 101

Palestinocentric view, *Aliya;* Certificates, Palestine; Jewish Agency, Socialist-Zionists, 63-64, 235ff, 241ff

Papal nuncio, See Bernadini, Fillippe; Paraguayan Papers, See also Huigly, Consul; Latin American papers, 102-103, 173, 203, 252

Paraguayan Papers, 102, 103, 252

Paris, 247, 260

Parliament (London), rescue resolution, 177, 180ff

Particularism (Concern for special groups or individuals), See also *Klal,* 45, 68, 73

Passports, See also "J"on, 186, 194; Latin American papers, 15-16

Pat, Jacob, See also Jewish Labor Committee, 71

Pearl Harbor, 76, 155

Pehle, John (Head of WRB), See also War Refugee Board, 7, 8, 38-41, 137-139, 151, 153

Penn, William, 120

Perl, Dr. William R., 261

Perlmutter, Rabbi Avraham (shtadlan), 22

Perlow, Rabbi Nachum (Admor of Novominsk), 158

Pisaro, Duchy of, 89

Pittsburgh Conference (Jan. 1943), See also American Jewish Conference, 95f, 162f

Pius XII, Pope, See also Vatican, 106, 213, 276, 280

Ploesti (Rumania), 282

Poalei Agudah, 233

Poland, See also Citizenship papers, 195, 202, 262, 263; Consulate in Bern, 201ff; Deportations from, 29, 200; Illegal pouch, 29, 55, 58, 73, 81, 105, 109, 111, 120, 126, 160, 161, 190, 197, 203ff, 234; Polish Government-in-Exile; 7, 12, 29, 58, 59, 60, 80, 84-87, 90, 126, 130, 131, 132, 133, 134, 149, 152, 160, 161, 173, 183, 184, 192, 202, 205, 234, 246, 256, 257, 262

Polish refugees, 50, 73, 76, 129; in Hungary, 164, 257; in Shanghai, 223

Portugal, 3, 46, 84, 172, 173, 187, 192

Portugal, Rabbi Zusha (Admor of Skulen), 234

Posner, Chaim, 207, 208

Postwar plans, 78, 79

Postwar reconstruction, 3

Prague, 152, 204, 240, 248

President Advisory Committee, 67

Proskauer, Judge Joseph (American Jewish Committee), 96f

Protocols of the Elders of Zion (Antisemitic work), See also Antisemitism, 76, 123

Quakers, 120

Quotas, Immigration (US), 128

Rabbis (Orthodox), See also Influence of, 6-13, 16-17, 19, 35-42; Jewish diplomacy, 24, 35-44, 50, 108; Orthodox Rabbis; Roshei Yeshivah; in Vienna, 258ff

Rabbis' March on Washington (1943), 71, 99ff, 140f

Ransom, See also Europa Plan; Jewish diplomacy, 18ff, 35-44, 56, 57, 58, 59, 72, 73, 74f, 80, 81, 108, 109, 110, 111, 116, 117, 147, 194, 198-199, 265ff, 272ff

Rashi (Biblical Commentator, 1040-1105), 12

Rathbone, Lady Eleanor (MP), 71, 176, 181

Rationalism, See also Secular Jewish ideologies, 43

Ravensbrueck (Concentration camp), 113, 227

Rayburn, House Speaker Sam, 100

"Reb Binyamin," 246

Red Cross, American, 55, 133

Red Cross, German, 58, 257, 262

Red Cross, International, 106, 112-113, 117, 175, 185, 214, 233, 249, 251, 252, 253

Red Cross, Irish, 172, 174-175

Red Cross, Spanish, See also Reichmann, 30, 58, 75, 249ff

Red Cross, Swedish, See also Wallenberg, Raoul, 113, 236

Red Cross, Swiss, 55, 236, 249

Talmudic students, See yeshivah students
Tangier (Sp. Morocco), 30, 190, 231, 247ff
Tartakower, Aryeh (World Jewish Cong.), 92
Tashkent, (Russia), 131, 132, 133, 147
Taub, Rabbi Shaul Yedidya (Admor of Modzitz), 158
Taubes, Rabbi Dr. Zvi, 207
Tchecheval, Rabbi Moshe, 167f
Teheran, 132, 133
Teitelbaum, Rabbi Joel (Admor of Satmar), 106, 158, 263, 269
Teitelbaum, Rabbi Yaakov, 156
Teller, Judd, 124
Temple, Dr. William (Archbishop of Canterbury), 180
Tenenbaum, Dr. Joseph, See also Joint Boycott Council, 51, 74, 85ff, 149
Tenzer, Herbert, 32
Tetuan (Spanish Morocco), 253
Theresienstadt (Concentration camp), 117, 118, 185, 211, 212, 214, 251, 253; from, 55, 80, 111-113, 151, 198
Tiso, Monsignor Josef (Pres.— Slovakia), 277, 278
Tittmoning (Detention camp), See also Vittel, 8
Torah (Meaning, both written Scriptures and Oral or talmudic law and tradition), See also Orthodox, 4, 43, 194, 228, 229
Torah Umesorah (day school movement), 130
Trading With the Enemy Act, See also Jewish diplomacy; legalism; Money transfer to occupied territory, 18, 38, 54-56, 107, 184
Transfer Agreement, See *Haavarah plan*
Transnistria (Rumania), 83, 236, 237, 238
Transylvania, 207, 210
Travers, Mr. K. (Visa Division), 163
Treasury Department, See also Morgenthau, Henry, Jr., 7ff, 37, 54, 55
Tress, Mike (Elimelech) (Chairman, Agudath Israel Youth), 31, 32, 125-126, 154ff, 167f
Tropp, Rabbi Naftoli, 132
Trujillo, Rafael, L., 76
Turkel, David, 156
Turkey, See also Istanbul, 24, 28, 71, 164, 174, 190, 202, 231, 232ff, 257; Jewish community of, 89

UJA (United Jewish Appeal), 62
UN, See United Nations
Ungar, Rabbi Shmuel Dovid, See also Weismandl, Rabbi Michoel Ber, 18, 26, 41, 139, 246, 272, 275, 278
Union of American Hebrew Congregations (Reform), 97
Union of Orthodox Hebrew Congregations, (London), 179

Union of Orthodox Rabbis of the U.S. and Canada (parent body of Vaad Hatzalah), See also Vaad Hatzalah, 31, 91, 98-99, 125, 139, 144, 153
United Jewish Appeal, See UJA
United Jewish War Effort, 133
United Palestine Appeal, 96
United States, As a haven, 7, 36, 202, 204
Universalism, See also Secular Jewish ideologies, 43-45
UNRRA (United Nations Relief and Rehabilitation Administration), 55, 151, 183
USSR, See Russia

Vaad Hahatzalah of the Jewish Agency, See *Moetza*, 27, 28, 30, 71, 104, 105, 164, 231, 232ff, 235, 245
Vaad Hatzalah (Orthodox rabbis rescue committee), See also Kastner train, 106-109; Orthodox, rabbis; individual names, 3, 4, 26, 31, 32, 39, 55, 58, 60, 67-68, 71, 72, 73, 81, 83, 90-91, 94, 100; Sternbuch-Musy-Himmler-negotiations, 109ff; Sweden, 221, 223f, 225f, 227f; Tangier, 248ff; train from Theresienstadt, 111-114; transfer of concentration camps, 113, 116, 125, 126, 127, 128, 129ff, 138f, 140-142, 145, 146, 148ff, 162, 163f, 176, 190, 193, 195, 203, 234, 239, 240, 246, 261
Vaad LePikuach Nefesh, 162
Vance, Cyrus, 150-151
Vatican, See also Pius XII, Pope; Roncalli, Cardinal; 118, 137, 139, 174, 185, 213, 223, 236, 277, 278
Venice, Jews of, 21
Vienna, See also Austria, 13, 140, 176, 177, 178, 179, 248, 255, 256, 258ff
Vilna, 154, 226
Visser t'Hooft, W.A., 208
Vittel, See also Individual countries, 7, 8-11, 59, 102ff, 109, 114, 172f, 190, 225; Latin American Papers; Mantello, George Mandel
Vladivostok (Russia), 130, 222, 242
Vogt, Rev. Paul, 208, 209f
Volunteers, 31-32, 153f, 154, 155, 156, 157, 158, 159
Vorhand, Rabbi Victor, 152, 240
Vrba, Rudoph (Walter Rosenberg), See also *Auschwitz Protocols*, 104ff, 206

Wagner, Senator Robert, 127
Wahrhaftig, Zorach (Mizrachi leader), 130
Wallace, Vice-President Henry, 100, 137
Wallenberg, Raoul, 59, 103, 106, 115, 116, 120, 215, 257
War Department, U.S., 138

War Refugee Board, See also McClelland, Roswell; Pehle, John; 7, 8, 10, 11, 37-41, 55, 56, 58, 71, 72, 73, 81, 83, 101f, 104-105, 112, 115, 116, 137, 138, 151, 153, 164, 165, 198, 207, 233, 234, 238, 239

Warren, George (State Dept.), 9

Warsaw, 57, 226, 283; deportations from, 91

Warsaw Ghetto, 60, 173, 191, 192, 200

Washington, D.C., 32, 38, 103, 163

Wasserman, Rabbi Elchonon, 155

Wasserstein, Bernard, 2

Wehrmacht, 113

Weisfogel, Rabbi Alex, 134-135, 137

Weissmandl, Rabbi Michoel Ber, 2, 4, 12, 18, 19, 26, 27, 28, 29, 30, 34, 35, 52, 53, 57, 60, 71, 72, 80, 81, 99, 110, 115, 158, 163, 176, 180, 188, 190, 191, 197, 234, 246, 264ff, 271ff; plea to bomb rail lines to (and) Auschwitz, 29, 34, 36, 41, 42, 56, 104ff, 116, 138, 139, 164, 172, 190, 206, 230, 234, 265, 266, 270, 282

Weizmann, Chaim, 63, 64, 172

Welfare state, See also 66, Liberalism; New Deal; Roosevelt, Franklin D., 66

West, General F.M., 209

Westerbork (transit camp), 262

Wetzler, Alfred (Josef Lanik), See also *Auschwitz Protocols*, 104ff, 206f

White Paper, British (1939), See also *Aliya*; British Mandate Government; 63, 94, 100, 170f, 237, 241, 242; Jewish Agency; Zionists

Wilhelmina, Queen (Holland), 60, 260

Williamsburg (Brooklyn), 128, 281

Winant, Ambassador John (U.S.), 102-103, 205

Wise, Rabbi Jonah B. (Reform), 49,

Wise, Rabbi Stephen S., 3, 29, 49, 62, 65ff, 70, 71, 74, 76, 77, 82, 87, 88, 90-98, 100-101, 135, 136, 146, 162

Wisliceny, Dieter, See also Slovakia; Weissmandl, Rabbi Michoel Ber, 18, 28, 41, 267f, 271ff

Wohlgelernter, Rabbi Solomon P. (Mizrachi), 229

Wolbe, Rabbi Shlomo, 220f, 223ff, 225, 227f

Woods, Sam, 189

Working Group, See Slovak Jewish Underground

World Agudath Israel, 58, 126, 160, 216, 261

World Jewish Congress, See also American Jewish Congress; Wise, Stephen S., 3, 29, 56, 61, 70, 74, 92, 102, 105, 136, 172, 188, 219, 238, 272, 273

World War I, 64, 258; World War II, 54, 64, 194, 262

Wyman, David, 101, 138, 270

Yad Vashem, 2, 195

Yavneh, 25

Yehudim, 62; See also German Jews

Yeshivah Etz Chaim (London), 179

Yeshivah Heichal Hatalmud (Tel Aviv), 149

Yeshivah Ner Israel, 221

Yeshivah of Baranovich (Poland), 155

Yeshivah of Jassy (Rumania), 244

Yeshivah of Kletzk, 132, 143, 155, 222

Yeshivah of Lubavitch, 222, 225

Yeshivah of Mir (Poland), 133, 220, 221, 222, 225, 236

Yeshivah of Nitra, See Nitra, Yeshivah of

Yeshivah of Radin, 132

Yeshivah of Slobodka (Poland), 149

Yeshivah of Slutzk, 144

Yeshivah Ohr Yisrael (London), 178f

Yeshivah Rabbi Jacob Joseph, 130

Yeshivah students (Talmudic Scholars), See also Rabbis, 41, 67-68, 76, 128-133, 144, 147, 154, 157, 203, 222, 241, 262, 263

Yeshivos, See also Yeshivah students, 67, 68, 125, 128, 129-131, 145, 226, 244, 245, 257; closing of (U.S.), 158

Yishuv, See Eretz Yisrael

Yochanan ben Zakkai, Rabbi, 25

Young Israel Movement (U.S.), See also Bunim, Irving, 31, 129, 140, 148, 167

Yugoslavia, 84, 86, 204

Zaks, Rabbi Mendel, 151

Zeirei Agudath Israel, See Agudath Israel Youth

Zikman, Lew, 77

Zionism (in general), See also Ben Gurion; Revisionist-Zionists; Silver, Abba Hillel; Socialist-Zionists; Wise, Stephen; Zionist Organization of America; 3, 23, 45, 46, 52-53, 64, 77; U.S., 64, 94

Zionists (in general), See also England, 52; Hungary, 106; Jewish Agency; Revisionist-Zionist, 1, 22, 26, 28, 29, 51, 56-57, 61, 64, 65, 70, 71, 82, 87, 94-99, 149; Socialist-Zionists

Zionists, U.S., See also American Jewish Committee; Jewish Labor Committee, 94-99, 162, 163

Zuber, Rabbi Yaakov Yisroel, 221, 224f; Mendel, 221, 224f

Zurich, 173, 202, 261

Zuroff, Efraim, 68

Zygelboym, Shmuel (Bund), 161